Languages and Nations

New Perspectives on Indian Pasts
General Editor: Saurabh Dube

Other titles in the series:
Thomas R. Trautmann
Aryans and British India (paperback edition)

David N. Lorenzen
Who Invented Hinduism?
Essays on Religion in History

A.R. Venkatachalapathy
In Those Days There Was No Coffee
Writings in Cultural History

Languages and Nations

The Dravidian Proof in Colonial Madras

Thomas R. Trautmann

YODA PRESS

YODA PRESS
G 93, Connaught Circus
New Delhi 110 001

Published in India
by YODA PRESS

First published 2006

ISBN 81-903634-0-9

For sale only in India, Pakistan, Bangladesh, Myanmar, Bhutan, Nepal and Sri Lanka.

Typeset in Sabon 10/13
By Excellent Laser Typesetters, Delhi 110 034
Printed & bound by Raj Press, R-3 Inderpuri, New Delhi 110 012
Published by Parul Nayyar and Arpita Das, YODA PRESS
G 93, Connaught Circus, New Delhi 110 001
Distributed by Foundation Books Pvt. Ltd.
Cambridge House, 4381/4, Ansari Road
Daryaganj, New Delhi 110 002

For Baskaran and Thilaka

Contents

Series Editor's Foreword

An irony pervades our present. The past is urgently in the air today, from controversies over textbooks and monuments to contentions over the heritage of nations and communities. At the same time, in recent years academic history writing has come under searing, searching scrutiny: from questions of the inadequacy of historical narratives to represent the experience and suffering of social subjects through to queries considering the complicities of historical knowledge with formations of modern power. Apparently, we are at a crossroads concerning the craft of history, doubly burdened by emphatic criticisms of the discipline and endless claims on the past. The tensions warrant unraveling.

LESSONS FROM HISTORY

Across the past decade, there has been acute interrogation not only of the formative procedures of academic history writing but of the aggrandizing attributes of historical thought itself. The criticism has addressed how such endeavors and ideas actively ignore, and often anxiously obscure, their pervasive limitations in explaining social worlds and historical subjects only to assiduously frame, even shape, these subjects and their worlds in routine and ready ways. Unsurprisingly, such considerations have emerged linked to a wider questioning of the collusions of historical scholarship with authoritative, normally exclusive, visions of the state and nation, the West and modernity, and the colony and post-colony. Under debate is the very nature of historical knowledge in the past and the present, from its presuppositions and procedures to its politics and partisanship.

The debate has been internal to the discipline of history as well as covering much broader intellectual terrain.

Equally clearly, the past has returned to haunt the present, finding novel manifestations and escalating assertions in our ageing modern world. Today, terms such as culture, identity, and tradition are not merely intellectual devices. Rather, these terms have been seized upon by their objects of analysis, the very people the concepts purported to describe. From indigenous communities in Australia to Asian immigrants in North America to religious militants in the world at large, here are subjects who have zealously claimed tradition, identity, and culture, articulating them in intriguing ways, many times living and dying in the name of these categories and entities. In different ways, demands on the past have been central to such procedures. Unsurprisingly, representations of history regularly find shifting yet salient configurations—as contested territory, ambivalent resource, ready motif, and settled verity—turning the past into a combustible element and a burning issue within public discourses. On the one hand, consider dalit demands for social justice and indigenous claims for their own rights. They reveal vigorous mappings of history among subaltern subjects that construe anew the violence of the past as a revision of the present. On the other hand, think of the belligerent and bigoted Bharat of Hindu nationalist imaginings and the increasingly intolerant "freedom" conjured by the radical right in the US. These register aggressive forgings of national history with universal pretensions that rework afresh the glory of the past as a measure of the present. From the fourth world through to the first world, there is no turning away from the past, no simple shrugging off of the burden of history.

None of this is to claim that the very nature of the historical discipline has not been severely questioned before. Nor is it to deny that the past has loomed large, including monstrously, in projects of unity and division in earlier eras, construed variously by states and empires and citizens and subjects. To attribute an entirely exceptional character to the present would be to succumb to a formidable contemporary conceit, one that the Haitian historical anthropologist Michel-Rolph Trouillot identifies as the invasive tendency to "overplay the uniqueness of our times." This arrogance readily refuses lessons from worlds before we were born. At the same time, precisely by learning from the past while training our eyes on the present, it is possible to detect something of the particularity of contemporary worlds.

Let us, then, stay a little longer with the two sides of the irony surrounding history in our present. The criticisms of academic history writing today build upon prior critical traditions but equally intimate emphases that are specific to our own age. Such critiques include edgy denouncements and reckless refusals of historical knowledge, based on anti-modernist premises, which nonetheless contain valuable lessons, issues to which I shall return. Here the point concerns more responsible critical engagements with historical scholarship, including explorations of colonial cultures and expressions of postcolonial perspectives, which have unraveled productive possibilities. These possibilities inhere in a wider propensity to carefully query the categories and entities—for example, modernity and history, nation and democracy, human rights and rational knowledge—that shore up our worlds, while cautiously affirming the potential of such concepts and processes in the past and the present.

The dispositions that I am describing do not simply celebrate particularity, contingency, and difference within social worlds and their scholarly understandings. Nor do they merely castigate the universal proclamations, enduring patterns, and practices of power at the heart of these domains. Instead, in different ways they attempt to think through the mutual entailments and common exclusions of the particular and the universal, of the contingent and the enduring, and of difference and power. This can further mean not to only oppose and criticize foundations of knowledge and authority but to cultivate and affirm categories and worlds in the wake of such questioning. Here are to be found orientations that acknowledge and articulate the revisable, open-ended, and contingent nature yet the necessary, ethical, and unavoidable character of vital conceptualizations of the world and ourselves. It is such protocols of prudent probing and dispositions toward critical affirmation that I have elsewhere called a *history without warranty*.

The insistent and contending claims on history in the here and now also signal something specific about contemporary worlds. Indeed, emphatic expressions of tradition, culture, and identity—including their demands on the past—are far from being primordial patterns or recalcitrant residues that modern and global processes of capital and consumption and state and citizenship have been unable to stamp out. Rather, the pervasive presence of these concepts and resources indicates their salience within schemes of modernity. Such salience and schemes have been seized upon today by historical subjects of distinct persuasions, from Native American groups to African proletarians to the Al Qaeda, as they articulate on the ground modernity and history, capital and globalization, the West and nation—in everyday spaces and public places. None of this might be entirely new, but it has acquired enormous urgency in the present. At stake, then, are distinct manifestations and critical articulations of the configurations and consequences of modernity as ideal and ideology and as process and history.

Understood in this way, the sustained play of the past in our present confronts contemporary discourses of crusaders of capital that rework history unto their own ends. It not only probes projections of the end of history, which track an irrevocable trajectory toward a post-historical world where incontrovertible terms of global, liberal democracy would work in tandem with the benign market of the liberal, global economy. It also makes possible the holding of a mirror up to the assumptions and anxieties shoring up representations of the all-conquering Goliath of globalization and the magical Midas of the market, revealing that such fables can reify the past and cultural difference yet equally turn their backs to the past to transform thereby historical difference into mind-numbing sameness. Taken together, here is what the irony under examination suggests: while requirements of the past and ruses of history have never been mere matters of work in the study and the seminar, their assertive and conflicting enunciations today are to an important extent peculiar to the contemporary world.

Arguably, something of the notion of having arrived at a crossroads has informed the responses of several historians and other academics as they have confronted criticisms of history and claims on the past. Unsurprisingly, such scholars have often endorsed the idea that can inhere in the image of a crossroads, one of following an already, unambiguously laid out pathway, tending toward a singular direction and an exclusive destination. Thus, faced with the proliferations of pasts proposed by the untrained, the unlettered, and the unwashed, historians have thrown up their hands in despair and demanded a return to rigorous procedures of disciplinary history. The call has come with its justifications, but it has also run the risk of turning history into a touchstone of truth, now located in a terrain unaffected by moral choices and political power, often equally excising the productive possibilities of plural contentions within history writing. Similarly, many members of the historical profession have responded no less impatiently to the critical questioning of historical knowledge, explicitly or implicitly emphasizing the necessity of continuing with the business-as-usual of history writing, frequently also begging key questions concerning the internal differences that are formative of the disciplines. Still other intellectuals have admitted to the theoretical sophistication of newer renderings of history and acknowledged the persuasions of the past in the present. But they have juxtaposed these renderings and such persuasions to find in the former little more than procedures of endless demystification, and to use the latter to express nostalgia for the old-fashioned virtues of the historical craft. On the other side of the apparent epistemic breach yet vigorously stamped by the hierarchical oppositions of modern knowledge, a flurry of annoyed critiques and ready dismissals of historical knowledge have flowed forth. They have demanded, for instance, the overthrow of conventions of history and their replacement by subversions of myth. Such anti-modernist measures can be doubly ironic: not only do they reinstate the exact oppositions of modernity, albeit now as representations in reverse, but they do so through a quest for novelty that is itself a central attribute of modernist desires, although one that paradoxically pervades postmodernist sensibilities.

To write sharply of these contending tendencies is not to pointedly discard them, nor to languidly legislate on them. Instead, it is to critically learn from these expressions, acknowledging that they can all offer valuable lessons, including important insights contained within their very practice of history writing. At the same time, the learning of such lessons requires the rethinking of the vocation of history, a project significantly underway in a multitude of manners. This might also be to discover that the notion of being at a crossroads can have some relevance as a figurative device if it is seen as signifying the twin tasks of carefully questioning and critically affirming the writing of history in the present, procedures that lead to many pathways. Here are to be found protocols that equally engage and prudently probe contentious discourses on the past, recognizing their particular presence in former worlds while registering their insistent claims in contemporary ones. It warrants emphasis that popular struggles over the past and disciplinary reconfigurations of history do not occupy entirely separate terrain. Yet it is also the case that to trace the conjunctions and disjunctions between such popular struggles and disciplinary reconfigurations is to raise new questions and to think through prior puzzles regarding the sustained interplay between social worlds and their academic apprehensions.

QUESTIONS OF HISTORY

All of this makes palpable a host of considerations. Let me outline four overlapping sets of questions, which derive from the wide-ranging intersections of historical writing with anthropological endeavor, critical thought, and social theory. In the first place, it has been increasingly noted that forms of historical consciousness vary in their degree of symbolic elaboration, their ability to pervade multiple contexts, and their capacity to capture people's imaginations. Such recognition neither falls back on oppositions involving cyclical notions of the past as characteristic of the East and linear conceptions of history as constitutive of the West, nor does it merely measure distinct notations of time across cultures with the latter projected as separate, bounded entities. Rather, it precisely probes such overwrought schemes, which carve up social worlds into enchanted terrains of myth and disenchanted domains of modernity, through the tracking of apprehensions and articulations of history as made up of interleaving, conflict-ridden processes of meaning and authority. On offer are explorations of the variability and mutability that can inhere in the perceptions and practices of history of a single group as well as enquiries into the persistence of oppositions between myth and history and ritual and reason in authoritative projections—explorations and enquiries that are attentive to the incessant interchange between power and difference.

The second consideration follows. For sometime now it has been variously admitted that history does not just refer to events, structures, and processes out there, but that it exists as a negotiated and reworked resource at the core of shifting configurations of social worlds. As mentioned earlier, close to our times, shaped by the stipulations of modernity, the clamour over the past in assertions of authority and alterity has provided a further twist to these patterns. To foreground such appropriations and enunciations of the past as important issues for the discipline of history is not to submit to a view that each of these visions is equally true. Instead, it is to track the uses of the past and their contending validities in the making of worlds and to trace the presence of power in the production of history.

This brings me to the third concern. Imaginative explorations of pasts of subaltern peoples and elite groups—constructed, recall, within larger, overlaying matrices of meaning and power—combined with energetic interrogations of univocal conceptions of universal history have made for compelling consequences. There has been an opening up of critical questions considering the coupling of history writing with the idea of the nation under modern regimes: Must all histories be national histories? Why does historical endeavour, including its critical manifestations, continue to be shaped by the impress of the nation? What should be the forms taken by an alternative practice of history writing? Such queries have been accompanied by sustained examinations of the haunting presence of a reified West in widespread beliefs in historical progress and at the very core of academic practice: Is the record of history mainly a register of the work of progress in some societies and of its lack in other ones? How are we to comprehend underlying expectations of progress in the past and of development in the present, the passage forward in time framed as the hallmark of history, in scholarly schemes and quotidian understandings? What has been the place of Europe as entailing the point of departure and arrival on the road to progress and modernity in academic and everyday perceptions in Western and non-Western arenas? In short, all of this has put a question mark on pervasive projections of the West and the nation as history, modernity, and destiny. Such terms of discussion have engaged and extended philosophical critiques of an adjudicatory reason and the enduring oppositions of modern and colonial knowledge. They have equally formed part of critical, imaginative renderings of state and nation and modernity and globalization, renderings that have rescued such concepts and entities from a resolute formalism in order to map their contingencies and contradictions on the ground.

In the fourth and final place, it has become evident that to draw on and participate in such a many-sided critical endeavor is not necessarily to shy way from the task of writing history. No doubt, questions concerning the historical enterprise shall continue to be raised in principally philosophical or overwhelmingly theoretical ways. But other terms of discussion are possible. In approaching the past and the present, these bind the impulse to cautiously probe and affirm with the desire to carefully narrate and describe, while being responsible about the challenge of thinking through intractable issues such as those of memory and trauma. Such endeavors take truly seriously requirements of evidence and fidelity to facts. Yet they can also sieve historical evidence through critical filters and construe facts unexpected that speak in the uneasy echoes of limiting doubt rather than deal in the aggressive certainties of a legislating knowledge. Such efforts are very visible today. Of course, we must learn to look.

THE SERIES AND THE WORK

New Perspectives on Indian Pasts is founded on the possibilities of critical ferment and creative expression in history writing. It does not call for a single pathway as the true measure of historical scholarship. Nor does the series demand any adherence from its authors to the proposals and procedures that have been proffered in this foreword. *New Perspectives on Indian Pasts* invites varieties of history, based on the belief that plural perspectives, intellectual disagreements, and ethical contentions—each resting on responsible dialog—are necessary for scholarly and public worlds. The series seeks to concretize these proposals by presenting a range of works: from historical biographies to labour histories; from discussions of art worlds to explorations of political cultures; from renderings of pasts of empire and nation to renditions of histories of the social sciences and the humanities; from analyses of memory to understandings of trauma; and from translations into the English of salient studies in other Indian languages to texts presenting important archival materials. The inventory is indicative. The point is that *New Perspectives on Indian Pasts* does not limit itself to cutting-edge scholarship, burdened with novelty. It wishes to draw in endeavors, empirical and theoretical, that expand the critical and creative and democratic and ethical horizons of history writing. The series is especially interested in presenting the work of younger authors. But senior scholars are also very welcome.

It is a particular pleasure to present *Languages and Nations* by the remarkable scholar Thomas Trautmann. This is his second title in this series. Before I say something about the book, a word on the author is in order. Thomas Trautmann's impressive scholarship has combined a generous vision with a graceful style to straddle the disciplines of history and anthropology, articulating abiding philological, linguistic, and literary issues. Trautmann worked for the PhD degree at the School of Oriental and African Studies in London. His doctoral research entailed a statistical-linguistic analysis of the authorship of Kautilya's *Arthashastra*. The thesis and the published book that followed firmly established that Kautilya's text was written by multiple authors who probably lived in somewhat different periods. Trautmann took up his first teaching position in the School of Oriental and African Studies. Soon he moved to the University of Michigan, Ann Arbor, where he has worked for more than thirty years, assuming in addition to his teaching responsibilities numerous other positions, including until recently the editorship of the major journal *Comparative Studies in Society and History*.

Across the 1970s and 1980s, Trautmann continued to write on questions of kingship while conjoining these concerns with the study of kinship. This resulted in his landmark account of Dravidian kinship that not only contains technical discussions of kinship terms and relations but includes an original account of the interplay between the cross-cousin marriage system dominant in South India and the relatively stable political history of the principal royal dynasties in this region. Trautmann's studies on kinship also led to a book in the history of anthropology discussing Lewis Henry Morgan's work on the kinship system of the Iroquois and pointing out the important influence of the Mosaic chronology—to conjoin Trautmann's related ideas of the "short chronology of the Bible" and the "Mosaic ethnology"—on Morgan's ideas about the early history of mankind. Subsequently, he has written and edited works on issues of time, while exploring the Orientalist projects and the ethnological knowledge of the British in India. Emblematic of these researches are both the present study and Trautmann's earlier *Aryans and British India*, the first international paperback edition of which had initiated *New Perspectives on Indian Pasts*.

In a short description it is difficult to do justice to the several accomplishments of Thomas Trautmann and his wide-ranging scholarship. But it would be quite unfair not to mention the critical continuities in his writing. These have large implications. Trautmann does not sever off as separate entities diverse worlds of knowledge or various ways of knowing. He seeks to think through their linkages and differences. Thus, Trautmann's deliberations on Morgan's understanding of Iroquois kinship bring these in relation to his own study of Dravidian kinship; and he finds the Mosaic chronology to be at work in the formation of the idea of the Aryan in late-eighteenth century British Orientalism in Bengal as well as in Morgan's ideas about the distant pasts of humankind. Equally, in Trautmann's hands Dravidian distinctions shore up the specific style of scholarship of the Madras school of Orientalists as well as his own account of kinship in southern India; and these distinctions are crucial for the differences in British knowledge about India between the Calcutta school and Madras school of Orientalism. All of this means that Trautmann's writings explore intellectual history in metropolitan locales and colonial theatres by bringing them together as crisscrossing terrain. Precisely by undertaking scholarly journeys that traverse India, America, and Britain, does he make distinctive contributions to the history of anthropology and to understandings of the imperial archive, British Orientalism, and their constitutive heterogeneity.

It should be no surprise, therefore, that *Languages and Nations: The Dravidian Proof in Colonial Madras*, focusing on the English scholar-administrator Francis Ellis and the Madras school of Orientalism, is a seminal study. Put simply, the work demonstrates the creation in southern India of a specific school of Orientalist knowledge, which rested on the study of the Dravidian language family. This style of knowledge was distinct from that of the well-known Orientalist school, based on the study of Sanskrit and Persian, which had developed slightly earlier in Bengal, and which Trautmann explored in his *Aryans and British India*. At the same time, the implications of the present account as of its preceding volume—the reach of their materials, arguments, and emphases—extend rather farther. To begin with, Thomas Trautmann's incisive explorations of what he calls the "languages-and-nations project" reveal the twinning in European thought of nations and languages, "in such a way that the histories of both were governed by genealogical relations", patterns with their bases in a Mosaic ethnology and a universal history. This meant that historical relations among languages came to signify historical relations among nations, an idea "applied worldwide through the expansion of European power in the eighteenth century", further leading to "an explosion in the grammar factory, which also continues to this day." Second, these correlations were profoundly productive in South Asia, precisely on account of the critical conjunctions between European and Indian traditions of language analyses, the acute entanglements between the knowledge schemes of the colonizer and the colonized. Here, the "Dravidian proof", formulated in Madras under Ellis between 1812 and 1819, has an especially important place, not least because of the immense archive that underlies it. Third and finally, the book deals throughout with contentious questions, also enormously resonant in our contemporary worlds, concerning Western repre-sentations and Indian traditions, Orientalist discourses and non-Western understandings, and racial theories and their denouement. At each step, Trautmann addresses such issues of imperial power and modern knowledge through protocols of rigorous research, judicious argument, wide-ranging reading, elegant writing, and even-handed analyses.

Languages and Nations is the fourth title in this series. Hopefully, a new arrival in *New Perspectives on Indian Pasts* once more signals a fresh departure in the grappling with history that characterizes the present, especially by working toward a broadening and deepening of intellectual conversation.

Mexico City **Saurabh Dube**
October 2006

Illustrations

Preface

I have long wanted to write this book.

Some years ago I began to investigate the way in which languages and nations are twinned in European thought such that the historical relations among languages become signs of the historical relations among nations—ethnology by means of linguistics, so to say. This idea was applied worldwide through the expansion of European power in the eighteenth century. It became exceptionally productive in India, where it encountered a tradition of language analysis that was rich and deep. The most spectacular result was the proposal, by Sir William Jones, of a historical relationship joining Sanskrit to the languages of Europe and Iran—the concept of what we now call the Indo-European language family, which became the foundation for comparative philology and the gold standard of historical linguistics.

This breakthrough formulation from British India has been discussed in nearly every history of linguistics, and there would be little purpose in adding to what has already been said, and said well, by the experts in the discipline that emerged from the developments it set in train. But two features of those narratives have made me think that historians should not leave this matter to the histories of linguistics. In the first place, since the comparison of languages initiated in the eighteenth century had a larger, *ethnological* character—to construct a genealogical tree of *languages*, not as an end in itself but as a means of access to the genealogical tree of *nations*, recovering the lost memory of the relations among nations—viewing this project and its discoveries through a history of linguistics framing that treats language as a self-contained object of study cannot capture the whole picture. In the second place, in these narratives the place of India has tended to be constructed as a source of *data* for European *theory*, as a passive receptacle rather than a source of theory in its own right, whereas in fact (or so it has seemed to me) elements of Indian linguistic theory were silently and, in the end, largely unconsciously folded into the new science of comparative philology. I have thought it highly probable that the Indo-European breakthrough was in some fashion a result of the conjunction of the two traditions of language analysis, European and Indian, that the conjuncture therefore needs examination, and that it was the richness of the Indian tradition of language analysis that made India an especially productive terrain for the European project of languages and nations. That is, it was not an accident that spectacular results came out of British India, including the conceptions of the Indo-European, Malayo-Polynesian, and Dravidian language families, and the identfication of the Romani language of the Roma, or Gypsies, as an Indo-European language from India.

The first result of what I think of as my "languages and nations" project was a book, *Aryans and British India* (1997), that focuses upon Sir William Jones's formulation of the concept of the Indo-European language family at Calcutta and the subsequent studies of India's languages as means of recovering its ethnological history. In the course of making the book I came across the remarkable early (1816) paper that first proposed the concept of the Dravidian language family, published by Francis Whyte Ellis, collector of Madras, a figure as obscure as Jones is famous, and in the book I devoted a few pages to this important and intriguing text, which was also, in its way, a scholarly breakthrough.

When I received a first copy of the finished *Aryans and British India* from the publisher, I was in Chennai, working at the Tamil Nadu State Archives, pursuing further material on Ellis and his colleagues, Indian and English, at the College of Fort St. George, where the South Indian languages had been taught to arriving British civil servants. I had already unearthed unpublished material by Ellis and his associates in the British Library and the National Library of Scotland. And on my way back from India, I found additional sources at the British Library and the Bodleian Library. I had more than enough material for the book I now wished to write on Ellis and Dravidian languages and British-Indian Madras. Moreover, the records I had found would allow me to bring out to some extent the interactions among British and Indian scholars, and between their respective traditions of language analysis, which was the context for Ellis's formulation of the idea of the Dravidian language family, the "Dravidian proof" as I call it in this book. However, even before I reached home I had been asked to accept the editorship of a journal I greatly admired as well as an administrative job in my university that I could not well refuse. These put the writing of the book on hold for five years. During that time I advanced the languages-and-nations project through a series of articles on aspects of the problem: "Inventing the history of South India," "Hullabaloo about Telugu," "Kinship, language, and the construction of South India," "Dr. Johnson and the pandits," and "Explosion in the grammar factory" (1999a, 1999b, 2001a, 2001b, forthcoming). I was also working on the relation of the European languages-and-nations project to the formation of a racial theory of history in the work of Arthur de Gobineau, but that is for another time. Following release from administrative detention, I got time off for good behavior in the form of a year of research leave, with sabbatical support from the University of Michigan plus a grant from the American Council of Learned Societies, the National Endowment for the Humanities, and the Social Science Research Council, for which I am immensely grateful. In the course of this leave I made a return visit to India, with help from the American Institute of Indian Studies, for a further, highly fruitful spell in the Tamil Nadu State Archives and a few days at the Asiatic Society of Mumbai. This gave me access to important materials I had not previously seen. Though I had drafted the book before revisiting Chennai, I rewrote it after returning home.

Languages and Nations, then, forms a pair with *Aryans and British India*. It is not a continuation of it but is complete in itself. As the *Aryans* book is a book about Calcutta, this is my Madras book, so to say. It is an examination of the same phenomenon from a different perspective and in a different local expression: Madras during the Ellis years, especially the years from the founding of the College of Fort St. George in 1812 to the untimely death of Ellis in 1819. I believe that in that brief period the most interesting interactions between Indian and English scholars about languages and nations were taking place in Madras, resulting in a distinctive school of Orientalism that stood in some degree of dissension with the pronouncements of the Calcutta Orientalists. I call this formation the Madras School of Orientalism. The body of work that constitutes this Madras school is more extensive than I can show here, and is in any case formed by two separate but related projects, that of Ellis and his Indian head masters at the College of Fort St. George, and that of Colin Mackenzie and his Indian assistants, growing out of the survey of the newly conquered territory of Mysore. It will take a team of scholars to recover the history of the Madras school in its fullness. In this book I take the most spectacular and durable result of that intellectual production, the Dravidian proof, and leave the many other results of the Madras school for another time.

For reasons that will be explained in these pages, the interactions between Indian and British scholars, and between the Indian tradition of language analysis and the languages-and-nations project of the British, were captured, in part, in the Madras colonial record leading up to the publication of the Dravidian proof. This record, and the more fully argued character of the Dravidian proof itself, allow us to see much more clearly the nature of this conjuncture than is possible in the case of Jones's proposal of the Indo-European concept, or indeed in any other of the remarkable outcomes of the languages-and-nations project in British India. It is this conjuncture and the largely unseen incorporation of Indian language analysis into that of Europe that I hope to explore and explain.

This book has many debts, which I am unable to repay but which I acknowledge with pleasure. Robbins Burling, Nicholas Dirks, and James Clifford read the manuscript through and gave an abundance of helpful comments and suggestions. I have had the benefit of Madhav Deshpande's boundless knowledge of Sanskrit, as before, and, in this book particularly, his mastery of the commanding heights of *vyākaraṇa* and *prātiśākhya*. Velcheru Narayana Rao gave me invaluable help with Telugu matters, as did K. Venkateswarlu, Lisa Mitchell, and Rama Mantena. I got many useful ideas from discussions with Romila Thapar, Sumathi Ramaswamy, Carla Sinopoli, Dilip Menon, David Lorenzen, Philip Wagoner, M. S. Pandion, V. Geetha, and Virchand Dharamsey, among others. A. R. Venkatachalapathy has been a valued intellectual companion during the final stages of making the book.

I am most grateful to Theodore Baskaran and Thilaka Baskaran for many kindnesses through the years, and for making my visits to Chennai so pleasant and protable. I am grateful to the Madras Institute of Development Studies and its director, Professor V. K. Nataraj, for allowing me to air my ideas in seminar there. Dilip Menon kindly invited me to speak about my research at the Delhi University History Department seminar. I had met him in the Tamil Nadu State Archives during my first visit, during which he organized a lunchtime seminar at Balaji Woodlands, and I followed his good example by reviving the seminar on my second visit. I am grateful for discussions there with Dilip, Sumathi Ramaswamy,

David Arnold, Rahula Aluhja (first edition), and (second edition) Bhavani Raman, Senthil Babu, Easwaran, and Srinivasa Rao—not to forget Sekar, who took a paternal interest in my nutrition. François Gros and M. Kannan of the Centre for Contemporary Tamil Studies of the Institute Français de Pondicherry kindly hosted a seminar there, organized by Senthil Babu and Bhavani Raman.

In addition to the sources of institutional support already mentioned I thank Pradeep Mehendiratta and Pappu Venugopala Rao for invaluable help with arrangements. My former colleague at the University of Michigan, the late John D'Arms, greatly benefited all humanities scholars by improving the funding of research in his brief but energetic stint at the American Council of Learned Societies, during which he shed light and good cheer all around. I think of the fellowship I got from the ACLS as the last of many good things owing to him. I am grateful to the many new staff members at the University of Michigan Library and the William L. Clements Library (especially Brian Dunnigan), the British Library (especially the agreeable and efficient staff of the Oriental and India Office Collections), the Bodleian Library, the National Library of Scotland (especially Ian McIver), the Roja Muthiah Research Library (especially the director, G. Sundar), the Tamil Nadu State Archives, and the Asiatic Society of Mumbai for their help. I thank my research assistants, Maittri Aung-Thwin, Sarah Womack, and Sudipa Topdar, and Jeanette Diuble, for typing.

Stanley Holwitz of California University Press guided this book (and two previous ones) through the acceptance process, and Cynthia Fulton of California University Press saw the book through press; I am most grateful for their expert care. I was unusually fortunate to have Carolyn Bond as my copy editor. Her knowledge of Sanskrit, the acuteness of her editorial eye, and the sensitivity of her literary ear saved me from many errors and infelicities. Errors that remain are surely mine.

The University of Michigan Photo Services supplied the photographs for figures 1–5 and 9, plus those of the Dravidian proof in appendix B. The photo in figure 6 is from Michigan State University Library.

CHAPTER I

Explosion in the Grammar Factory

In the European thought of the eighteenth century, languages and nations were understood to be parallel, in that the histories of both were viewed as governed by genealogical relations and linked; therefore, the genealogical relations among languages could serve to extend the reach of historical memory concerning the relations among nations and to repair it where it was defective. Language history in this sense became a new tool for ethnology on a universal scale, producing original and unexpected groupings of kindred languages that have in many cases endured to the present. To supply this new ethnological project with the raw material on which it operated required the production of grammars and dictionaries virtually without limit and covering the entire world—an explosion in the grammar factory that continues to this day.

Several of these new and still-valid groupings are associated with British India: the Indo-European language family, which is the best known and the pattern for all the others; the Malayo-Polynesian language family; the Indo-Aryan origins of the Romani language; and the Dravidian language family. Of these four cases, the emergence of the concept of a Dravidian language family has the richest archive, available in hitherto unexamined colonial records of Madras. The first published proof of the Dravidian language family appeared in British-Indian Madras in 1816, the product of a circle of scholars associated with the College of Fort St. George. In this book I examine the languages-and-nations project that the British brought with them to India in the light of the Dravidian proof, and vice versa; that is, this book moves on two planes, using each to illuminate the other. The premise of the book is that the exceptional productiveness of British India as a terrain for the languages-and-nations project of Europe had to do with the exceptional development of language analysis in India since the times of Pāṇini and earlier. The conjuncture of these two traditions of language analysis in British India can be examined at close quarters through the Dravidian proof.

The first two chapters concern, respectively, the European and Indian traditions of language analysis. In the remaining chapters the discussion turns to Madras and the Dravidian proof. In the present chapter I examine well-known material, including the formation of the Indo-European concept, but from a new direction, and interpret it in a way that departs considerably from the received view. I begin with the idea of what I call locational technologies, the more inclusive set that includes the languages-and-nations project and its genealogical scheme of locating particulars in relation to one another.

TECHNOLOGIES OF LOCATION

The propensity to exaggerate the originality of one's thoughts is a failing that is perhaps most acute among those who do not work in teams as the laborers in the vineyards of the natural and social sciences do. Humanities scholars, given to the solitary mode of production, most often work in caves or in studies—like St. Jerome who, as translator of the Bible into Latin, an immensely successful book, is something of a patron saint of scholars. We have two images of St. Jerome. In one he is shown living in a rough cave, with ink and paper at hand, smiting his breast with a stone, saying to himself, as I imagine it, "I *must* finish my book!" The scholar in agony is paired with another image, of which Albrecht Dürer has made so appealing a rendering, that of the great scholar in his study, a tame lion at his feet, sunlight streaming through the window: the scholar happy in his work. I think of these two opposed images, of scholarly agony and pleasure, as St. Jerome before and after tenure. In both, the scholar is—not counting the lion—utterly alone.

For historians and others writing in solitude (I include myself), it is all too easy to be seduced by the pleasing notion of one's own originality, lured by its inherent sweetness and egged on by romantic ideas of individual work of literary genius and the individual scientific breakthrough. Through the distorting optic of an exaggerated sense of individual originality, the social and the historical pass out of view, and a single self occupies the center of the field of vision. It takes special effort to remember that every intellectual project derives its meaning in relation to larger, collective projects that long preceded and will long outlive the individual, and that the text written by an individual contains within it many voices of a continuing conversation. When we open out the field of vision to its widest extent, the individual work becomes a speck in a larger intellectual project that is the work of many hands across many nations and centuries, It is in relation to this wider field that the efforts of individuals are rendered significant and lasting.

One such project of the *longue durée* is the charting of the heavens, a project that has been underway since the times of the ancient Sumerians, perhaps longer, and which we have every reason to think will continue in process as long as there is a human race to carry it on. Astronomy above all seems to have a unitary history that combines the work of countless individuals of many nations over a very long time. John Playfair, speaking at the end of the eighteenth century, put it nicely when he said that the successive developments in the observation of the heavens and the reasoning about them comprise "an experiment on the human race, which has been made but once" (Playfair 1790:136). It is this compelling sense of singularity that puts astronomy at the heart of ideas about science as a progressive accumulation of knowledge that is universal.

Another such project is astronomy's inverse, the mapping of the earth's surface. Yet others are the construction of a unitary chronology of the past, and the classification of nations and languages—the topic of this book. We may call all of these locational projects because they define representational spaces and represent entities as locations within those spaces.

The space of each of these locational projects of the *longue durée* is defined by what, for want of a better word, I will call a technology of location. The star chart is a good example. It defines its space by dividing the sky as seen from earth with lines of declination and right ascension. Within that space one determines the placing of each heavenly body in terms of degrees (or hours), minutes, and seconds. Those units bear witness to the Mesopotamian origins of this locational project: 360 degrees in the whole circle of the sky (or 24 hours), 60 minutes in a degree, 60 seconds in a minute, in the base 60 numbering system of the Sumerians. Every star in the heavens has its position fixed by a pair of numbers. The star Aldebaran, for example, is at right ascension 4 h. 30 m., declination 16°19'. The relation between any pair of stars is a derivative of their positions within this space.

The star chart, like the other locational projects, arose in the deep past and is very much in use today. This long-term intellectual venture, carried forward by the incremental contributions of innumerable individuals over many centuries and across many different countries and cultures, this vast and largely anonymous collective effort, is, like the others, a part of the living core of modernity. Yet precisely because it is so very central it is practically invisible. No deep rupture, no Kuhnian paradigm shift, has cast it aside. Not even the famous shift from an earth-centered, Ptolemaic conception of the planetary system to a sun-centered, Copernican one has upset the structure of the star chart.

The space of the star chart first developed as a fiction that, though false, turns out to be highly useful: the useful fiction that the sky is the interior of a titanic sphere, on the surface of which the stars are hung. This imagined sphere was then marked off into sectors by a rectilinear grid as a locational technique to fix the heavenly bodies in place for study. Or perhaps, in the beautiful metaphor of an ancient Sumerian poem, the sky is the tablet of lapis lazuli upon which the goddess Nidaba inscribes cuneiform signs, the stars, which tell the destinies of human beings down below.[1]

For the study of the earth, this imagined celestial sphere was projected back onto the real sphere, or spheroid, of the earth, for which it is both useful and a reasonably true representation. The earth, in turn, was divided into sectors by degrees of longitude and latitude, which define a related locational space. Thus the earthly space was theorized through astronomy. It was *astrology,* however, that was the connective tissue between the two projects of mapping the stars and mapping the earth, the belief, that is, in the influence of the heavenly bodies upon earthly destinies—for what the goddess Nidaba writes on the tablet of the sky is the destinies of humans, if only we can read it. The desire to read that sky tablet of our futures was a powerful motivation for the entire enterprise from the start, but it was the locational projects themselves that survived the ultimate casting out, from the table of recognized sciences, of the ages-old project of astrology that first set these sciences in motion.

Ptolemy of Alexandria, in Roman Egypt of the second century A.D., wrote works of astronomy, astrology, and geography that became canonical for later ages and had an immense influence in the Christian West, the Muslim Middle East, and beyond, into Central Asia and India.[2] Al-

1. I thank Piotr Michalowski for this information. See Michalowski 1992.

2. The main astronomical work of Ptolemy is the *Syntaxis,* called the *Mathematical collection* or *The great astronomer.* His *Geography* has already been mentioned. His main

though Ptolemy was not the inventor of the highly theorized space of the locational projects of astronomy and geography, he raised the science of Mesopotamia, Egypt, and Greece to a higher level, and it was through his writings that this tradition was transmitted to future ages. We know the names of some of his predecessors in the development of this space, such as Marinus, Hipparchus, and Poseidonius. But the names of the many Mesopotamians and Egyptians who had made celestial observations for two thousand years before Ptolemy are largely unknown. There is a certain justice in calling this astronomical and geographical space Ptolemaic, and I shall do so in this book, but it must be understood that it was not his invention; it was the culmination, in his works, of a long-continued effort by many, many people.

The Ptolemaic grid of declination and right ascension for the mapping of objects in space from the viewpoint of earth, and the grid of longitude and latitude for the mapping of objects on the earth's surface as seen from space, have become the taken-for-granted frameworks within which those mappings proceed as a steady accumulation of knowledge by increments—our surest example of progress in knowledge. Such locational devices are not mere metrics, like the meter stick that stands inertly in the corner until it is taken up to measure something. The grid defining Ptolemaic space is, rather, like a vessel that is meant to be filled; it has, as it were, the project of its filling engineered into it. There is nothing passive about the grid. It *asks* to be filled up with an infinite number of points of information, put into meaningful relation to one another through their locations in the grid. It is a project engineered into a tool for its accomplishment, a locational project embedded within the locational technology for carrying it out.

While the locational *project* of mapping the earth has an event-filled history that we can partially capture, the locational *technology* is the enduring, defining frame for the project. One might suppose that Ptolemaic space has had a continuous existence from antiquity to the present, but that is not the case. Most of the first printed atlases produced in Europe and many early Arab maps were Ptolemaic, in the double sense that the maps were framed by the Ptolemaic grid of longitude and latitude, and the maps themselves depicted the features of the earth's surface as rep-

work of astrology is called, simply, the *Tetrabiblos (Four books* or *Fourfold book)*. Although histories of science usually deal only with his astronomical and geographical works, his astrological work was part and parcel of his life project, as was the case for most astronomers of the ancient world.

resented in the tables of places and their longitudes and latitudes given in the text of Ptolemy's *Geography* (see figure 1). But it is a question whether the maps attributed to Ptolemy and attached to his *Geography* are truly his or are of later design. Moreover, many maps of antiquity and of the European middle ages were clearly made in a quite different space that is not Ptolemaic; examples are pilgrimage maps and the well-known T-O maps, in which a circular earth is divided into three continents by a T-shaped watery body: Asia at the top, Europe to the left, and Africa to the right. For a very long time many, indeed most, maps were not constructed within the Ptolemaic space, especially in the middle ages.

Moreover, there were serious alternatives to the Ptolemaic space that had possibilities for cumulative, scientific mapping and that might have displaced it. A leading example comes from the *portolan,* or harbor-finding, sea charts for sailors developed in Catalonia and coastal northern Italy in the thirteenth century. These charts had wind roses, or compass roses, with lines (called rhumb lines or loxodromes) radiating outward from their centers. The four-sided figures formed by the intersection of lines from several compass roses at standard locations could define the position of any point in the open ocean and fix the locations of the coastline for purposes of navigation, just as latitudes and longitudes could. We have several surviving examples of the transferal of these principles to the mapping of the world as a whole, in competition with the Ptolemaic maps (see figure 2). The space of the *portolan* maps still survives today, marginally, in the navigational charts used at sea, but always in combination with the now standard Ptolemaic coordinates of longitude and latitude.

Again, the Ptolemaic map of the world, and Ptolemy's tables of locations which the map illustrates, contained many errors which were exposed and corrected by the new knowledge accumulating through European seagoing. Since the new knowledge contradicted Ptolemy's tables and his highly theorized world map, it is not surprising that we have early printed maps based on the new knowledge that cast aside the Ptolemaic grid of longitude and latitude along with the Ptolemaic map. The history of mapping in Europe since the first printed atlases of the Renaissance in brief is the story of how the map of Ptolemy was ushered out and replaced by the knowledge newly acquired on the ground, even as the Ptolemaic grid was made the standard frame for the space of that new, improved mapping. We may say that Ptolemaic space survived not only the overthrow of Ptolemy's planetary system by that of Copernicus but also the demise of his own map of the world. Everything became obsolete but

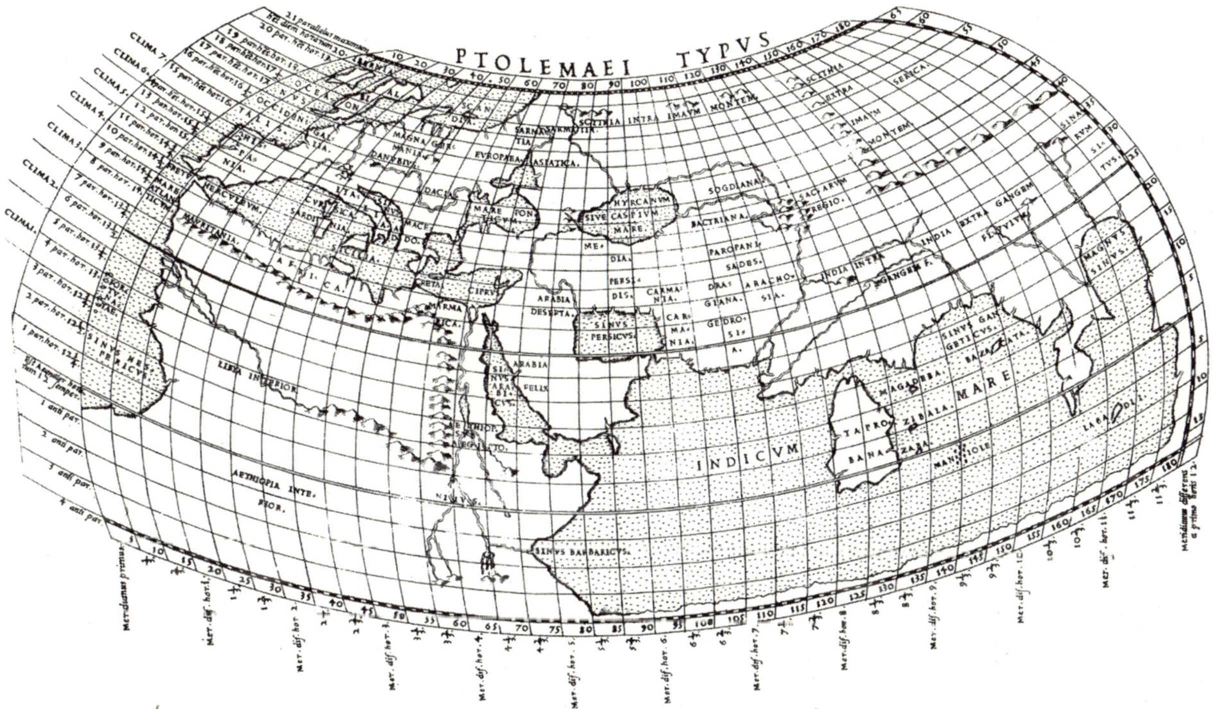

Figure 1. The world map of Ptolemy, according to a Venetian editor, 1561. Longitude is in fractions of hours east of the Fortunate Isles and latitudes in the number of hours in the longest day of the year. (From Brown 1949: 55.)

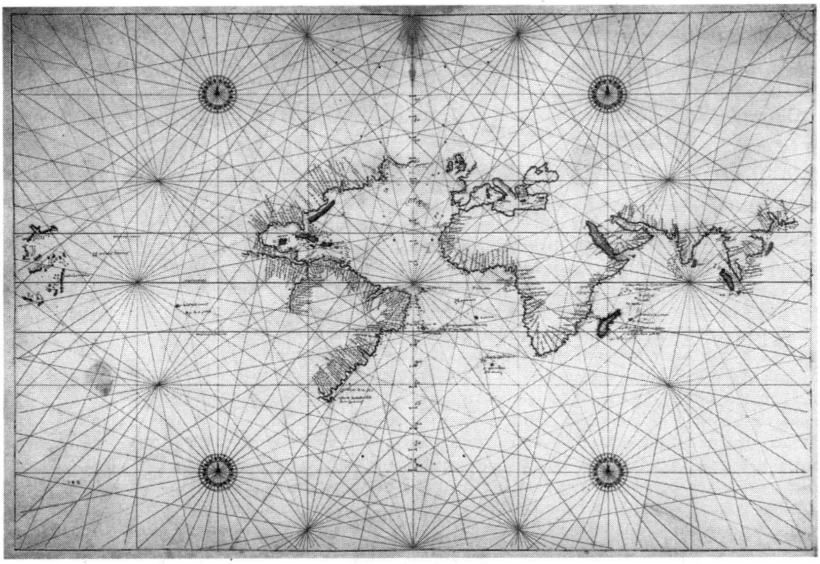

Figure 2. A *portolan* map of the world by the Genoese mapmaker Battista Agnese, c. 1536. (From Whitefield 1994: 59.)

the framework, while the framework itself has proven exceptionally enduring and, indeed, indispensable. Cheap hand-held Global Positioning System devices, drawing upon hugely expensive geosynchronous satellites circling the earth many times a day, now routinely locate objects of all kinds in Ptolemaic space.

We are all familiar with the graticule of longitude and latitude because it appears on maps and globes and is taught in school. The comparable technology for the location of historical events, however, is not well known, being a more dispersed entity with a more backstage existence. Yet all written history depends upon the chronologies that ancient nations worked out for themselves and the synchronisms among the national histories established by the Christian chronologers of the early centuries after Christ. It was Eusebius, in the fourth century A.D., who constructed a chronological canon or table that synthesized national chronologies into a single whole for the writing of a history of Christianity. This table is the foundation of world-historical chronologies to this day.[3]

3. I discuss the Eusebian grid of chronology more fully in Trautmann 1987:206–9.

The Eusebian chronological canon is a locational technology for time. It is a simple device in which events in the chronologies of the various ancient nations are put side by side in columns, such that each horizontal line represents a year of synchronic time. Thus, reading across the columns one finds the synchronisms between events in the various national histories. It was by this means that biblical history was synthesized with the Greek chronological system of Olympiads, and these plus the national histories of the Romans, Chaldeans, Egyptians, and others were brought into a synoptic table that rendered possible the writing of a history across nations—a universal history.

The familiarity of the Ptolemaic grid of longitude and latitude contrasts with the near-total obscurity of the Eusebian chronology. Very few historians who are not historians of the ancient world, let alone members of the general public, will even have heard of the chronological canon of Eusebius, and yet it is the source of all current dating of historical events. What is more, we have no complete surviving example of the chronological canon in the original Greek and know of it only through secondary sources and translations. It is a paradox of history that the locational technology upon which all dating in universal-historical time depends has been handed down only through fragments preserved by the later Greek chronologers, such as Gregory Syncellus, or in translations, especially the Syriac one edited by Josef Karst and the Latin one by St. Jerome, which supplied the chronological grid for historians in western Europe from very early on. Yet despite its dispersed, virtual state, the Eusebian grid for historical chronology has grown through the ages. We continue to lengthen its columns by the addition of earlier and later events, and to widen its reach by integrating into it the chronologies of more different national histories, even if we do not know we are doing so.

It is well to stress the theoretical, highly constructed character of the Eusebian chronology and the concept of historical synchronicity embedded in the structure of the table. Without that locational technology there is no basis in synchronism for the construction of histories across nations. It was the transnational spread of Christianity that occasioned the need to map the histories of the nations upon a unitary plan defined by the horizontal lines of synchronism and the before-and-after logic of the columns.

We come now to the third locational technology of this discussion, the one which especially concerns the topic of this investigation into lan-

Figure 3. The Mosaic ethnology. The descendants of Japhet, son of Noah, as depicted in the *Nuremberg Chronicle*. (From Schedel 1493: fol. 16.)

guages and nations. It is the Tree of Nations, or, as I like to call it (since it comes from the Book of Genesis in the Bible, attributed to Moses), the Mosaic ethnology.[4]

In Genesis, the ten patriarchs from Adam to Noah are succeeded by a branching tree of Noah's sons, Shem, Ham, and Japhet, followed by their sons, and so forth, comprising a large family tree of patriarchs whose progeny are the nations of the earth. The names of the patriarchs are the names of the nations. Thus, for example, the patriarch Eber is the father of the Hebrew people, and the patriarch Javan gives his name to the Greeks, that is, the Ionians ("Yauna" in Persian, "Yavana" in Sanskrit) (see figure 3).

4. For more detailed discussion of the Mosaic ethnology, see Trautmann 1997, ch. 2, "The Mosaic ethnology of Asiatick Jones."

The underlying treelike branching structure is built up from relations of kinship. Not all kinship relations are used, however, but only patrilineal ones, relations of descent through males only. Thus relationships of kinship are sculpted by abstracting only the patrilineal ones to make a tree that ramifies endlessly and does not return into itself. This ramifying figure is maintained by suppressing the representation of descendants through females and the marriages that would otherwise intertwine the branches of the Tree of Nations. Such a structure is what the anthropologist E. E. Evans-Pritchard (1940) called a *segmentary lineage*, and it is of a kind widely used in North Africa and the Middle East, including the biblical lands, to represent and regulate relations among lineages.

The Mosaic ethnology is a simple locational technology for determining the relations among peoples, conceived as branching lineages of the human family tree, as relations of near and far. It is quite capable of worldwide extension and has been the basis of ethnological classifications for a very long period of history. It is quite different from the Hegelian psychohistorical calculus of Self and Other that is so important a construct for theorizing today, since in the Mosaic ethnology every human being is related to every other, but in varying degrees of nearness. This device was widely used by all the Peoples of the Book—Jews, Christians, and Muslims. It was *the* framework within which newly discovered peoples were fitted, to give order and meaning to the rush of new ethnological knowledge that came with the expansion of Islam, and, later, with the European expansion from the Renaissance onward. Thus Muslim scholars found it a matter of importance to determine whether the Chinese are descended from Ham, Shem, or Japhet, and Columbus brought with him to the New World a Morisco who knew Arabic and Hebrew to determine whether the American Indians were descended from the Lost Tribes of Israel. Because they are all based on the Mosaic ethnology, universal histories in the Islamic Middle East and India, on the one hand, and in Christian Europe, on the other, have a family likeness at a fundamental level. However fraught their relations became, Christians and Muslims in the middle ages and the early modern period shared an intellectual culture built upon common structuring principles that they did not share with peoples of nonbiblical religions. This commonality included the Mosaic ethnology as well as a master narrative of universal history, according to which the world was created but a few thousand years ago and peopled from a single central point, and the nations multiplied following the confusion of tongues by God at the Tower of Babel. The fanning out of lineages from a point of origin indexes the figure of the patrilineal Tree of Nations.

The Mosaic ethnology is the main technology of location to be found in universal histories of the Peoples of the Book from the Bible itself down to the eighteenth century. It survives, and indeed flourishes, to this day, but in a transmuted, secularized, and scientized form, as the structuring principle of historical linguistics (while ethnological analysis has turned to the Hegelian frame of Self versus Other). This adaptation of the Mosaic ethnology to linguistic history deserves our attention.

It is something of a scandal for linguists that the roots of their science are planted in the Bible, and this fact has been the object of repeated attempts at erasure and willed forgetting. Histories of linguistic science written within the discipline have represented its rise as a rupture from the past, a breakthrough moment when science emerged, miraculously, from nonscience. Carryovers from the prescientific age into current usages, such as the names "Semitic" and "Hamitic"—taken from names of Noah's sons—for linguistic groups are interpreted as nothing more than vestiges of older, nonscientific conceptions now scientifically reconceptualized. But in spite of its collective suppression in the charter myth of the discipline of linguistics, the Mosaic ethnology continues to shape the work of historical linguistics to this day. The radiating structure of the Tree of Nations, now under the new-old scientific name of "cladistics," underwrites the grand projects of linguistics, such as George Grierson's *Linguistic survey of India* (1903–27) and Antoine Meillet's *Les langues du mond* (1952). The attempt to unify languages into a finite set of families through the conception of a radiating movement in time, and the ambition to unify all these families into a gigantic superfamily by discovering connections among them at ever-deepening levels of past time, ran strong in the project of Joseph Greenberg, whose books on the languages of Africa (1955) and the Americas (1987) were complemented by his work on Eurasian languages (2000), completed just before his death, as well as in Illich-Svitic's work on Nostratic (Manaster Ramer 1993).

There is a mystery here that needs exploring, one that we will not get at through the "history of linguistics" narrative. It is the mystery of how a framework for the classification of *peoples* becomes transformed into one for the classification of *languages*. Solving this problem is crucial to understanding why languages and nations came to be twinned in European thought, and I will shortly propose a solution. Before turning to that matter, however, a few final comments are needed about the three technologies of location we have been examining: the Ptolemaic grid of space, the Eusebian grid of chronology, and the Mosaic ethnological tree. They appear to be concerned with, respectively, space, time, and ethnology. But, in fact, all three are concerned with locations in both space and time at once, or, shall we say, in space-time. They differ not in their media but in their objects. The Ptolemaic grid may seem to be purely about space, but in fact space and time are mutually convertible at fixed rates of exchange, so to say, such that 15 degrees of longitude equals one hour's difference of time. The borders of the Ptolemaic world maps regularly defined longitude by both degrees of arc and hours of distance from a meridian, and the various latitudes by both degrees of arc from the poles and hours of daylight at midsummer. Indeed, the interconvertibility of time and space measures is essential to this locational technology. In the Eusebian chronology, time is the vertical axis, and space—that is, the geographically dispersed nations—is the horizontal one. And in the Mosaic ethnological tree, the vertical axis again is of time, while the horizontal one tracks the spatial dispersion of the nations. The three locational technologies are directed at different kinds of objects in unitary space-time: geographical objects, historical events, and human communities or nations.

LANGUAGES AND NATIONS

We come, then, to the main business of this chapter, which is to excavate the meaning of the twinning of languages and nations in European thought. We do so by attempting to solve the mystery of how the Mosaic ethnology, a classification of *peoples,* was transformed into a framework for the classification of *languages*. This is not, however, a mystery of which anyone has written before, and so I must first persuade the reader that there is indeed a mystery here to be solved, and explain why the mystery itself has been hidden.

As we have seen, one explanation for why the mystery has not hitherto been addressed is historical linguistics' nonrecognition of the Mosaic ethnology, the biblical Tree of Nations, as the source of the genealogical trees of language. A collective unwillingness to find the roots of linguistic science in religion, as well as to acknowledge the origin of the discipline in what is now the separate discipline of ethnology, is the reason the problem is not posed in autohistories of linguistics.

From that beginning, I direct the reader's attention to Sir William Jones's proposal of the idea of the Indo-European language family in British-Indian Calcutta, in order to examine closely how it came about and why it came about at a particular point in history and not earlier. I do so for a couple of reasons. In the first place, after Jones, the study of Indo-European languages quickly became the most intensely cultivated field in comparative philology, supplying models and standards for other fields. In the second place, Jones provided the breakthrough moment for the disciplinary autonarrative of a bounded linguistic science miraculously emerging from the nonscience that preceded it, a narrative that exerts a strong pull upon any investigation of the event in question. I have already suggested that this narrative is defective, and we need to explore the matter more deeply.

Accounts of the history of linguistics almost invariably quote a certain passage of Sir William Jones from the "Third anniversary discourse," on the Hindus, which Jones delivered to the Asiatic Society at Calcutta, as its president and founder, in 1784. The overall scheme of these annual discourses marking the anniversary of the Society's founding was to examine the five "stock nations" of Asia, namely, the Hindus or Indians, Arabs, Persians, Chinese, and Tartars, one by one, and determine their relations to one another. The examination focused on four features: language and letters, religion and philosophy, architecture and sculpture, and arts and manufactures. This is the famous passage:

> The *Sanscrit* language, whatever be its antiquity, is of a wonderful structure; more perfect than the *Greek,* more copious than the *Latin,* and more exquisitely refined than either, yet bearing to both of them a stronger affinity, both in the roots of verbs and in the forms of grammar, than could possibly have been produced by accident; so strong indeed, that no philologer could examine them all three, without believing them to have sprung from some common source, which, perhaps, no longer exists; there is a similar reason, though not quite so forcible, for supposing that both the *Gothick* and the *Celtick,* though blended with a very different idiom, had the same origin with the *Sanscrit;* and the old Persian might be added to the same family, if this were the place for discussing any question concerning the antiquities of Persia. (Jones 1788d:422–23)

The conception expressed here is astonishingly modern. It specifies five ancient languages and posits that they have "sprung from some common source, which, perhaps, no longer exists," and so constitute a family of languages. This is, of course, the Indo-European family, although the name had not yet been invented, and the inferred lost common source is now called Proto-Indo-European. This passage *does* have a breakthrough quality to it. The grouping of languages it propounds was without precedent, both in Europe and in India, and the idea that languages of Iran and India are closely related to European ones created an entirely new sense of deep history. The literatures of these languages preserved no recollection of a common origin and the migrations it implies, but the language themselves preserved proof of it where historical memory had left no trace. It was just this ability of philology to restore a lost history through comparison of languages that was the most spectacular of its powers. Moreover, the historical relationship Jones here proposes has proven durable, and the idea remains valid today, more than two centuries hence.

When this famous passage is abstracted from one narrative, the "Anniversary discourses," and inserted into the narrative of the rise of linguistics as a self-contained field of scientific study, in the process its reading is changed. When we examine it in its original context, the breakthrough quality is not entirely lost but it is considerably qualified. The main thing to grasp about the "Anniversary discourses" is that they were an *ethnological* and *historical* study, not a linguistic one as such; thus the language data function in the argument as evidence for propositions about historical relations among nations or races, not for propositions about historical relations among languages as an end in itself.

Far from constituting the study of languages as a self-contained discipline, Jones treats languages as a means, and just one of many means, to disentangle ethnological relationships. It is a paradox that someone so gifted in languages regarded languages as mere instruments of knowledge and not objects of knowledge in themselves, and used the word "linguist" to mean simply a knower of languages, not a scholar of a self-contained object of knowledge. We see at work here the common presumption of his age: that languages and nations are inextricably connected, so much so that relations among languages index the relations among nations, and historical relations among nations can be inferred from relations among languages. Even when, in later years, comparative philology acquired a body of works all its own, the connectedness of language with issues of nation and race remained so deeply presumed that it was not available for discussion and debate. It was not until more than a century after Jones that Europeans declared, as a surprising new discovery, that the connection between languages and nations is contingent not necessary.

As we zoom out from Jones's passage on Indo-European and look at the "Anniversary discourses" as a whole, the picture changes considerably.[5] This early formulation of the Indo-European language family has

5. The ten anniversary discourses were published in the first four volumes of *Asiatic researches*. They may also be found, collected together, in the *Works* of Jones, of which

several inclusions which are by no means acceptable today: the ancient Egyptians, for example, and the Chinese, and even the Incas and Aztecs of the New World. On the other hand, Jones does not include some languages universally acknowledged to be Indo-European today, most notably the Slavic, which he classifies with the Tartar language. Eventually one becomes aware that the scheme has an underlying structure, as follows:

Shemites	Religion
Hamites	Arts and sciences; civilization
Japhetites	Nomadism

In the conclusion of the "Anniversary discourses" Jones finds that the five principal nations of Asia are reducible to three: the Indians (which includes the Persians and the Chinese), the Arabs, and the Tartars—corresponding to Noah's sons, Ham, Shem, and Japhet, respectively.

This structure of associations was taken over from Jacob Bryant's *Analysis of antient mythology* (1744–76; see Trautmann 1997:41–46). It is somewhat eccentric, in that it identifies the Indians, and hence the Persians and Europeans, as Hamites, in place of the more usual view that Europeans descended from Japhet. It did not succeed in overturning the latter view, and indeed "Japhetic" was a common label for the language family that came to be called Indo-European. The organizing idea of the Bryant-Jones scheme is that all the arts and sciences of primitive times are attributable to the Hamites, who were also the first to turn from the true religion, known to all mankind in the times of Noah, to idolatry; while it is among the Shemites that true religion was preserved, and the Japhetites fell out of the agrarian life established by God in Eden into a life of nomadism. Jones extends this scheme around the globe: for the New World, for example, he has a two-nation theory, such that the nomadic, hunting American Indians are Japhetites, but the Aztec and Inca civilizations are Hamitic. One becomes aware, by the end of the "Anniversary discourses," that the whole scheme is a rational working-out of the story of the peopling of the world from a single stock by the descent of Noah, in a past contained within the chronology of Archbishop Ussher, according to which the world was created no further back than 4004 B.C. and human beings spread across the earth after the universal

the 1807 edition is the most widely available, or the newly published edition of Garland Cannon (1993).

flood, dated to 2349 B.C. The assumption, then, was that within the short time span of the biblical chronology, the human family split up into descent lines and fanned out rapidly across the face of the earth.

This brief look at the larger scheme of the "Anniversary discourses" is useful not so much in the way of drawing attention to Jones's errors as in providing a critical distance on the normal view: that the idea of Indo-European arose immediately from the apprehension of similarity among Latin, Greek, Sanskrit, and Persian, and that historical linguistics came into being by a kind of spontaneous combustion in the mind of Jones. Jones himself promotes that view when he says of Sanskrit, Latin, and Greek, that "no philologer could examine them all three, without believing them to have sprung from some common source." Taken literally, the statement implies a strict empiricism, according to which the historical relationship of the languages is directly seen in the languages themselves and requires only that they be placed side by side for this deeper seeing to take place. This is the "discovery" narrative at its simplest, and it shuts down further investigation into that account's true nature before any inquiry can begin.

If the narrative of simple discovery were true, the Indo-European language family would have been brought to light long since, in antiquity. The Greeks, Persians, and Indians had dealings with one another, and there were undoubtedly many opportunities for the kind of direct comparison that, by Jones's account, would have led spontaneously to the positing of a common ancestry. Yet not only did the ancients fail to discover the Indo-European language family, the Greeks took almost no interest in recording matters to do with languages in their accounts of Persia and India, such as the *Persika* of Ctesias or the *Indika* of Megasthenes. Jones remarks on this Greek indifference to other languages at the beginning of the "Third anniversary discourse": "It is much to be lamented, that neither the *Greeks,* who attended ALEXANDER into *India,* nor those who were long connected with it under the *Bactrian* Princes, have left us any means of knowing with accuracy, what vernacular languages they found on their arrival in this Empire" (Jones 1788d:421–22). Nor did the sophisticated linguistic science of the Indians take any notice of Greek, beyond a few vague references to the language of the barbarians *(mleccha).* Those for whom the similarities of the ancient languages should have been most telling failed entirely to come to the conclusion that Jones represents as springing directly from the simple juxtaposition of languages.

The truth of the matter is that the brute facts of language similarity do not interpret themselves, and indeed are subject to any number of interpretations. That this is so is proven by the many competing interpretations of these facts in the eighteenth and nineteenth centuries. Nathaniel Brassey Halhed, a friend of Jones, for example, had come to a similar conclusion about the historical relationship of Sanskrit and Greek somewhat earlier, in his *Grammar of the Bengal language* (Halhed 1778; Rosane Rocher 1983). On the other hand, Dugald Stewart, the leading philosopher of his generation, followed the lead of Christoph Meiners (*Historia doctrinae de vero Deo,* 1780) and Gottlieb Siegfried Bayer (*Historia regni Graecorum Bactriani in qua simul Graecarum in India coloniarum vetus memoria explicatur,* 1738) and made a fool of himself by publishing, as late as 1827, when the comparative philology of Indo-European was well on the way to its greatest successes, an elaborate demonstration that Sanskrit was similar to Greek because it *was* Greek, overheard by the wily brahmins from Alexander's soldiers during their incursion into India, and adapted by them as a kind of pig Latin with which to mystify the people and hold them in subjection to their priestcraft (Stewart 1827:110; Trautmann 1997:124–26). In the meantime Friedrich Schlegel (*Über die Sprache und Weisheit der Indier,* 1808) had accepted the Indo-European idea, but with a difference from the formulation of Jones that was deeply consequential, according to which Sanskrit is not the co-descendant of a lost ancestral language with Greek, Latin, Gothic, Celtic, and Persian, but is *itself* the ancestor and source of the other Indo-European languages. It was Schlegel's program to reengineer the conception of ancient India as the pure source of a lost, primitive innocence and ancient wisdom—the India of Romanticism, an India that embodied the childhood of the human race. While Franz Bopp (1816, 1833, 1845–53), the great pioneer of Indo-Europeanist comparative philology, resisted this view and held to the one Jones had expressed—that Sanskrit was the sibling and not the mother of the other Indo-European languages—other writers, perhaps the majority of them in the early nineteenth century, held some version of Schlegel's view. Thus the comparative examination of Sanskrit and Greek has led to three quite different interpretations: the identity of Sanskrit with Greek, the co-descent of the two from a common ancestor, and the derivation of Greek from Sanskrit.

Perhaps the most telling case that helps us free ourselves from the naturalizing narrative of the discovery of Indo-European by the mere inspection of Sanskrit, Latin, and Greek is that of the Jesuit missionary Gaston-Laurent Coeurdoux, who spent his whole adult life in South India. Only now, thanks to the work of Sylvia Murr (1977, 1987), do we have a full appreciation of this fine scholar-missionary's Indological work, which, as Murr has shown conclusively, was recycled (to put it politely) by the Abbé Dubois in the well-known and much reprinted work *Hindu manners, customs and ceremonies* (3d ed., 1906). Father Coeurdoux also conceived a form of the Indo-European idea, and he did so before Jones, in a letter to the Académie des Inscriptions written in 1768. However, his ideas were only published in 1808—after his death and after Jones had published the "Third anniversary discourse"—thanks to the efforts of another French Indologist, Abraham-Hyacinthe Anquetil-Duperron.

After providing a number of examples of Latin, Greek, and Sanskrit words, Coeurdoux interprets the similarities among them in this way:

> The Samskroutam language is that of the ancient Brahmes; they came to India from the north of that country, from Caucasia, from Tartary, which had been peopled by the descendants of Magog. Of the sons of Japhet, some spoke Greek, others Latin, still others Samskroutam. Before their total separation, their languages were somewhat mixed because of the communication they had among each other; and there remain vestiges of that ancient intercourse, in the common words which still exist, and of which I have reported a part. (My translation of a passage in Coeurdoux c. 1768:666; see also Murr 1987, pt.1, ch.7)

While Coeurdoux, like Jones, interprets the similarity among the three languages in biblical terms, that is, in the terms of the Mosaic ethnology, we see in this passage that this particular technology of location does not operate as an iron frame leading always to identical results. For Jones, the three nations of this passage are Hamites, but for Coeurdoux they are Japhetites; moreover, for Coeurdoux the brahmins of India are of the descendants of Japhet called Magog, who had migrated to Central Asia, whence the brahmins migrated to India. He accounts for the similarity of the three languages not by co-descent from a single ancestor language, as in Jones, but by mutual borrowing among languages long neighboring one another, though originally distinct. One supposes the author means that God made these languages completely different from one another following the building of the Tower of Babel, and thereafter they grew similar because of their communications with one another.

From this passage we can draw several conclusions. First, both Father Coeurdoux and Sir William Jones, independently of one another, observed similarities among Sanskrit, Latin, and Greek through comparison, and sought for interpretations from the Genesis narrative of the Confusion of Tongues and the Dispersal of Nations, in short, from the Mosaic ethnology. Second, they located the nations speaking these languages differently, Coeurdoux making them co-descendants of Japhet, Jones making them co-descendants of Ham. The way in which the Mosaic ethnology is applied is thus underdetermined, and the outcomes of its application are not predictable, though both Coeurdoux and Jones place the three nations in a common descent line. Third, we come to the crucial move: from the genealogy of *nations* to the genealogy of *languages*. Here Coeurdoux and Jones again differ, showing two very different totalizing conceptions. Coeurdoux gives an explanation of language similarity through *mixture,* positing a movement from original distinctness toward similarity. Jones gives an explanation of language similarity through *co-descent,* positing a movement from original unity to difference—a movement that mirrors the movement of the Tree of Nations from generation to generation of patrilineal descendants. Jones applies the figure of the Tree of Nations directly to language as a model of language history, and by his doing so language history becomes a remedy and substitute for the lost memory of the history of nations. Language, like the DNA in our cells, contains, unknown to its speakers, the hidden history of the human race. Thus for Jones, and not for Coeurdoux, the shape of language history tracks the shape of the history of the nations. It is the explanation of Jones that became the foundation of comparative philology.

The reason why the ancient Indians, Persians, and Greeks did not discover the Indo-European language family is now clear. The underlying technology of location, the Mosaic ethnology, did not come from the ancient Greeks, Persians, or Indians, but from the Bible.

The question remains, however, why the Indo-European conception did not arise earlier among those who did have the locational technology of the Mosaic ethnology, the Peoples of the Book: Jews, Muslims and Christians. One would especially expect it to have been made by Muslim scholars when the expansion of Islam brought them into contact with various branches of the Indo-European family. One thinks, for instance, of the great scholar al-Biruni, who had lived and studied in India and knew both Persian and Sanskrit. The writings of Muslim historians did make abundant use of the Mosaic ethnology to give meaningful location to the many foreign peoples they encountered—a fact that was very consequential for Orientalist scholarship in British India, for it was largely through Persian, the language of diplomacy and learning for the Mughal empire, that the British acquired knowledge of Indian civilization in the early days. Muslim histories of India—and so also Muslim interlocutors of British scholars in British India such as Jones—used the familiar Mosaic technology to determine the ethnological location of India. For example, a history of India written in Persian by Firishtah was translated and published at Calcutta in 1768 by Alexander Dow; in it we learn that Japhet had sons named Turc, Chin, and Rus, from whom the Turks, the Chinese, and the Russians are descended, while the Indians are descendants of a patriarch named Hind, not named in the Bible but reckoned as a son of Ham, and that he had sons named Purib, Bang (i.e., Bengal), Decan (Deccan), Narwaal, and so forth, who founded the nations of India (Firishtah 1768:7–9). Similarly, in Abu'l Fazl's *Akbar nama,* Ham has sons named Hind and Sindh (both names of India), and Japhet, called the most just of Noah's sons, is said to be the ancestor of the Mughal emperors (Abu'l Fazl 1908, vol. 1, ch. 1; first English translation by Gladwin 1783–80). These texts, among others, would have reinforced Jones in his adoption of Hamitic ancestry for the Indo-Europeans.

In short, Muslims, Christians, and Jews shared the Mosaic framework for ethnological classification, and in that sense belonged to a common intellectual world. Our problem is to account for the fact that the application of methods for determining the historical relations among nations was applied to the problem of finding the historical relations among languages, and to explain why using language history as an index of the historical relations among nations appears only late in the day, and only among the Europeans.

COMPARATIVE VOCABULARY, OR THE METHOD OF THE WORD LIST

To see how language history became an index of the history of nations we need to zoom out still further and see Jones and the project of the "Anniversary discourses" in a yet larger context.

It is a curious fact that the famous text of Jones in the "Third anniversary discourse" does not display the means by which the comparison of languages was undoubtedly accomplished the comparative vocabulary. The "Anniversary discourses," he makes us understand, being oral performances to mark an occasion, were no place for the extensive recitation of evidence, and like any good lecturer Jones knew to present listeners with plenty of conclusions without troubling them overmuch with tedious evidence.[6] But his sketch of the Indo-European conception

6. At the end of the eighth anniversary discourse Jones says that in the ninth discourse "I shall resume the whole argument concisely and synthetically; and shall then have con-

rested upon inspection and comparison of the languages in question, and we may be sure from every parallel of his day—and they are abundant—that such a comparison was given focus and direction by the means, simple but effective, of the word list: arranging the words of several languages in columns against a standard list of categories.

The simplicity of the word list lends itself to the empiricist view, against which I have been arguing, that the mere comparative inspection of languages leads to the apprehension of their historical relationships. It seems the word list merely orders the material of languages in ways that make comparison possible and are more user-friendly than older methods, such as the polyglot Bibles or polyglot collections of Pater Nosters that began to be published almost as early as the introduction of print in Europe. It takes an effort to see that the simple word list is not, after all, simple. The comparative vocabulary is not a neutral enterprise but an abstraction from living languages that freezes and organizes certain aspects of them for a certain purpose.

It is unfortunate for our purposes that Jones did not publish the word lists upon which his comparison of the Indo-European languages surely rested, for we would like to examine them at this point in the argument. We know for a certainty that they existed, and we see something of their content in the later work of Alexander Hamilton—a contemporary of Jones who learned Sanskrit at Calcutta and went on to become the first professor of Sanskrit in Europe, at the East India College in England (at Hartford Castle, later Haileybury)—particularly in Hamilton's review of Franz Bopp's important first work on the comparison of Indo-European languages (Bopp 1816; Hamilton 1820; see also Rosane Rocher 1961). We are obliged to look elsewhere for an example to analyze, but we can make a virtue of the necessity by turning to two important short papers, written at more or less at the same time as Jones's "Third anniversary discourse," by William Marsden, another member of the Asiatic Society and also in the employ of the East India Company.

William Marsden is chiefly remembered for his *History of Sumatra* (1783, 1966), his dictionary (1801, 1812a) and his grammar of Malay (1812b), and the collection of 3,447 coins he gave to the British Mu-

densed in seven discourses a mass of evidence, which, if brevity had not been my object, might have been expanded into seven large volumes with no other trouble than that of holding the pen; but (to borrow a turn of expression from one of our poets) 'for what I have produced, I claim only your indulgence; it is for what I have suppressed, that I am entitled to your thanks.'" (Jones 1807, 3:185).

seum (cf. Marsden 1823–25). He contributed extensively to linguistics, but (as he observed bitterly) his philological work was better appreciated on the Continent than in England, where the brilliant reputation of Jones had thrown Marsden's work into the shade.[7] How true this is can be seen in the *Dictionary of national biography* entry for Marsden (s.v.), which describes him as "orientalist and numismatist" and does not mention one of his greatest achievements, the first demonstration of the Malayo-Polynesian family of languages, and barely mentions his paper on the Indian origin of the Gypsies. These two accomplishments, which remain valid today, were realized by the method of the word list.[8]

Marsden shipped out to Bencoolen, Sumatra in 1770. On 5 March 1780, having just returned to England at age twenty-five, he wrote a letter to Sir Joseph Banks, president of the Royal Society, subsequently published as "Remarks on the Sumatran languages" (Marsden 1782). The centerpiece of that article is a vocabulary of fifty English words, against which are listed in columns the equivalent words in thirteen languages (see figure 4). Six of these languages are Sumatran: Malay, Achenese, Batta, Lampoon, Nias, and Rejang. The remaining languages are Javanese, Malagash (of Madagascar), Mongeray, Macassar, Savu, Tahitian, and Chinese, although Chinese does not play much part in the analysis. Marsden's purpose in drawing up this chart, he says, was, first, to

7. "About the period at which I first submitted to the notice of the literary world such information as a residence in Sumatra had enabled me to acquire on the subject of the languages spoken by the inhabitants of that and other of the Eastern Islands, it happened that the richer and more important mine of SANSKRIT learning had been opened by the labours of WILKINS and of JONES. To this the attention of persons who took an interest in Oriental studies was almost exclusively directed, and little encouragement was given to philological (though much to physical) researches in the maritime and less civilized regions of the East. In latter years, however, a disposition has been shewn, especially amongst our continental neighbors, to bring these languages within the scope of critical investigation, to examine their structure, their analogies, ascertain the extent to which they prevail, and, if possible, to deduce their origin" (Marsden 1834, art. 1, "On the Polynesian, or east-insular languages," pp. 1–116).

8. Marsden's publications and manuscripts show abundant interest in the comparison of languages. The published works I may mention include: *A catalogue of the dictionaries, vocabularies, grammars and alphabets of all languages and dialects* (1796), *Bibliotheca Marsdeniana philologica et orientalis, a catalogue of works and manuscripts collected with a view to the general comparison of languages and to the study of Oriental literature* (1827), and articles on the languages of Polynesia ("The Polynesian, or east-insular languages") and on the romanization of Oriental languages ("On a conventional Roman alphabet, applicable to Oriental languages") in *Miscellaneous works* (1834), art. 1, pp. 1–116, and art. 2, pp. 1–27. Among the manuscripts of Marsden at the School of Oriental and African Studies of the University of London there is, for example, a collection of lists of fifteen numerals, common nouns, and adjectives in languages of all parts of the world (MS 12283–12304).

English	Malay	Acheen	Batta	Lampoon	Neeas	Rejang
One	Satoo	Sah	Sadah	Sye	Semboaa	Do
Two	Duo	Dua	Duo	Rowah	Demboaa	Dooy
Three	Teego	Tloo	Toloo	Tulloo	Tuloo	Tellou
Four	Ampat	Paat	Opat	Ampah	Oopha	'Mpat
Five	Lumo	Lumung	Leemah	Leemah	Leema	Lemo
Six	Anam	'Nam	Onam	Annam	Oonoo	Noom
Seven	Toojoo	Toojoo	Paitoo	Peetoo	Pheetoo	Toojooa
Eight	Slappan	D'lappan	Ooalloo	Ooalloo	Ooalloo	Delapoon
Nine	Sambilan	Sakoorang	Seeah	Seewah	Seewa	Sembilan
Ten	Sapooloo	Saploo	Sapooloo	Pooloo	Phooloo	Depooloo
An hundred	Sa-ratoos	Sa-ratoos	Saratoos	Saratoos	Oghoo	Sotoſe
Huſband	Lackee	Lackaye	Morah	Cadjoon	Dongagoo	Sacky
Wife	Beenee	Beenaye	Aboo	Cadjoon	Seealavee	Sooma
Father	Bapa	Bah	Ammah	Bapa	Amah	Bapa
Mother	Mau	Mau	Enang	Eenah	Eenah	Indo
Brother	Sadarroo	Addooeh	Ahhah	Adding	Talleephooſoon	Cacoon
Head	Capallo	Oolou	Ooloo	Ooloohi	Hugu	Oolou
Eyes	Matto	Matta	Mahtah	Mattah	Huru	Matty
Noſe	Eedong	Eedoon	Aygong	Eerong	Eeghoo	Eeoong
Hair	Ramboot	Oh	Oboo	Booho	Boo	Boo
Cheeks	Peepee	Meung	Oroom	Bechum	Bo-oogh	Cubbole
Belly	Proot	Proot	Buttoohah	Tunnaye	Talloo	Tennuay
Hand	Tangan	Iarrooay	Tangan	Chooloo	Tanga	Tangoon
Legs	Cakee	Buttees	Paat	Binto	Apeh	Bettees
Garment	Badjoo	Badjow	Ahbee	Caway	Baroo	Badjow
Day	Aree	Ooraye	Torang harree	Rannee	Loo-oh	Beely Iooeng
Night	Mallam	Mallam	Borgning	Beenghee	Boong-ee	B. calemmoon
White	Pootee	Pootee	Nabottar	Mandack	Aphooſee	Pootea
Black	Etam	Hetam	Nabeerong	Malloom	Aytoo	Meloo
Good	Baye	Gaet	Dengan	Buttie	Sooghee	Baye
Die	Mattee	Mattay	Mahtay	Jahal	Maté	Mattooee
Fire	Appee	Appooy	Ahhee	Aphooy	Aleetoo	Opoay
Water	Ayer	Eer	Ayck	Wye	Eedano	Beole
Earth	Tana	Tano	Tana	Tanno	Tano	Peeta
People	Orang	Oreeoong	Halla	Ooloon	Neegha	Toon
Coconut	Clappo	Oo	Crambee	Clappah	Bunneeo	Neole
Teeth	Geegee	Geguy	Ningee	Eeſſan	Eephoo	Aypen
Hog	Babee	Booy	Babee	Babooye	Bavee	Sooeetemba
Bird	Boorong	Cheechim	Peedong, Manook	Boorong	Foopho	Benono
Egg	Telloor	Boh	Peerah	Tullooy	Adoolo	Tennole
Fiſh	Eecun	Incoor	Dekkay	Ewah	Eeagh	'Conn
Rice	Bray	Breeagh	Dahans	Beeas	Booragh	Blas
Potatoes	Oobee	Gadoong	Gadong	Cutillah	Govwee	Ooby
Sun	Matto Aree	Mattowraye	Matah haree	Matta rance	Seeno	Mattu beely
Moon	Boolan	Booloon	Boolan	Boolan	Bowa	Booloon
Stars	Beentang	Beentang	Bintang	Bintang	Doophee	Beetang
I	Ambo, Sayo	Ooloon	Apoo	'Gnah	Eeow	Ookoo
Yes	Eeo	Nyoh	Olo	Eea	Eh	Aou
Come hither	Maree ſeenee	Jah knnyi	Maré toſone	Eja dejah	Einee undeh	Comeendi
God	Allah tallah	Allah	Daibattah	Alla Talla	Lowa langee	Oola tallo

Figure 4. William Marsden's comparative vocabulary of twelve Malayo-Polynesian languages and Chinese. (From Marsden 1782: facing p. 154, table 1.)

trace, if possible, a common origin among these far-flung languages, and, second, to determine whether the languages spoken by the "various independent and unconnected nations" of the interior of Sumatra are radically different, "as is generally supposed by the Europeans resident there," or are different dialects of a single language.

The vocabulary appears to be a mere list, and its evidence is offered modestly by the young author, with but a minimum of analysis, in deference to what the wiser heads of the Royal Society will make of it. But the list is, in fact, carefully constructed and has a theory behind it. It

Javan	Malagaſh	Mongeraye	Macaſſar	Savu	Otaheite	Chineſe
Seejee	Eraike	Eeſakoo	Saydee	Uſſe	Atahay	Cheed
Roro	Dooe	Lolaye	Dooa	Rooe	Erooa	No
Tulloo	Teloo	Looleetoo	Tulloo	Tulloo	Torhoo	Sanh
Papat	Ephat	Lopah	Pa-me	Uppa	Attaa	See
Leemo	Leemoo	Leemo	Leema	Lumee	Ereema	Go
Nanam	Enena	Daho	Anan	Unna	Aono	Lacq
Peetoo	Pheetoo	Pheetoo	Peetoo	Petoo	Aheetoo	Shit
Oloo	Valoo	Apho	Arrooa	Aroo	Awarroo	Peeh
Sanga	Seevee	Seewa	Aſſarra	Saio	Aceva	Caow
Sapooloo	Phooloo	Tooroo	Sapooloo	Singooroo	Ahooroo	Chap
Satoos	Tatoo		Sangatoos			Chepé
Lanang	Laké laké	Namee	Baronee		Tane	Ang
Ooadone	Ampela	Jah	Makoonraye		Huaheine	Poh
Paman	Appa	Bapa	Ambo		Medooa tane	Enteeah
Beeang	Nenay	Mau	Endo		Med. waheine	Neha
Sadooloor	Ranowla	Noko	Sadjee		Teine	Suotee
Endaſs	Loohah	Jahé	Ooloo		Oopo	Toucah
Matta	Meſſoo	Nana	Mattaye	Madda	Matau	Buxu
Eerong	Oorong	Meenee	Eengana	Sivanga	Eahoo	Peeh
Ramboot	Vooloo	Jahé	Gummanna	Row	Eraowroo	Toumo
Peepee	Takoolaka		Dowcheelee	Cavaranga	Paparea	Sheepay
Oouattung	Keeboo	Ataliba	Allay	Dùlloo	Eoboo	Pueto
Lungan	Feletanan	Tanaraga	Tapha-lamay	Wùlalea	Ereema	Tehoo
Seekeel	Toongoota	Eetee	Aajiengna	Baibo	Awy	Cahcoot
Calambee	Ahanzoo	Moortana	Cabadja	Cova	Aihoo	Sanh
Deena	Hareeanroo	Ooſa	Aſſo		Mahana	Ieet
Oongee	Haree Vah	Gamoo	Bunnee-ee		Eaoo'	May
Pootee	Phootee	Bootee	Pootee		Tea	Pay
Eerung	Minetee	Metam	Lotong	Bulla	Ere ere	Oh
Saye	Sooah	Row	Macleching		Myty	Hoh
Mattee	Mattee	Hoomoo	Mattee		Matte	See
Geennee	Aphoo	Atta	Appee		Wahaa	Whoey
Banneeo	Rano	Eera	Ooaye		Avy	Choee
Lumma	Tana	Tano	Bunnoo		Fenooa	Toh
Wong	Ooloo	Anoonoo	Taow	Momonne	Tata	Lang
Clappo	No Word	Ooata	Calookoo		Taro - Aree	Eea
Oontoo	Neephee	Oaſſee	Aſſunna		Eneehees	Cheekee
Cheling	Lamboo	Baye	Babee	Vavee	Booah	Tee
Mano	Voorong	Olo	Manoomanoo	Dolula	Manoo	Cheow
Endo	Atoodee	Aſſowa	Tello	Dulloo	Aouero	Nooey
Eewa	Pheeah	Appee	Iooco-edja	Nudoo	Eya	Hee
Bras	Varay	Reta	Bra	Arree		Bee
Cuſtela	Oovee	Jammais	Oobee		Oomarrah	Whunchee
Surningee	Maſſoo anroo	Ooatoo	Matangaſſo		Mahana	Jettaou
Oolan	Voolan	Ooroo	Oolang	Wurroo	Maruna	Gooay
Ooeentang	Vintan	Eepee berray			Efaitoo	Schay
Coula	Zaho	Anee	Eedee		Waow, Mee	Gooa
Inghee	No word	Eeo	Eeay-na	O	Ai	Hoh
Mareenee	Aveeah	Maoo	Sakomaye		Harre mai	Layeno
Dewah	Dernakaree		Allah tallah		Eatua	Teehn tay

consists of words "of universal use from the nature of the ideas they express," namely, the numbers from *one* to *ten* and *one hundred;* kinship terms *(husband, wife, father, mother, brother);* parts of the body *(head, eyes, nose, hair, cheeks, belly, hands, legs);* garments; *day* and *night; white* and *black; good; die;* the elements *(fire, water, earth); people;* foodstuffs (*coconut, hog, bird, egg, fish, rice, potatoes*—with the word *teeth* randomly stuck in); heavenly bodies *(sun, moon, stars),* and a miscellany *(I, yes, come hither, God)*. The vocabulary, then, is not a random sample of the abundance to be found in a living language or a dictionary but is comprised of what are conceived to be the simplest, most primitive and necessary conceptions that languages must name at their very creation—words which constitute, for that reason, the native core of those languages.

From this simple-seeming device Marsden then abstracted the most obvious cognates, constructing a second list that reversed the order of the original word list, putting the cognates first and the English glosses second. These "examples of words in the Sumatran and neighbouring languages[,] corresponding in sound and significance with others in places remote from thence" (see figure 5) and consisting of about half the words of the original vocabulary list, display correspondences across languages from Madagascar to New Zealand and Easter Island. Marsden, with a show of diffidence, says that though he has been only mildly successful in tracing a common origin among the languages in question, the only general inference that can be drawn is that "from Madagascar eastward to the Marquesas, or nearly from the east coast of Africa to the west coast of America, there is a manifest connexion in many of the words by which the inhabitants of the islands express their simple ideas, and between some of the most distant, a striking affinity." This is the very first statement of the bounds of the language family we now call Malayo-Polynesian.

Marsden goes on to suggest that Central Asia ("Tartary"), that *officina gentium,* or womb of nations, may have been the source of the peoples of the archipelago, and a knowledge of Siamese, Lao, Cambodian, and Peguan—languages lying between Central Asia and the islands whose languages he has been studying—would be the "readiest clue to a discovery of that kind." A few decades later John Leyden, also of the East India Company, published two short works on the languages of the Indochina Peninsula, as if in response to this expressed need (Leyden 1810, 1812). The theory of a Central Asian origin of these languages—a Japhetic origin, in Mosaic terms—did not prove useful. Nevertheless, Marsden had accomplished a basic demonstration of the relatedness of many of the languages making up the Malayo-Polynesian family, mostly from materials collected by himself, as he says, from the mouths of natives (excepting those for Savu and Tahitian) and not from books. It was a stunning accomplishment, equal in every way to Jones's proposal of the Indo-European concept.

Marsden's discussion, brief as it is, throws much light on the underlying assumptions of the whole enterprise of collecting words against a standardized word list. Regarding the second question he had set out to examine, the relationships among the languages of the Sumatran interior, he regarded his table as showing them to be dialects of a single language, against the view prevailing among Europeans there, and among the Sumatrans themselves, that the languages were unrelated. To be sure—

and here Marsden gives the arguments of the opposing view—the fact that several of these languages had writing systems all their own seemed to prove that the languages were of different origins and that the similarities among them had been produced by the borrowing of words from one another. The different Sumatran peoples do not comprehend one another's language, are different in their persons, and their manners and customs are "as unlike as those of the most distant nations." But, Marsden replies to his own objection, the words they have in common "are radical and such whose correspondent ideas must have existed and been described prior to all intercourse with either remote or neighbouring people; as will appear from an inspection of the comparative specimens, and consequently that the dissimilarity, not the similarity, must have been induced by degrees" (Marsden 1782:156). The critical aspect of the proof is that the vocabulary is made up of words that are radical, that is, root words native to each language.

In this passage we see Marsden considering the two great alternatives of interpretation for similarity among languages: *mixture* of languages through borrowing versus gradual *differentiation* of languages sharing descent from a common original language. He decides that language similarity is, on the whole, the vestigial evidence of co-descent and not the product of linguistic mixture and convergence. This is the very issue that separates Jones and Coeurdoux in the interpretation of the resemblance among Indo-European languages, Jones arguing (correctly, in this case) for co-descent and Coeurdoux arguing (wrongly) for convergence due to borrowing. The issue is inescapable in any comparison of two or more languages for purposes of determining historical relations, and the method of the word list is a kind of technology for getting at relations of co-descent. It does this by what it aims to include—radical (root) words of the language, as Marsden puts it. But it also operates by what it excludes from the list, namely, those words corresponding to more complex ideas, words of art and science that develop late through commerce with other nations and the combination of simple ideas into complex ones. The philosophical distinction between simple and complex ideas, as well as Locke's conception of words as names of ideas and his developmentalist, progressive notion of knowledge (Aasleff 1982), are the theoretical underpinnings of the simple vocabulary list as a strategic method for uncovering relations of co-descent.

The second paper by Marsden, "Observations on the language of the people commonly called Gypsies" (1785), offers further testimony to the efficacy of the comparative vocabulary as a tool by which reliable new

Malay	Mattee	Die, Dead	Otaheite	Matte
Acheneſe	Mattay		Garageeco	Mattee
Batta	Mahtay		Madagaſcar	Mattee
Neas	Mate		Buggueſs or	Mattee
Rejang	Mattooee		Macaſſar	
Javaneſe	Mattee			
Malay	Matto	Eyes	Otaheite	Matta
Achen.	Matta		Savu	Madda
Batta	Mahtah		Garageeco	Matta
Rejang	Matty		Buggueſs	Mattaye
Lampoon	Mattah		Eaſter iſland	Matta
Javan.	Matta		Marqueſas	Matta
			Amſterdam	Matta
			N. Zealand	Matta
			Malicolo	Maitang
Malay	Babbee	Hog	Otaheite	Booa
Achen.	Booy		Marqueſas	Booa
Batta	Babee		Amſterdam	Booacha
Neas	Bavee		Savu	Vavee
			Mongeraije	Baye
			Malicolo	Brooas
			Tanna	Boogas
Batta	Manook	Bird, Fowl	Otaheite	Manoo
Lampoon	Manoo		Eaſter Iſland	Manoo
Javan.	Mano		Amſterdam	Manoo
			Tanna	Manoo
			N. Caladonia	Maneek
			Buggueſs	Manoo manoo
Rejang	Neole	Coconut	Amſterdam	Eeoo
Neas	Bunneco		Chineſe	Eea
			N. Caladonia	Neeo
Malay	Eecun	Fiſh	Otaheite	Eya
Neas	Eeagh		Eaſter Iſland	Eeka
Rejang	Eewah		N. Zealand	Eeka
Javaneſe	Eewah		Amſterdam	Eeka
			Madagaſcar	Pheeah
Malay	Ayer	Water	Buggueſs	Ooaye
Achen.	Eer		Mongeraye	Eera
Batta	Ayck		Otaheite	Avy
Lampoon	Wye		Eaſter Iſland	Evy
			N. Caladonia	Ooee
Malay	Oobee	Potatoes and	Otaheite	Eoohe
Neas	Gooee	Yams	Eaſter Iſland	Oohe
Rejang	Ooby		Amſterdam	
			N. Caladonia	Oobe
			Madagaſcar	Oovee
Malay	Orang	Man	Chineſe	Lang
Lampoon	Oooloon	Perſon	Madagaſcar	Ooloo
Javan.	Wong	People		
Achen.	Appooy	Fire	Madagaſcar	Aphoo
Lampoon	Aphooy		Chineſe	Whooee

Figure 5. William Marsden's list of cognate words in Sumatran and neighboring languages. (From Marsden 1782: facing p. 154, table 2.)

Malay	Duo	Two	Otaheite	Erooa
Acheneſe	Dua		Savu	Rooe
Batta	Duo		Madagaſcar	Dooee
Neas	Dembooa		Bugueſs	Dooa
Rejang	Dooy		Eaſter Iſland	Rooa
Lampoon	Rowah		Marqueſas	Aooa
Javaneſe	Roro		Amſterdam	Eooa
			Tana	
Malay	Teego	Three	Otaheite	Torhoo
Achen.	Tloo		Savu	Tulloo
Batta	Toloo		Madagaſcar	Telloo
Neas	Tuloo		Bugueſs	Tulloo
Rejang	Telou		Eaſter Iſland	Toroo
Lampoon	Tulloo		Marqueſas	Atoroo
Javan.	Tulloo		Amſterdam	Toroo
Malay	Ampat	Four	Otaheite	Atta
Achen.	Paat		Savu	Uppa
Batta	Opat		Madagaſcar	Ephat
Neeas	Oopha		Eaſter Iſland	Faa
Rejang	Mpat		Marqueſas	Afaa
Lampoon	Ampah		Malicolo	Ebat
Malays	Toojoo	Seven	Otaheite	Aheetoo
Achen.	Toojoo		Savu	Peetoo
Batta	Pailoo		Madagaſcar	Pheetoo
Neas	Pheetoo		Mongeray	Pheetoo
			Marqueſah	Aeeheetoo
Malay	Sambilan	Nine	Otaheite	Aeeva
Batta	Seeah		Savu	Saio
Neas	Sewah		Madagaſcar	Seevee
			Eaſter Iſland	Heeva
Neas	Adooloo	Egg	Savu	Dulloo
Lampoon	Tulloy		Bugueſs	Tello
Malay	Papateel	A Tool	N. Zealand	Patoo patoo
Malay	Telingo	Ear	Malicolo	Talingan
Malay	Tapa	Sole of Foot	Otaheite	Tapooy
Javan.	Eerung	Black	Otaheite	Ere ere
Malay	Momotong	Cut	Otaheite	Motoo
Malay	Paya	Fatigued	Otaheite	Paya Faeea
Neas	Talloo	Belly	Savu	Dulloo
Malay	Bray	Rice	Savu	Arre
Achen.	Breeagh		Madagaſcar	Varay
Neas	Booragh		Bugueſs	Bra
Rejang	Blas		Chineſe	Bee
Lampoon	Beeas			
Javan.	Bras			
Malay	Bapa	Father	Otaheite	Papa

Comparisons of the Gypsey and Hindostanic languages.

	English Gypsies.	Turkish Gypsies or Chinghiarès.	Cingari vel Errónes Nubiani.	Hindostanic.
One	Aick, yek	Yeck		Aick, ek, yek
Two	Dooee	Duy		Do, dow
Three	Trin	Trin		Teen
Four	Stau, staur, shtar	Shtiar		Chaur
Five	Pange	Panch		Paunch
Six	Shove	Shove		Chäye, chey
Seven	Heftau	Eftâ		Saath, saut
Eight		Oktô		Aath, aut
Nine	Henya	Enia		Noh, no
Ten	Desh	Desh		Dus, dosh (Bengalese)
Man	Räye, gajo	Rom, manush	Manusch	Maanóosho (Bengalese) Mannoos (Mahratta)
Woman or Lady	Raünee, gaujee	Romee		Rendee, raunee
Head	Bol-shuroo, sharo	Shero	Scheiro	Seer, sirr
Eyes	Yack-au, yock	Yack	Jaka	Aunk, choke, okhyo, (Bengalese)
Nose	Bol-nok	Nack	Nak	Nauck
Hair	Ballau, bolau	Bal	Bal	Baul, bal
Teeth	Dan-au	Dan		Daunt, dont, (Bengalese)
Ear	Kananä		Can	Kaun
Good	Questo	Latchò		Acha
Day	Dewas, devas, dévus;	Deeves		Deen, deewus, (Mahratta)
Night	Rautee	Ratee		Raut, raat
White	Pauno	Parnee		Paandra, (Mahratta)
Black	Kaulo	Caglee		Kaulla
Fire	Yaug	Yagg	Yag	Aug
Water	Paunee	Pagnee	Pani	Paunee
Dead	Mullo, mouläy	Moolo		Mooah, maylay, (Mahratta)
Cow	Gouvinee		Curcumni	Gauee
Sheep	Baukro		Bakro	Bhare
Hog	Baulo	Balò	Palo	
Fish	Matcho	Matcho		Matchee, mutchee
Bird	Chereko, chillakoo	Chiricklo		Chereah
House	Kair		Ker	Ghurr
Knife	Chooree			Chooree
Moon		Chonn	Chon	Chaund
Salt	Lone			Noone, (Bengalese)
Gold	Soona-kai			Sonna
Silver	Roop			Roopau
God	Me-devel	Devlaa		Dawa, (Bengalese)

Figure 6. William Marsden's comparative vocabulary of Romani and Hindustani. (From Marsden 1785: 386.)

scientific knowledge could be achieved. From a specimen of words of the Cingari, or Gypsies, in a history of Ethiopia by Ludolphus, "which he had collected from these people in his travels, with a view of determining their origin," Marsden was surprised to find many words familiar to him from his knowledge of Hindustani. The similarity seemed so extraordinary, he says, that he suspected an error in the publication, "which might have arisen from a confusion of obscure vocabularies in the author's possession," but he verified its accuracy by gathering further vocabularies from Gypsies in England and, through a correspondent, in Turkey. He displayed the results in a table using a vocabulary very similar to that of his article on the Sumatran languages, but slightly shorter (39 words) (see figure 6). He observes also that some of the Gypsy words correspond to words in Marathi and Bengali, and that "it is not a little singular that the terms for the numerals *seven, eight* and *nine,* are purely *Greek,* though the first five, and that for *ten,* are indisputably *Indian.*"

Since the name "Gypsy" was a corruption of "Egyptian," some scholars thought the Gypsy language might be traced to Coptic, a view which Marsden was able to disprove: only a single word bore a resemblance to Coptic. Thus in a second brief article, Marsden had established the Indian origin of the Romani, or Gypsy, language, by means of the vocabulary list. More or less at the same time Jones stated, on the basis of Grellman's recently published dictionary, that the Gypsy language "contains so many Sanscrit words, that their Indian origin can hardly be doubted," giving a list of such words "pure Sanscrit scarce changed in a single letter" ("The eighth anniversary discourse," delivered 24 Feb 1791, Jones 1807, 3:170–71).[9]

These three accomplishments of the 1780s, the first formulation of the Indo-European concept by Jones, the first formulation of the Malayo-Polynesian concept by Marsden, and Marsden's identification of the Indian (or as we now say, Indo-Aryan) origin of Romani, share a number of characteristics with one another and with a fourth publication, also associated with the East India Company, that is the central object of this book: F. W. Ellis's 1816 proof of the unity and non-Sanskritic origin of the South Indian languages, now called Dravidian. Each of these discoveries, as also others like them in the eighteenth and early nineteenth centuries, was truly new and unexpected, revealing historical connections among languages for which there was no historical memory that have proven sound and remain valid today.

The word list, then, has been a deceptively simple, highly effective tool for eliciting historical relations among languages as indices of historical relations among nations. How did it come about that European travelers to Asia and elsewhere took with them a more or less standardized word list, with a view to participating in the great revolution in ethnological knowledge that resulted from its use? No doubt the sources of this program were many, but a short text by G. W. Leibniz, published in 1718, shortly after his death, is of critical importance and may well be the model for subsequent lists, including Marsden's.

The text in question is Leibniz's "Appeal concerning languages of

9. According to the 11th edition of the *Encyclopaedia Britannica,* s.v. "Gipsies": "Ruedinger (1782), Grellman (1783) and Marsden (1783) almost simultaneously and independently of one another came to the same conclusion, that the languages of the Gipsies, until then considered a thieves' jargon, was in reality a language closely allied with some Indian speech." Jones identified in Grellman's list Romani words corresponding to Sanskrit *aṅgāra,* "charcoal," *kāṣṭha,* "wood," *pāra,* "a bank," and *bhū,* "earth." His contribution to the question of Roma origins has not been previously noted.

peoples," a letter of inquiry he sent to the imperial interpreter.[10] It begins: "As nothing throws greater light indicating the ancient origins of peoples than the collation of languages, I often wonder that geographers and travelers neglect to write of languages, and but rarely exhibit specimens of them." His request for information amounts to instruction to travelers about how such linguistic specimens should be collected (Leibniz 1718:49). He asks for collections of Pater Nosters in foreign languages, a well-established practice—he tells us that we have examples of the Pater Noster for the languages of the Poles, Serbs, Dalmatians, Croats, and Russians, all of the Slavonic (i.e., Slavic) family, and of the Wallachians, Cettos and Livonians, Turks, Persians, and Chinese. He asks for texts with interlinear translations into languages known to Europeans. But he also asks—and this seems to be new—for "a few examples of their words, expressing common things," which he spells out in detail:

Names of numbers: *one, two, 3, 4, 5, 6, 7, 8, 9, 10, 20, 30, 40, 50, 100, 1000.*

Relatives and ages: *father, mother, grandfather, son, daughter, brother, sister, father's brother, husband, wife, father-in-law, son-in-law, man, woman, child, youth, old man.*

Parts of the body: *body, flesh, skin, blood, bone, head, brow, nose, eye, pupil, ear, beard, mouth, tongue, tooth, chest, heart, throat, jaw, foot, finger, hair, belly, breasts.*

Necessities: *food, drink, bread, water, milk, wine, herbs, fruit, salt, fish, ox, sheep, horse, clothing, hide, house, wagon, sword, bow, arrow, lance, slingshot.*

Naturalia: *god, man, heaven, sun, moon, star, air, rain, thunder, lightning, cloud, frost, hail, snow, ice, fire, heat, light, smoke, earth, field, mountain, valley, sea, river, stone, sand, dog, wolf, deer, bear, fox, bird, snake, mouse.*

Actions: *to eat, to drink, to speak, to see, to be, to stand, to go, to strike, to laugh, to sleep, to know, to pluck,* and so forth.

It is striking that Marsden (who does not mention Leibniz or indeed any prior authority for his list) uses much the same, though not identical,

10. I am grateful to Hans Aarsleff for drawing my attention to this work, which is discussed in his book, *From Locke to Saussure* (1982), a work of profound scholarship. On this text of Leibniz, see also Gulya 1974.

categories in much the same order: numbers, kinship terms, parts of the body, necessities, naturalia. Other of the innumerable examples of the comparative vocabulary bear a family resemblance to this one, and it is possible that it is the ultimate source for them all.

Leibniz's formulation of the vocabulary list was contained within a definite program, as we can make out from the terms of his request. As a northern European he seeks information on the northern peoples who lie to the east and who, since much of Asia and part of Europe received colonies from such northern peoples, he considers most worth knowing yet are known least of all. He especially wants to explore the relations between the Germanic and Slavonic, or Slavic, language families to determine whether there are other language families that belong to neither. He seeks, for example, linguistic specimens from Transylvanian Saxons "not as cultivated men speak, but as the common people speak, that they may be compared with the language of our Saxons. It is said that there are among the common people many words neither Hungarian, nor Slavonic, and moreover which generally cannot be understood by other Germans." He also asks for information about an enclave of Germans in Crimean Tartary, "or rather of the ancient Goths," who, according to a report by an imperial ambassador to the Ottoman court, use a dialect of German. He requests information about non-Slavic languages of the Muscovite Empire: the languages of Siberia, the Black Sea, and other places. He wonders whether records can be had about a certain Hungarian Jesuit, made captive in Tartary and sold to barbarians beyond the Caspian Sea, who discovered that the language there was related to Hungarian. He asks whether in Albania and Bulgaria there is to be found any language completely different from Slavonic, Hungarian, Greek, and Turkish. The point of all these questions is evident: his program is to map the entire ethnological history of Eurasia through its languages and to determine the place in that history of the German language and people.

In the course of this brief letter—less than three pages in print—we see that Leibniz has engineered into, and out of, his word list a number of characteristics: the language of common people, not the learned; words that are necessary for the immediate needs of life, not the more complex notions of art and science; primitive words rather than recent ones; simple rather than complex words; native words rather than foreign borrowings. Those are the attributes of the native core of a language that the vocabulary seeks to capture.

It follows that the conception of the language is an abstraction from the living language; a thick abstraction, perhaps, but an abstraction nevertheless, that is formed by identifying its core and removing from consideration the late, learned, foreign, borrowed, complex accretions of later ages. The method of the word list constitutes in its seeming simplicity the first, surgical move of historical linguistics: the cutting away of the later, borrowed, and complex accretions to reveal the native core of language, so that the operation of comparison can be performed on the authentic body of the language. This allows the historical relations among languages to be figured as the radiating branches of a tree, since the borrowings or mixtures that would make the branches grow into one another have been discarded by analysis. It is well to keep in mind the conception of language that undergirds the genealogies of languages in historical linguistics.

We are now in a position to answer the question why it was in eighteenth-century European thought, and not earlier in the Christian West nor among Muslim scholars of the great age of the expansion of Islam, that the twinning of languages and nations took such a decisive turning, thereby completely rewriting the deep history of the world. It was in this time and context that a method was devised—the word list—that could put the posited close relation of languages and nations to work, such that language relations could be elicited even in the absence of historical memory and so serve as a key to ethnological relations, that is, the history of nations.

Initially, comparative vocabulary showed the way to the ancient, native core of languages. Comparative grammar followed, offering, if anything, a surer way into the native heart of languages. Already in Jones we see vocabulary *and* grammar providing evidence of historical relatedness among languages, and the comparative grammar of Indo-European was systematized by Franz Bopp, who made it his life's work.

The pairing of languages and nations or races, a strong tendency in biblical thought and in European thought from late antiquity, became intensified only at the moment when it was given a rational, scientific method, the method of the vocabulary. The application of this seemingly simple means in an age of worldwide expansion of European power yielded astonishing results, whose very durability tells us that they hold a great deal of truth. The presumption upon which this pairing rests—that the native core of a language is intimately bound to the nation that speaks it—was unquestioned in the age of its invention. It was only later, in the mid-nineteenth century, that one begins to hear a growing chorus of voices asserting, as a new and surprising truth, that race and language do not necessarily coincide with one another (see chapter 7). Hitherto, for millennia, the assumption had been that they did.

GRAMMAR MANIA

Examining the text of Leibniz, we come to see that behind what appears to be a *mere* word list is a formative theory that determines what gets included in the list and what does not. The word list, with its names for numbers, kinship terms, parts of the body, forces of nature, and objects of common use, incorporates within it a conception of the primitive core of a language, as distinguished from its later accretions, and sets up a series of binaries (primitive/recent, native/foreign, common/learned) that are used to accomplish the first move of the emerging analytic: the identification of the primitive core and the removal, for purposes of analysis, of everything that is not part of the core.

I say again that this method has been highly effective, astonishingly so and out of all proportion to its low level of complexity. Even before a satisfactory and unitary scientific standard of etymology had been found through the recognition of lawlike regularity in sound shifts within languages, beginning with Grimm's law in the early nineteenth century, the word list was the means to new discoveries that have endured. Simple as its form is, outmoded as is the biblical frame of historical time within which it was conceived, lacking as it does a method of determining which similarities count as signs of relationships and which do not, or a method of discerning relationships among words that do *not* look similar yet are cognate (the greater analytic power achieved when comparative philology arrived at the laws of sound shifts)—despite all these shortcomings, the method of the word list, even in its simplest, eighteenth-century form, must be close enough to the truth of things to have been able to deliver so much knowledge that was new and lasting.

The word list is the middle term that allows for the complete assimilation of language to the terms of the Mosaic ethnology, permitting languages to be treated as kinsmen in the branches of a segmentary lineage and as growing ever more different and distant, like lineage segments of the Nuer or Arabic-speaking Muslim lineages in Yemen (Dresch 1988, 1989) or Libya (Davis 1987).

Jones presented his pioneering statement about the Indo-European languages not as an end in itself, as a finding about languages, but as an objective means to make up for defective historical memory. For Jones, the three faculties of the mind were *memory, reason,* and *imagination*—the respective sources of history, science, and the arts (Jones 1788b:xiii). History, then, is founded on memory, which is to say that to know the history of India one must consult the historical memory of the Indian nation as captured in histories written by Indians. Jones and his British colleagues had sought Indian history in the texts called *purāṇas* (antiquities), and one of the earliest texts composed in Sanskrit at British request, written before Jones arrived in India, was a synopsis of the *purāṇas*, titled *Purāṇārthaprākaśa*, by Radhakanta Sharma (see Ludo Rocher 1986, text published in Rocher and Rocher 1994–95). Yet the high hopes with which the British pursued history through the *purāṇas* were only partially fulfilled. Jones himself believed that the *purāṇas* contained a genuine recollection of the flood of Noah and thus corroborated the truth of the Bible, for example. But the *purāṇas'* genuine memory of civil history in India prior to about 200 B.C., in his view, "is involved in a cloud of fables" (Jones 1788d:421). To make good this defect, then, four means could be introduced from outside the national memory, namely, the study of languages and letters, the study of philosophy and religion, study of the remains of old sculpture and architecture, and study of the written texts of the sciences and arts. It is in the context of the first of these that Jones made his famous statement about Indo-European; that is, language comparison functions as an exterior means by which to recover a history obscured by "fable." If the method was useful in India, with its long and ancient literary tradition, how much more useful it must be as a way of finding history in places were there was no writing in which memory could be made fast.

Such a program for recovering the history of the nations of North American Indians had been proposed before, in 1744, by the Jesuit missionary Francois-Xavier de Charlevoix. He argued that previous writers had compared the morals, customs, religions, and traditions of the American Indians with those of Old World cultures to determine their origins but had neglected the one means that would solve the problem: comparison of their languages. For languages change but slowly and remain distinct from one another, so that if the American languages could be shown to have the features of the mother languages, they could be traced back to the creation of different languages at the Tower of Babel and so prove that America had been peopled by the great-grandchildren of Noah (Charlevoix 1994, 1:153–54). This program was restated by Thomas Jefferson in *Notes on the state of Virginia* (c. 1782) and put into effect by means of a printed vocabulary, similar to the one of Leibniz, which may still be seen in the library of the American Philosophical Society, against which were recorded the words of different Indian languages in columns. This project was carried forward and completed by Stephan Du Ponceau, protégé and successor of Jefferson in the presidency of the American Philosophical Society (Du Ponceau 1838).

At the same time as Jefferson and Du Ponceau were investigating the history of the New World nations through the history of their languages, Catherine of Russia, with the help of a vast imperial bureaucracy, was collecting a comparative vocabulary of her empire, a vocabulary she hoped would encompass the whole world. Here again the word list had a Leibnizian form, and the result was published by Pallas in 1786–89, in the two-volume work grandly called *Linguarum totius orbis vocabularia comparativa*—at the very moment, one might say, that Jones was proposing the Indo-European concept before the Asiatic Society in Calcutta. Thus the project of Jones was not at all singular but was part of a broad movement that, because of the worldwide expansion of European power in the eighteenth century, reached the far corners of the earth.

By means of the theory encoded in the structure of the comparative vocabulary, languages and nations or races were understood as being so closely identified with one another as to have no gap between them—like adjacent stones in one of those cyclopean walls of the Incas or the Pyramid of Cheops. Every statement about the relations among languages was a statement about the relations among nations. This was the first effect of the full assimilation of language to the locational technology of the Mosaic ethnology.

The second effect was the radical redefinition of what a language is. Eighteenth-century European discussions still had room for distinctions between stock, or primitive, languages and mixed languages formed from the blending of stock languages. But the logic of the word list tended away from that kind of thinking and toward identification of the primitive core as constituting the authentic language itself. Though mixture is an aspect of every natural language, for a natural language to enter into the historical-linguistic tree, it must first give up its borrowed clothes and get naked. Much as ancient genealogists learned to sculpt the relations of kinship to form beautiful, treelike branching structures by throwing away all relations of descent and marriage except those that pass exclusively through males, modern linguists could map languages onto such structures only after the languages had been thinned down, carved out, and abstracted from all that time, proximity, and communication do to make neighboring natural languages, such as the languages of India, resemble one another. It will be well to keep in mind the highly artificial nature of both these effects, and to remember that they flow from the word list and its theory. While in the eighteenth century there was considerable vacillation between mixture and genealogy as the explanation of similarity among languages, the inexorable tendency, or at any rate the tendency that won out, was the latter, epitomized in the slogan of the Young Grammarians of the mid-nineteenth century: there is no such thing as a mixed language *(Es gibt kein Mischgesprach)*. The audacity of this statement is breathtaking, for in truth there is no such thing as a pure language, a language that is not mixed, if we are speaking of natural, actually existing languages spoken by human beings rather than artificial languages abstracted from them for purposes of comparative study.

It has become customary to the point of cliché, when examining the pairing of languages and nations in European thought, to invoke the words and thoughts of Herder. The idea that Herder is at the bottom of this has been overdone, and we need to focus, rather, on Locke and Leibniz.

Locke's *Essay concerning human understanding* (1689) discusses language at length but not languages, *langue* but not *parole*, and it did not generate a program for research into the world's languages. But Leibniz's *Nouveaux essais sur l'entendment humaine* (1765, published posthumously; see Leibniz 1981), which was inspired and provoked by Locke and is a sort of commentary on Locke's book in the form of a dialogue between two speakers, one a surrogate for Locke and the other for Leibniz, does develop such a view and, indeed, imagines the explosion in the grammar factory before it occurred. It is useful, therefore, to take the two together. Briefly, what Locke's view of language supplies to Leibniz is the idea that a language is not created once for all time by God but is an historical entity growing and becoming progressively more copious in vocabulary as it develops complex ideas through the cumulation of experiences of nature and commerce with other nations. The growth of ideas from simple to complex is tracked by the growth of language from rude to polished, savage to refined.

The following is what Leibniz builds upon that Lockean base: "Languages in general, being the oldest monuments of peoples, earlier than writing and the [practical] arts, best indicate their origins, kinships and migrations." It is for this essentially ethnological reason that it is useful and important to study etymology. But in doing so one must show the relationships among various peoples and should not make leaps from one nation to another remote one without solid confirming evidence, especially that provided by intervening peoples. Etymologies should not be trusted without a great deal of corroborating data; to do otherwise is to "goropize," that is, emulate the absurd etymologies of the Dutch scholar

Goropius Becanus, who proclaimed Dutch as the original language (Leibniz 1981:285). When European scholars have used up the ancient writings of the Romans, Greeks, Hebrews, and Arabs, there will be the Chinese, Persians, Armenians, Copts, and Brahmins to supply materials for further progress. "And when there are no more ancient books to examine, their place will be taken by mankind's most ancient monument—languages. *Eventually every language in the universe will be recorded, and contained in dictionaries and grammars; and comparisons will be made amongst them*" (emphasis added). Thus does Leibniz predict the explosion in the grammar factory. The comparison of languages will extend the genealogy of nations beyond the reach of written histories. Study of foreign languages will be useful for the study of *things,* "since their properties are often reflected in their names (as can be seen from the names of plants among different nations)" and for the knowledge of the *mind* and the variety of its operations, but above all it will also be useful for searching out the origins of *peoples,* through etymologies, which can best be ascertained through language comparison (Leibniz 1981:336–37).

By the end of the eighteenth century, as Leibniz predicted, a veritable explosion in the grammar factory had occurred in Europe, by which I mean an impulse to blanket the world in grammars and dictionaries. This impulse was indeed borne around the globe by mercantile and imperial expansion. The explosion in the grammar factory is still underway today. We continue to think it obvious that languages, whether written or not, have a grammar, and that linguists would want to write grammars and dictionaries for every language in the world and would give their books titles like *Les langues du monde* (Meillet 1952)—a late echo of the *Linguarum totius orbis vocabularia comparative* (Pallas 1786–89).

It was not always so. A remarkable passage from an unpublished manuscript in the British Library brings out clearly how very characteristic the explosion of grammar- and dictionary-making was of modern-era Europe, and how different it was from Europe's supposed ancestors, Rome and Greece. The passage is from a text of another East India Company servant and Orientalist, John Leyden, of whom I will have occasion to speak later. In a proposal to the governor-general seeking sanction for an ambitious plan of making a whole set of grammars and dictionaries for the languages of India and Southeast Asia, Leyden lays out the value of languages of the region for administration, diplomacy and trade, and goes on to consider the importance of studying all languages, not just the useful ones, "in a literary point of view," which is to say, a purely scholarly one:

> Almost all the languages and dialects of India have been more or less cultivated by writing. Almost all of them contain a variety of compositions and untill these compositions be examined by Europeans the history of the tribes and nations to which they belong can never be elucidated in a satisfactory manner. India is as it were the literary property of the English nation. The facility of research is in their hands and in their[s] alone, as it is only by the individuals of this nation that the literature and languages of India whether of primary or secondary importance, can be properly investigated. The peculiar advantages therefore which the English enjoy, render them responsible to the general commonwealth of letters and pledged to all posterity as long as civilized men shall exist in the earth. The fame of some great conquering nations and in particular of the Romans is deeply sullied by their inattention to the literature of the nations they conquered. The sanguine flood of Roman glory not only swept away ancient nations but obliterated the accumulated records of the primeval times. The Roman warriors trod under foot the arts and sciences of Etruria and left nothing but the fragments of their vases to demonstrate the existence of former civilization. The ancient literature of Spain the monuments of the Carthaginians and Phoenicians & the venerable institutions of the Druids of Gaul & Britain they extinguished, and [of] the literature of ancient Egypt, they left us nothing but the hieroglyphics as a riddle to perplex future ages, a cypher of which they destroyed the key. Roman literature as it is preserved, is a ruin of ruins, a military trophy, raised from the fragments of ancient monuments. (Leyden, "Plan for investigating the languages, literatures, antiquities and history of the Dekhan"; BL Add. Mss. 26,567, ff. 112v–113)

This passage is remarkable for its frank imperialism, but, given the tendency of the British to imagine themselves in togas, it is remarkable as well in condemning the Greeks and Romans for failing to preserve knowledge of the Etruscan and ancient Egyptian languages. Leyden is quite right to point out the Greeks' and Romans' utter indifference to the languages of others, in the sense of failing to make grammars and dictionaries of them and conserve knowledge of them for the future.

The explosion in the grammar factory, then, is a specifically European phenomenon, and one in which its biblical heritage is a crucial ingredient that is absent from ancient Rome and Greece. The twinning of languages and nations begins in Genesis, with its seventy-two patriarchs and seventy-two languages, as St. Augustine has it. The explosive growth of grammars and dictionaries in the eighteenth century is perhaps a late outcome of the missionary tendency of Christianity; for both the translation of the Bible into the vernaculars stimulated by the Protestant Reformation, and the making of grammars and dictionaries for missionary purposes stimulated by the Counter-Reformation, with the great Jesuit projects in the vanguard, were important precursors of the eighteenth-century explosion. No doubt there were other causes. Benedict Anderson, noting the dramatic increase in the writing of grammars and dictionaries for European languages beginning in the eighteenth century, makes a powerful case for the connection of this growth industry with nationalism and the means of its propagation: print capitalism (Anderson 1991:70–82). Bernard Cohn, describes the grammar- and dictionary-writing fever in early British-Indian Calcutta and makes a powerful case for the connection of this growth industry with British colonial rule and the urgent need to master the languages of India in order to master India itself (Cohn 1985). But nationalism and colonialism do not encompass the field constituted by *all* languages, however distant and obscure. The explosion in the grammar factory is fired by the forces of national self-love and colonial utility, no doubt, but it exceeds them as well. Nor is it a natural product of these forces. It has a history, and it began rather recently. It is not a constant of history.

CHAPTER 2

Pāṇini and Tolkāppiyar

Could it have been a coincidence that the European languages-and-nations project, which was carried to every corner of the globe by the worldwide spread of European power, was especially fruitful in British India? I believe that it was not a coincidence, but rather that India's own tradition of language analysis, highly developed from ancient times, played an important role, indeed, that the new knowledge being produced in British India came about precisely because of the conjuncture of these two traditions of language analysis, European and Indian. It is the purpose of this book to show that this was the case.

The matter has only to be stated for it to be seen to be highly probable. The likelihood is so evident that the greater question is not whether it is true, but what has kept this evident truth hidden. The culprit, in a word, has been the powerful tendency in modern thought to treat India as a mere supplier of data for European theory in the production of knowledge. This idea, "No theory outside the West," was developed especially by James Mill in Britain and G. W. F. Hegel on the Continent, both of them theorists of Europe as the metropolitan center of universal knowledge. The position was developed explicitly in opposition to early Orientalists in British India and quickly became hegemonic, crowding out earlier appreciations of the achievements of Indian science, Indian philosophy, and Indian theory. The view that there is no theory worth considering outside ancient Greece and modern Europe survived Marx's transformation of Hegel, so that it dominates the spectrum of European thought from edge to edge, right to left. As a consequence, whenever theory is invoked in modern discussions of India, ancient Indian theories become data in respect of contemporary, living theory. We need, therefore, to do some remedial work against this tide of presumption to make evident the strength of language analysis in India before colonization by the British.

The material of this chapter is complex, and readers will have to be patient. What is central to the argument of the book here is the formation in the Indian tradition, specifically among the grammars of the Prakrit languages, of categories of words according to their type of derivation from Sanskrit roots *(tatsama* and *tadbhava)* or their nonderivation from those roots (*deśya,* among other terms). This is the focus of the first section of the chapter. The second and third sections concern Indian phonology and its universalization through Sir William Jones.

LANGUAGE ANALYSIS IN INDIA

We have seen that leading ideas of language analysis in the West, at least in respect of language history and comparative philology, have their roots in religion, specifically in the biblical story of the Tower of Babel, which links language diversity with the proliferation and spread of the nations across the face of the earth. The project of extensive language comparison in the service of the history of nations met, in India, another religiously derived tradition of language analysis. To situate this Indian tradition in the configuration of high learning in ancient India we can examine briefly its place among the Vedic sciences, taking "science" in a broad sense to mean any formalized body of knowledge. Language analysis dominates the standard list of six sciences that subserve the Vedic religion of sacrifice. These *vedāṅgas,* or "limbs" of the Veda, are: ritual *(kalpa),* phonetics *(śikṣā),* prosody *(chandas),* etymology *(nirukta),* grammar *(vyākaraṇa),* and astronomy *(jyotiṣa).* The prominence of language analysis in this set of sciences—four out of the six—is striking. The great motivating force here was the desire to reproduce the Vedic hymns exactly, and the sciences of language were the means by which the Vedic texts could be perfectly understood and reproduced without error and without change.

These six Vedic sciences developed through the classical period of Indian civilization and from them other sciences evolved. Ritual led to the formation of a large body of religiously oriented law *(dharmaśāstra),* with its own technical terminology and rules of interpretation. And astronomy, which in the Vedic period was especially concerned with the construction of the calendar for the determination of religiously significant times, developed greatly in the post-Vedic period in connection with mathematics (computation) and astrology, rather similar to the (Mesopotamian) sciences we find clustered together in the work of Ptolemy. In addition to law, linguistics, and the astronomy-astrology-mathematics complex, other bodies of formalized learning emerged subsequent to the Vedic period. Poetics, or literary criticism *(alaṅkāraśāstra),* for example, is a field in which the ancient Indians excelled, and which deserves to be better known in the West (see, e.g., Selby 2000, introduction).

Law, language analysis, and astronomy-astrology-mathematics form a triad of highly elaborated sciences with roots in the Vedic period. Of these, the science of law is of great importance in studying Indian civilization but is perhaps by its very nature the most India-specific and least universalizable in its results. The astronomy-astrology-mathematics complex is the opposite; here Indian achievements have entered into the daily lives of peoples around the world. The so-called Arabic numerals, really Indian ones, mark the Indian contribution to place notation and the concept of zero, the most visible fruit of India's pioneering work in computational methods, which included algebra and the beginnings of trigonometry. These entered European practice through the intermediacy of Arab mathematicians and replaced the roman numerals in the middle ages.

Language analysis falls somewhat between the India-specificity of law and the universalism of mathematics and the number system, for Indian linguistics was above all devoted to the fixing and illumination of the language of the Vedic hymn collections, not language in general. Yet though it has a very India-specific object, it nevertheless manages by its profound analysis of this single language, Sanskrit, to say much that illuminates language generally. As such, it was the basis for grammars of other Indian languages, such as Telugu, Tamil, and the Prakrits. And it proved exportable, shaping the writing systems and grammars of countries in Central Asia, East Asia, and Southeast Asia, which Indian learning reached through the spread of Buddhism and Hinduism. It also reached the West, but not until relatively late, during the period of British colonization.

In these two areas, then, Indian sciences of the ancient period have made important, indeed fundamental contributions to modern life. The profiles of the two are quite different, however. In respect of astronomy-astrology-mathematics, in some sense its history is unitary; as Playfair has said, the progress of astronomy is an experiment upon the human race which was made but once, a single experiment involving a multitude of nations. Getting a true fix on India's place in the process is vexed by the opposing excesses of anti-Orientalists, such as James Mill of the nineteenth century, and the "Vedic mathematics" enthusiasts of the twenty-first. Neither is informed by the rare combination of skills needed to get at the relation of Indian astronomy, astrology, and mathematics to those of other early nations. The writings of David Pingree (1963, 1979), whose control of the science and of the many languages involved have made him the leading expert in this subject, are indispensable here. From Pingree one gets the picture of India lying on the edge of a large intellectual world in which the ancient Greeks participated, but of which the center and origin were located in Mesopotamia and the Middle East. With these other cultures India participated, intermittently and across this vast territory and over long periods of time, in a larger conversation about these sciences. Pingree identifies successive periods of Babylonian, Greco-Babylonian, Greek, and Islamic waves of influence on Indian astronomy and related sciences. India returned the favor with interest through the westward spread of its number system and algebra. It was also a purveyor of its astronomy-astrology-mathematics to regions further afield of this Mesopotamian center, especially in Southeast Asia, and in Central and East Asia as well.

In language analysis, by contrast, India did not participate in any extra-India conversations or borrowings that we know of. As far as one can see at the present state of knowledge, Indian language analysis was wholly homegrown and, initially, consumed wholly at home as well. The other early analysis of language, at Babylon, consisted of glossaries and grammatical paradigms motivated by the problems of writing the cuneiform script in a dead language, Sumerian, by Akkadian-speaking scribes (Jacobsen 1974; Michalowski 1992). The first stirrings of a formalized science of language in Mesopotamia, then, belonged to a scribal culture dedicated to the production of texts that were mainly political, economic, and legal in nature, and tied to the cuneiform script. The beginnings of language analysis in India, as we have seen, were quite different, being closely tied to the performance of Vedic ritual and its liturgy, in the absence, at first, of any form of writing. As it developed, language analysis in India shaped the formation of Indian scripts and attached itself to the literatures of other religions—Buddhism and Jainism—and to the production of courtly poetry in Prakrit and other languages. Eventually it, too, was exported in part to China, Japan, and Korea, to Central Asia, and especially to Southeast Asia, where it played a great role in the formation of scripts.

GRAMMAR

Eighteenth century Europeans, then, came to India with a well-formed project in hand, to pursue the genealogy of nations by means of the genealogy of languages, and they encountered there a long-elaborated tradition of language analysis. One might suppose that they quickly took to the study of the Indian grammarians, such as the great grammarian Pāṇini, whose *Aṣṭādhyāyī* (c. 400 B.C.) is an intellectual accomplishment of the first magnitude. And indeed they did so indirectly, since the entirety of the tradition of Sanskrit grammar, even its non-Paninian schools, are influenced by this work. But the difficulty of Pāṇini is notorious. H. T. Colebrooke, the first European to master the text, remembers that Sir William Jones (who had studied the *Siddhāntakaumudī* of Bhaṭṭojidīkṣita, a Paninian text) called Pāṇini, when studied without a commentary, "dark as the darkest oracle" (Staal 1972:34). As J. F. Staal has said, the study of Pāṇini has long been regarded as a hyperspecialist occupation pursued by a subset of the specialists of Sanskrit philology, and even linguists treated Pāṇini as a subject for Indology rather than as "a deceased colleague of great genius." Staal believed the opposite should be, and was coming to be, the case: "It is now generally recognized that Pāṇini, despite his exclusive preoccupation with Sanskrit, was the greatest linguist of antiquity, if not of all time, and deserves to be treated as such. Accordingly, linguists, dissatisfied with mere lip service, are beginning to turn to him and to the Sanskrit grammarians, just as logicians turn to Aristotle" (Staal 1972:xi).

This assessment may have been too optimistic. Linguists *should* engage with Pāṇini as their Aristotle, no doubt, but there is little sign that they are doing so, and the discouraging confinement of Pāṇini within a special branch of Indology in the imaginaire of linguists continues. There are some obvious reasons why this should be so. Besides the difficulty of the text itself, it must be said that most of the literature produced by the specialists is readable only by other specialists, and even overviews of the history of grammar in India presuppose a knowledge of that which is being surveyed. One approaches the task of providing such a sketch with fear and trembling, knowing that it can only scratch the surface of a complex subject.[1]

The desire to render the Vedic text correctly and reproduce it with-

1. Belvalkar's brief survey (1915) is still useful and quite accessible. Hartmut Scharfe's (1977) includes discussion of Tamil and other South Indian grammars not covered by Belvalkar, and is more up-to-date. I have made use of both, as well as Deshpande's works on

out change was, as I have said, the motive that impelled the close scrutiny of its language. But that motive emerged late in the day, as the current speech changed and grew more distant from the language of the Vedic hymn collections. It was probably that growing difference that made the need to investigate language urgent. Etymology *(nirukta)*, or the explanation of difficult words and names, was one of the earliest forms linguistic investigation took; another was phonology *(śikṣā, prātiśākhya)*, having to do with pronunciation of the Vedic verses. Grammar *(vyākaraṇa)* was perhaps not the starting point of formal linguistics in India, but it reached astonishing heights at a very early date with the work of Pāṇini. It is quite clear that in Pāṇini's time Sanskrit was a living language, but it had changed distinctly from the language of the Veda in many ways so that the Vedic text was growing ever more obscure.

Pāṇini treats Vedic and Sanskrit as two registers of a single language. His project is to reduce the whole of this language to two things only: a list of roots *(dhātus)* and a set of transformational rules *(sūtras)* which, when applied to the roots, generate the universe of Sanskrit words. Thus, in the first place, Pāṇini's text consists of the transformational rules set out in the *Aṣṭādhyāyī* (eight-chapter text), in the form of very terse rules that number just under 4,000, plus the *Dhātupāṭha* (a list of verbal roots) which gives nearly 2,000 verbal roots, meant to be an exhaustive list, divided into ten morphological classes to which the rules of transformation apply differentially. Any linguistic analysis of a language must consist of a grammar and a dictionary, and Pāṇini's grammar thus has an associated dictionary. But the division between grammars and dictionaries can be differently made. In this case the dictionary is pared down to bare roots, with no inflectional forms, and all of the morphological changes which turn roots into words are specified in the grammar.

A few additional ancillary texts are necessary to the fulfillment of Pāṇini's project, most notably the list of morphologically significant classes *(gaṇa)* of substantives, the *Gaṇapāṭha*. This is not an exhaustive list. While Pāṇini holds to the doctrine that all substantives as well as verbs derive from verbal roots, the classes of substantives so derived that must be specified as the objects of particular transformational rules of grammar have an uncountable and unlimited number of possible words making up their contents. This uncountability was acknowledged. As the Indian grammarians of old used to say, when the gods Indra and Brahmā

---

phonology (1993) and sociolinguistics (1997), Misra (1996), Renou ed. (Pāṇini 1966), and Katre ed. (Pāṇini 1987).

tried to name all the words, uttering them one by one in turns, even they were unable to reach the end of the list. The ability to generate new substantives, including the making of compounds (on the formation of which the rules of Sanskrit put no limits), escapes the otherwise closed universe that Pāṇini posits and articulates in the form of rules.

The ambition of this project, and the brilliance of Pāṇini's execution of it, might be enough to account for the fact that his recondite work has drawn the admiration and interest of scholars for over two thousand years, and continues to do so. But Pāṇini has given his work an added degree of elegance and difficulty by the great economy of expression he sought and achieved.

The *sūtra* form itself, which was the prevailing genre when Pāṇini was writing, is an incitement in that direction, consisting of short prose rules meant to be committed to memory and no doubt accompanied by a teacher's oral explanation, if not a written commentary to elaborate a form of expression so concise that it cannot be understood without outside assistance. The grammarian's joke was that the maker of *sūtras* rejoices more in the saving of half a syllable than in the birth of a son. That was only a slight exaggeration. Pāṇini's four thousand *sūtras* are many, no doubt, but each one is very brief indeed. The first *sūtra* is but four syllables: *vṛddhir ād aic,* expressing what in English takes many syllables more: "The technical term *vṛddhi* denotes the vowel *ā* and diphthongs *ai, au*" (1.1.1, after Katre). The others are much the same length. The very last *sūtra* of the entire work is famous for its minimalism, consisting of just two short vowels: *a a* (8.4.68). The explanation of this cryptic text illustrates the complexity that can be compressed into so short an expression: "The vowel short *a* (which was treated as an open vowel in the whole of the text to this point) is replaced by short *a* (which is a close vowel)," that is, for purposes of the transformational rules the short vowel *a* had been treated in the text as if it were open and homophonous with long *ā* so that they could be classed together for inclusion under certain rules, but that "as if" is now canceled and the close nature of *a* is affirmed (after Katre, Pāṇini 1987:1066).

The means by which this hypereconomy of expression is achieved are several. One of them is the formation of classes to which the *sūtra* rules apply, the classes themselves being detailed outside the text, in separate treatises. I have already mentioned the list of verbal roots in classes *(Dhātupāṭha)* and classes of substantives *(Gaṇapāṭha),* to which we should add the list of primary nominal affixes for the formation of noun stems from verb stems (the *kṛt* affixes, listed in the *Uṇādisūtras*).

Speech-sounds	Anubandhas
1. a i u	ṇ
2. ṛ ḷ	k
3. e o	ṅ
4. ai au	c
5. h y v r	ṭ
6. l	ṇ
7. ñ m ṅ ṇ n	m
8. jh bh	ñ
9. gh ḍh dh	ṣ
10. j b g ḍ d	ś
11. kh ph ch ṭh th c ṭ t	v
12. k p	y
13. ś ṣ s	r
14. h	l

Figure 7. The *Śivasūtras* of Pāṇini's grammar. The *anubandhas* are end-markers of a series beginning with one of the speech sounds. (After Staal 1972: 278.)

A second means of economy is the formation of abbreviations of a certain kind (called *pratyāhāra*) indicating ranges of sounds to which rules applied. We have already given the example of the opening of Pāṇini's text, in which *āt (ād)* stands for the long vowel *ā* and *aic* stands for the group of diphthongs *ai, au*. Such abbreviations are formed by arranging the letters of the alphabet into an artificial order convenient for forming groups of sounds that are the objects of certain rules of transformation. Marker consonants *(anubandha)* are inserted at strategic points into that order to mark the ends of groups. This is laid out in the fourteen *Śivasūtras* (also called *Maheśvarasūtras* or *Pratyāhārasūtras*) prefixed to Pāṇini's text (figure 7). The notational method is to name the first letter of the series followed by the marker consonant; thus the abbreviation *ak*, for which *k* is the *anubandha*, signifies the vowels *a, i, u, ṛ, ḷ* in all lengths and accents, with and without nasality, while *ik* denotes the series *i, u, ṛ, ḷ* (the *ak* series minus letter *a*), and *uk* denotes *u, ṛ, ḷ (ak* minus *a, i)*. These markers and conventions of naming could generate hundreds of abbreviations for groups of sounds, but in practice only forty-one or forty-two of them are needed for the formulation of the *sūtras*. The great compression achieved by naming large classes of sounds with made-up words of a single syllable was purchased at the cost of the difficulty of mastering that list of abbreviations with its arbitrary marker consonants and the non-normal alphabetical order in which the *Śivasūtras* place them.

A third means of economy is the principle of *anuvṛtti,* by which some *sūtras* are made to govern following ones so that words of the governing *sūtra* are tacitly supplied. The most extensive case of *anuvṛtti* occurs at the beginning of the third chapter. It consists of a single word (3.1.1.: *pratyayā́ḥ,* "The technical term *affix* . . . , " after Katre) that governs all the *sūtras* of chapters 3, 4 and 5, such that every *sūtra* in those chapters is deemed to begin with that word.

These are the leading means of economy, and there are others. Perhaps the most difficult is the order in which the various parts of Sanskrit grammar are taken up, which is not the order of a primer, in which the grammar is delivered in digestible servings, starting with the easier bits, or in a reference grammar in which the parts of speech are discussed one after the other. Here again, the *Aṣṭādhyāyī* seeks economy rather than ease of understanding. To be sure, we can identify in it a succession of thematic groupings, but they are of a rather peculiar kind. They are, as named by V. N. Misra: general definitions and rules of interpretation (chapter 1); substitution and purpose of declension (chapter 2); primary suffixes (chapter 3); suffixes addable to the nonverbal stem to form secondary stems and declensional suffixes (chapters 4 and 5); morphophonemics at the level of the word (chapters 6 and 7); and miscellaneous topics (chapter 8) (Misra 1966:22–23). Nevertheless, the internal organization of chapters follows the logic of economy remorselessly. Thus, the order of rules follows a logic of its own which allows the briefest possible expression, moving from transformational rules applied to the largest possible classes, followed by exceptions affecting smaller classes.

The result is astonishing in its achievement, but even the hyperspecialists who understand and admire Pāṇini have occasionally suggested that he has sacrificed too much in his pursuit of economy. A passage which Staal quotes from Max Müller's *Sanskrit grammar for beginners* (1866) is so very good an example of the extremes that I cannot resist quoting it again here as a case which, as we see at the end, even the pandits found remarkable. It concerns the transformation of the vowel *ṛ* of a verbal root before the aorist tense of verbs ending in *iṣam,* etc., and whether the vowel is to take its augmented form called *guṇa* (i.e., becoming *ar*) or the further augmented form called *vṛddhi* (i.e., becoming *ār*). What is significant in the example is not the particular outcome but the opposing effects of the application of different rules of Pāṇini before the final result is achieved.

> The grammatical system of the Hindu grammarians is so peculiar, that rules which we should group together, are scattered about in different parts of their manuals. We may have the general rule in the last, and the exceptions in the first book, and even then we are by no means certain that exceptions to these exceptions may not occur somewhere else. I shall give but one instance. There is a root *jāgṛ*, which forms its Aorist by adding *iṣam, īḥ, īt*. Here the simplest rule would be that the final [vowel] *ṛ* before *iṣam* becomes [the consonant] *r* (Pāṇ. VI. 1. 77). This, however, is prevented by another rule which requires that final *ṛ* should take Guṇa before *iṣam* (Pāṇ. VII. 3. 84). This would give us *ajāgariṣam*. But now comes another general rule (Pāṇ. VII. 2. 1) which prescribes Vṛddhi of final vowels before *iṣam*, i.e., *ajāgāriṣam*. Against this change, however, a new rule is cited (Pāṇ. VII. 3. 85), and this secures for *jāgṛ* a special exception from Vṛddhi, and leaves its base again as *jāgar*. As soon as the base has been changed to *jāgar*, it falls under a new rule (Pāṇ. VII. 2. 3), and is forced to take Vṛddhi, until this rule is again nullified by Pāṇ. VII. 2. 4, which does not allow Vṛddhi in an Aorist that takes intermediate *i*, like *ajāgariṣam*. There is an exception, however, to this rule also, for bases with short *a*, beginning and ending with a consonant, may optionally take Vṛddhi (Pāṇ. VII. 2. 7). This option is afterwards restricted, and roots with short *a*, beginning with a consonant and ending in *ṛ*, like *jāgar*, have no option left, but are restricted afresh to Vṛddhi (Pāṇ. VII. 2. 2). However, even this is not yet the final result. Our base *jāgar* is after all not to take Vṛddhi, and hence a new special rule (Pāṇ. VII. 2. 5) settles the point by granting to *jāgṛ* a special exception from Vṛddhi, and thereby establishing its Guṇa. No wonder that these manifold changes and chances in the formation of the First Aorist of *jāgṛ* should have inspired a grammarian, who celebrates them in the following couplet:
>
> > *guṇo vṛddhir guṇo vṛddhiḥ pratiṣedho vikalpanam* |
> > *punar vṛddhir niṣedho 'to yaṇ pūrvāḥ prāptayo nava* ||
> >
> > Guṇa, Vṛddhi, Guṇa, Vṛddhi, prohibition, option, again Vṛddhi and then exception, these with the change of ṛ into a semivowel in the first instance, are the nine results. (Staal 1972: 138–39)

What are we to make of a set of rules that is so compressed, and ordered in such a way, that one cannot generate from it a single Sanskrit word until one has mastered it from the beginning to the end? What are we to make of a grammar without time, *akālakam vyākaraṇam*, as it was called by Candravṛtti (Sharfe 1977:114)? The economy and the precision—in a word, the elegance—of the text is breathtaking, and it reminds us of nothing so much as computer software. In this case, of course, the central processing unit, the hardware for this software, is the human brain. We may truly say that it has taken Europeans till the age of computers to see the astonishing beauty of Pāṇini's accomplishment rather than seeing it as an oddity or even a monstrosity. More than one person has remarked that the contemporary success of software engineering in India and among Indians must have some connection with Sanskrit grammar and, however indirectly, with Pāṇini.

The software analogy takes us even further away from pedagogy. But it would be quite wrong to infer that because students today find Pāṇini impenetrable, it was not meant for young students. Only it is a different kind of pedagogy than that to which a primer or topically organized grammar is directed. Economy was directed at ease of memorization, and children are good at that. As Kātyāyana has said, "The fame of Pāṇini extends to children," which can only mean that Pāṇini was studied by children. Long after Sanskrit had ceased to be anyone's first language and had to be learned from a teacher, so that mastering Pāṇini was rendered considerably harder, the seventh-century Chinese Buddhist pilgrim-scholar Hsüan Tsang, who spent years studying in India, said that boys of seven study the science of language first—a science he elsewhere attributes to Pāṇini (Staal 1972:5–6). It is well to keep in mind that the compression of Pāṇini's text served the demands of a different kind of learning than is followed today, one based on memorization of whole texts. This difference, however, makes the text more difficult for those who approach it today without having those skills that were common for students in the past.

Every text has a history, and does not appear suddenly from outer space like a meteorite, even a work as truly exceptional as Pāṇini's *Aṣṭādhyāyī*. It was not completely without precedent, nor was it the perfect realization of its own program. There were texts before it that paved the way, and after-texts that attempted to complete the program. But, like many a great work of ancient times, the success of Pāṇini's grammar eclipsed those of his rivals so that their works ceased to be reproduced and became lost. Our main source for knowledge of their existence is their mention by Pāṇini himself. From Pāṇini and his commentators we have the names of eleven schools of grammar, most of them extinct, namely, Aindra (the school of Indra), Śākaṭāyana, Āpiśali, Śākalya, Kāśakṛtsna, Gārgya, Gālava, Kāśyapa, Senaka, Sphoṭāyana, and Candravarmaṇa. It is "beyond doubt that Pāṇini stood at the culmination point of a rich grammatical tradition" (Mishra 1966:14–15). Pāṇini's great project followed in the wake of others and had the benefit of earlier linguistic work in etymology and phonology as well. Of that earlier work we have only a shadowy knowledge, for the surviving texts are few, and most have been revised or replaced by later productions.

As for the texts that followed, two are of such importance that they are regularly studied along with Pāṇini to elucidate the difficulties of a notoriously difficult text. The first of these is by Kātyāyana, a critic of Pāṇini whose *Vārttikas* are meant to correct and perfect some 1500 of Pāṇini's *sūtras*. The second is by Patañjali, whose *Great commentary (Mahābhāṣya)* explicates the better part, though not every *sūtra*, of Pāṇini's text, and of Kātyāyana's corrections as well. Patañjali's commentary mentions Puṣyamitra Śuṅga, founder of the Śuṅga dynasty that succeeded the Mauryas, 187–151 B.C., which gives a fairly firm chronological horizon for the close of this formative phase. These two, with Pāṇini himself, are the three sages of Sanskrit grammar and complete the Paninian system, though many other treatises followed.

Language analysis in India, then, had a most precocious beginning, going back to the late Vedic period, and was so intensely pursued by so many scholars that it quickly reached a level of sophistication without parallel in the ancient world. This was the matrix in which Pāṇini composed his amazing work. Pāṇini and the Paninians dominated the field of grammar thereafter, but there were other, non-Paninian developments as well, some of which may have had their roots in the pre-Pāṇini schools. The great nineteenth-century Orientalist A. C. Burnell attempted to show that many of the surviving non-Paninian schools have a common lineage and are traceable to the Aindra school of grammar, which is older than Pāṇini's school (Burnell 1875). Whether or not there was a single Aindra school, Burnell's demonstration of the similarities among the non-Paninian grammars is elegant and persuasive.

Burnell had searched for evidence for the Aindra school in Sanskrit grammars of the South without success, but then he came across a description of the *Tolkāppiyam*, the oldest surviving grammar of Tamil and attributed to one Tolkāppiyar, as *aintiram nirainta*, "in accordance with the Aindra grammar." This comes from the preface, written by one Paṉambaraṉ (whom Burnell takes to be a contemporary), who says it was read out in the assembly of King Pāṇḍiyaṉ and approved by a critic, which was the formal means of publishing a book in those days and, indeed, till just a couple of centuries ago. Burnell then compared the order of topics in the *Tolkāppiyam*, which differs from the order in Pāṇini, with those of two other grammars, the Sanskrit grammar called *Kātantra* and the

Pali grammar of Kaccāyana, finding that they coincided minutely, across and within the gross order of *sandhi,* nouns, verbs, and *kṛt*-affixes, due allowance being made for the fact that the structure of Tamil is very different from that of Sanskrit and Pali, which accounts for some divergences of the *Tolkāppiyam* from the other two.

Burnell's comparison of non-Paninian grammars convincingly established the influence of the *Kātantra* grammar of Sanskrit upon the grammars of Tamil in South India and Pali in Sri Lanka. The *Kātantra* is more user-friendly than Pāṇini both in its simpler ordering of topics and its brevity—it was comprised of only 1,400 *sūtras* against the nearly 4,000 of Pāṇini. Having established the influence of the *Kātantra* tradition in the grammars of three different languages, and given evidence of a linkage to the ancient Aindra school, Burnell proceeded to show how the technical terms of these Aindra grammars differ from those of Pāṇini and the Paninians. In the non-Paninian grammars of this tradition the technical terms are mostly ordinary words used with a specialized meaning, such as *nāma,* "name," for noun, and so forth. In Pāṇini, on the contrary, the technical terms specific to the text are for the most part "highly artificial abbreviations or letters used with a particular conventional value assigned to them; they are not, in short, really words" (1875:11–12). These would include the abbreviations of groups of sounds listed in the *Śivasūtras,* and made-up words in Pāṇini that have no ordinary meaning, like *sup* and *tin.* Burnell shows that while Pāṇini uses existing technical terms, which we may presume were taken from his predecessors because they are also found in the non-Paninian grammars, he also uses what we can infer to be newly coined abbreviations and terms, easily distinguishable by their artificiality and lack of simple meanings in the language. Burnell also demonstrates, very convincingly, that many of the technical terms of the *Tolkāppiyam* and of later Tamil grammars are simple translations of Sanskrit ones he attributes to the Aindra school or to other pre-Paninian texts. For example, a vowel is called *uyir,* "breath" or "life," and a consonant *mey,* "sense" or "body," resorting to ordinary Tamil words. The "happy little allegory of consonants being the body and vowels being the life" has been invented by European students of Tamil grammar, in ignorance of the fact that these words are translations of the Sanskrit *svara,* "sound" or "breath," for vowel and *sparśa,* "touch" for consonant, which are ordinary words used in a special sense in the grammars. Hence we must infer that the Tamil words are simple translations of the Sanskrit ones.

Burnell's fine study may have overdrawn the case for a single Aindra school encompassing all of the non-Paninian grammars, but he succeeded in establishing the importance of the *Kātantra* grammar of Sanskrit, whose presence or influence in places as distant as South India and the Deccan, Sri Lanka, Bengal, and Kashmir describes an arc of territory around the Vedic middle country of the Panjab and the upper Ganga valley and at a distance from it. This distribution tends to confirm Albrecht Weber's view that the *Kātantra* was meant for those approaching Sanskrit not as native speakers but through one of the Prakrit languages (in Belvalkar 1915:82). Burnell also determined the approximate place of the *Tolkāppiyam* in the history of grammar in India, namely, in the non-Paninian tradition that goes back, ultimately, to the simpler analysis (in the sense of being closer to natural speech in its technical apparatus, its metalanguage) of the early, early days of language analysis in India. It is clear that the *Tolkāppiyam,* like the *Aṣṭādhyāyī* of Pāṇini, did not fall from the sky, but achieved its precocious sophistication by making use of the earlier language analysis that had been developed for Sanskrit (Subramaniam 1953–57).

Of Tolkāppiyar, the author of the *Tolkāppiyam,* we know nothing certain; he may have been a Jain, or a brahmin. His text is not only the oldest surviving grammar of Tamil, it is probably the earliest work of Tamil literature to survive in its entirety (Zvelebil 1992:x; 1995:705). Its *sūtras* (Tamil *cūttiram*) are arranged under three broad headings, *eḻ uttu,* "letters"; *col,* "words"; and *poruḷ,* "substance"—or phonology, morphology, and poetics. David Shulman shows how deeply interconnected were grammar and poetry in South India (Shulman 2001). Only the first two books of the *Tolkāppiyam* correspond to the *Kātantra.* The third book bears a close relation to the surviving classical literature of ancient Tamil, the poetry of the Sangam. Although the final form of the *Tolkāppiyam* may not have been fixed till about 500 A.D., its earliest form is probably to be placed in the first century B.C. (Zvelebil 1995:705–6).

The texts of the non-Paninian schools (Belvalkar 1915:57 ff; Scharfe 1977:162 ff.) include the grammars of the Buddhists and Jains, whose linguistic object is quite different, being concerned with the Pali and Ardhamagadhi languages, respectively, in which their early scriptures were written. Followers of both religions ultimately wrote texts in Sanskrit, and Buddhists such as Candragomin, and Jains such as the author of the *Jainendravyākaraṇa* and the great polymath Hemacandra, wrote grammars of Sanskrit. However, since they were not interested in explaining the older, Vedic register of Sanskrit, the number of *sūtras* needed was less than the nearly 4,000 *sūtra*s of Panini—closer to 3,000. Hemacandra added a chapter on Prakrit to his Sanskrit grammar (the *Prākṛtavyākaraṇa,* Hemacandra 1997; also the *Apabhraṃśavyākaraṇa,* 1994), which necessitated further *sūtras*. The Pali grammar of Kaccāyana, as I have already said, is in the same tradition as the *Kātantra*.

In the matter of Sanskrit grammars written by others besides Jains and Buddhists, because of the rebarbitive nature of Pāṇini it is not surprising that grammars were subsequently composed that were topically arranged and simplified for beginners. In addition to the *Kātantra* at 1400 *sūtras,* there was Bopadeva's *Mugdalabodha* (fl. 1250 A.D.) which had 1200 *sūtras,* and the *Sārasvata-sūtrapāṭha* (c. 1300 A.D.), with a mere 700. When Englishmen came to Bengal and began learning Sanskrit, it was from these easier schoolbooks, though Jones took up the Paninians. The *Aṣṭādhyāyī* itself was only mastered by Colebrooke in the next generation.

The number of Sanskrit works on linguistics that have survived through the ages is voluminous, and Pāṇini is their centerpiece. Pāṇini continues to be studied by highly able scholars, who regard his text as the commanding heights of Sanskrit and of linguistic knowledge, as we have seen in the foregoing tribute of Staal. George Cardona's bibliography of something like a thousand works on Paninian grammar in print in European languages (Cardona 1976) attests to the continuing fascination that Pāṇini's incredible intellectual achievement holds for the learned members of this most difficult hyperspecialty.

The many languages of India were touched by this thick body of work on Sanskrit grammar, and as I have already mentioned, grammars for Pali, the Prakrits, and Tamil were composed in ancient times upon Sanskrit models. There is, however, a great difference among them: While the *Tolkāppiyam* explains Tamil grammar using some of the analytic techniques of Sanskrit grammar, it does so in terms of Tamil alone and without reference to the Sanskrit language. The grammars of the Prakrit languages, on the other hand, formulate second-order rules that are additional to the rules of Sanskrit grammar, that is, they treat the Prakrit languages as derivable from the Sanskrit roots via the rules of Pāṇini and include further rules specific to the Prakrits that address the non-Sanskrit-derived aspects of those languages. The means that the Prakrit grammarians formulated rules for identifying the Sanskritic and non-Sanskritic components of the Prakrits that would prove essential to the Dravidian proof, as we shall see in chapter 5. To that end we need to understand the logic of the Prakrit grammars.

The Prakrit languages are all historically related to Sanskrit, with names, such as Maharashtri, Shauraseni, and Magadhi, that associate them with particular regions or peoples; yet it is not the languages of ordinary speech but the literary forms of the different Prakrits used in poetry and in Sanskrit drama that form the object of the Prakrit grammars.[2] In the drama, the Prakrits tend to appear not as the regional languages their names suggest but as different registers of language belonging to different social classes, while only high-caste males are presented as speaking Sanskrit. The Prakrit grammarians do not write distinct grammars for the distinct literary Prakrits; rather, these languages are conceived to be on a continuum from Sanskrit in an ordered series from near to far. By convention Maharashtri is considered the model Prakrit language, perhaps because of its reputation as a language of fine art poetry, especially love poetry, at the court of the Sātavāhana king Hāla, whose name is attached to a famous anthology that is a model for others. Thus, in a Prakrit grammar Maharashtri is treated first, in *sūtras* that account for the features of the language in relation to Sanskrit, as if a Maharashtri word were a further transformation to which a Sanskrit root is subject after forming a Sanskrit word. The first surviving Prakrit grammar, Vararuci's *Prākṛtaprakāśa,* states at the end of the section on Maharashtri that the remaining portion must be learned from Sanskrit grammar *(śeṣaḥ saṃskṛtāt,* quoted in Acharya 1968:47), showing very clearly the dependence of Prakrit grammar upon Sanskrit and the conception of Prakrit as being somehow a form of Sanskrit—both the same and different at once. Subsequent chapters give rules additional to those given for Maharashtri, governing successively more distant Prakrits. In Vararuci's grammar, for example, the rules for Shauraseni are followed by the rule *śeṣam mahārāṣṭrivat,* "the remaining portion should be taken to be the same as Maharashtri" (ibid.). In this way the various literary Prakrits were treated as a series, arranged according to their degrees of departure from Sanskrit.

Prakrits were certainly spoken languages and languages of courtly writing from the time of Aśoka, as evidenced in the inscriptions attributed to him. The body of Prakrit work surviving is mainly courtly art poetry (anthologies and portions of the Sanskrit dramas) and royal inscriptions, in addition to the religious literature of Buddhists in Pali, which is not called a Prakrit but falls in the same class, and of Jains in Jaina

2. I make heavy use of Krishna Chandra Acharya's excellent overview of the Prakrit grammars, found in the introduction to his edition of Mārkaṇḍeya's *Prākṛtasarvasva* (1968), in my treatment of the subject. I am grateful to Madhav Deshpande for bringing this to my attention.

Prakrit, usually called Ardhamagadhi. The relations between Sanskrit and the Prakrits implied by the Prakrit grammars are structural rather than historical, a matter of the different registers of a single field of variation. But they also imply a historical derivation of the Prakrits from Sanskrit, or, perhaps we should say, the Prakrit grammars can be read in terms of such historical derivation.

When it comes to the Dravidian languages of South India, as we have seen, the Tamil grammar tradition, though it draws upon the analytical means of Sanskrit grammar, is self-contained in its treatment of Tamil. This, however, is exceptional; the other Dravidian languages for which grammars have been composed in premodern times are treated in those grammars as deriving from Sanskrit. The presence of large numbers of transparently Sanskrit and Prakrit words in Telugu, Kannada, and Malayalam—more so than in Tamil—was no doubt an inducement to do so, and the scripts of those languages, again unlike Tamil, represent the whole range of Sanskrit phonology as well as sounds peculiar to the Dravidian languages. The singularity of Tamil grammar and of the Tamil script was crucial to the formulation of the conception of the Dravidian language family in modern times.

One of the most important developments of the Prakrit grammars, and one that is very significant for the story I wish to tell, is the analysis of vocabulary into three main sets. Sanskrit words that are employed largely unchanged except for the use of Prakrit word endings are denoted by the technical term *saṃskṛtasama,* or *tatsama,* that is, "same as Sanskrit." Those that have internal changes as well—that have, in other words, been Prakritized—are called *saṃskṛtabhava,* or *tadbhava,* that is, "similar to Sanskrit" (Acharya 1968:56). All such words can be considered to derive from Sanskrit roots. The residue of words that cannot be readily explained as derivatives from Sanskrit are called *deśi* or *deśya,* "country words," with tinges of both being local to a region and being less refined than Sanskrit words. Besides these three crucial categories there are sometimes others, such as *grāmya* ("village words," vulgarisms beyond the pale of grammatical analysis), *antardeśya* ("exotic words," a subset of *deśya*) and *mleccha* (foreign words, barbarisms). This analytic, which was mainly understood in structural terms, was also applied to grammars of Telugu, Kannada, and Malayalam.

Indian linguistic analysis is strongly structural in its orientation, so the Indian tradition took the distinctions of *tatsama, tadbhava,* and *deśi* largely in structural terms, or as different registers of language having greater or lesser prestige. In contrast, European scholars connected with early colonial India, who were pursuing the genealogical connections among languages as a key to the history of nations, read those same terms historically, and found in them a ready-made technology for sorting out the Sanskrit *(tatsama)* and Prakrit *(tadbhava)* loanwords from an indigenous, Dravidian *(deśya)* core of South Indian languages. This is the major argument of this book. As I will demonstrate in chapter 5, what made it possible for Ellis and his team at Madras to formulate the Dravidian concept was the fact that existing grammars treated Telugu like a Prakrit language, while Tamil grammar treated Tamil as a self-contained entity and largely ignored Sanskritic and Prakritic elements in the language.

PHONOLOGY

The complexity of the *Aṣṭādhyāyī* tells us that Pāṇini built upon and transformed earlier forms of language analysis. These earlier analyses had a more natural ordering of topics and a technical terminology drawn from the natural language. Even if this earlier literature had not survived, and even if no non-Paninian schools had continued through time side by side with the Paninian one, we would probably be forced to infer the existence of these simpler and more natural forms of language analysis and pedagogy to explain how Pāṇini's text came about in the first place. But a significant portion of that earlier literature does survive, as do the later, non-Pāṇinian texts such as the *Tolkāppiyam,* enough to provide rich materials for the reconstruction of the history of language analysis in India.

The earliest achievements of that language analysis—and very solid achievements they are, as is readily apparent to this day—lay in phonology. While Pāṇini's text was and remains the pinnacle of Sanskrit grammar, scaled only by specialists and approached only gradually by European Indologists in modern times, phonology is the aspect of the Indian tradition of language analysis that was immediately available for universal application. The accuity of that analysis can be perceived in the very order of the alphabet. Indeed, the first lesson in Sanskrit, which usually concerns the alphabet—or a lesson in any of the many scripts derived from the ancient Brahmi script, whose alphabetical order is shaped by this ancient phonological analysis—is a lesson in phonology.

To show how a linear series such as the order of the alphabet can encode and teach a form of phonological analysis, it is helpful to consider an analogy in the interpretation of Old Babylonian grammatical texts as discussed by Thorkild Jacobsen (1974). Such texts are in the form of columns of words, some of them giving different grammatical forms of the same word. Jacobsen shows how the grammatical analysis of Old Babylonian words into paradigms can be inferred from such bare lists. Consider, he says, the noun paradigm for a Latin word, *insula,* "island":

	singular	plural
nominative	*insula*	*insulae*
accusative	*insulam*	*insulas*
genitive	*insulae*	*insularum*
dative	*insulae*	*insulis*
ablative	*insula*	*insulis*

Such a paradigm could be rendered as a single column of words in two different ways:

singular	nominative	*insula*
	accusative	*insulam*
	genitive	*insulae*
	dative	*insulae*
	ablative	*insula*
plural	nominative	*insula*
	accusative	*insulas*
	genitive	*insularum*
	dative	*insulis*
	ablative	*insulis*

or

nominative	singular	*insula*
	plural	*insulae*
accusative	singular	*insulam*
	plural	*insulas*
genitive	singular	*insulae*
	plural	*insularum*
dative	singular	*insulae*
	plural	*insulis*

ablative	singular	*insula*
	plural	*insulis*

Either way, the analysis of the noun declension by means of a grammatical paradigm could be inferred from the word order of a bare column of such words, even if the labels for number and case are stripped away. In this way the grammatical analysis of Old Babylonian can be reconstructed from columns of unlabelled words. In a similar way, the ancient phonological analysis of the sounds of Sanskrit is sedimented into the bare alphabetical order, and is conveyed by the ordering itself. It is important to bring this out, because the superior ordering of the alphabet in Indian scripts and those non-Indian scripts derived from or inspired by Indian ones is not generally captured in the "history of the alphabet" literature.

Phonology was pioneered in the texts called *śikṣā* and *prātiśākhya* (Deshpande 1997). These were attached to particular Vedic schools and directed their efforts to the explication of the phonological details of the Vedic liturgical text to which their school was devoted. In this they were different from the schools of grammar, which addressed themselves to the explanation of the Sanskrit language and the language of the Vedic texts in general, and were not limited to a particular Vedic school and its hymn collection, or *saṃhitā*. The minute examination of the sounds of a particular Vedic *saṃhitā,* then, was the object for early phonological study, but the results of such fine-grained study were nevertheless among the first fruits of the analysis of the Sanskrit language generally. This analysis seems to have operated without the benefit of writing, for the Brahmi script that emerges later is shaped and ordered by the analysis. Thus the ancient phonologists of India created an alphabetical order before they had a written alphabet; indeed, they had an alphabet before they had a script, we may say.

The alphabet as we find it in the phonological texts attributable to about 700 B.C., according to Madhav M. Deshpande, is given in figure 8. Deshpande, whose excellent discussion of the subject I rely on (Deshpande 1997), says that this listing of sounds is accepted with only minor variations by all the *śikṣās* and *prātiśākhyas.* First come the simple vowels *a, ā, i, ī, u, ū,* ordered back to front by place of articulation, namely, throat *(kaṇṭha),* palate *(tālu),* and lips *(oṣṭha);* then come vocalic *ṛ, ṝ, ḷ* (and a long version of vocalic *ḷ* in some traditions); all these being the *samāna,* "simple" vowels. They are grouped in pairs of short and long, the pairs being called *varṇa,* such that, for example, the *a-varṇa*

vowels:	a ā i ī u ū ṛ ṝ ḷ e o ai au				
consonants:					
sparśa	k	kh	g	gh	ṅ
	c	ch	j	jh	ñ
	ṭ	ṭh	ḍ	ḍh	ṇ
	t	th	d	dh	n
	p	ph	b	bh	m
antaḥstha	y	r	l	v	
ūṣman	ś	ṣ	s	h	
additional sounds:					
anusvāra	ṃ				
visarga	ḥ				
jihvāmūlīya	ḫ (before k, kh)				
upadhmānīya	ẖ (before p, ph)				

Figure 8. The Sanskrit alphabet *(akṣara-samāmnāya)*. Compare this alphabetical order with the one in the Śivasūtras (figure 7). (After Deshpande 1997: 39.)

consists of *a* and *ā* (and also the extra-long form, *a3*, as well as all three of these *a*-sounds both with and without each of the three Vedic accents). The remaining vowels are usually called *sandhyākāras,* "compound vowels," the first two *(e, o)* often called monophthongs, the last two *(ai, au)* often *dvi-varṇa,* "having two sounds," or diphthongs, the two pairs again articulated in a back-to-front order in the mouth.

The ordering of the consonants, the *sparśa,* "contact sounds," or stops and nasals, again shows a close analysis of such things as place of articulation, voicing, and aspiration. The five rows of the table of *sparśas* in figure 8 correspond to five groups called *vargas:* the *ka-varga* (guttural), *ca-varga* (palatal), *ṭa-varga* (retroflex), *ta-varga* (dental), and *pa-varga* (labial). That is, the rows progress down the table according to place of articulation, from the back of the mouth to the front. Within each *varga* there are pairs of unaspirated and aspirated stops, the first pair being voiceless, the second pair voiced; each is followed by the homorganic nasal. These comprise the five columns of the table.

Deshpande has shown that some theorists have reduced the number of primitive sounds by analyzing the contents of these *vargas* as having been formed by conjunctions of primitives. Thus in the *ka-varga, k* would be considered a primitive consonant, from which the next sound, *kh,* is derived by addition of the aspiration-primitive *h, jihvāmūlīya* (whence it becomes *soṣman,* "having a spirant"); again, the next sound, *g,* is derived by adding the primitive of voicing *(ghoṣa)* to *k,* so that it becomes *ghoṣavat,* "with voice." The sound *gh* is derived by adding voiced aspiration to *g.* The nasal at the end of the *varga* is derived by adding the primitive voiced nasal *ṃ (anusvāra)* to the primitive consonant *k.*

The remaining consonants of the alphabet are the semivowels or "in-between sounds" *(antastha, antaḥstha): y, r, l, v,* and the spirants *(ūṣman,* "aspiration sounds"): *ś, ṣ, s,* and *h,* both sets again observing the back-to-front convention of ordering.

This splendidly reasoned alphabetical order (a revelation to students raised on late daughters of the Semitic scripts, such as the roman script in which this book is written, with its irrational *a, b, c* order) is encoded in the Brahmi script, first attested in the inscriptions of Aśoka in the third century B.C. All the indigenous scripts of modern India are traceable to Brahmi, which was shaped by the phonological analysis of the Vedic tradition. This alphabetical order is also perpetuated by the daughter scripts of Brahmi, which is to say, most of the scripts of South Asia, Tibet, and Southeast Asia, and has influenced the scripts of East Asia. The origin of Brahmi remains an issue which divides the community of scholars. Most European scholars believe it was inspired by a Semitic model, whether Phoenician, Aramaic, or Sabaean (cf. the classic treatment of Bühler 1907). Among these choices, Aramaic is the most probable, because Aramaic inscriptions of the Mauryas have been found in South Asia, and Aramaic was a language of government records for the Achaemenian kings of Iran, whose power for a time extended to the Indus Valley. Many South Asian scholars hold that Brahmi was derived by modification from the logographic script of the Indus Civilization. But whatever may be the origin of the graphic matter from which the shape of the signs was made, the script as a system of sounds was made by the phoneticians of Sanskrit. This fact is not sufficiently appreciated in the scholarly literature on the history of the alphabet, and indeed is generally obscured by the manner of exposition. Isaac Taylor's influential nineteenth-century work, *The Alphabet* (1883), for example, which was a model much followed thereafter, has as its main theme the Semitic origin of most of the currently surviving scripts of the world, and gives stemmas showing the derivation and relationship of the letter *m,* for example, in the alphabets of the world. For Taylor, then, Brahmi and the scripts of South and Southeast Asia deriving from it are interesting only as further instances of the various changes in individual letter-shapes from an original Semitic script. What is missed completely is how the ancient Indian phonological analysis of Sanskrit transformed the graphic material, whether Semitic or other, and presented it in a novel alphabetical order.

Because this order is so reasoned, the learning of the Brahmi script or any of its many descendant scripts is a first lesson in phonology. And Brahmi has spread widely. Within South Asia it is the ancestor of the Devanagari, Gujarati, Gurmukhi, Bengali, Oriya, Kannada, Telugu, Malayali, Tamil, and Sinhalese, to list only scripts in use today, which is to say, virtually all the scripts of South Asia except the Perso-Arabic script used for Urdu. With the spread of Indian religions and court culture to Southeast Asia, Brahmi-based scripts were developed for Burmese, Thai, Lao, and Khmer, that is, virtually the whole of the Indochina Peninsula except for Vietnam and Malaysia, and they predominated in Indonesia until the introduction of the roman script in recent times. The survey of K. F. Holle (1877, cited in Kuipers and McDermott 1996:474–76) registered 198 different scripts deriving from Brahmi, stretching from India through Southeast Asia, a great many of them in the various islands of Indonesia and reaching eastward as far as the Philippines. Brahmi-based scripts have flourished in Central Asia as well, notably the Tibetan script, but also Khotanese, Mongolian, and others.

The effects of Brahmi and the phonological analysis congealed in its alphabetical order upon East Asia seem to have been considerable. Buddhist texts have been found in Central Asia in which a Brahmi-derived script is used to render Chinese phonetically (Emmerick and Pulleyblank 1993), but these are few and marginal. Far and away the most important effects of Indian language analysis upon Chinese seems to have been to stimulate methods of phonological analysis of Chinese. Sir William Jones himself remarked that "the order of *sounds* in the *Chinese* grammars corresponds nearly with that observed in *Tibet*, and hardly differs from that, which the *Hindus* consider as the invention of their Gods" (Jones 1788d:424). However, it was not in grammars but in the dictionaries of rhymes that Indian language analysis seems to have had its greatest effect on China, and its effect was mostly through phonology rather than grammar.

Rhyme books, according to William Baxter (1992:33), are known by title as early as the Wei-Jin period (A.D. 220–420), but the most important of them are the rhyming dictionaries, beginning in 601 A.D. with the *Qièyùn* of Lù Făyán. Pronunciations in the rhyme books are shown not by adopting a foreign, phonetic script such as Brahmi but by analyzing the sounds of words through a specially devised form of spelling, in which the word is represented by two characters, the first having the same initial consonant as the word itself, the second having the same sound as the final sound of the word. These phonetic initials and finals are arranged into tables, forming classes of rhyming words. This form of phonetic spelling, called *fănqiè (fan ch'ie),* which arose in perhaps the second century A.D., was influenced by Indian phonology (ibid.), specifically, by an Indian Brahmi-derived script (Scharfe 1977:79) at the time of the expansion of Buddhism in China. In the rhyme tables the initials are ordered in a systematic way which, although it is not the same as the Sanskrit order of the Brahmi script, is similar and may have been influenced by it, though in a way suitable to the Chinese language. Thus the order of columns in the rhyme tables is *p, ph, b, m, t, th, d, n, ts, tsh, dz, s, z, k, kh, g, ng, glottal stop, x, γ, ny, n,* which approximates the groupings of consonants (the *vargas*) in the alphabetical order of Sanskrit, except in reverse order—from the front to the back of the mouth, from lips to throat. There are also retroflex initials (represented by Baxter as *tr, trh, d*), which are put in the same columns as the series *t, th, d,* and retroflex and palatal affricates and fricatives *(tsy, tsry, dzr, xr, zr,* and *tsy, tsyh, dzy, sy, zy),* which are put in the same columns with the series *ts, tsh, dz, s, z* (Baxter, personal communication; see also Karlgren 1926, 1963). The rhyming dictionaries and the *fănqiè* spelling system were tools that enabled the development of a highly sophisticated Chinese philology aimed at the understanding of classics of Old Chinese such as the *Book of Odes,* whose rhymes no longer rhymed because of the phonological changes that had overtaken Middle Chinese. These tools overcame the handicap that a nonphonetic script posed for the phonological analysis of the language. The rhyming dictionaries of the Chinese philologists, which had been written to illuminate the classics of Old Chinese, and the rhymes of the classics themselves, furnish modern linguistics with its most important means for the study of the phonology of Old Chinese (Karlgren 1926, 1963; Baxter 1992) Thus the effects of Indian phonology upon China appear to have been enormously productive and long-lasting. They continue to this day.

In Japan and Korea, the influence of the Indian phonologists seems to have been different again. The Japanese developed a phonetic script, Kana, better suited to the multisyllabic nature of Japanese language yet parallel to the Chinese-derived logographic script, Kanji, and both are in use today. Kana is by no means a descendant of Brahmi in a direct way. But like Brahmi it is a syllabary, and the dictionary order of symbols is in the alphabetical order of Sanskrit and the Brahmi script, so it is reasonable to suppose that exposure to Sanskrit and Indian scripts through Buddhism was involved in the formation of Kana. The hybridity of Japanese writing was completed by the admission of Romaji, or roman script, for some purposes (Smith 1996). In Korea, the Hankul script was invented by King Seycong in 1444 A.D. This highly sophisticated script, based on a close analysis of the Korean phonology, is also highly original, basing the shapes of signs on the shapes of their places of articulation in the mouth. But "there may still be reason to believe they looked to scripts of Indic descent for the alphabetic idea" (King 1996:225), particularly to the 'Phags pa script. This script was devised by a Tibetan Buddhist monk of that name, national preceptor to the emperor Qubilai (Kublai Khan), who ordered him to devise a script in which all the languages of his empire could be written, including Tibetan, Uighur, Mongolian, and Chinese; it was completed in 1269 A.D. The Tibetan script itself is a descendant of Brahmi, and Indic aspects of the 'Phags pa script include the inherent vowel *a* in consonants, different forms for vowels in initial and noninitial positions, and the Indic alphabetical order (van der Kuijp 1996).

While Brahmi and its descendant scripts reached China with Buddhism early in the first millennium, knowledge of them in the West began very much later, perhaps 1500 years later, more or less with the expansion of European power in Asia after the Renaissance. As in China, the effects of these scripts on the West, if we follow the estimate of J. R. Firth, were also hugely productive and durable.

According to Firth, the work of Sir William Jones, specifically his "Dissertation on the orthography of Asiatick words in Roman letters" (1788a), forms an epoch between the great English scholars of language in the Royal Society at the time of the Restoration and the true foundation of what Firth calls the English school of phonetics (Firth 1957) in the nineteenth century by Henry Sweet. Jones gave an immense stimulus to phonetics and general linguistics, Firth says, and through him Indian language analysis greatly influenced the English scholars of phonetics: "Without the Indian grammarians and phoneticians whom he introduced and recommended to us, it is difficult to imagine our nineteenth-century school of phonetics." In another passage he puts it baldly: "Modern grammar and phonetics are founded on the Indian sciences" (Firth 1957:111 n. 1). W. S. Allen, whose *Phonetics in ancient India* gives a systematic account of Indian phonetic doctrine that can be used by phoneticians today (treating the Indian analysts as contemporaries), strongly concurred with Firth's assessment of the influence of the Indian phoneticians upon Europe via Jones, especially upon William Dwight Whitney and A. J. Ellis (Allen 1953:4). In fact, he thought the Indian tradition of phonetic analysis was greatly superior to the European tradition:

> In phonetics, we all too rarely look back beyond the great names of the nineteenth century—Henry Sweet, A. J. Ellis, Alexander Melville Bell—except occasionally to honour a few lonely and half-forgotten figures of the immediately preceding centuries. We justify some of our more grotesque and inadequate terminology (e.g. "*tenuis*" and "*media*") by tracing it back to the Latin grammarians, sometimes as far as Dionysius Thrax or even Aristotle: but generally speaking the expressions of ancient phonetic thought in the west have little to repay our attention or deserve our respect, whereas Indian sources as ancient and even more ancient are infinitely more rewarding. (Ibid., 2)

This tradition has been made available to the West through Jones's article, in which "the whole order of treatment and descriptive technique is clearly based on Indian models" (Ibid., 3).

Viewing these developments as a panorama, it appears that Indic scripts and the phonological analysis expressed in their alphabetic order have been powerfully influential in Asia and Europe and that their effects are very much with us today. It is also apparent that this influence was variously received and put to use. In South Asia, Southeast Asia, and Central Asia the Brahmi script gave birth to other scripts more or less on the same lines though often tinkered with to accommodate the phonological features of other languages, and it provided scripts for languages which hitherto had none. Where the Chinese script prevailed, the Indian scripts and phonological tradition were consumed quite differently. In Japan they influenced the formation of a phonetic script to supplement the Chinese-based Kanji, and in Korea they influenced the invention of an entirely new script, closely tailored to the phonology of the language. In China they served the study of the classics through the elaboration of a philology based on phonological analysis. In Europe they contributed to the formation of a scientific phonetics and comparative philology that aimed at a comprehensive, worldwide collection and analysis of languages that has become an integral part of modernism.

Just at the moment when the European program of recovering the genealogy of nations through the genealogy of languages was getting underway, scholars found the tools of etymology ready to hand in India.

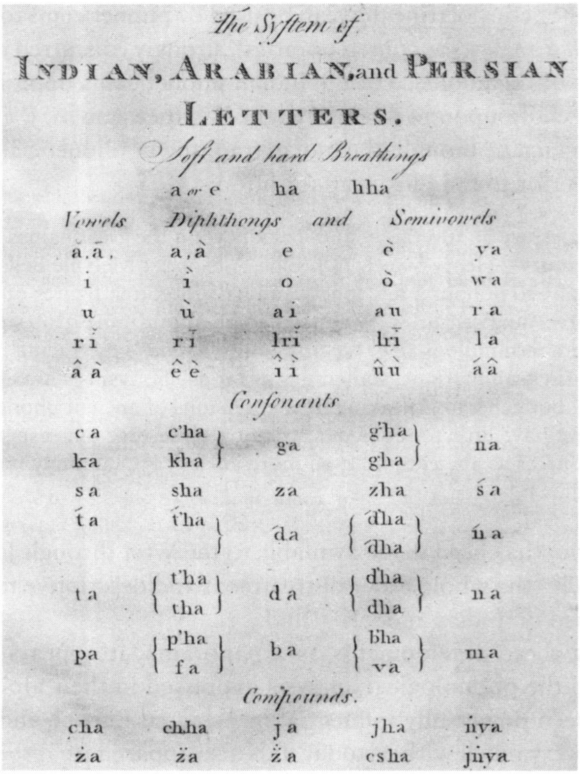

The System of
INDIAN, ARABIAN, and PERSIAN
LETTERS.
Soft and hard Breathings

a or e	ha	hha

Vowels	Diphthongs	and	Semivowels	
a, ā	a, à	e	è	ya
i	ì	o	ò	wa
u	ù	ai	au	ra
ri	rì	lri	lrì	la
â à	ê è	î ì	û ù	á â

Consonants

ca ka	c'ha kha	ga	g'ha gha	ṅa
sa	sha	za	zha	śa
ṭa	ṭ'ha	ḍa	ḍ'ha ḍha	ṅa
ta	t'ha tha	da	d'ha dha	na
pa	p'ha fa	ba	b'ha va	ma

Compounds.

ċha	chha	ja	jha	ṅya
ża	ża	ża	csha	jṅya

Figure 9. The romanization of Sanskrit, Persian, Arabic, and other Asian languages, in the system of Sir William Jones. (From Jones 1787a: facing p. 1.)

"VOWELS AS IN ITALIAN"

The first outcome of the conjuncture of the two traditions of language analysis in British India—the very first article of the first volume of *Asiatic researches*—was an article by Sir William Jones on the transliteration of words in Asian languages, "A dissertation on the orthography of Asiatick words in Roman letters" (1788a). It is entirely understandable that phonology should be the area where these traditions first met, as the mastery of an Indian script and its phonology is the first step in learning an Indian language. Strictly speaking, though, Jones's system is not a phonetic transcription but a transliteration, which is a representation of a script rather than a system of sounds as such. Since the Devanagari script, a direct descendant of the ancient Brahmi script, was the pattern for

Jones's transliteration, however, the work of the ancient phoneticians was contained within it, and through it, transmitted to Europe.

In the article Jones addresses the problem of representing words from Asiatic languages in roman script and expressly considers two alternatives: a phonetic transcription and a transliteration, in which letters of the roman script stand for specific letters of the target scripts. The latter are the scripts of Arabic, Persian, and Sanskrit, languages in which Jones worked and for which he had devised this system of transliteration as his own. In a notebook of Jones's first lessons in Sanskrit—now in the Harry Ransom Library at the University of Texas-Austin—which appears to be in his own hand, the romanization is influenced by Bengali pronunciation, for instance, *tobo* for *tava,* "thy," "of thee." Perhaps it was his later knowledge of the true phonological value of the sounds of the Sanskrit alphabet and their difference from the sounds of Bengali that led him to prefer a transliteration to a phonetic transcription.

Jones's article follows the alphabetical order of the Devanagari script, which "is more naturally arranged than any other" (ibid., 13), as the basis for the discussion of the transliteration of Arabic, Persian, and Sanskrit. And the order in which he takes up the sounds in the narrative and presents them in his table follows the alphabetical order of Sanskrit, the *akṣara-samāmnāya* of the *śikṣās* and *prātiśākhyas.* Thus the phonological analysis of the late Vedic period scholars is built into Jones's scheme of transliteration.

The scheme itself (figure 9) was very influential, and is the basis of the transliteration scheme for Sanskrit now in use, only slightly altered from that of Jones. Among the features of his system are the use of diacritics to differentiate between the two sets of "t" and "d" sounds, the retroflex and the alveolar ones; Jones distinguishes the retroflex sounds with an accent mark, while today we use a subscript dot, or full stop *(ṭ, ṭh, ḍ, ḍh, ṇ).* Again, for aspirated consonants he adds an *h* but inserts an apostrophe to indicate that it is not a conjunct character consisting of consonant plus *h* but a single character, for instance, *t'h.* This convention of the apostrophe was often written as a comma or a straight, vertical, short subscript line, but was eventually dropped altogether, since the combination of a consonantal stop plus the letter *h* does not occur in Sanskrit, so that confusion can never arise. Long vowels are marked for length, but short ones are unmarked (unlike, for example, the transliteration of Charles Wilkins, who marks all the short vowels for quantity as well).

It is in the representation of the vowels that the system of Jones has been especially influential, for he decided not to provide normal English equivalents but to use essentially the Italian equivalents. Jones's practice here was widely followed by missionaries and others in the nineteenth and twentieth centuries in writing grammars of languages all over the world. "Vowels as in Italian, consonants as in English" puts in a slogan the system of Jones.

The overall goal of Jones was to produce a system from which "each original sound may be rendered invariably by an appropriate symbol, conformably to the natural order of articulation, and with a due regard to the primitive power of the *Roman* alphabet" (1788a:1). English is notorious for departing from that primitive power of the roman alphabet, Jones says, especially in the matter of the vowels. "Our English alphabet and orthography are disgracefully and almost ridiculously imperfect," and it would be impossible to render Indian, Persian, or Arabic words in roman letters "as we are absurdly taught to pronounce them" (ibid.). Thus, the sound of the first vowel *(a)* "in our own anomalous language" is often represented by our (English) fifth vowel *(u)*. Yet we also represent it by a variety of vowels and diphthongs, as in the phrase, "a mother bird flutters over her young," in which the Sanskrit vowel is represented consecutively by *a, o, i, u, e, ou*. "Vowels as in Italian" was in large part a decision to follow a Latin standard for romanization rather than an English one. In a sense the Great Vowel Shift of Middle English separates the modern orthography of English vowels from their original, more Roman-like pronunciation, and renders English values for the roman vowels very unhelpful in a transliteration, especially if it is to be understood by Europeans speaking languages other than English. To these reasons for the adoption of the Italian standard for the transliteration of vowels one may perhaps add a sentimental reason. Sir William and Lady Jones were fond of Italian poetry and used to read it together in the evening in Calcutta. "Vowels as in Italian" was, as they say, overdetermined for Jones.

As a result of this decision concerning the vowels, however, a gap opened up in the representation of Indian names and words in English between the vernacular representations, which followed English pronunciation of the vowels, and learned ones, which followed Jones. This led to a doubling of representations, as in the pairs of variant spellings: *Hindoo, Hindu; pooja, puja; Poona, Pune; Lukshmi* (or *Lucksmi*), *Lakshmi* (rhymes with *luck*, not *lack*); *pundit, pandit* (rhymes with *pun,* not *pan*); *Punjab, Panjab.* The learned spelling *Hindu* eventually replaced *Hin-*

doo, but the learned spellings have not been uniformly successful in replacing vernacular ones because they are not intuitive. Vernacular spellings continue to be used in renderings of Indian place names and personal names. Some of that doubling, then, persists unresolved. The spelling of some non-Indian words has also been affected by the Jonesean system, such as the spelling of *tabu* for *taboo.* In other cases the learned system has lead to a change of pronunciation, such that when American radio journalist Lakshmi Singh gives her name, she pronounces it as if it rhymed with *lack* instead of *luck.*

One feature of the Jonesean system for the transliteration of vowels that is no longer followed is the occasional use of *e* for *a* in certain environments, such as before a nasal. This is to accommodate the transliteration scheme for Persian, in which the letter *zeber* has that value, varying from something like "a" to something like "e" according to the sounds that follow, and Jones allowed this to influence his transliteration of non-Persian words. This was a great misfortune. The name of the compiler/author of the lawbook Jones translated, "Manu," becomes by this rule "Menu." The colossal statue of Jones in St. Paul's Cathedral, or worse, in the dining hall at Harrow School of which he had been a student, where he is shown holding a book containing the word "Menu," can be mocked by the irreverent as depicting a waiter holding a menu. This odd deviation from the "vowels as in Italian" standard was dropped by later scholars. (For further details of this curious wrinkle in the Jonesean system see Trautmann 1998:104–5.)

This influential article by Jones, then, appearing at the launching of the *Asiatic researches* and widely read, admired, translated, and pirated in Europe, marks the first effect of Indian language analysis on European scholarship. The scheme which resulted was offered as a simple means for rendering Asian words in English narrative in such a way that scholars could unerringly restore the original spelling in the Arabic, Persian, or Sanskrit (Devanagari) scripts. In the course of doing so, the Sanskrit alphabetical order also provided a standard for a scheme of representation that allowed for the *synoptic* representation of *many* languages—useful, for example, in comparative vocabularies intended as tools for the determination of language histories, such as Jones himself undoubtedly used to determine the siblingship of Sanskrit, Greek, Latin, and the other Indo-European languages. It was an invaluable tool for the languages-and-nations project.

Thus, though the scheme of Jones was a transliteration, because it was based on a phonologically devised script it pointed the way forward to a universal system of phonetic representation, culminating in the International Phonetic Alphabet, which represents *sounds* directly rather than *scripts*. Thus the phonological analysis of ancient India has had a very long reach, shaping not only the scripts of South, Southeast, and East Asia but the scientific linguistics of today.

CHAPTER 3

Ellis and His Circle

Having examined the structure of the European and Indian inputs into the British-Indian conjuncture, we turn now to the Dravidian proof. In this chapter I introduce the leading personnel associated with the emergence of the Dravidian conception; in the next, I will analyze the College of Fort St. George, which was the institutional context of its publication.

This chapter is a collective biography of the persons involved. The key figure is Francis Whyte Ellis (1777–1819), Collector of Madras and senior member of the College of Fort St. George, which was his brainchild and which brought together the scholars and the different scholarly skills needed to formulate a proof of the Dravidian language family concept. The chapter also presents Ellis's two close friends, William Erskine and John Leyden, partly to show how the archive surrounding the Dravidian proof was formed, but mainly to identify the personal projects of each of them. The specific characteristics of Ellis's scholarly trajectory become clear when seen both in relation to those of his two friends, and also in relation to the other large project undertaken at Madras, that of Colin Mackenzie. The chapter also brings forward information about the three leading scholars in Ellis's circle at Madras: A. D. Campbell; Pattabhirama Shastri, the leading head master at the College; and Sankaraiah, Ellis's sheristadar, or head of staff, at the Collectorate of Madras. Although Ellis is the primary figure in the story of the Dravidian concept, in that he authored the published proof, it will become clear that it was the work of many hands.

FINDING ELLIS

Some of the most profound and lasting intellectual effects of British colonial rule in India have been on the conception of India's deep past. Here colonial philology and archaeology have made fundamental contributions that have augmented the existing textual bases of Indian history—the *purāṇas,* epics, and royal genealogies—recovering new material for history through the study of inscriptions, coins, monuments, and bringing India's deep past into relation with the pasts of other ancient nations. The fundamental contributions were, again, the concepts of the Indo-European language family, announced by Sir William Jones in 1786, and the Dravidian language family, published by Ellis in 1816, plus the formulation of the concept of the Indus Civilization, first published by Sir John Marshall in 1924. These are the three fixed points of ongoing scholarly inquiry into the origins of civilization in South Asia. The last is also the topic of a public debate currently raging in India about the linguistic and religious identity of the Indus Civilization.

Both from a world-history perspective, then, and from the perspective of the history of Indian civilization, Jones and Ellis had roles of immense importance. But while Jones is well known and much written of, Francis Whyte Ellis is nearly forgotten.

One of the reasons for the nearly total obscurity into which the memory of Ellis has fallen is that his most notable achievement, the published proof that the Dravidian languages are interrelated and are not derived from Sanskrit, was superseded by the publication, in 1856, of Robert Caldwell's *A comparative grammar of the Dravidian or South-Indian family of languages*. Caldwell's magisterial comparative study of the Dravidian family has become a classic, and it is still in print. It is a great work of scholarship and a landmark in its field, wholly deserving of the high esteem in which it continues to be held. But Caldwell was not excessively generous in giving credit to his predecessors, and Ellis in particular gets much less than his due in Caldwell's preface to the first edition. Caldwell writes: "The first to break ground in the field was Mr. Ellis, a Madras Civilian, who was profoundly versed in the Tamil language and literature, and whose interesting but very brief comparison, not of the grammatical forms, but only of some of the vocables of three Drâvidian dialects, is contained in his introduction to *Campbell's Telugu Grammar*" (Caldwell 1856:iv).

One notes the minimizing language in which Caldwell frames this recognition of Ellis's priority: the comparison is interesting but *very brief,* and *not of grammatical forms* but *only some of the vocables.* Readers may judge for themselves whether this does justice to Ellis when we examine the Dravidian proof in chapter 5. Caldwell goes on to speak of the Rev. Dr. Stevenson's work on the identity of the non-Sanskritic element in the languages of the Deccan, judging his papers to be too sketchy to be of permanent philological value, though "decidedly in advance of everything which had hitherto been published on this subject." He avers he was not aware of the contributions of Ellis and Stevenson to Dravidian comparative philology when he began his own work on the subject; "and when at length I made their acquaintance, I felt no less desirous than before of going forward, for though I had lost the satisfaction of supposing myself to be the discoverer of a new field, yet it now appeared to be certain that the greater part of the field still lay not only uncolonized, but unexplored" (ibid.). Thus, grudgingly, he acknowledges the priority of Ellis and Stevenson, while averring that their work did not influence his and magnifying his own accomplishment at the expense of theirs. In the third edition of Caldwell's work (1913), which is the one currently in print, this preface does not appear at all, and no acknowledgment of Ellis's priority remains. Indeed, Ellis is mentioned only three times in the book, and only concerning points on which Caldwell disagrees with him. Caldwell seems to be telling us that his book is virtually without predecessors, and that what came before was only a history of error. This was not, to be sure, the first or the last time an author was less than generous toward opinions other than his own. Because of the well-earned success of Caldwell's book and the absence of reference to Ellis and others in the latest edition, the understanding has become virtually universal that the Dravidian language family was established as a scientific entity by Caldwell in 1856. Very few people today know that it was established in print exactly forty years previous, by Ellis.

In my earlier researches I too began with the belief that Caldwell was the discoverer of Dravidian. As seventy years had separated Jones's announcement of the Indo-European idea and the publication of Caldwell's book, I wondered what ideas about languages and nations had been proposed in that long interval. It was then that I came upon Ellis's Dravidian proof, included as a note to the introduction to Campbell's grammar of Telugu, published by the College of Fort St. George at Madras for its students in a small edition (reproduced here in appendix B). It became clear to me that this work, scarce and little known as it now is, nevertheless had an effect on British Indian scholarship and stimulated wide-ranging comparisons of the non-Indo-European languages by such scholars as the missionary John Stevenson in Bombay (Stevenson 1841–44 a, 1841–44b, 1843, 1849–51, 1853a, 1853b, 1853c) and Brian Houghton Hodgson in Nepal and Darjeeling (Hodgson 1833, 1847, 1848, 1849; see also Waterhouse 2004). During the seventy-year interval from Jones to Caldwell, then, the existence of a Dravidian language family had been shown by Ellis, and others had sought to determine whether all the other non-Indo-European languages of India fell into a single family or not. The true accomplishment of Caldwell, in fact, was not the discovery of the Dravidian family of languages but the determination of its true extent, and the fact that it is *not* the same as a second non-Indo-European language family of India, the Kolarian or Munda or Austroasiatic language family. It is with Caldwell that the modern consensus that there are three main language families in India proper was established (see Trautmann 1997:149–64).

There is plenty of evidence that the work of Ellis had an effect upon his successors, and so upon Caldwell himself, directly and indirectly. His pioneering work in Tamil literature is remembered in the Tamil country. N. Venkata Rao, head of the Telugu Department in Madras University during the 1950s, published a series of articles that showed with admirable clarity and detail the role of Ellis in the publication of the Dravidian concept (Venkata Rao 1953–54, 1957, 1957–58).[1] Burrow and Emeneau recognized the priority of Ellis in their preface to the *Dravidian etymological dictionary* (1961:v). As one looks more closely, then, one sees that the memory of Ellis was not entirely lost. In 1997 I published a short account of Ellis and his Dravidian proof in *Aryans and British India.* That, as well as the reprinting of the Telugu grammar in which his Dravidian proof first appeared (Ellis 1816), has begun to reestablish the importance of Ellis's contribution.

There is another reason for Ellis's obscurity today. Ellis died suddenly, in India, at a fairly young age, and in the settling of his estate his personal and scholarly papers literally went up in flames. At the time of his death he had been on tour in Madurai, staying with the collector there, Rous Petrie, when he accidentally poisoned himself by taking something he thought was medicine for an unnamed ailment, probably a stomach problem of some kind (in a letter he complained of chronic dyspepsia). Walter Elliot, himself a civil servant and notable scholar of South Indian

1. I am most grateful to Professor K. Venkateswarlu of Visakhapatnam for bringing these excellent articles, which I had not known about when writing my previous book, to my attention.

antiquities, and a great admirer of Ellis who felt that his accomplishments had not gotten the recognition that they deserved, took steps to recover his work and publicize his life. Elliot said that all of Ellis's papers were "lost or destroyed" and recorded it as current report that "they served Mr. Petrie's cook for months to kindle his fire and singe fowls." The thought of this fine scholar's life work, which one would so love to be able to read, going up in smoke, page by page, is deeply melancholy for me. It calls powerfully to mind the story of Guṇāḍhya of ancient times, who read and burned, leaf by leaf, the great collection of stories he had written in the language of the demons, the *Bṛhatkathā,* out of pique because the king disdained a work in such a debased language, while the animals listened with pleasure and watched with horror.

What makes this image especially distressing is that Ellis had made it his life plan to publish nothing until he had become a ripened scholar at forty years of age. This resolve did not allow for an untimely death, and, as it happened, he died at age forty-one. Very little of his work had been published at that point, when he was on the brink of a series of publications that would undoubtedly have been important contributions to the scholarly study of South India. The loss is no less tragic for being virtually unknown.

When I set out in search of this lost Orientalist, therefore, the prospects were bleak in the extreme. The inventory of Ellis's publications at the time of his death stands thus: There is the Dravidian proof, an article-length note in the introduction of a Telugu grammar published by the College, of which Ellis was the creator and over which, as senior member of the Board of Superintendence, he presided. Another work, the *Treatise of mirasi right,* on the land tenure of the Madras region, Ellis had written in the line of duty as Collector of Madras, as a report to the Board of Revenue, without any view to its publication; the Board, however, so liked it that they recommended it for publication by the Government of Madras (Ellis 1818; reprinted in C.P. Brown 1852, and in Bayley and Hudleston 1862). This unintended publication is important in the history of land tenures in British India, because the *Treatise of mirasi right* lay athwart the path of the introduction of the ryotwari system by Thomas Munro and his associates. For this reason Ellis is known and discussed in the literature on land tenure, including a detailed treatment by Eugene Irschick in his book *Dialogue and culture* (1994). At the time of Ellis's death a third work of his, left incomplete, was being printed at the College, again for the use of students: a translation of the Tamil classic collection of moral aphorisms, the *Tirukkuṟaḷ* (c. 1819). Another work, completed but published only after his death in the *Asiatic researches,* is an excellent exposé of the *Ezour Vedam,* a "Veda" which Ellis shows to have been concocted by Christian missionaries.

Besides the two, or two and two-thirds, printed pieces that appeared in Ellis's lifetime, and the few more that made it into print after his death, the probability of finding unpublished letters and papers was poor indeed. It is rare for the private papers of persons who are not public figures of great visibility to end up in archives, very rare indeed, and according to the testimony of Walter Elliot the Ellis papers had been lost or destroyed. Nevertheless, I went to the India Office Library, which has since become the Oriental and India Office Collections of the British Library, hoping to find a few scraps of information on this great scholar, with one slender reference to an Ellis item in the papers of William Erskine from Eugene Irschick's book (1994:224 n. 25, which he in turn got from Dharampal).

I was rewarded beyond all expectation. It turned out that William Erskine of Bombay was a fellow Orientalist and a good friend of Ellis, and the Erskine Collection on close examination was found to contain a number of items from Ellis, both letters and, to my great surprise and delight, handwritten copies of unpublished papers. These finds led to others, and the hunt took me to Edinburgh. Erskine's papers had been divided among the India Office Library, the British Museum, and the National Library of Scotland by his son, C. J. Erskine, and each of these collections contains Ellis material. In particular, in the Erskine collection in the National Library of Scotland I found twenty-two letters of Ellis to Erskine, many of them long, most of them containing Orientalist shoptalk, filled with particulars of Ellis's scholarly work. Erskine had saved all these letters, perhaps in an album, preceded by a character sketch of Ellis. Erskine, moreover, was a close friend and literary executor of another lost Orientalist, John Leyden of Calcutta, who knew and respected Ellis. The Leyden material in the Erskine collections led me to examine the voluminous Leyden collections in the British Library and the National Library of Scotland, where I found yet more Ellis items. The India Office Library contains a long letter of Ellis to Leyden that is especially valuable. Other Ellis material is found in the papers of Colin Mackenzie in the Oriental and India Office Collections (OIOC) of the British Library.

Walter Elliot himself played an important role in rescuing Ellis's material from destruction. Besides publishing a couple of previously unpublished papers of Ellis's and memorializing his life, Ellis found and preserved two extensive drafts of a work by Ellis on Tamil prosody among papers of the College of Fort St. George. These are now in the Elliot Collection of the British Library (OIOC). Elliot bequeathed to another Tamil scholar, the missionary G. U. Pope, other extremely valuable drafts of Ellis's from the College, which he found among discarded papers there. Pope gave them to the Bodleian Library at Oxford. I learned of these papers through Pope's entry for Ellis in the *Dictionary of national biography.* The reference is cryptic, and the papers are not listed in the main catalogue of the Bodleian. I searched through six sublibraries till I found them in the seventh, the Oriental Reading Room. These papers include a rough draft of a history of Tamil language and literature that would have been Ellis's masterwork, had he lived.

Finally, of course, in addition to these private papers and letters, there is Ellis's work in the colonial archive. Ellis was a hardworking civil servant, and his name appears frequently in the colonial record, especially the proceedings of the Board of Revenue, the district records of Madras District during his period as collector (1810–1919), and the proceedings of the Public Department of the Madras Government (called Madras Public Consultations) concerning projects for dictionaries and grammars of the South Indian languages and the reports of the College of Fort St. George from its founding in 1812 till Ellis's death in 1819. All of these records, handwritten with steel nib pens and bound in large, quarto volumes, are found at the Tamil Nadu State Archives in Chennai. Duplicates of the Board of Revenue Proceedings and Public Consultations were made and dispatched by clipper ship to England for the archive of India House, and are now in the OIOC. The volume of the British-Indian official archive is enormous; for example, Public Consultations of Madras, a single department in the three provincial governments of British India, contains over ten thousand volumes. One cannot but be impressed by the huge amount of labor and care that was devoted to the creation of such an archive, and that continues to be devoted to its preservation. And scholars cannot but be, at times, oppressed by its sheer size.

The workaday records of government transactions may seem unpromising places in which to search for Orientalist scholarship in the strict sense, but they proved a treasure trove for the purposes of this book, for several reasons.

For one thing, Ellis was a nearly perfect embodiment of Orientalism as colonial policy. Orientalist policy, which aspired to rule India in accord with Indian culture, required investigation of that culture through the study of Indian languages and the reading of Indian texts that were its repositories. At Calcutta a triangle of institutions consolidated the power of Orientalism as colonial policy: the Government itself, and especially the courts, in which matters of marriage and inheritance continued to be governed by Hindu law and Muhammadan law throughout the colonial period; the Asiatic Society; and the College of Fort William, begun in 1804, to school the arriving junior civil servants in the languages of India. It was this entrenched power of the Orientalist establishment in Calcutta that Thomas Babington Macaulay and Charles Trevelyan attacked with such success in the 1830s. Similar institutional triads were created at Bombay, where William Erskine was closely involved as founding secretary of the Literary Society of Bombay, and at Madras, where Ellis virtually single-handedly created the College of Fort St. George, and was one of the founders and a leading light of the Madras Literary Society. Working in this setting and deeply committed to the Orientalist way of knowing and ruling India, Ellis sought always to align the work of Government servants, including himself, with a deepening knowledge of India, and the key to this was language. Thus the utilitarian records of the colonial government tell us much about Ellis, and many of his most interesting works of scholarship lie unpublished in the colonial archive.

For another thing, during the first two decades of the nineteenth century, Ellis's era in Madras, the Government of Madras was actively interested in investigating the languages of South India and in promoting the publication of grammars and dictionaries. Having taken on vast responsibilities to extend the network of land revenue collection and the courts of law across the inland territories of South India newly acquired by the conquest of Tipu Sultan in 1799, the Government was much concerned with the problem of providing collectors and judges with adequate language training and with grammars and dictionaries. Ellis was thickly involved with this effort. He virtually created the College of Fort St. George for the instruction of arriving young civil servants, and he was the head of its Board of Superintendence. Moreover, the Government offered subsidies for the publication of bilingual grammars and dictionaries, and convened committees to review proposals submitted to it in search of such subsidies. The reports of these examinations, often very lengthy ones, are preserved in the colonial archive. Thus, quite without expecting it, I found a thick seam of linguistic scholarship in the improbable matrix of the Madras Public Consultations for those years. At the same time, Madras was the storm center of the new proposals to settle the land revenue with the peasantry (ryotwari) rather than with the lords of many villages (zamindari). Ellis's involvement with the Board of Revenue and his being collector of Madras gave him a direct interest in such matters, over which he marshaled his scholarly skills to make important interventions.

Thus, this lost Orientalist is not lost at all. His work is scattered through the pages of the colonial archive, like so many pressed flowers forgotten but preserved, and in the papers of his friends, Erskine and Leyden, as well as represented in the handful of works published during his brief life or after his death. The record from which we can know of the life and work of Ellis, and through it of his associates, Indian and British, is actually quite extensive.

THREE FRIENDS: ERSKINE, LEYDEN, ELLIS

Even if Ellis's papers had been wholly lost, the governmental record remains, and a good deal of Ellis's life and work can be recovered from that remarkable archive. But the private papers preserved by Erskine are especially valuable, as they speak directly to Ellis's scholarly interests outside the heavy obligations of his work life and the formality of official correspondence. As I have said, it is exceptional that private papers should end up in public archives, and in the case of Ellis we owe their survival to the admiration in which he was held by Walter Elliot and to his friendship with William Erskine. Indeed the archive that Erskine formed was built around the friendship of Ellis, John Leyden, and himself. Both Ellis and Leyden died before their time, Leyden of fever in Java in 1811. Leyden had accompanied the expeditionary force when the British took over the island from the Dutch during the Napoleonic Wars, going along as interpreter and taking all his papers with him. Erskine was Leyden's literary executor, and he went to great lengths to retrieve Leyden's papers from Thomas Raffles, who held on to them for a long time; in 1813, Ellis wrote to Erskine, wondering whether it was possible that Raffles had dared to appropriate them, which, if so, would be the "vilest felony," for he could not use them as they ought to be used, and would prevent their being used by others, a "grand larceny on the reputation of the dead" (Ellis to Erskine 25 Aug 1813, NLS, f. 84).[2] In the end Erskine did acquire the Leyden papers, and they form a very extensive collection in the British Library. Had Ellis had the prescience to name Erskine *his* literary executor, Erskine might have saved those papers that got burned up by Rous Petrie's cook. Even so, Erskine kept Ellis's letters and the papers

2. Raffles' history of Java was first published in 1817, four years after this letter (reprint, Raffles 1965). It contains two references to Leyden, in vol. 1, p. x, and vol. 2, p. clxi. Erskine's fear that Raffles was plagiarizing Ellis does not seem to be borne out, as far as I can tell.

he sent him, and these are extremely valuable. (Unfortunately, Erskine seems not to have preserved copies of his own letters to his friends, so that we have to make out the conversation from one side of it.) Erskine, unlike his two friends, lived to nearly eighty years of age, though his life was clouded by disgrace, as we shall see in a moment. Because he outlived his friends, because he preserved materials from them, because he became Leyden's literary executor, because his son Claude saw to it that his father's papers ended up in the India Office Library, British Library and the National Library of Scotland—these are among the reasons that, against the odds, this valuable archive of private papers was formed and is preserved to us.

William Erskine (1773–1852) was educated at Edinburgh University, where he met and became friends with Leyden. After several years of struggle to establish himself as a lawyer, he accepted an invitation from Sir James Mackintosh, who had been appointed Governor of Bombay, to accompany him to India as a private secretary, with the promise of the first appointment in his gift. Erskine accepted, departing at the end of 1803 for Bombay, arriving in May 1804. In this way, rather exceptionally, he became an Indian official without having been made a member of the civil service. He was appointed clerk to the Small Cause Court, later became a stipendiary magistrate and, in 1820, Master in Equity in the Recorder's Court.

Not long after arriving in Bombay, on 26 November 1804, Mackintosh and others formed the Literary Society of Bombay, with himself as president and Erskine as secretary. Orientalist scholarship and the life of the Literary Society became Erskine's great passions. One can follow the Society's progress from its slender beginnings through Erskine's minutes, still preserved in manuscript at the Society, which has now, after several transformations of name, become the Asiatic Society of Mumbai.

The minutes and the letters of Ellis to Erskine that survive allow us to make out the two men's interactions in some detail. Ellis, who visited Erskine in Bombay in 1808, was elected to membership of the Asiatic Society of Bombay the following year (Minute Book 29 May 1809) having been proposed by Erskine and seconded by Mackintosh—at a meeting attended by only five people. Erskine visited Ellis at Madras in September-October of 1809. The minute book of the Society and the letters of Ellis to Erskine show continuing scholarly exchanges. Ellis wrote a Tamil tract about the smallpox vaccination, and a plan for compiling and translating a body of Hindu law suited to the south of India with a preliminary overview of the *dharmaśāstra* authorities recognized in the

South, both of which were read by Erskine at a meeting on 13 January 1812. On 22 April 1817 Erskine read Ellis's paper on the forgery of the *Ezour Vedam,* a paper which was also read to the Asiatic Society in Calcutta and published in their journal, the *Asiatic researches,* after Ellis had died (Ellis 1822). Ellis was greatly interested in the Literary Society of Bombay, and doubtless his knowledge of it contributed to the formation at Madras of a literary society in 1812. In turn, once the College of Fort St. George had been created in Madras, also in 1812, Erskine was interested in the details of its structure as a possible model for a similar college at Bombay. In other letters, Erskine discusses the *Prabodhacandrodaya* of Kṛṣṇamiśra, an allegorical drama propounding the Advaita philosophy, as translated by John Taylor of the Society, a work which Ellis had already read in the original and in a Tamil translation as well, and Ellis helps get subscribers for the Society's plan to publish Taylor's translation of the *Līlāvatī.* In another letter, Ellis gives detailed comments on two inscriptions from Ceylon, which appear to be those which the Minute Book says were received from one Major Franklin (Ellis to Erskine 9 Sept 1810; Minute Book 26 Sept 1815).

In this connection I mention a most intriguing letter of recommendation for one Haji Mahammed, a Turk from Smyrna, which Ellis wrote to Erskine (3 April 1817), which shows that Ellis and Erskine shared the further bond of being Masons. Haji Mahammed, "found his way to Calcutta and, being one of the order, came recommended to us from the masons there." This is one of but a few tantalizing suggestions of a connection between Freemasonry and Orientalism in India.[3]

Erskine's expertise lay in Persian, and the great project that he carried through his life was to write a history of the great Mughals from Baber to Aurangzeb—"A History of the House of Timur" as his son Claude put it in a letter (BL Add. Mss. 39,945). The first volume to appear was a kind of preliminary to the history proper, namely, a translation of the memoirs of Baber, done jointly with Leyden. Erskine began it early in his Bombay years, and he published it on his return from India, in 1826. He had completed a translation of the Persian text of the

3. The connection between British Orientalists and Freemasonry is an intriguing question. As I have noted elsewhere (1997: 61), the first grand lodge was established in Calcutta as early as 1740. I do no know whether Sir William Jones was a mason, but I have discovered that H. T. Colebrooke was, as indeed was the Governor-General and most of the notables of Calcutta and the French leaders of Chandernagore, according to an article in the *Bombay Courier* (22 Jan 1814, "Calcutta intelligence"). Madras and Bombay also had active lodges. I understand from Vahid Fozdar that he is writing a book on Freemasonry in British India.

memoir some ten years previous, while Leyden was translating it from the original Turki. When Leyden died, his translation was less than half finished, and it came to Erskine in 1813. He compared and corrected the two translations, and when Elphinstone supplied him with a manuscript of the Turki text, he compared the whole to the original, and supplied it with notes. It was a most laborious and time-consuming project, complicated by Leyden's death and the fact that the latter's translation was incomplete and still rather rough. The first installment of the history proper was the *History of India under Baber and Humayun,* completed in 1845, according to the date of the preface, but not published till 1854, after Erskine's death. Erskine's life project, the "History of the House of Timur" up to the death of Aurangzeb, remained unfinished. He left many translations and summaries of Persian manuscripts bearing on this project, as well as 486 Persian manuscripts, 195 of which his son sold to the British Museum.

In addition to this great project, Erskine published five articles in the two volumes of *Transactions of the Literary Society of Bombay,* which, as secretary, he prepared for press. These were on a variety of topics: burial urns from the Persian Gulf; a landmark treatment of the Elephanta cave temple with beautiful illustrations and ground plan; the religion and texts of the Parsis, with discussion of the "Zend" language, or Avestan, a substantial early contribution to the study of this important subject; a disproof of the authenticity of two texts supposed to be of high antiquity, the *Desatir* and *Dabistan,* which the author shows to have been composed in Mughal times, though Sir William Jones had relied upon them as works of much greater age; and a paper on the relative antiquity of the Buddhist, Jain, and Vedic religions, contributing to the discussion of a question that remained unsettled till the work of Brian Hodgson and Eugène Burnouf put the history of Indian Buddhism on firm footing.

Although he did not suffer the early death to which so many British-India hands were vulnerable, and which deprived him of his two good friends, Erskine suffered a catastrophe of a different kind which darkened his life. Shortly after his arrival in Bombay, Sir Edward West, judge of the Recorder's Court, was proposed and elected to membership in the Literary Society of Bombay (Minute Book, 26 Feb and 26 March 1823). Shortly after that he removed Erskine from judicial offices on charges of defalcation. The deed sent shock waves throughout the British community in India. And it set off a storm of protest from Erskine's many friends and supporters, who included Monstuart Elphinstone, the Governor of Bombay. The Erskine affair became a *cause célèbre,* the reverberations of which lasted for decades. Warring texts were published in the newspapers of the day and continued to appear as late as 1900 (Douglas 1900, *Glimpses of old Bombay,* siding with Erskine) and 1907 (Drewitt's sympathetic memoir of West, Drewitt 1907:105). The case against Erskine alleged excessive and fraudulent charges extorted from Indian suitors at the Small Claims Court; Erskine blamed his Indian clerk, to whom the business of the office was entrusted because of his own poor health. One cannot at this great distance of time be sure of the rights and wrongs of the case. My sense of it is that, on the one hand, Erskine conceded that wrongs had been done by his office and, on the other, that his sudden and shocking removal was the result of a savage rectitude. In any case, the toll on both parties was terrible. West's biographer says that he endured a hostile press and a hostile governor, that "he was never forgiven by those whom he was obliged to expose" and was subjected to slights and insults. "Attempts were made . . . to drag him into duels, and after his death his memory, as was to be expected, has been severely handled by the admiring biographers of his opponents" (Drewitt 1907:54). For his part, Erskine recorded in his diary, *anno* 1827, that five years, "years of sadness & sorrow unmixed," had passed since he had last made an entry in his diary. It was, he said, a period of horror and suffering upon which he did not dare to turn his eye. What he had thought were impossibilities had occurred—the destruction of his peace of mind and his station in life gone forever. He desired death. "I may long for, but will not hasten, the end of my miseries. There is now but one port of rest for me" (BL Add. Mss. 39,945, f. 4). Erskine's departure from India was abrupt. Shortly after, at a meeting of the Literary Society, upon the motion of the Elphinstone, president of the Asiatic Society of Bombay and Governor of Bombay, and seconded by the archdeacon, it was unanimously resolved to send Erskine a letter expressing the high esteem in which the Society held his service to the Society and his scholarship, and the Society's hope that "the interest of Literature will be materially promoted by [his] now being relieved from the interruptions of official business" (Minute Book 30 July 1823). This was a highly visible show of support for Erskine and, although it said nothing of the affair, was by implication a rebuke to West by the Society of which both were members (West was not present at the meeting). It was further resolved that Erskine be requested to sit for his portrait at the expense of the Society, and that the painting would be placed in its rooms. The sitting seems never to have come about. After returning from India, Erskine resided on the Continent for many years at Pau and Bonn; later he traveled to

Edinburgh, where he became rector of St. Andrews University, a kind of public vindication. He wrote occasionally for the *Edinburgh review* and worked at his life project. In 1923 a marble bust of Erskine was presented to the Society by his descendants, and it may be seen in the vestibule leading to the library (Bombay Branch of the Royal Asiatic Society 1954: 3).[4]

Turning now to John Leyden (1775–1811), the third in this trio of Orientalists, we find him to be very different from Ellis and Erskine, indeed, in many ways one of a kind: a man with a brilliant gift for languages, eccentric in the extreme, a vivid character with a buccaneering impetuosity of manner and a high opinion of his own accomplishments, and a non-stop talker with a "screech voice" which did not endear him to everyone. Indeed these qualities divided people sharply, some finding him (taking him at his own always generous estimate) a genius and endlessly entertaining, others finding him hard to bear and difficult to escape. Erskine and Ellis were both friends of Leyden, but in different ways and degrees. Erskine was immensely fond of Leyden and deeply mourned his loss. With Ellis it was much more complicated; his relation to Leyden was marked by reserve and criticism of what he saw as the fault of coming too quickly to scholarly judgment. It could hardly have been otherwise. Leyden landed in Madras in 1803, took up Tamil quite soon, and began developing his great project of mapping the languages of South and Southeast Asia—of blanketing them, as it were, with grammars and dictionaries, which is to say, he was working in very much the same vein that Ellis was, so that an element of competition and rivalry was inevitable. He was a quick study, and impatient to rush into print. Ellis, as we have seen, was of the exact opposite temperament, perfecting his knowledge through long years of study and intending not to publish before age forty. The two marched at completely different tempi, and inevitably their relations, while friendly enough, were cool rather than warm, being based more on shared intellectual interests than on personal chemistry. Leyden soaked up information for his own use and put it out quickly as his own. And he was a one-man self-publicity machine. Ellis disapproved of the speed and the clatter, and was not as admiring of Leyden as Leyden was.

Nevertheless Ellis asked Leyden to consider him "one of the warmest of your friends" in the closing of a long letter (Ellis to Leyden 7 Aug–28

4. I am grateful to Virchand Dharamsey, historian of Orientalism and cinema, for pointing this out to me.

Sept 1808, OIOC Mss. Eur.D.30, p. 141), and calls Leyden "our friend" in a letter to Erskine after Leyden's death (Ellis to Erskine 25 April 1812, NLS Mss. 36.1.5, f. 72). His letters to Leyden were probably few, judging by the one which did survive (a very long, detailed letter, it must be said), in which he speaks of having chanced upon a letter from him, turning over old letters and papers, written four years previous, which he had not answered till that moment. Ellis was critical of Leyden's published work on "Indo-Chinese" (of which more later), and his general disapproval of Leyden's rushing to judgment colors his comment to Erskine: "I agree with you most sincerely in your regrets for Leyden; we regret in him, in part, the loss of a personal friend, but any friend of Literature has great cause for unmixed regret; had his life been extended I have no doubt that the latter part would have been much more valuable than the former, for age, which paralyzes less sanguine natures, would have moderated his ardour, without impairing his vigour." This evaluation comes from one who valued moderation, the steady, systematic accumulation of knowledge, and a well-matured scholarly judgment.

Born the son of a poor shepherd, John Leyden nevertheless got himself into Edinburgh University by dint of his evident talent and some helpful patronage from the local laird. Along the way he had acquired something of a reputation as a poet, an editor, and a collector of border ballads for Sir Walter Scott; in fact in Scottish letters he was a figure of some note whose reputation would only have grown had he remained in Scotland. At the conclusion of his studies in Edinburgh he was licensed to preach in the Church of Scotland and took up a post, but he was not suited for the life because of his various tics, including above all his piercing voice, which, by all accounts, was startling to hear. Learning of an opening for the position of surgeon in the East India Company, he quickly completed the remaining requirements for an M.D. degree at St. Andrews in only six months. He was chosen for the service and shipped out to Madras, arriving in 1803.

Upon reaching Madras, Leyden was put in charge of the general hospital for four months, during which time he studied the languages. It is probably Ellis of whom he speaks when he says in a letter to Erskine that he had been completely unable to find reliable information on the languages of South India before leaving Britain and found himself on arrival completely in *terra incognita,* but "I fortunately was introduced by accident to one of the few young men that in this Presidency have a literary turn, which circumstance was of great importance in directing my future exertions" (15 Sept 1804, BL Add. Mss. 26,651, f. 50). He became friends with Ellis and also Colin Mackenzie, and toured Mamallapuram with them and Sir Thomas Strange, judge of the Supreme Court, "gentlemen whose company and conversation I was sure would amply compensate for any disappointment which I might experience from the view of these ancient caves & ruins" ("Tour to the Seven Pagodas," BL Add. Mss. 26,568, f. 6). He made a favorable impression on the governor, Lord William Bentinck, and was appointed surgeon and naturalist to the commissioners who had been appointed, under Mackenzie, to survey the large territories of the South Indian interior that had fallen to the British by the defeat of Tipu Sultan. He was very ill much of the time, and although he drew up reports on the geology, diseases and medicines, and agriculture and languages of Mysore, the results of his labors were rather preliminary and limited. Because of ill health he proceeded to Kerala to recuperate, where he remained four months. He took ship for Penang in October, where he resided till the beginning of 1806, during which time his health improved and he also made friends with Raffles, the governor, and later Governor of Java.

Leyden returned to India in February, this time to Calcutta since his health did not permit a return to Madras. In October of 1807 Bentinck proposed to Calcutta that Madras be authorized to create a Civil Institution, matching the Military Institution at which cadets learned Persian and Hindustani, to teach younger civil servants the native languages, and that John Leyden be appointed its superintendent, but somehow this did not come to pass and Leyden remained at Calcutta. He was elected professor of Hindustani at the College of Fort William, a post which would have made use of his formidable skill and great interest in languages, and he became a member of the Asiatic Society. Soon after, however, the newly arrived governor-general, Lord Minto, appointed him judge of the Twenty-Four Parganas, where he spent his energies capturing, trying, and imprisoning bandits, at which he appears to have been very good. Ellis reports, "By his account of himself when last here, he appeared to have thrown away a good deal of his time entirely in hunting Decoyets, who might probably have been as officiously hunted by one less gifted than himself" (Ellis to Erskine 25 April 1812, NLS Mss. 36.1.5, f. 72). Two years later (January 1809) he became one of the commissioners of the Court of Requests at Calcutta, which made ample, if not good, use of his linguistic talents. In March of 1811 he sailed with Lord Minto as translator for the expedition to Java, but it took him to an early grave. Not long after arriving in Java, as it says in a memorable passage of the *Dictionary of national biography,* he entered "an unventilated native library" and, "fever supervening," he died. He became a martyr to Orientalism.

Because Leyden was such a colorful character I cannot forbear quoting some of the better remembrances of him. One of these is by Henry Cockburn, who captures Leyden well in his admirable sketches of Edinburgh worthies, *Memorials of his time:*

> John Leyden has said of himself, "I often verge so nearly on absurdity, that I know it is perfectly easy to misconceive me, as well as misrepresent me." This was quite true; especially the vergency on absurdity. He cannot be understood till the peculiarities to which he alludes are cleared away, and the better man is made to appear. His conspicuous defect used to be called affectation, but in reality it was pretension. A pretension, however, of a very innocent kind, which, without derogating in the least from the claim of any other, merely exaggerated not his own merits, nor what he had done, but his capacity and ambition to do more. Ever in a state of excitement, ever ardent, ever panting for things unattainable by ordinary mortals, and successful to an extent sufficient to rouse the hopes of a young man ignorant of life, there was nothing that he thought beyond his reach; and not knowing what insincerity was, he spoke of his powers and his visions as openly as if he had been expounding what might be expected of another person. According to himself, John Leyden could easily in a few months have been a great physician, or surpassed Sir William Jones in Oriental literature, or Milton in poetry. Yet at the very time he was thus exposing himself, he was not only simple, but generous and humble. He was a wild-looking, thin, Roxburghshire man, with sandy hair, a screech voice, and staring eyes—exactly as he came from his native village of Delholm; and not one of these not very attractive personal qualities would he have exchanged for all the graces of Apollo. By the time I knew him he had made himself one of our social shows, and could and did say whatever he chose. His delight lay in an argument about the Scotch Church, or Oriental literature, or Scotch poetry, or odd customs, or scenery, always conducted on his part in a high shrill voice, with great intensity, and an utter unconsciousness of the amazement, or even the aversion, of strangers. His daily extravagances, especially mixed up, as they always were, with exhibitions of his own ambition and confidence, made him be much laughed at even by his friends. (Cockburn 1974:172–73)

"Whatever he did, his whole soul was in it," Cockburn goes on to say. "His heart was warm and true." Many responded to that ardor, and evidently Cockburn was one of them, Erskine, another.

Lord Minto, Governor-General of India at the time of the takeover of Indonesia from the Dutch during the Napoleonic Wars, has left us another sketch of Leyden, every bit as lively as Cockburn's and worth quoting at length. It comes in a letter to his wife and daughters at Calcutta while on shipboard with Leyden, bound for Java:

> Dr. Leyden's learning is stupendous, and he is also a very universal scholar. His knowledge, extensive and minute as it is, is always in his pocket, at his fingers' ends, and on the tip of his tongue. He has made it completely his own, and it is all ready money. All his talent and labour indeed, which are both excessive, could not, however, have accumulated such stores without his extraordinary memory. . . . It must be confessed that Leyden has occasion for all the stores which application and memory can furnish. I do not believe that so great a reader was ever so great a talker before. You may be conceited about yourselves, my beautiful wife and daughters, but with all my partiality I must give it against you. You would appear absolutely silent in his company, as a ship under weigh seems at anchor when it is passed by a swifter sailer. Another feature of his conversation is a shrill, piercing, and at the same time grating voice. A frigate is not near large enough to place the ear at the proper point of hearing. If he had been at Babel he would infallibly have learned all the languages there, but in the end they must all have merged in the Tividale How [Tiviotdale twang], for not a creature would have got spoken but himself.

He adds: "The only little blemish I have sometimes regretted to see in him is a disposition to egotism; not selfishness—but a propensity to bring the conversation from whatever quarter it starts round to himself, and to exalt his own actions, sufferings, or adventures in a manner a little approaching the marvelous" (Kynynmound 1880:253–55). Clearly, Leyden was a strong dose, and some were powerfully attracted while others wished only to get safely out of earshot.[5]

Leyden's life, though it was cut short even before Ellis's, is the better known of the two. In addition to the memorials just mentioned by contemporaries who knew him personally, we have a memorial by Sir Walter Scott (Leyden 1858), an article by G. Smith (1848), and substantial biographies by James Morton (Leyden 1819) and P. Seshadri (1912), as well as a doctoral thesis from Edinburgh University of over five hundred closely typed pages by I. Brown (c. 1967) that is very useful. Leyden left a few published works and a great many manuscripts, scholarly papers, and letters, most of them now in the British Library and the National Library of Scotland. The difficulty in interpreting his life is that it went

5. Regarding Leyden's famous voice, John Malcolm, a fond friend, put it as gently as he could: "He was fond of talking, his voice was loud and had little or no modulation, and he spoke in that provincial dialect of his native country; it cannot be surprising therefore that even his information and knowledge, when so conveyed, should be felt by a number of his hearers as unpleasant if not oppressive" *(Bombay courier* 2 Nov 1811).

in so many directions and so requires an array of special skills on the part of the biographer which perhaps only he united in one person. In the absence of expertise in some aspects of his work, one inevitably tends to take his own interpretations at face value. Yet as we have seen, Leyden was continually overestimating what he had done and would do in the future, and on many points we have only his testimony. It is on the Oriental side of his work that the difficulties are greatest because his work was spread over so large a surface and over so many languages and scripts.

Leyden had dozens of projects underway at any given time, and some of them reached print, notably, his translation of the *Shajrat Malayu*, edited by Raffles and published posthumously under the title of *Malay annals* (Leyden 1821), also his unfinished translation of Baber's memoir, which was completed, revised, and annotated by Erskine (Erskine and Leyden 1826). But amid the dozens of smaller projects there was one big project that was the centerpiece of Leyden's work in India and Southeast Asia. Even though little of it reached print, manuscripts of the project allow us to discern the overall direction of Leyden's life work, or at any rate the Orientalist part of it, and it is valuable for our purposes as a clear expression of the languages-and-nations project described in chapter 1. Leyden's big project was an ambitious comparative study of the structure and genealogy of languages in India and Southeast Asia, described in great detail in several manuscript versions that are currently in the British Library (BL Add. Mss. 26,564–67, 26,600). I will call it, simply, the Plan. The Plan had the following four parts:

1. Plan for investigating the languages, literature, antiquities, and history of the Deccan
2. Plan for investigating the languages, literature, antiquities, and history of the Indo-Persic nations
3. Plan for investigating the languages, literature, antiquities, and history of the Indo-Chinese nations
4. On the comparative utility of the Dekkani, Indo-Persic, and Indo-Chinese languages, and the works most necessary for facilitating their acquisition

The three regions over which this inquiry is spread are, essentially, South India and the Deccan, North India, and Southeast Asia (which he calls Indo-China, but which includes Indonesia).

It is in the fourth part that Leyden sets forth the rationale of the Plan, showing full awareness that he is participating in a worldwide project. He stresses the value of the cultivation of Indian languages from the commercial, political, economic, and literary points of view but identifies himself especially with the literary, which is to say the scientific, objective. It is important "in the literary point of view," he says, to study *all* languages, even the obscure ones that have no written literature, because of their importance in mending the imperfections in the historical record contained in written texts. And he quotes Samuel Johnson's dictum: "The similitude and derivation of languages afford the most indubitable proof of the traduction of nations, and the genealogy of mankind. They add often physical certainty to historical evidence; and often supply the only evidence of ancient migrations, and the revolutions of ages which have left no written monuments behind them" (13 Aug 1766 in Boswell 1791:374).[6] Johnson's observation is highly pertinent to the present state of Indian records, Leyden comments, as "even the unwritten languages and dialects of the rudest tribes of India acquire an adventitious importance from the light they are likely to throw on ancient migrations and conquests and the authenticity they are likely to confer on historical investigation (BL Add. Mss. 26,600, f. 114v). He refers to the parallel project of Catherine of Russia, published by Pallas (1786–89, discussed

6. The passage by Samuel Johnson begins, "I am not very willing that any language should be totally extinguished," and continues, "My zeal for languages may seem, perhaps, rather over-heated, even to those by whom I desire to be well-esteemed. To those who have nothing in their thoughts but trade or policy, present power, or present money, I should not think it necessary to defend my opinions; but with men of letters I would not unwillingly compound, by wishing the continuence of every language, however narrow in its extent, or however incommodious for common purposes, till it is deposited in some version of a known book, that it may be always hereafter examined and compared with other languages, and then permitting its disuse" (13 Aug 1766 in Boswell 1791:374). It reminds us that the "explosion in the grammar factory" expands as the number of spoken languages shrinks, and that there is an aspect of salvage scholarship to the project. There is a strikingly similar passage in Jefferson: "A knowledge of the several languages [of the American Indians] would be the most certain evidence of their derivation which could be produced. . . . It is to be lamented, then, very much to be lamented, that we have suffered so many of the Indian tribes already to extinguish, without our having previously collected and deposited in the records of literature, the general rudiments at least of the languages they spoke. Were vocabularies formed of all the languages spoken in North and South America, preserving their appellations of the most common objects in nature, of those which must be present in every nation barbarous or civilized, with the inflections of their nouns and verbs, their principles of regimen and concord, and these deposited in all the public libraries, it would furnish opportunities to those skilled in the languages of the old world to compare them with these, now, or at any future time, and hence to construct the best evidence of the derivation of this part of the human race" (c. 1782:510–11).

in chapter 1), and, in the vein of the work of Jefferson and Du Ponceau on the comparison of American Indian languages, he mentions Barton's *New views on the origin of the tribes and nations of America* (1797) and Volney's *View of the climate and soil of the United States of America* (1804). The argument of the piece is that since the British are, for the moment, in charge of the government of India, it is incumbent upon them to promote the scientific investigation of India's past.

Coming to specifics, Leyden states that the first and most necessary work is the making of a grammar and "radical vocabulary," and that where languages are obviously related to one another there is much advantage in treating them comparatively. An elementary work of this kind would include (1) a series of alphabets, from the most ancient to the present, "confirmed and illustrated by inscriptions"; (2) comparative tables of the inflections of nouns, pronouns, verbs, and verbals of ancient and modern dialects; (3) exposition of syntax with specimens of varieties of style; and (4) a radical comparative vocabulary of nouns, pronouns, verbs, and particles, to which could be added "an historical account of the rise and progress of the language and notices of its present extent" (BL Add. Mss. 26,600, f. 115).

Second in sequence and importance would be dictionaries of the languages. I give here the huge list of works that Leyden, with full confidence in his superhuman powers, proposed to write and asked the Government to fund, grouped into the three categories of Dekkani, Indo-Persic, and Indo-Chinese or, as we would say, South Indian, North Indian, and Southeast Asian.

IN THE DEKKANI LANGUAGES

1. Comparative grammar and radical vocabulary of Tamil, Telugu, Kannada, Malayalam, Sinhalese, and Tuluva languages, "all of which are intimately connected"; 800 pages quarto
2. Comparative grammar of Marathi, Konkani, Oriya, and Gujarati, "which, though not so intimately connected, have yet considerable resemblance in their structure"; 400 pages quarto
3. A polyglot dictionary of Tamil, Telugu, Kannada, Malayalam, Sinhala, and Tuluva languages, "in which I conceive two thirds of the whole of vocables would be found to be the same in all, which would greatly diminish the extent of the work"; about 2000 pages

4. A polyglot lexicon of Marathi, Konkani, Oriya, and Gujarati; about 1200 pages
5. History of the languages and literature of the Deccan; about 500 pages
6. A supplement on the languages of secondary importance or materials that are more difficult to procure; about 400 pages

IN THE INDO-PERSIC LANGUAGES

1. Comparative grammar and radical vocabulary of Pahlavi, Pashtu, and Baloch; 500 pages
2. Comparative grammar and radical vocabulary of Kashmiri and Panjabi, and perhaps also Braj Bhasha and Marwari; 600 pages

IN THE INDO-CHINESE LANGUAGES

1. Comparative grammar and radical vocabulary of the Pali, Prakrit, and Zend languages; about 1000 pages
2. Grammar and glossary of Malay, Burmese, Thai, and Vietnamese (the "Anam language"); 400 or 500 pages quarto
3. Grammar and glossary of the Mon Khmer and Lao languages; 400 pages
4. Grammar and glossary of the Javanese, Buggis, Bima, Balla, and Tagalog languages; 500 pages
5. Dictionary of Malay distinguishing words of Sanskrit and Arabic origin from the native terms of the language; 600 pages quarto (ibid., ff. 116v–117r)

To this a supplementary volume might be added on other languages of the eastern islands. Leyden has "no hesitation in stating that I could undertake to complete the whole of them in five years and any part of them in a proportional length of time" if health permitted and adds that "from him who professedly aims at little, much can never be expected" (ibid., f. 117v).

Leyden submitted the Plan to the Government at Calcutta, but he took it back a few days after submitting it for reasons we do not know; perhaps someone intimated that it would not be well received. In any case, his grand project was not funded. Nevertheless, it is clear that two of the few works he did complete were derived from part 3 of the Plan: a small book called *A comparative vocabulary of the Barma, Maláyu and T'hái languages* (1810) printed at the Mission Press of Serampore, and a very long article that appeared in *Asiatic researches* after his death, "On the languages and literature of the Indo-Chinese nations" (1812). It is to the latter (in an earlier, manuscript version presumably) that Ellis directed his criticisms, to which I will return later.

The superhuman rate of production which Leyden proposed to impose upon himself would have relied both on his quickness in acquiring languages and on peculiar methods of study described by his friend John Malcolm, who published a memorial tribute in the *Bombay courier* (2 November 1811). They are of interest both in explaining Leyden's style of his scholarship and, more importantly, showing something of his relation with Indians. We might call these methods extractive. Malcolm says of Leyden:

> When he read a lesson in Persian, a person near him whom he had taught, wrote down each word on a long slip of paper, which was afterwards divided into as many pieces as there were words, and pasted in alphabetical order, under different heads of verbs, nouns, &c. into a blank book that formed a Vocabulary of each day's lesson. All this he had in a few hours instructed a very ignorant native to do, and this man he used in his broad accent to call "one of his Mechanical aids."

Besides the difference of temperament, perhaps the greatest difference between Ellis and Leyden was in their attitude toward Indians and India. We shall shortly examine Ellis's working relations with Indians such as Sankaraiah and Pattabhirama Shastri; here I need only say that there was nothing of the "mechanical aid" in his conception of them. Moreover, Ellis greatly admired Indian literature—excessively, Erskine thought—and one of his major purposes was to assist in its revival. As to religion, the Rev. Dr. Taylor thought Ellis an atheist. Leyden, on the other hand, had been a minister of the Scottish church, advanced the cause of the Serampore missionaries with his friend Lord Minto, the governor-general, detested Hinduism, and considered its effects on the Indian people pernicious: "Indeed the moral character of the Hindus—'the blameless, mild, patient, innocent children of nature,' as they are ridiculously termed by gossiping ignoramuses, who never set eyes on them—is as utterly worthless and devoid of probity, as their religion is wicked, shameless, impudent, and obscene" (quoted by Morton in Leyden 1819:lxv).

Quite different was the attitude of Ellis, of whom Erskine said:

> He was remarkable for the proficiency he had made in the various languages of Southern India, and for his thorough acquaintance with the

> manners, customs and literatures of the Hindus. He is said to have written the Tamil with great elegance, and was a poet in that tongue. . . . He was eager to improve the condition of the natives, but had perhaps too high an opinion of their literature and acquirements. . . . He lived much among the natives & had a perfect knowledge of their habits of thinking.

Thus while Orientalist scholarship rested on knowledge of Indian languages and the authority of Indians and their texts, the relations of British Orientalists with Indian scholars were subject to varying degrees of cultural inhibition and degrees of respect.

THE MADRAS CIRCLE: ELLIS, CAMPBELL, PATTABHIRAMA SHASTRI, SANKARAIAH

On 11 May 1797, the Court of Directors of the United East India Company received a petition from Francis Whyte Ellis to be admitted to the service in the manner required of aspiring writers (there are dozens, perhaps hundreds, of such petitions in the Oriental and India Office Collections of the British Library), both as an example of his penmanship and as a formal request for appointment:

> To the Honourable the Court of Directors of the United East India Company.
>
> The humble petition of Francis Ellis
>
> Sheweth
> That your petitioner has been educated in Writing and Accounts and humbly hopes he is qualified to serve your Honours.
> He humbly therefore prays your Honours will appoint him a writer in the ______ Establishment, and should he be so fortunate as to succeed he promises to behave himself with the greatest diligence and fidelity, and is ready to give such Security as your Honours may require.
>
> And your Petitioner will ever pray.

The blank in the petition was filled by another hand with the name of the post to which he was to be sent: "Madrass."

A few days earlier (9 May), Ellis, "late of Compton in Bedfordshire, but now of London" had signed a sworn statement attesting the year of his birth to be 1777, according to his parents, no certificate of birth having been found. A few days later (17 May) a bond of £500 was made by Sir James Wright of Bedford Street, Covent Garden, Baronet, and Roger Palmer of Oxford Street, with the Company on behalf of Francis Ellis of London, Gentleman, "Appointed a writer and Covenant Servant at Fort

St. George in the East Indies" (OIOC O/1/4, ff. 55–57). The terms of his indenture were standard: he was to serve for five years at a mere five pounds sterling a year. Ellis entered the service at the tail end of an era in which Company servants were paid poorly but given rights of private trade by which they could make fortunes on the side in India while working for the Company. The structural corruption of the system became notorious and gave way to a more orderly and bureaucratic form of government with high salaries and the abolition of private trade.

The final item in the collection of papers about Ellis's appointment is a certificate from one Robert Roy of the Academy, Burlington Street, attesting that Ellis "has acquired an extensive knowledge in classical Learning—He has studied with much success the French Language, Mathematics and particularly Arithmetic Writing &c. and his Manners are polite manly and regular." This completes what we know about Ellis's birth and education before his arrival in India, nearly a year later, on 7 April 1798 (OIOC J/1/16, ff. 514–17).

There is no book-length biography of Ellis; we have only brief summaries of his official career (e.g., Dodwell and Miles 1839) and scholarship (Wilson n.d.), and the short pieces by Elliot (1875, 1878). The following is a summary of the civil service career of Ellis, as it appears in official lists:

1798	Assistant under the Secretary to the Board of Revenue
1801	Deputy Secretary to the Board of Revenue
1802	Secretary to the Board of Revenue
1806	Judge and Magistrate of the Zillah of Masulipatam, in the Telugu country
1809	Collector of Land Customs
1810	Collector of Madras
1819	Died, 9 March, while on leave at Ramnad, in the southernmost part of the Tamil country

Ellis's career was somewhat exceptional in that he mostly resided in Madras city, the seat of government, except for three years at Masulipatam. When he arrived, Lionel Place was Collector of the Jagir, the large tract of territory surrounding Madras that had been granted to the Company by the Nawab of the Carnatik in 1760 but had come under the Company's direct administration only in 1786. The Company had hitherto had only an imperfect report on the land tenures of the jagir, made by Colonel

Thomas Barnard in the 1770s. During Place's short, vigorous, and contentious period as collector, he assembled a massive report, with detailed information on jagir land tenures. Place's report was an important prior text to Ellis's *Treatise of mirasi right,* which Ellis submitted to the Board many years later as Collector of Madras. About the same time, the Company, in the course of its war with Tipu Sultan, acquired new inland territories to which the revenue machinery was extended through the settlements imposed by Captain Alexander Read and his associates, including Thomas Munro. Thus Ellis got an education in the intricacies of land revenue at the very beginning of his career, a time when knowledge of South Indian land tenures was rapidly increasing and colonial policy was rapidly changing, especially around the introduction of a ryotwari settlement. His close involvement with revenue would continue when he later became Collector of Land Customs and then Collector of Madras, that is, the enlarged, twenty-six-square-mile territory including the Fort and the city, garden suburbs, and farming villages, which had been under British control for a long time and through which colonial knowledge of Indian land-revenue practices had been developed prior to the conquest. Ellis's knowledge of and involvement with land tenure was to put him and the Board of Revenue on a collision course with Thomas Munro, chief architect of the ryotwari system and, at the time of Ellis's death, Governor of Madras.

Following his apprenticeship with the Board of Revenue, Ellis, in his very first judicial appointment, was sent to open up a new court in territories recently come under British administration, under the treaty with the Raja of Tanjore. He was posted to Tanjore in 1806, to be judge and magistrate at the zillah court of Kumbakonam (Judicial Department, 13 May 1806), a posting so brief and so disastrous that it was omitted from the lists of his postings in the *Madras almanac* and other civil service handbooks. In a letter to Leyden he says that his "removal from Tanjore and consequent banishment from the southern provinces" was a violent shock (BL OIOC Mss. Eur.D.30, p. 127).

The affair involved two incidents, of which the first was his arrest of a servant of the Raja of Tanjore. According to a petition submitted to the court by one Ayam Perumal Padaiyachi dated 1 November, a certain Savandaiyan Pillai, who superintended the garden lands of the Raja of Tanjore in Kumbakonam, had sought to collect from the petitioner taxes due the raja by some other party for whom he was mistaken, and Savandaiyan's peon had "put bruised chillies on my eyes, sprinkled water on them, & placed Ketticals on my hands & ordered a man to press them down by trampling on them with his feet" (OIOC BC F/4/268 no. 5895, p. 7).

Hearing that a complaint of torture had been made against him, Savandaiyan Pillai took refuge in one of the raja's palaces, which was used as a prison and so had a guard of sepoys. When Ellis, in his role as magistrate, sent an officer to serve a summons, Savandaiyan Pillai used the raja's guard against Ellis's authority. The peon who did the torture on Pillai's orders was later seized under a warrant from Ellis, but he had to be taken by force from sepoys of the raja, under whose protection he had placed himself.

Ellis wrote to Captain William Blackburne, the Resident at Tanjore, about the matter, who wrote back requesting him very earnestly to suspend further proceedings against the king's two servants, as "His Excellency's mind is disturbed in a very extraordinary degree." The Raja was, indeed, so disturbed that he wrote Governor Bentinck he "never would have signed any Treaty however advantageous to me in other respects if it had contained any clause by which I might be considered to be personally amenable to the Jurisdiction of this Honorable Company's Courts" (ibid., p. 334). The Government of Madras tabled Ellis's report on the subject, but the matter reached the Court of Directors in London, who reacted strongly, recognizing the "youthful inexperience" of Ellis but nevertheless censuring him for lack of discretion, and the Government of Madras for tabling the matter.

The Government of Madras had tabled the matter because by the time it came before them, Ellis and another youthful judge thrown into the maelstrom of introducing Company justice into Tanjore, Daniel Crauford, had already been whisked away and reassigned to distant Masulipatam and Rajahmundry, respectively, the Government censuring their conduct "for impeding the collection of the public revenue in Tanjore" (MJC 8 Nov 1806 IOL). This second affair involved the monopoly the British government at Madras asserted over the sale of betel leaf, for which it issued a cowle, or contract, to the renter or revenue farmer who purchased the right. This renter was given powers to enforce sales by betel growers at a fixed price, including powers to issue fines and to enter and search private dwellings to find sequestered stocks of betel from growers who were holding out for a higher price. The protests of local growers of betel against the novel monopoly and the oppressive actions of the renters led Crauford and, apparently, Ellis to halt the actions of the renters, finding as they did that the issuance of cowles for this monopoly was not authorized by a published Regulation from the Board of Revenue. A higher court, the Court of Sadr and Faujdari Adawlet, ruled against Crauford, who seems to have been the principal in the matter, though both he and Ellis are named in a minute of the governor following the court's decision. In that minute Bentinck said,

> I cannot persuade myself that either Mr. Crauford or Mr. Ellis could have had the intention of throwing any unnecessary impediment in the way of the public service or of acting from the wish to make a vain display of superior authority. I have too good an opinion of these Gentlemen, to attribute to them any such motives. But it is impossible for me to acquit them of an extraordinary degree of indiscretion and I cannot be insensible to the ill effects that their conduct must have upon the authority of the Collector of the Revenues. (MJC 7 Nov 1806)

Ellis and Crauford were accordingly transferred.

Ellis felt this "banishment from the southern provinces," that is, from the Tamil country to the Telugu-speaking region, was a disgrace and an exile. But it must have had the unintended benefit of forcing him to master Telugu, which certainly contributed to the formulation of the Dravidian proof. It also put him in connection with an important Telugu scholar there, Mamadi Venkayya, a remarkable Komati trader who had retired to a life of scholarship. Venkayya was writing dictionaries of Telugu and Sanskrit in which Ellis had a great interest and which, under his urging, the College of Fort St. George later sought to purchase and publish. Ellis had already spent a few months, in the winter of 1804–5, in the Northern Circars of Andhra, "with a view to qualifying himself for a judicial station to which Lord William Bentinck had it in contemplation to promote him"; now he spent three years in Andhra, at Masulipatam. He speaks of this period, in the above-mentioned letter to Leyden, as one in which he was "continually in motion," as having "scarcely been out of tents for three months together," as he rolled through the Company's territories from Jagannath to Kanya Kumari, holding court and dispensing justice (Ellis to Leyden 7 Aug 1808, OIOC Mss. Eur.D.30, p. 127).

Another benefit of the otherwise painful Tanjore interlude was that he came to know Sankaraiah, with whom he was to have a long connection, and who would play an important role in the Madras School of Orientalism. Sankaraiah was sheristadar, or chief of staff, to Ellis and his successors at Kumbakonam, and later joined the Collectorate of Madras, shortly before Ellis took charge in 1809, and they worked closely together.

Ellis was appointed Collector of Land Customs, or Land Customer, toward the end of 1809, and the office was soon combined with that of Collector of Madras, in charge of the land revenue and other matters. It was a large, complex job, two jobs indeed. On the one hand, like that of other district collectors, his jurisdiction was divided into several taluks (Mylapore, Egmore, Pudupaukam, Tandiarpalla) under amildars, for the collection of the revenue upon agriculture; on the other hand, the job entailed overseeing the departments of Arrack and Toddy, Company's Land, Quit Rent, Home Farm, Salt Revenue, and Fencible Corps (list of establishment of servants, Madras District Records 4 June 1810). Much the greater part of the work, and the receipts of revenue, lay in the control and taxation of commodities, including the harsh business of enforcing the Company's monopoly rights over salt, liquor, and tobacco, which involved advertising and issuing licenses to renters, dealing with smuggling, and preventing and punishing corruption among Government servants in his charge. When Ellis took on this position, Sankaraiah was a writer in the Arrack and Toddy Department at the miserable pay of 23 pagodas monthly (ibid.), which was nevertheless the second highest salary in the establishment; Ellis soon made him sheristadar, increasing his monthly pay to 40, then to 60 pagodas, the highest the Board of Revenue would permit. As sheristadar, Sankaraiah was in overall charge of the native Government servants of the Madras District cutchery.

Ellis seems to have been a very good at his work, and to have been held in the highest esteem by the Board of Revenue, to whom he reported. The Board noted with satisfaction that his amalgamation of the two positions into one had resulted in a decided savings in costs, and that in his first year the receipts of revenue exceeded those of every previous year but one. This good report reached the Governor in Council, who forwarded it to London. The Court of Directors, in their dispatch to Madras, noted that the overall savings through reduction of staff and salary, amounting to 7,707 pagodas annually, but went on to complain that the pay of the collector, which was a percentage of the revenue receipts, at 9,228 pagodas, was too high, and should have the same limit of a collector of an unsettled district, namely 7,500 pagodas; but they "abstained from giving the orders above recorded a retrospective operation in consideration of the increase which has been already affected in the Revenues of the Presidency under the judicious management of Mr. Ellis" (general letter 6 Jan 1814 in MDR Aug 1815). The combination of praise for raising the revenue and cutting his salary to increase the profits of the Company did not sit well with Ellis, and he contested the matter before the Board, arguing that the passage in the general letter applied only to the emoluments of the Collector of Madras, not to the (larger) emoluments of the Collector of Land Customs, which were "confirmed to him by the regulation by which the duties themselves are imposed and can only be abolished by the revision of such part of the regulation as relates to them" (MDR 27 April 1816). The Board was sympathetic, and the existing rate continued for a time while the matter was referred to higher authority. My overall impression is that Ellis was highly efficient and effective in his work as Collector and Land Customer, doing what amounted to two jobs and getting an unusually large salary, commensurate, he seems to have felt, with the work he did.

It is worth remarking that the very large difference between Ellis's large compensation and the small compensation received by his chief of staff, Sankaraiah, was the pattern in British Indian government since the ending of private trade: a small body of civil servants, paid well to put them beyond the temptations of corruption, supervising a vast army of low-paid Indian government servants. This kind of asymmetry was a structural feature of Orientalist scholarship in British India as well, shaping the relations between British and Indian scholars.

It was during this very busy period of his life, from late in 1809 until his death in early 1819—less than a decade—that Ellis came into his own as a scholar through the founding of the College of Fort St. George in 1812 (which we will examine in the next chapter) and the creation of the Literary Society of Madras, in which he was highly active, the same year. And in the group of scholars who came together around Ellis, none are more important than A. D. Campbell, Sankaraiah, and Pattabhirama Shastri, whom I must now introduce.

Alexander Duncan Campbell (1789–1857), was something of a protégé of Ellis. Born at St. Andrews, a son of the second laird of Fairfield and educated at the High School of Edinburgh, Campbell acquired an appointment in India and arrived in 1808. During his early career he served at the Board of Revenue in Madras, and was made secretary to the College at its founding, so that all of the College's official correspondence with the Government of Madras at that time is signed by him. In the course of a long career in the service, till his retirement in 1842, he served variously as secretary to and later member of the Board of Revenue, Collector and Magistrate of Bellary District, judge of the Sadr and Faujdari Adawlet courts, and member of the Board of Superintendence at the College. He wrote an important survey of native schools in South India, gave testimony on the land systems of the South to a Parliamentary committee at the renewal of the East India Company's charter in 1832, and composed a three-volume *Code of regulations for internal govern-*

ment of Madras, published in 1843, among other things. After resigning from the service he lived with his wife in London till his death.

Upon his arrival in India, Campbell lived frugally on his 60 pagodas per month and worked hard at languages. From 8:00 in the morning to 10:00 in the evening he "fagged at business and study," winning the prize of 1,000 pagodas for proficiency in Hindustani (which he had begun in Scotland, under Gilchrist, before embarking for India) in May of 1810, and for proficiency in Telugu in September, 1813.[7] Immediately after winning the prize, he commenced writing his grammar of Telugu with the help of Udayagiri Venkatanarayana, from whom he had learned the language, and he presented the text to the Government of Madras in May of 1814. Printed by the College Press two years later, toward the end of 1816, the work went into second and third editions before it was overtaken by the Telugu grammar of C. P. Brown—who had first learned Telugu from Campbell's grammar. In his grammar Campbell argues for the non-Sanskrit origin of Telugu, and he uses the method of the word list in making his case. His views are very much in tune with Ellis's interpretation of the Indian grammarians and the concept of Telugu as an original language, and it is in Campbell's grammar that Ellis's introductory note is found that contains the Dravidian proof. Campbell also composed a Telugu dictionary, drawing upon the manuscript dictionaries of Mamadi Venkayya and one drawn up in French by the Jesuits. It was published in 1821, on the draft of which Ellis, in the last days of his life, composed a critique on behalf of the College Board. Both works claim to render into English the work of the recognized Telugu grammars of the past, and they cite them by name. Underlying the dictionary entries is the categorization of nouns according to the etymological categories of the Indian grammarians: *tatsama, tadbhava, deśya,* and *grāmya.*

Indians do not appear so frequently, and their lives are not so sharply etched, in the colonial record as the British civil servants. In the case of Sankaraiah (1771–1817), however, we have a pretty full outline of his lifetime of service to the Company because in 1816 the Board of Revenue asked Ellis to submit a detailed list of native servants of the Madras

7. I am grateful to Angus Campbell of Manila, the Philippines, for giving me a copy of the diary of his great-grandfather Alexander Duncan Campbell, from which this passage comes. The diary makes repeated reference to an album of letters that included some from Ellis and from Udayagiri Venkatanarayana, but this album, unfortunately, no longer exists. The official career of this interesting and admirable figure is summarized in Prinsep 1885:22.

District cutchery (MBR 3 Dec 1816). Sankaraiah, whose proper name was Bomakonti Shankara Shastri, was "a Bráhman of the Telugu nation" of the Ātreya *gotra* and Smarta sect. His family had moved to the South, that is, the Tamil country, first to Cuddalore, but for three generations had been settled at Madras. At the writing of the list, Sankaraiah had been in the Company revenue service for twenty-three years, beginning in 1788 or 1789 as a writer to the Resident of Tanjore, and serving successively as accountant and interpreter to the Collector of Tanjore; then in the Guntur collectorate; then superintending accounts at Masulipatam under the deputy paymaster; from 1806 serving as sheristadar to the successive judges at Kumbakonam, beginning with Ellis's brief and troubled stay there; and finally with Ellis in the Madras District cutchery, rising quickly to the position of sheristadar. For a brief time he served as Head English Master in the College of Fort St. George, where the pay was better, but then was reappointed to his previous position.

Ellis says of Sankaraiah, "He understands well the Telugu, Tamil, and English, which he writes and speaks with much correctness, and has a considerable knowledge of the Sanscrit, with the literature of which, the legal writings especially, he is well acquainted" (ibid.). Ellis commented further that Sankaraiah was conversant in accounts, in judicial and revenue affairs, the Regulations of Government in both branches, that his information was extensive and his industry and diligence afforded satisfaction to his superiors. "Of the perfect integrity and the correctness of the sentiments and conduct of this very respectable man, on all occasions, during the period I have known him, I can speak with the confidence of entire conviction" (ibid.). Writing within the constraints of the high formality of official correspondence, Ellis is here expressing, one feels, a considerable warmth of feeling toward his long-time associate. Sankaraiah died before Ellis, not long after this was written. Sankaraiah played an important role in the Dravidian proof, as we shall see, and was discussing these matters with Ellis over a considerable period of time. Sankaraiah's writings on mirasi land tenure in the Madras area are published in the *Treatise of mirasi right* (1818), which appeared after his decease.

Of Vedam Pattabhirama Shastri (1760–1820), whose role in the Dravidian proof was crucial, as we shall see in chapter 5, we find less in the colonial record, but that little is telling. He was a brahmin of the Puduri *śākha*, coming from Viruru village, Atmakur taluk, Nellore district (Venkata Rao 1957:22). He was appointed head master for Sanskrit and Telugu at the inception of the College of Fort St. George. His teaching duties were extensive: he taught *tarka* (logic), *vyākaraṇa* (Sanskrit grammar), and *dharmaśāstra* (law) to the Indian students, as well as Telugu grammar to the Telugu students studying to become teachers of Telugu. He served the College in that capacity from 1812 till his death in 1820. Significantly for our purposes, he wrote a most valuable *dhātumāla,* or dictionary of roots, for Telugu, which was an essential ingredient in the Dravidian proof. A copy of the manuscript exists in the Government Oriental Manuscript Library (no. 1227), made after his death, in 1826; parts of it were copied by a successor at the College, Paravastu Chinnayasuri (1806–62) and published long after, in 1930, mistakenly attributed to the latter, as Venkata Rao notes (1957:24). Pattabhirama Shastri also wrote a commentary in Telugu prose on the Sanskrit grammar attributed to Nannaya, the *Āndhraśabdacintāmaṇi,* and a grammar of Telugu in verse, presumably for use in teaching Telugu grammar to Indian students in the College, since published (1951) by Venkata Rao (ibid.).

Both Pattabhirama Shastri and Sankaraiah are found in an interesting list of "respectable inhabitants" of Madras of 1813, which names the leading brahmins, "Gujarati" traders, Baniyans, Telugu traders ("Gentoos and Coral Merchants"), Mudaliars, and Pillais (MPC 26 Oct 1813). But they both also appear, in a very different light, in the *Sarvadevavilāsa.*

This rare and precious Sanskrit text, edited and published by the great Sanskritist V. Raghavan, gives a picture of the notable patrons, scholars, and artists of Madras in a different perspective from the one we find in records of the colonial government (Raghavan 1957–58). It is a poem, a *campu-kāvya,* or poem written in a mixture of prose and verse, in which two pandits visit the leading patrons of the city (these being the various gods, *sarva-deva,* of the title) and describe to one another the parties these godlike wealthy patrons throw for musicians and scholars, and the religious festivals they host (the pleasures, *vilāsa,* of the title). The patrons are not rajas, as they would have been in the past, but, in the new era of international trade and colonial rule, wealthy Indian merchants and dubashes (agents) to the Company, during the moment of their greatest wealth and influence around the beginning of the nineteenth century, as ably described by Susan Neild-Basu (1984). The influence and wealth of the dubash class would fade, as did that of the Vijayanagara rulers before them, and new institutional forms would become the custodians of South Indian high culture; in particular, as we shall see (chapter 6), the College of Fort St. George itself aspired to be an institutional patron of Indian literature and played an important role in the development of a print culture for Tamil and Telugu classics. In terms of fast-changing conditions for high culture, the *Sarvadevavilāsa* gives a freeze-frame picture of a vanishing moment.

In this poem the patrons include the leading trinity, likened to Brahmā, Śiva, and Viṣṇu, namely, Vedacala Mudaliar, a Tuluva Vellalar agent of the East India Company; Kalingaraja, a wealthy patron about whom little is known; and Sriranga, a Telugu brahmin. Other patrons mentioned include Deva Nayaka Mudaliar, from a family of dubashes to the Company since 1725 (Raghavan 1957–58, pt. 2, 65–80). The anonymous author paints appealing word pictures of musicians, poets, and scholars performing new works and being rewarded generously in the parties hosted by the patrons in their homes in the garden suburbs of Madras, and of temple festivals subsidized by the patrons as administrators *(dharmakartā)* of Madras's great temples. What makes this record is so appealing is that what the colonial archive foregrounds, the work of government and commerce, is here put in the background. The East India Company is present in the *Sarvadevavilāsa,* but merely as the source of wealth and influence of the patrons, whose liberality and good taste create the cultural and religious performances the text describes.

I was pleased to find Pattabhirama Shastri and Sankaraiah among the learned and influential brahmins *(paṇḍitān vipra-prabhūn)* holding important positions in the Company, who are described as both scholars and patrons (ibid., pt. 1, 409). Pattabhirama Shastri is the first of this group to be mentioned; he is likened to Śiva meditating at the foot of a banyan tree and is called a master of all shastras and a great scholar (ibid.). Sankaraiah appears as Śaṅkara; he is the last to be mentioned, where the text breaks off. He is said to have first become eminent in religious scholarship *(vaidika)* and subsequently to have excelled in worldly affairs *(laukika)* and been held in high esteem by all rulers (ibid. pt. 1, 414; pt. 2, 87–88).

Raghavan made good use of the colonial archive to identify the Madras notables spoken of in the text. His study of the text is invaluable, but he does not identify Pattabhirama Shastri and Sankaraiah. The text is not dated, but Raghavan shows that persons mentioned in the text are dateable to the late eighteenth and early nineteenth centuries, and gives evidence showing that the text could not have been written earlier than 1787 or later than 1817. He thinks it belongs to about 1800. Had he known the identity of Pattabhirama Shastri and Sankaraiah he might have dated it somewhat later, in their heyday, around 1815. Further comparison of this text with the colonial record, especially the Madras District Records and the Public Consultations, would almost certainly be profitable; for example, the important patron Kalingaraja may be the A. Collingaroya Moodelliar, who is included in the previously mentioned 1813 list of respectable inhabitants of Madras along with Pattabhirama Shastri and Sankaraiah. In any case the enchanted world of the *Sarvadevavilāsa* gives us valuable insight into the cultural and religious life of the Indian elite of Madras at a time when patronage was in the hands of wealthy merchants and bankers, since royal patronage was going into terminal decline, and scholarship was sustained by those who were servants of the Company.

Returning to Ellis, it remains to explain the peculiar circumstances of his passing away before turning to the analysis of his life project.

Ellis died suddenly on 9 March 1819, not of disease, as many Englishmen in India did, but of a fatal accident. He had gotten a medical certificate attesting to attacks of dyspepsia accompanied by considerable derangement of the liver and recommending "a change of air towards the cooler climate of the interior" to restore his health (MDR 18 Nov 1818). Dyspepsia appears to have been a chronic ailment, for in his 1808 letter to Leyden, Ellis had written of "a damnable fit of Dyspepsia, which has tormented me for the last five months, and I fear will ultimately drive me either to England or out of the world." Instead of heading for the cooler climate of the hill stations, however, he went south to carry out his researches, and was residing with the Collector of Madurai, Rous Petrie. During a trip to Ramnad in the southernmost tip of India, while medicating himself for his ailment, he took something poisonous by mistake and died. Erskine suggests the poison was laudanum "or some other noxious liquid," but of course Erskine was not on the scene and his information would have been at secondhand at best (Erskine, NLS Mss. 36.1.5, f. 21).

Ellis died slowly and inexorably over a period of several hours and wrote a will as he contemplated his own untimely end. He bequeathed his property to his mother and left legacies to a brother and the family of an aunt, to four servants, and to his dubash. Having named no executor, and having no kin in India, the estate was administered by the Supreme Court of Judicature, Madras. His household goods and personal effects were sold at public auction in Madurai and Madras, including an excellent library of books and manuscripts of over five hundred items, which must have been one of the best personal libraries of European works in Madras. As mentioned previously, according to Walter Elliot, Ellis's private papers were "lost or destroyed" and according to current report were used by Petrie's cook "to kindle his fire and singe fowls."

Erskine's sketch of Ellis, quoted in the previous section, contains this description of his temperament:

> He was very learned & ingenious but shy, irritable, proud & obstinate. His peculiarities were injurious only to himself. He was eager to improve the condition of the natives, but had perhaps too high an opinion of their literature and acquirements. He was an excellent & attached friend; liberal to his servants & dependents, and had his mind ever open to conviction. He was an excellent classical scholar, & his ideas on the accent & prosody of the ancient languages, derived from his study of Sanscrit &c seemed to me new and ingenious. His death was an irreparable loss to Indian Literature, especially at Madras. (NLS Mss. 36.1.5, f. 21v)

Shy and proud at once, irritable and obstinate, Ellis's peculiarities were indeed occasionally injurious to himself, as at Tanjore and on other occasions; but also an excellent and attached friend, and superb scholar: this was Ellis, to the life, according to one who knew him well.

THE DISSERTATIONS

Ellis was a true Orientalist in the full sense of the word, who fulfilled the ideal type of the scholar-administrator better than anyone I know of. He was very good at his work, but there is no mistaking that what he really loved was the scholarship, and that all his ambitions rested on it. In this section I will try to specify the overall direction of that scholarship—his big project—much as I have done for Erskine and Leyden. What that big project, involving what he called the dissertations, was and was not Ellis explained in a letter to Erskine dated 3 July 1809.

In the letter Ellis discusses the problem of history in India, specifically what he calls "Hindu history," in distinction from Erskine's grand project of writing a history of the (Muslim) Mughals from Persian sources, and he makes it clear that he is actively involved in the problem as it affects South India. He begins by correcting an impression he had given his friend in a previous letter which has not survived:

> In speaking of the possibility of composing a History of the two Dynasties of Vijayanagaram, I never meant to say that I intended to undertake it. I had indeed at one time some idea of giving some account of Crishna Rayalu, not as a Regular History, but as a dissertation for the Bengal or some other society. Anything in the form of regular History respecting the Hindu Dynasties, though much information has been obtained, is in my opinion premature. So much is yet to [be] learned, so many facts are yet in doubt, and so many points are yet to be ascertained, that were a person to set down now to [write] a Regular History either of this or of any other Hindu Dynasties,

> he would probably have to rewrite it more than once, before he could make it satisfactory even to himself. (NLS Mss. 36.1.5, Ellis to Erskine 3 July 1809, ff. 42–43)

Ellis continues by identifying two projects for the history of South India then underway: Colin Mackenzie's ambitious collection of historical materials, using a small army of Indian assistants working out of Madras, which produced a mountain of material on inscriptions and local histories; and Colonel Mark Wilks's history of Mysore, which came to be published in three volumes (Wilks 1810–17). Ellis had a hand in both of these projects, and some few traces of his interactions with them remain. Erskine records that Ellis helped Mackenzie with the decipherment of his collection of inscriptions (NLS Mss. 36.1.5, f. 21), and Wilks notes the help Ellis gave with Sanskrit texts showing that the ancient Hindu king was not the owner of all the land (Ellis 1810).

"All that can now be done" on the Hindu history of South India, Ellis says, "is in progress, and in very good hands. Major Mackenzie is digesting the very extensive information he possesses, and more is daily collecting." He advises Erskine "to select some detached portion of Hindu History (I do not mean Fable by that word though they are often synonymous)" as a potential project, such as the transactions of the Hindu Maratha kings, connected with the downfall of Bijapur, as Wilks has already done, "whose story, springing from the decline of the Vijayanagaram government, must necessarily contain many circumstances connected with this event: & this I am endeavouring to do, by bringing together all that I know (though that all is not much) regarding the Tamil principalities." While stressing the importance of recovering the history of South India, Ellis nevertheless distinguishes his own project from it:

> We should endeavour, however, to impress on those it may interest, that India is not entirely without history, referring for the proof to what time must inevitably embody, whoever be the operator. For my own part, though somewhat ambitious of literary reputation, I do not think that history will be my walk, I have naturally so strong an inclination to fable, that if the subject could be adorned by it, I scarcely expect myself capable of resisting the temptation to fabricate. (Ellis to Erskine 3 July 1809, ff. 43–44)

The reference to fabrication is not entirely facetious, as we shall shortly see when we speak of the *purāṇa*-like Tamil text Ellis composed on the smallpox vaccine. In the meantime, what is to be noticed is that history was not to be his "walk." This is a surprising statement for someone whose scholarship is so deeply historical. What it really means is that his contribution would not be to the writing of *political* history, for when we come to the part of the letter in which he defines what his walk *is,* we see that history of a kind is central to it.

Ellis opens that discussion with mention of his work on the prosody of Tamil verse, in connection with which he speaks of his intention to write four dissertations. The work on prosody, he says, is nearly finished and requires only to be arranged. But he wishes to preface it by an account of Tamil, of its dialects "which pervade the whole of Southern India," and of its literature. This, he says, proceeds slowly and even the ultimate shape of it is uncertain. Ellis has the notion of four dissertations being necessary to complete the subject, namely:

1. On the history of the countries in which the Tamil is spoken
2. On the Tamil language and its ancient and modern dialects
3. On the rhythmic measures of the Tamil, i.e., the work on prosody
4. On Tamil literature

He fears that carrying out this plan will result in a heavy book instead of a series of dissertations (articles, we would say). For the present, he intends to complete the first and the third topics—history and prosody—in a couple of papers, leaving the last one, on Tamil literature, for a "regular and separate work, to be accumulated as I proceed through the language and to be hereafter digested when a sufficiency of materials were procured." He adds that the Jesuit missionary and Tamil scholar Constantius Beschi—"I have mentioned this extraordinary man to you, as holding a high rank among Tamil Authors"—had an intention of composing such a work but unfortunately never carried it out. The four dissertations together, we can say, would have formed a history of Tamil language and literature, to give a name, which Ellis does not, to the big project of his life as he conceived it at that stage. It is telling of his admiration for Beschi that he thinks of his own project as identical to that which the great Italian Jesuit scholar of Tamil did not live to accomplish.

Nearly eight years later, as we see in a letter to Erskine dated 24 March 1817, the project has developed and broadened into a large work of comparison, and the dissertations are identified somewhat differently. Now Ellis is actively producing a set of dissertations on the major languages of southern India, not just Tamil, and the plan is "to illustrate the origin and connection of the dialects." There are now to be five dissertations (which perhaps are meant to include the earlier project on Tamil):

1. On the alphabetic writing of India in general and South India in particular, including notices of the alphabets of the Sinhalese and those of Burma and Java, which can be demonstrated to derive from the Tamil
2. On low and high Tamil
3. On Telugu
4. On Malayalam
5. On Canarese (Kannada) and the minor dialects Kodagu, Tuluvu, and so forth

At the time, the dissertation on Telugu had been printed ("not *published,*" Ellis specifies) at the College of Fort St. George, and the one on Malayalam was being printed. This seems to mean that they were printed as separate papers for the use of the students of the College. None of these original papers has survived in that form. Ellis sent copies of them to Erskine, but they are not in the Erskine collections at the British Library and the National Library of Scotland, nor have I found copies elsewhere. But both have been published. The dissertation on Telugu, included in A. D. Campbell's grammar of Telugu published by the College Press as a "Note to the introduction" (Ellis 1816) is of course what I call the Dravidian proof. The dissertation on Malayalam was published long after Ellis's death by Walter Elliot in the *Indian antiquary* (Ellis 1878). Erskine states, however, that the chief dissertation was that on the Tamil, "which I know not if he completed," and Elliot stated it as his belief that the Tamil dissertation was never printed. I have not found the dissertation on the scripts of South India nor the one on Canarese, and they may not have been written.

What one sees here is that Ellis's project of writing the history of Tamil language and literature, which remained his central objective, was contained within a larger, comparative Dravidian framework; or perhaps we should say, his central interest in Tamil opened out into a more ambitious program for the major Dravidian languages as a set. The framework itself mirrors the design of the College he built, as we shall see in the next chapter, and the pieces printed at the College Press were intended for the students, although they are far more than works of pedagogy.

Ellis's central interest in Tamil language and literature, particularly the impulse to understand it within the largest frame of comparative study, did not develop slowly through his life; it was present early on, as we see from a couple of remarkable letters Ellis wrote in 1800 to the Government of Madras (MPC 2 May and 27 June 1800). Responding to a notice that the Government would receive proposals for grammars and dictionaries of Marathi, Telugu, or "Malabar" (i.e., Tamil) languages, Ellis, then scarcely four years in India, boldly proposed to write a grammar and dictionary of Tamil. The Government expressed pleasure at this display of zeal and industry but maintained that he should first pass the examination in the Malabar language. This Ellis declined to do, and it is a curious fact that he never took the examination, or at any rate that his name does not appear on the surviving lists of those who did so. At that juncture his competence in Tamil was incomplete, he said, "as my course of study hitherto has been rather theoretical than practical," and he had little conversant acquaintance with it. He explains:

> Into [this] course of study I was originally led by conceiving the most perfect knowledge of this or any other Language might be acquired by founding practice on Theory, and from a wish rather to gain an insight into the Indian Dialects in general than to confine myself to one in particular. These Dialects are indeed so intimately connected that to obtain a perfect Grammatical knowledge of one is to obtain a knowledge of all, a few partial deviations of Phrase and Idiom excepted, and this is so much the case that in translating Malabar into Gentoo [i.e., Tamil into Telugu], or the reverse, the position of a single word in a thousand *need* not be changed. (MPC 27 June 1800; emphasis in original)

Thus already at this early stage Ellis had come to think, on theoretical grounds, that a full knowledge of the Tamil language would require the widest framework of comparison, and, specifically, he was already thinking about its closeness to Telugu.

Ellis's grand project, it need hardly be pointed out, is another instantiation of the European languages-and-nations project, as was Leyden's—the latter, of course, being shaped by Leyden's friendship with Ellis, whom he met in Madras just a few years after the letters just quoted from were written. The difference between the two projects reflects different casts of mind: Leyden's desire to quickly reach a grand overview, Ellis's scholarship deeply centered on Tamil using the most wide-ranging comparison to elucidate Tamil while also considering Tamil the key to elucidating the whole story of languages and nations in South India.

In the previously cited letter of 24 March 1817, Ellis says, "I made many years ago a resolution not to publish anything until I was forty years old and I have kept it pretty well considering, for I shall not have completed that age until the conclusion of the current year, and the only thing like a literary production I have yet printed is the dissertation [on Telugu] I shall send you." One cannot help feeling how very unfortunate that resolution was in the face of his impending death, and that the non-completion of his grand project was, as Erskine believed, "an irreparable loss to Indian literature, especially at Madras." As a result, what did not make it into print was the central project itself, the history of Tamil literature, and what did make it into print was material peripheral to that central project, though important insofar as it treated of the larger, theoretical frame. Ellis's publications, then, are a periphery without the center, which would have been a splendid history of the Tamil language, literature, and people.

Nevertheless the fragments of the grand project and other writings of Ellis that survive are substantial, if we include the manuscript materials from private papers and the colonial archive as well as the published works. To begin with, the grand project itself is not entirely lost. Besides the published dissertations on Telugu and Malayalam, rough drafts of the dissertation on Tamil were rescued from among the discarded papers of the College by Elliot, bequeathed to G. U. Pope, and deposited by Pope in the Bodleian Library. The drafts give a good sense of how the work would have proceeded. Moreover, Elliot preserved the very long manuscripts of his work on Tamil prosody, two versions of which are in the Elliot Collection of the British Library (OIOC); in his letter to Erskine, Ellis had said the work was effectively complete.

In the bibliography I give a list of all the published works of Ellis, most of them published after his death. Within his own lifetime, besides the dissertation on Telugu published in Caldwell's Telugu grammar, a "Note, by Mr. Ellis, on the 239th and 243d verses of the eighth chapter of Menu" was printed as an appendix in Wilks's *Historical sketches of the south of India,* arguing against the theory of Oriental despotism (royal ownership of all the land) and in favor of the view that private property in land existed in ancient India (1810). To the same effect was the so-called *Treatise of mirasi right* (1818), on the property rights of peasant joint-proprietors of a village. This had not been intended for publication; it had been submitted to the Board of Revenue in answer to a circular request for answers to a list of questions about ownership rights of persons called mirasidars. It is an important and much-discussed production, incorporating both Ellis's and Sankaraiah's treatments of mirasi land tenure, with translation, notes, and supportive documentary evidence, including texts and translations of inscriptions and land contracts of various kinds, and the Board of Revenue thought it so good that it deserved to be published for the use of the service. At the time of Ellis's death. another piece of his was going through the College Press, but was not completed; this is Ellis's annotated translation of the *Tirukkuṟaḷ* of Tiruvaḷḷuvar, which was intended for the use of the students but was also, surely, another step toward his big project on the history of Tamil literature. Copies of this rare work exist (Ellis c. 1819), and it has since been published (Tiruvalluvar 1980). G. U. Pope completed a translation of *Nālaḍiyār* that Ellis left incomplete at his death (Naladiyar 1963).

A major article by Ellis appeared posthumously in *Asiatic researches,* the journal of the Asiatic Society at Calcutta; the article had been read before the Asiatic Society, as well as before the Bombay Literary Society, several years earlier (Ellis 1822). It is a splendid analysis of the *Ezour Vedam,* a text famous in Europe because it had been cited by Voltaire to show that a just apprehension of God was not confined to Christian thought. This strange text, kept in the Jesuit library in Madurai, is in bad Sanskrit written in roman script. Ellis gave an elaborate demonstration that it was a hoax, probably of the missionaries; he thought it the work of Roberto Nobili. The exposure of this missionary hoax—and the perpetration in the colonial interest of a hoax of his own ("The legend of the cow-pox," discussed below)—may have been on his mind when Ellis made his lighthearted remark to Erskine about his own inclination to fable.

Two other posthumous publications are a lengthy piece on the Sanskrit lawbooks authoritative in the South that contains abbreviated versions of lectures on the topic Ellis gave before the Literary Society of Madras (Ellis 1827), and an analysis of the copper-plate grant of the Jewish community of Cochin, edited by Elliot, who says it was found "among some old papers in the College" (Ellis 1844).

In addition to these publications, there are several unpublished works. The most intriguing of these is "The legend of the cow-pox," an English translation of a text Ellis says he composed in Tamil concerning the smallpox vaccine, which had just been developed by Jenner and was about to be introduced into Madras. The text being so very curious, I have included it here in appendix A. It is in the form of a colloquy between the Goddess (Śakti) and Dhanvantari, the physician to the gods. The Goddess describes the new vaccination, derived from the teat of a cow infected with cowpox, as a new, sixth *gavya,* or sanctifying product of the cow (the canonical *gavyas* being milk, butter, yoghurt, urine, and dung), to protect humankind against the fearful disease. Besides being very cleverly done, the story is a perfect example of Orientalism as both a philologically based scholarship and a colonial practice. It was intended to convince Indians of the goodness of the new vaccine and to support the vigorous program of reaching the whole population with it. This text, the Tamil original of which I have not been able to find so far, is preserved in the papers of Erskine and Leyden, to whom Ellis sent copies. Ellis speaks of writing other texts in Tamil, but he does not give us the details. He was perhaps following the example of Beschi, whose Tamil writings are well known.

Finally, the colonial archive, preserved at the Tamil Nadu State Archives and in the British Library's Oriental and India Office Collections, contains a number of scholarly pieces by Ellis amid the dry details of taxation, customs on arrak, toddy, and tobacco, road mending, the perennial problem of encroachments, and suchlike details of his life as Land Customer and Collector of Madras. These include, besides the published *Treatise of mirasi right,* a long minute on systems of land revenue in South India by the Board of Trade, in the making of which he probably played a role and to which he certainly contributed the information for the section on the Tamil country (MBR 5 Jan 1818). He wrote a number of interesting short minutes on *inam* and other indigenous categories of the Tamil land system (MDR 20 Apr 1817). He also wrote a most learned minute on the right and left divisions among the castes of South India, with abundant quotations from *āgama* texts, in which he ventures an hypothesis about the origin of this important classification. He produced this paper in the wake of serious riots of right- and left-hand castes in Madras (MPC 6 March 1812, written 20 Aug 1810, Brimnes 1999). But by far and away the most important colonial records involving Ellis concern the language problem and the solution for it that Ellis had devised and which he supervised, the College of Fort St. George, which we must now examine.

CHAPTER 4

The College

Having met the leading personnel involved in producing the new knowledge about South India, we must now examine the College of Fort St. George, which was the main locus for this process. This chapter is not a history of the College as such (though such a history is very much to be desired). It is, rather, an inquiry into the relation of the College to the Dravidian proof. As such, our examination is limited to the period from the College's founding in 1812 till the death of Ellis in 1819.

MADRAS BEFORE THE COLLEGE

The College of Fort St. George was the brainchild of Ellis, and as senior member of the Board of Superintendence from its inception, he lavished on it his best knowledge and care. It filled his thoughts and ambitions, and was more important to him than the full-time day job he had as Collector of Madras. From a letter of his successor it appears that Ellis had rooms at the College where he kept books, as a result of which the cutchery, or court, of the Collector of Madras did not possess a complete set of the Regulations of Government when he died (MDR 29 May 1819, nos. 215, 256). From this we can infer that Ellis was accustomed to doing much of his scholarly work at his College rooms.

The College was proposed as a solution to the problems of language in colonial Madras, and so I need to begin with a word about the language situation at Madras, and in British India generally, prior to the College's founding.

Madras had been in possession of the East India Company since 1639, and the Company's servants had been trading there since that time without producing a single grammar or dictionary of the languages of South India. The dictionaries and grammars that were available for Europeans had largely been made by Jesuit missionaries, and most of these circulated in manuscript form. By and large, the Company worked through Indian agents, or dubashes (people "having two languages," though they were much more than translators), who by the end of the eighteenth century had acquired considerable power through their ability to manipulate the local political situation. Brahmins opened schools for teaching English of a sort to those who aspired to this profession. Some Englishmen learned Hindustani or Portuguese (the latter was in use along the coasts for quite some time as a language of trade, and has left a deposit of loanwords in many Indian languages), and Persian was cultivated as a language of diplomacy and continued as a language of government for the Company into the nineteenth century. The use of Persian and Hindustani largely perpetuated the pattern of the Mughal empire, to which the Company was to some degree the heir. In the first century of the East India Company's occupation of Madras, Englishmen rarely learned the Dravidian languages indigenous to the South except, one supposes, a few phrases needed in the kitchen, the garden, and the bedroom. They barely even knew the names of the South Indian languages, calling them Malabar and Gentoo languages, or Malabars and Gentoos, rather than Tamil and Telugu, up to 1800 or so.

The situation was similar at other East India Company factories and did not change till some while after the defeat of the Mughal power in Bengal (1757), when the Company assumed the administrative powers (diwani) of the Bengal government (1765) and faced the complex demands of administering the land tax for large areas of the Indian countryside. Though the English had acquired from the Mughals a firman, or charter, permitting them to trade in Bengal as early as 1634, it was not till after the all-important transition from trading company to ruling power that the first grammar of Bengali was published, in 1778, by an Englishman, Nathaniel Brassey Halhed. At that time, Halhed said, Bengali was utterly unknown in Europe and, indeed, "it is scarcely believed that Bengal ever possessed a native and peculiar dialect of its own" distinct from "Moors" (Hindustani or Urdu), which had been thought to prevail over all of India (Halhed 1778:ii). Halhed tells us that Europeans arriving in India, "reduced to a necessary intercourse with Mahometan servants, or Sepoys, habitually acquire from them this idiom [Urdu] in that imperfect and confined state which is the consequence of the menial condition of their instructors." Contrary to the general supposition of Europeans, this language was unintelligible to villagers in Hindustan and Bengal, being used only in large towns frequented by Muslims and foreigners (ibid., xiii–xiv).

Halhed's preface to *A grammar of the Bengal language* is a very important text for us, as it is the first account in English concerning Sanskrit and its relation to other languages, and presents some of the general views of Sanskrit that prevailed at the Orientalist establishment at Calcutta. He describes Sanskrit as "the grand Source of Indian Literature, the Parent of almost every dialect from the Persian Gulph to the China Seas . . . a language of the most venerable and unfathomable antiquity," which, though now shut up in the libraries of brahmins, "appears to have been current over most of the Oriental World" (ibid., iii). Traces of it are still to be found in almost every part of Asia. Halhed was astonished to find Sanskrit's similarity with Persian and Arabic, and even Latin and Greek—not in the technical and metaphorical terms, which, he says, belong to a higher stage of civilization and thus might have been borrowed from other languages, but in "the main ground-work of language, in monosyllables, in the names of numbers, and the appellations of such things as would be first discriminated on the immediate dawn of civilization" (ibid., iii–iv). We see at work here the theory subtending the method of the word list examined in chapter 1. The resemblance extends to the similarity of scripts seen on coins of Assam, Nepal, Kashmir, and many other kingdoms, and the impressions of seals from Bhutan and Tibet. Another ground of resemblance lies in the alphabetical order of Sanskrit (discussed in chapter 2), which is "so very different from that of any other quarter of the world. This extraordinary mode of combination still exists in the greatest part of the East, from the Indus to Pegu, in dialects now apparently unconnected, and in characters compleatly dissimilar; but is a forcible argument that they are all derived from the same source" (ibid., iv)—an astute point which is, in fact, correct. Names of persons and places, titles and dignities, show traces of Sanskrit to the farthest limits of Asia, Halhed argues—as is still true, for example, of Thai and Indonesian personal names. In his enthusiasm engendered by discovering the wide scope of Sanskrit across Asia, Halhed goes overboard and speculates that even the ancient Egyptians got their sciences and education from the brahmins of India.

The three fundamental parts of speech in Sanskrit, Halhed tells us, are the roots of verbs *(dhātu)*, "original nouns" *(śabda)*, and particles *(avyaya*, indeclinables). He is aware of the rules of grammar *(vyākaraṇa)*, applying to verbal roots and nouns, in which "the art of the Grammarian has found room to expand itself, and to employ all the powers of refinement." He says, "Not a syllable, not a letter can be added or altered but by regimen; not the most trifling variation of the sense in the minutest subdivision of declension or conjugation can be effected without the application of several rules; and all the different forms for every change of gender, number, case, person, tense, mood or degree are methodically arranged for the assistance of the memory" (ibid., vii). What he goes on to say is of great importance as an expression of what I call "the linguistic unity of India" view that dominated Calcutta, a mistaken view against which the Dravidian proof had to make its way:

> To this triple source [Sanskrit verbs, nouns, and particles] I conceive that every word of truly Indian original in every provincial and subordinate dialect of all Hindostan may still be traced by a laborious and critical analysis; and all such terms as are thoroughly proved to bear no relation to one of the Shanscrit roots, I would consider as the production of some remote and foreign idiom, subsequently ingrafted upon the main stock. A judicious investigation of this principle would probably throw a new light upon the first invention of many arts and sciences, and open a fresh mine of philological discoveries. (ibid., viii)

The idea that every truly Indian word was traceable to a Sanskrit verbal root, original noun, or particle, and that all others not traceable to them were later and foreign imports, was a historicizing reading, perhaps, of the pandits' doctrine of Sanskrit as an eternal language.

The Company's transition from trading venture to ruling power after the conquest of Bengal promoted the study of India's languages for the directly instrumental purposes of colonial rule. But the cultivation of languages had also to do with the fact that the transition to ruling power brought into the service of the Company, for the first time, a lot of people with university education, such as Halhed himself, and also William Jones. These men brought with them an interest in the languages-and-nations project of European high culture, which, in a sense, could now use colonial institutions as a vehicle for its global spread, just as earlier it had used the missionizing projects of Catholic orders, especially the Jesuits.

The Orientalist establishment at Calcutta consisted of three interconnected institutions: the Government itself (in particular, the courts of law which administered Hindu and Muhammadan law, based on Dharmaśāstra and Shariah texts, in matters of marriage and inheritance), the Asiatic Society (formed only in 1784), and the College of Fort William, which was established in 1804 to train arriving civil service recruits in Indian languages under the supervision of Orientalists of the Asiatic Society such as H. T. Colebrooke. This pattern, as I have said before, served as a model for Madras and Bombay in the times of Ellis and Erskine.

The College of Fort William was created by the governor-general, the Marquess Wellesley (Kopf 1969; Das 1978). It was his "University of the East," and all arriving writers were to spend three years there in study before taking up their postings in Bengal, Madras, or Bombay. The course included the three classical languages (Arabic, Persian, and Sanskrit), and the six modern languages (Hindustani, Bengali, Telugu, Marathi, Tamil, and Kannada); in other words, most of the major languages of India, both north and south, were to be learned at this single center. In the original conception of the College of Fort William, Calcutta was to be *the* educational center for the entire India civil service, including those who were to be posted to Madras and Bombay. It was to be a production center for a usable knowledge of the languages of all of India, and a flood of teaching grammars and dictionaries accompanied its growth.

But in forming this centralizing and ambitious plan the governor-general acted on his own initiative, without first seeking the authorization of London, and the result did not sit well with the Court of Directors (Farrington 1976). For one thing, members of the Court of Directors enjoyed lucrative powers of patronage, collecting large fees from the parents of young lads they recommended to the service. For another thing, a committee led by Charles Grant had recommended the creation of a school for Company servants in England, so they could get a good education in British patriotism and Anglican religion on British soil and not go "unfortified against erroneous and dangerous Opinions" when they were first exposed to what were viewed as the moral dangers of India (East India Company 1804, cited in Trautmann 1997:115). As a result, an East India College was established at Hertford Castle, and later moved to permanent quarters at Haileybury, offering the first two years of education to young writers, with a full course of study, including Indian languages, mainly Persian, Hindustani, Bengali, and Sanskrit, prior to their arrival at Calcutta and entering the College of Fort William (Farrington 1976; Danvers 1894). Until the creation of the East India College, Indian languages had to be learned in India from Indian teachers; Company servants who had learned the Indian languages, though they retired to England, did not pass on that knowledge there. Calcutta had enjoyed a virtual monopoly of the production of new European knowledge of Indian antiquities. The founding of the East India College was the beginning of the end of that monopoly, and the formation of the Royal Asiatic Society in London completed the process. Calcutta's Asiatic Society became the Asiatic Society *of Bengal*.

Thus Calcutta's College of Fort William lost its centralizing role soon after its creation, and the requirement that new recruits spend time there before going to postings in Madras or Bombay was dropped, too, leaving them to make their own arrangements for language teaching. However, the changed situation did not prevent the Calcutta Orientalist establishment from continuing to present itself as a center of production of Orientalist knowledge within India, and to make pronouncements about all of India. This combination of circumstances led to some tensions between Calcutta, on the one hand, and Bombay and Madras, on the other. Madras created the College of Fort St. George and the Madras Literary Society in 1812, completing the Orientalist triangle on the Calcutta model; Bombay had founded its Literary Society much earlier, in 1804, and Erskine took Madras as a possible model for a college at Bombay.

Both of the leaders of Orientalist projects at Madras, Mackenzie and Ellis, were members of the Asiatic Society, and both published in its journal, the *Asiatic researches*. Ellis showed his allegiance to Calcutta's leadership in Orientalism in certain ways, for instance, by adopting the transliteration scheme of Sir William Jones in all his renderings of Indian languages in roman script; and we can often identify Ellis as the author of an anonymous report in the colonial archive of Madras by the spellings of words, for example, "Telugu" instead of "Teloogoo," and the use of diacritical marks in the representation of long vowels and aspirated consonants. Nevertheless, while Ellis in various ways situated himself as an adherent of the Calcutta model of Orientalism, he was also consistently critical of the way Calcutta Orientalists got the South wrong. Often they erroneously assumed that what was true of the North was true of India as a whole. It was around this sense of the inadequacies of the Calcutta model that there developed a Madras School of Orientalism, as I want to call it, around the Ellis and Mackenzie projects, a school that was both allied to and critical of the Calcutta school. The most telling instance of this critique of Calcutta occurred when Carey (1814) produced a grammar of Telugu from Calcutta (or Serampore, where the press was), and it was answered by A. D. Campbell's Telugu grammar (1816), published at Madras by its College, containing the Dravidian proof.[1]

I should now like to examine, through the eyes of Ellis, the state of the European study of Indian languages at Madras prior to the creation of the College of Fort St. George. We find an elaborate analysis of the attempts to promote knowledge of Indian languages among Company servants in a report dated 20 October 1811 of the Committee for the Examination of the Junior Civil Servants; Ellis is a signatory, and the text bears all the marks of Ellis having been its main author (MPC 10 Dec 1811). The report conveys, briefly, the results of recent language examinations over which the Committee presided, but it goes on to analyze at length the problems with the current arrangements for language instruction and to then outline a plan for the creation of the College of Fort St. George. I give the substance of the report in some detail.

The Madras Government, beginning 15 December 1797, offered a reward of 1,000 star pagodas to civil servants who showed proficiency in the study of native languages, and the purpose of the Committee was to set examinations and report the results for that purpose. The reward was substantial, being the equivalent of £400, and was twenty times the monthly salary of a beginning writer (50 pagodas) at the time of the report. Language instruction was offered by the staff of the Madrassah in Fort St. George to newly arrived junior servants, who came with two years at the East India College behind them. The Committee found these arrangements woefully inadequate.

The leading problem was that the number of students in Persian and Hindustani greatly outnumbered those "in the more useful dialects of the territories dependent on this Government," especially Tamil and Telugu, the "two most useful languages." The report includes a table of the twenty-two winners of the prize to date. Up to the end of 1809 there had been only eight for Tamil, three for Telugu, and one for Kannada; thereafter, there was not one in any of the "native dialects of the Peninsula"

1. I coined the term "Madras School of Orientalism" in an article published in 1999 (see also Trautmann 2001a) to designate the projects of Ellis and Mackenzie and their Indian and British associates in early nineteenth-century Madras. Ellis and Mackenzie had good relations and often exchanged information. Both of them avowed the Orientalist paradigm established at Calcutta and acknowledged Calcutta's leadership in this sense, but thought that Calcutta had gotten South India wrong and felt that they and their associates were called upon to correct it. On Mackenzie there are many studies (e.g., the standard biography, W. C. Mackenzie 1952, and Subramaniam 1953–57 on the temple inscriptions), but the current mini-boom of studies of his project was inaugurated by Dirks (1993, 2001), followed by Robb (1998), Mantena (2002), and Wagoner (2003).

(MPC 10 Dec 1811, paras. 12, 13). Through the whole period, however, the prizes for Persian and Hindustani were numerous.

The preference for Persian and Hindustani on the part of candidates, the Committee thought, was partly due to the existence of many excellent elementary books for their study published in the last few years—and, by implication, the lack of them for the languages of the South. But it was mainly attributable to the East India College at Hertford. The College opened in 1806, "and its operation on the Madras Service was felt immediately after the first set of Junior Servants who had passed through the College arrived in the Country in 1809" (ibid., para. 14). The effectiveness of the language training at Hertford was evident in "the short periods within which those who had studied in the College have been enabled to claim the reward" and the greater number of such examinations since 1809, at two a year, compared with one a year in the period before. But because the East India College had been connected with the College at Calcutta at the outset, its language offerings—Persian, Hindustani, Bengali, and Sanskrit—spoke to the needs of the Bengal service but paid no attention whatever to any of the languages peculiar to Madras (ibid., para. 15). Students arriving at Madras, finding "the same reward held out and the same prospect of rising in the Service" for Persian and Hindustani as for any of the "native dialects," had been biased to continue studies in the languages they had begun at Hertford, though these would be of no public utility "compared with the dialects peculiar to these territories" (ibid., para. 16).

Persian, the Committee said, "is no more useful than it has artificially been made by the recent introduction of the Mahomedan Criminal law" in Madras, and in any case the practice of writing court decrees in Persian could easily be dispensed with, given that Persian is known by scarcely one person in ten thousand living under the Madras Government. Hindustani was useful in every part of India as a lingua franca, and was the universal language of the army, but its public advantage for a civil servant was small. It enabled a judge or collector to communicate with native servants of his court, but for communication with the people, "a few Mahommedans in a few districts excepted," he would need an interpreter as surely as if he spoke only English (ibid., para. 18). In many districts even the Muslims did not use Hindustani, such as those deriving from the early Arab immigrations, the Tamil-speaking Labbies on the east coast, and the Malayalam-speaking Mapillais on the west coast. The Hindustani-speaking descendants of northern invaders of the peninsula under its partial conquest by the Mughals were now, "except where a solitary Mosque attracts a few ragged Fakirs," confined to larger inland towns or colonies, where some (Muslim) jagirdar or inamdar (holder of a land grant) might give them employment (ibid., para. 19).To rectify the bias without erring in the opposite direction of discouraging the study of Persian and Hindustani too much, the Committee recommended either raising the reward for the acquisition of Tamil, Telugu, and other South Indian languages or declaring that no one could receive the reward for proficiency in Persian or Hindustani without having *first* passed the examination in one of the native dialects of the South. Of the two, the Committee thought the second was the better path, and, indeed, probably because it did not raise the cost, it quickly won the sanction of the Madras Government.

The Committee then addressed two other measures: the provision of competent language teachers for the junior servants, and the provision of "elementary books" for the study of the "Southern dialects" (ibid., para. 23).

The native teachers who offered themselves for teaching at the time of the report were, the Committee judged, with very few exceptions, utterly incompetent. Their whole qualification consisted in having acquired an imperfect knowledge of English and an ability to write out a few meager vocabularies, mostly acquired from Indian headmasters of schools teaching English to aspiring dubashes. They knew little grammar, and of the art of teaching they knew still less. More often than not, the student directed the teacher, acquiring conjugations and declensions by interrogation. In fact, an intelligent student drilled his instructor "into a knowledge of the language more correct and regular than he before possessed" (ibid., para. 24). The Persian and Hindustani munshis were little better, and being generally ignorant of English, were even less capable of teaching beginners from England. This general lack of competence was due to poor pay and the uncertainty of employment. The Persian or Hindustani munshi seldom received more than 10 pagodas per month, and few teachers of the South Indian languages receive more than 5 or 6 pagodas. The prospect of continuing to earn even this small pay was inversely proportional to their exertions in teaching, for when the students became proficient in the language, the teachers were dismissed and their pay came to an end. By comparison, a very inferior writer-copyist in the Madras offices was earning 15 to 25 pagodas a month, and even more in the Revenue Department. As no one could make teaching a regular livelihood, those who taught did so as a temporary employment and quit on the first better opportunity that arrived. Only those who could not do better remained as teachers. At the time, four Hindustani or Persian munshis, one Tamil teacher, and one Telugu teacher were employed at the Madrassah in the Fort on salaries the highest of which was 15 pagodas for instruction of junior servants who sought instruction there. But as the munshis and teachers were not allowed to go to the junior servants' homes to give instruction, most junior servants hired munshis at their own expense and studied at home, so that the positions in the Madrassah were "little better than sinecures" (ibid., para. 28).

Thus the institution that the Government had created for language instruction was virtually useless. The Committee contrasted this situation with the school begun by the Jesuits at Pondicherry for the instruction of Indians in Latin, French, and Tamil. It produced a considerable number of well-educated Indians, and after the British capture of Pondicherry, the Company placed them in the courts and cutcheries of nearly all the districts south of Madras. The few good teachers of Tamil at Madras had been either educated at Pondicherry or taught by those who had been teachers at the College at Calcutta, which had been able to promote a high level of ability among its Indian staff.

As for the provision of textbooks of the South Indian languages, the Committee believed that although the Madras Government had hitherto done little to follow the example of the Bengal Government in encouraging their production, the materials were at hand and needed only the Government's liberal patronage to bring them into print. The Committee listed the books that could be immediately published "at no further expense than the charges for paper and printing." This list is a most searching survey of the materials by which Europeans might learn, and had learned in the past, the languages of the South. Notably, most of the sources were the productions not of the Government but of Christian and especially Catholic, more especially Jesuit, missions, before the suppression of the Jesuit order in 1773. Only some of this material was in print; most of it circulated in manuscript copies.

The Committee reported that for Tamil, "the principal dialect of Southern India," valuable books existed but had become scarce. Tamil, specifically high Tamil, was "the key to all the other dialects of Southern India"; some of the best compositions in it were the works of Catholic missionaries (ibid., para. 39), especially the eighteenth-century works by the Jesuit J. C. Beschi, of the Madura Mission.[2] I give in paraphrase the list of

2. Several of Beschi's works (1822, 1920, 1971, 1974) were translated into English by persons associated with the College of Fort St. George, but only after the death of Ellis, who thought the students should be able to read them in Latin. Some are still in print. A statue of Beschi has been installed on the Marina in Madras.

works as given in the report, following the wording fairly closely but abbreviating and summarizing at places:

1. The *Tonnul,* Beschi's Latin grammar of the "superior dialect" of Tamil, or "high Tamil," with sections on orthography, etymology, composition, prosody, and rhetoric. It is an original work but contains the substance of the *Tolkappiyam,* the *Nannul,* and other older treatises of Tamil grammar. The rules are in verse, accompanied by prose commentary. "A person moderately skilled in the low Tamil might soon make himself master of this Grammar." Although the work seems never to have been printed, there are many good manuscript copies available, both on cadjan (palm leaf) and paper.
2. The *Catur Akaradi,* a Latin dictionary of the "superior dialect" of Tamil composed by Beschi, consisting of four distinct dictionaries, under the titles of "Peyar" (meanings of words), "Porul" (words bearing the same meanings—synonyms), "Tokai" (technical and general terms of science and literature), and "Totai" (a rhyming dictionary). It was compiled from older dictionaries, of which a great number exist, but it is the only one entirely in alphabetical order [which the word *akārādi* ("*a,* etc.") indicates]. This work too has never been printed, but manuscript copies are very numerous and it is the best of the available dictionaries.
3. Beschi's Latin grammar of the high Tamil is not a self-contained grammar, but a supplement to his Latin grammar of the low Tamil (*Grammatica Latino-Tamulica, sive de vulgari Tamulicae linguae idiomate kotuntamil dicto,* a "complete Grammar of the low, and an excellent key to the high Dialect"; ibid., para. 44). This grammar was printed for the first and perhaps last time by the Protestant missionary press at Tranquebar in 1738; the Committee does not approve of the English translation recently published at the Vepery Press.

The Committee recommended that Beschi's low-Tamil grammar should be printed in the original Latin, along with his dictionary. The Committee members presumed that the junior servants would have been well educated in Latin at the East India College at Hertford (an assumption that was apparently too optimistic, since the grammar was subsequently translated into English and published by the College Press for its students).

Furthermore, Latin "is of all others the language best calculated for conveying grammatical instruction" (ibid., para. 45). Lastly, to translate it into English would spoil the grammar's scheme, in that the Tamil is compared with the Latin, and the arrangement and expression all have reference to the Latin. A literal translation would be virtually unintelligible.

4. The Danish missionary Christopher Theodorus Walther composed another work in Latin on the low Tamil language, intended as a supplement to Beschi's grammar and published (at Tranquebar, presumably) a year after. It is of limited use, as it frequently confounds the high and low dialects and makes errors of colloquial usage.
5. Beschi's Tamil-Latin dictionary, which is a complete dictionary of the "low dialect" of Tamil; this and his *Catur Akaradi* together constitute a perfect dictionary of the whole language. Different meanings of words are illustrated by using them in phrases; peculiar observances, manners, and opinions are explained. Translation would be valuable, but publication of the original would be desirable and necessary for the preservation of the work, which is not known to have been printed and of which only a few manuscript copies are known to exist.
6. Beschi's Portuguese, Latin and Tamil dictionary. In this the alphabetical arrangement follows the Portuguese, not the Latin. "It would form an excellent foundation for an English Tamil Dictionary, but in its present state could be of little utility, unless a knowledge of the Portuguese previously existed."

These grammars and dictionaries were the work of a man perfectly qualified for the task "by previous education, by long and intimate intercourse with the people of the Country, and by a radical knowledge of the two dialects of the language he has illuminated." The Committee expressed its surprise that "these works should have been allowed to fall into oblivion," given that the country where these two dialects of Tamil were in use was part of the British dominions, and the cultivation of this language "has long been of the first importance to our subjects and ourselves" (ibid., para. 49).

> These works indeed were the produce of religious enthusiasm and since the operation of that enthusiasm has been diverted from this quarter of the Globe, every interest of a worldly nature, all considerations of commerce,

> of politics, and of humanity have been too weak even to preserve a remembrance of them, much less to supply their place; two miserable dictionaries, and a still more miserable Grammar of the low dialect are all that have ever been composed in English in the Tamil Language. . . . There has recently been printed a vocabulary English and Tamil which is still more defective than the works here noticed. (Ibid.)

For Telugu, "though not cultivated in the same degree as the Tamil, which is scarcely exceeded by any language in the number and variety of its compositions original and translated," there were several grammars, all written not in Telugu but in Sanskrit, the main one being the *Āndhravyākaraṇa* of Nannaya Bhaṭṭa. The Committee thought that Nannaya's work would be a good foundation for writing a grammar of Telugu in English, making use also of other works of the same kind such as the *Āndhraśabdacintāmaṇi,* a commentary on the former, or rather, a larger work on the same plan. Many natives at Madras were perfectly competent to translate these works, and would do so for a suitable reward. Though the Committee thought that writing such a grammar would take considerable time to complete, this is exactly what was later done, at the College, by the secretary, A. D. Campbell, and it was published by the College Press in 1816. At the time, there were also various English translations of a small grammar of Telugu originally written in French. Though incomplete, the grammar contained nearly all the rudiments of the language and was correct as far as it went, the Committee said. It was, the Committee believed, superior in every way to the English grammar of Telugu edited by Protestant missionaries at Vepery and was widely used.

A complete and very excellent Telugu dictionary arranged alphabetically had recently been compiled at Masulipatam by a Komati of that area, Mamadi Venkayya (whom I have mentioned in chapter 3), called *Āndhradīpaka.* Being all in Telugu, it would not be useful to students till they had made considerable progress in the language. The Committee noted that a complete Telugu-English dictionary could eventually be made on the basis of this work, and with that in mind it should be immediately published, "saving, of course, the copyright to the learned and respectable author" (ibid., para. 54). Venkayya had also completed a dictionary of Sanskrit, in alphabetical order, in the Telugu script, which could be printed at the Egmore Press. There existed, in addition, a Telugu-Sanskrit-French dictionary which might assist the compiler of a Telugu-English dictionary but was of little use in its present form; the explanations were correct but brief, the Sanskrit was imperfect, and the words were arranged alphabetically according to the roman rather than the Telugu script.

As for Kannada and Malayalam, the Committee considered them "very inferior dialects." During the most flourishing period of the Canarese (i.e., Vijayanagara) empire, the Committee noted, Telugu (rather than Kannada) had been the language of court and literature; while the "mental slavery" to which the Nambudiri brahmins subjected the aborigines of Kerala prevented the development of Malayalam literature. Nevertheless, both languages were spoken by large populations under British rule, and so some provision had to be made for learning them. Kannada had at least one grammar plus a dictionary, but the Committee did not know of any grammar or dictionary of Kannada composed in a European language. The Committee had heard of works on Malayalam in both Dutch and Portuguese, but the only work any of the Committee members had seen was the grammar of Mr. Drummond, "which might be greatly improved here, for as this dialect is the immediate, though degenerate offspring of the Tamil, a knowledge of the parent language would afford great facilities in correcting and extending it" (ibid., para. 58). The lack at Madras of type fonts for the scripts of these languages also posed an obstacle.

The Committee's take on Sanskrit is most interesting. An extensive knowledge of Sanskrit grammar could not promote the learning of the southern languages, given that it has a different grammatical structure. Because of the many Sanskrit loanwords in the South Indian languages, acquaintance with Sanskrit was nevertheless useful, especially knowledge of the rules for forming words from roots and the meanings of various suffixes, which teachers could easily convey to their students. Junior servants, then, *should* be encouraged to pay some attention to Sanskrit, and elementary textbooks such as those recently published at Calcutta should be put at their disposal. The best Sanskrit grammar to date was Colebrooke's, of which the first volume had been published. It included all the rules for the formation of nouns and furnished all the information about Sanskrit that is useful for the study of the southern languages. Colebrooke had also translated the main Sanskrit "vocabulary," the ancient compilation of Amarasiṃha, the *Amarakośa*. William Carey and Charles Wilkins had each published complete grammars of Sanskrit, and Forster the first part of another, the second part of which was in press. The Committee recommended that a few copies of each should be deposited at the Madrassah for the use of both native teachers and British students.

This, then, is the Committee's assessment of the state of "elementary works." Besides reading it as a report to the Government by a committee, we can also read it autobiographically, as a statement by Ellis about his own formation. That Beschi was his hero is evident here and elsewhere in his writings, and it is evident as well that he went to great lengths to locate Beschi's writings in print and in manuscript. We can hardly go wrong to infer from the detail and warmth of the assessment of Beschi's contribution—especially alongside Ellis's early statement about how he learned Tamil, beginning with the higher register and taking a wide, comparative view of the South Indian languages (MPC 27 June 1800; discussed in chapter 3)—that Ellis drew deeply on the works of Beschi in his own education in Tamil, perhaps aided by some of those Indians educated at the Jesuit school at Pondicherry of whom he speaks so well. His interest in Telugu, second only to his interest in Tamil and, as we know indirectly, formed very early after his arrival in India, conforms as well to the profile of this report, and we may well suppose that his admiration for Mamadi Venkayya of Masulipatam was formed during his years at that city as judge of the zillah court. The subordinate character of his own interest in Kannada and Malayalam is also evident. What we cannot perceive from this report is how deeply knowledgeable Ellis became in Sanskrit literature. Shot through this survey, finally, is a series of ideas about the languages of the South that anticipate, indeed embody, Ellis's version of the idea of a Dravidian language family: the connectedness of the four major languages with one another, their derivation from Tamil, their nonderivation from Sanskrit, and the presence in them of Sanskrit words not as indigenous formations but as loanwords.

THE PLAN OF THE COLLEGE

What was the relation of the College to the Dravidian proof, which was published by the College Press four years after its founding? When I began this research I supposed that the College was the *cause* of the Dravidian proof, in the sense that it was the site where a synoptic view of the Dravidian languages became possible and a body of scholars who had the necessary skills for their comparison had assembled. I had in mind a pleasing correspondence between what I imagined to be the physical structure of the College, dispensing instruction in the languages of South India in adjacent classrooms, and by their very juxtaposition giving rise, in the mind of Ellis and his circle, to the Dravidian idea. That is, the need to provide teaching in the languages spoken in the territories under the Government of Madras led to the creation of the College, which required the collection of the scholars of South Indian languages in a centralized space where their vocabularies and grammatical structures were exposed and, inevitably, compared.

The conception of a homology between the structure of the College and the structure of the Dravidian idea proved to be correct, but, as we see from the Committee's report dated 20 October 1811, the causal relation is the other way around: the Dravidian idea is already evident in the report that proposed the creation of the College and gave it its structure. The College was not the cause of the Dravidian idea; rather, the Dravidian idea was the cause of the College's structure from the outset. We need, then, to examine the College not so much in its actual, historical functioning during its initial seven years under Ellis's direct influence, but in his *plan* for the College and the way in which the Dravidian idea is woven into it.

For the plan to be realized, it had to be made appealing to a government that had shown interest in promoting the study of languages by its junior servants but reluctance to spend very much money on it beyond the one-time rewards of 1,000 pagodas and offers to subsidize the publication of grammars and dictionaries that would be useful to the junior servants in their pursuit of these rewards. These feeble gestures had failed. The small number of junior servants successfully examining for the reward was disappointing by itself, and the pitifully low proportion of junior servants pursuing and winning rewards in the South Indian languages was more so. The Committee had an opening to propose a bold new departure but one that was not too costly—something like the College of Fort William but on a much cheaper plan. The project had to appear to be value for money to the Governor in Council at Madras, and above all to the Court of Directors in London.

The price tag for the College of Fort St. George was kept low by putting all the teaching in the hands of Indian teachers, instructed and supervised by Indian head masters whose salaries were modest, rather than appointing Europeans as professors at high salaries, as at the college in Calcutta. Overall supervision of the College was put in the hands of the Board of Superintendence, whose members included the official translators to government and a secretary, A. D. Campbell. All the supervisors had other full-time positions for which they were paid; I find no evidence that they drew any supplementary pay for overseeing the work of the College, and there is no provision for it in the financial statements submitted by the Board to the Governor in Council, excepting a salary of 50 pagodas for the secretary. While the proposal for a college inevitably involved some additional expense, therefore, the addition was not great when seen in relation to that of the College of Fort William. The College of Fort St. George was the functional equivalent of the latter and, at first glance, a smaller version of it. But on closer inspection we see that it was on quite a different plan. Moreover, the Committee proposing the college was able to subtract from the cost of a proper college the existing cost of the Madrassah, which was, they showed, largely a waste, since the junior servants were obliged to live so far away that they did not take instruction there. The increased cost would not be great, and the college would deliver the language learning that was so badly wanting.

To see how the idea of a Dravidian language family gave the College its structural logic, we need to consider the plan of the College in some detail, specifically, the provisions for Indian head masters and teachers, the course of study, and the College Press. I begin with a sketch of the governance of the College and the overall change in the language policy of the Madras Government that the proposal for the College introduced.

The Board of Superintendence generated voluminous reports to the Madras Government, including annual reports on the overall state of the College, reports on the twice-yearly examinations of the junior servants, reports on the training of the native teachers and law students, and others. For present purposes we will consult the first annual report, for the year 1812, submitted to the Government with the expectation that it would be forwarded to the Court of Directors in London. It is very long—289 paragraphs—virtually a book. It is dated 1 January 1813 and was entered into the Madras Public Consultations on 2 February. The College had by then become a reality, and the recommendations of the Committee had been elaborated into a structure governed by a set of proposed rules which were in actual use as they awaited the sanction of London (MPC 2 Feb 1813, para. 149).

Under these rules, the College was governed by the Board of Superintendence, consisting of the translators to government and other members appointed by the Governor in Council. Members submitted matters for consideration at meetings of the Board through the senior member present, who for the first seven years was Ellis, except for brief intervals when he was on leave and out of station. During deliberations the opinions of junior members were to be taken first, and other members according to rank; the senior member had the deciding vote in case of a tie. The Board was to meet twice monthly. The day-to-day supervision of the College was to have been undertaken by Board members on a rotation, but this proved impractical and in a fairly short time this rule was dropped and the secretary, who attended on a daily basis in any case, carried out this function, implementing the decisions of the Board and overseeing the head masters, teachers, and junior servants. The Board was to hold examinations of the junior servants twice a year, on the first Wednesday of June and December, and on subsequent days as needed. An annual report (which in practice incorporated the report on the December examinations) was to be submitted to the Government on the first of the year and forwarded to the Court of Directors.

The creation of the College brought about big changes in the lives of newly arrived junior servants, and not all of them may have been welcome. Hitherto, junior servants had been on their own, employed in minor roles in government offices of the city while presumably studying languages with a hired teacher in their rented lodgings in the cheaper suburbs and staying away from the Madrassah in the Fort. They were out of direct supervision after working hours, and if their pay was on the low side, their credit with moneylenders was good. Now the junior servant was to come under the charge of the College and its Board of Superintendence for a period of three years—following his two years at the East India College at Hertford—unless the Board of Superintendence recommended his removal to the Government at an earlier time, that is, if he reached the desirable level of language skills and was ready for full-time employment in the service.

What the Board had largely achieved was a supervisory control over the newest junior servants. The College did not at the beginning have its own building and had to rent cramped quarters, during which time the junior servants found housing where they could. But eventually the College became a live-in facility, and the supervision of the junior servants' lives became complete. The other great change was in keeping the junior servants in Madras for several years of full-time study and not sending them immediately to posts in the interior, or even to low-level jobs in government offices in the city. The withdrawal of as much as three years' labor at even low levels of skill was a large cost of the new system that did not appear in the various financial statements the Board submitted to the Government.

The Board was greatly concerned about the woefully inadequate starting pay for the junior servants at 50 pagodas, plus a mere 10 pagodas for housing, leading the junior servants into debt to moneylenders. The Board proposed that the pay be raised to 75 and 100 pagodas in steps, as students showed progress in the mastery of languages and other aspects of their education. This created an incentive to progress in learning languages in addition to the prize for proficiency. Each student was assigned a teacher of his own as he prepared for the twice-yearly proficiency examinations. The 1,000 pagodas reward for proficiency in a language was continued, but now the reward would not be granted for Marathi, Sanskrit, Hindustani, Persian, or Arabic unless the student had previously passed the examination in Tamil, Telugu, Malayalam, or Kannada (ibid., Junior Civil Servants, rule 7).

The result of all these developments was an enormous change, truly a linguistic revolution. For one thing, the creation of the College displaced the Madrassah, governed by the culture of the munshi, who was now reduced to a teacher of one language among many within a European-style college over which he had no say. For another, the restructuring of language preferences set aside the essentially Mughal pattern, centuries old, of treating Persian and Hindustani as the leading languages of governance. At the same time, Tamil, Telugu, Kannada, and Malayalam, which had played a distinctly subordinate role to Persian and Hindustani in government culture and practice, were brought to the fore and treated as a set of languages indigenous to the South, as distinguished from languages brought to the South by conquest. In this way a new pattern regarding language was set for British-Indian Madras, though the military service continued to promote the study of Hindustani and Persian in the manner of the Mughals.

A curious effect of promoting the languages we call Dravidian to the forefront of the training for civil servants was that it promoted the study of Sanskrit at the same time. This had to do with the language training available in England at the East India College. The Board of Superintendence was critical of the fact that junior civil servants came out of their two years at Hertford prepared, for the most part, in Persian and Hindustani. Of the languages taught at Hertford at the time of the report (1813)—these two plus Bengali and Sanskrit—the last was the only one of direct relevance for the South. They recommended that junior servants bound for Madras be advised to take up Sanskrit as a good background preparation for learning the languages of the South; the Government of Madras forwarded the recommendation to the Court of Directors in London, and it received their approval. The effects of this change were palpable. Some years later the Board of Superintendence remarked that the students now coming out of the East India College (by now at Haileybury) prepared in Sanskrit were progressing well, thanks to the merits of Alexander Hamilton, the Sanskrit professor there (indeed, Hamilton was the first professor of Sanskrit in Europe; MPC 14 Aug 1816). Thus the needs of the civil service at Madras consolidated the teaching of Sanskrit at Haileybury. And while the Southern languages were being foregrounded by the College, Sanskrit, too, was being singled out as an important language of South India, further contributing to the displacement of Persian and Hindustani in colonial Madras.

INDIAN HEAD MASTERS, TEACHERS, AND STUDENTS

While the purpose of the College was to give adequate language training to the junior servants newly arrived from England, in order to accomplish that purpose the College also became a training school for Indians, presided over by leading scholars and, as such, a center for the revival of letters in the languages of the South. As we shall see later, this was not an accidental or secondary consequence but one which Ellis had very much in view from the start. However, the creating of a machinery for the teaching of Indians was justified on the strictest grounds of necessity.

The principle evil which the College was invented to overcome was the poor quality of the language instruction available to the junior servants, and its cause was the teachers' lack of grammatical knowledge of both English and the languages they taught, as well as the fact that they were poorly paid, with little prospect of permanent employment. The first proposal the Committee made to raise the standard of teaching was to require all munshis and other teachers at the Madrassah to be examined, and to receive a certificate from a Madrassah committee appointed for the purpose in order to continue as teachers. The Madrassah committee in fact evolved into the Board of Superintendence, and the arrangement to create a body of qualified teachers quickly developed into the College of Fort St. George. Attracting a body of intelligent teacher candidates with the prospect of permanent employment at good pay and training them in grammar under able scholars was the nub of the matter.

Besides the need for teachers, therefore, there was need for a cadre of Indian head masters to teach "a correct, and grammatical knowledge of English, and of their own languages, which few profess" and which was not being conveyed in the schools for dubashes (MPC 3 Mar 1812, p. 1259), This being so, the College was to admit a body of Indian students aspiring to be teachers, place them under the tutelage of the head masters, and have them sit for examinations in hopes of gaining certificates that would allow them to teach the junior servants in the College. The College, then, was to be a school for Indians as well as British junior servants, a site at which grammatical knowledge of the South Indian languages was cultivated and disseminated.

When the College was first proposed, the Committee was at pains to suggest the highest pay for teachers that it judged would be acceptable to the Government while keeping the overall costs low. The highest salary, that of the head masters, would be fixed at 50 pagodas. This, the highest pay of the best-qualified and most senior Indian staff of the College, was the rate at which the junior servants *began* their careers at Madras, which, as we have seen, the Committee regarded as inadequate. Even so, the Committee seems to have anticipated difficulty from the Government and was at pains to muster its best arguments in making the case. This figure, the Committee held, was the minimum that could be offered with hope of attracting qualified persons, and even on this salary they apprehended much difficulty in procuring fully qualified native teachers (MPC 3 March 1812, p. 1261). The plan called for a full complement of head masters, one each for English, Tamil, Telugu, Sanskrit, Persian, and Hindustani, but only in the fullness of time. To get started, they said, it was not necessary to employ a single head master for each language. For one thing, the headship for Telugu and Sanskrit could be combined in one. Moreover, as the service was already well supplied with Persian and Hindustani teachers, the appointment of head masters in those languages could be postponed to the future, when it might be necessary to prepare a new generation of teachers. And they need only appoint an acting head English master, at half pay, for now. Thus the highest salaries were kept to a minimum. The Government grumbled but sanctioned the amount.

For the teachers it was essential to hold out the prospect of permanent employment and liberal pay, as "nothing less than these inducements could influence respectable Natives to pursue the particular studies requisite to the attainment of this object." Those who offered themselves for the situation of native teacher to junior servants were to be arranged in three classes. The first class consisted of those who were qualified to be teachers and needed no further training. The second class was made up of candidates studying under the head masters and preparing themselves for the examinations leading to the certificates which would allow them to be assigned as teachers to junior servants. These were to be paid. Teachers in the first class had a salary of 15 pagodas per month if they were attending one of the junior servants, to be increased to 20 or 25 if it was desirable to assign them to more than one person. Those in the second class were to be paid between 4 and 10 pagodas, as a kind of retaining salary so that prospective teachers would be assured of income while waiting for an opening in the teaching ranks, in response to the eight to ten junior servants arriving at Madras each year. The third class consisted of volunteer students who entered the College and received instruction from the head masters with hopes of eventually filling vacancies in the second class, but at no pay. "We have reason to believe, that numerous respectable Natives would be glad to place their younger relatives under the Masters. We think that great public advantage might be derived were some of those most respectably connected admitted to study at the institution, and the Masters allowed to accept of honorary gifts which at fixed periods of the year are customarily made by Natives to the Superior Class of their Instructors," a kind of *gurudakṣiṇa* (ibid., p. 1270).

By these modest arrangements the Committee was authorized to appoint three, or really two and a half, head masters. The most brilliant of these appointments was that of Pattabhirama Shastri, who in the *Sarvadevavilāsa* is called the foremost pandit in its list of influential brahmins (*vipraprabhu;* Raghavan 1957–58, pt. 1, 409). He was known to Ellis before, having supplied testimony to a committee on which Ellis served concerning aspects of the right- and left-hand division of castes which had rioted in 1809, in connection with which Ellis wrote a learned minute. The Tamil head master was Chidambara Vadiyar, a Pandaram. The half position was occupied by the young Udayagiri Venkatanarayana, who was eventually promoted to head English master. Persian and Hindustani had to do without a head master for the time being, and so suffered a kind of demotion. The Committee thought it sufficient to make Sayyid Abdul Qader the head Persian munshi, a gesture of recognition for his former status which put him at the front of the twenty native teachers comprising the first class, who were paid 10 pagodas. The second class, of native students, contained fourteen members, each at 4 pagodas, and there was an unspecified number of volunteer students.

Soon after its creation the College undertook to train Indians in Hindu and Muhammadan law, and teaching these subjects to Indian students was made a part of the head masters' duties. Law examinations were given that would qualify the students to become either pandits and munsifs in the courts, giving expert rulings on Dharmaśāstra and Shariah law, or pleaders. The junior servants were also to be given a rudimentary training in Hindu and Muhammadan law, as well as the Regulations of Government. But it is the teaching of law to Indian students that deserves to be noted. It is a little-known fact that the College of Fort St. George, in this way, became the first colonial educational institution in Madras through which Indians could enter the legal profession. Thus, while ostensibly being devoted to the training of the junior servants, the College from the start was a center of higher learning for Indians as well.

The headmasterships were positions of great authority and power, their holders presiding over the body of Indian students and supervising their training in grammar and law. The head masters were encouraged to write books that would serve the needs of their students, and the College Press undertook to publish them. It is likely that the new head masters were previously known to Ellis; Pattabhirama Shastri certainly was, as we have seen. He and the others contributed directly to the Dravidian proof, as we shall see in the next chapter. Udayagiri Venkatanarayana assisted A. D. Campbell in the making of his Telugu grammar. Ellis's sheristadar, Sankaraiah, later held the position of head English master, and, though he did not hold the position long, he in any case was closely involved in scholarly investigations with Ellis throughout their association. In short, we can suppose a close working relationship between the head masters and the British members of the Board of Superintendence, especially Ellis and Campbell, and the head masters' active involvement in new writing and publication in South Indian languages.

THE COLLEGE PRESS

In its report of 20 October 1811, as we have seen, the Committee identified a number of grammars and dictionaries of the four major languages of the South that should be printed with government assistance. The Committee gave no information about how this was to be accomplished, but subsequently, in the 29 January 1812 report of the Committee for the Improvement of Superintendence of the Studies of the Junior Civil Servants, also headed by Ellis (MPC 3 Mar 1812), it was proposed to place the Press under this committee's immediate inspection, for the complex nature of the books to be printed "will require an unremitted attention on our parts to secure even tolerable correctness" (ibid., p. 1273). This was followed by a surprising offer: "We have reason however to believe that with some assistance from Government this difficulty will easily be overcome. Our Senior Member has offered to place at the disposal of the Institution, the requisite printing presses, and a complete font of Tamil types." The senior member was of course Ellis. The intriguing information that he had printing presses and Tamil types of his own is not explained, and one wonders what he used them for. The inventory is given in the margin: one large press, one small press, "Europe Iron work for a large Press," a font of small letters weighing four hundred pounds, and a font of large types weighing two hundred pounds. In addition, the superintendent of the Government Press at Egmore had agreed to supply Telugu type, Telugu workmen, ink, and so forth, on condition of receiving some books for sale to benefit the Male Asylum, an orphanage for the sons of British soldiers who were trained as printers and did the printing of the *Madras almanac*. The Government would need to furnish paper and authorize the expense for a person to superintend the workmen, the Committee said. A font of English type, recently imported from Europe, "by far the best that [has] ever been brought to India, as a reference to the Commercial Circulater, the press work of which is executed by a font exactly similar, will demonstrate," could be had for about 2,000 pagodas. Evidently the Committee, and probably Ellis himself, had gone into the matter in considerable detail.

We see adjustments being made to this plan in the subsequent report, dated 1 January 1813 (MPC 3 Feb 1813). Five boys from the Male Asylum had been provided to the College Press by the superintendent of the Government Press, but the arrangement had not worked out; though well qualified as compositors, they were too young to undertake the harder labors of the Press. Instead it had been necessary to employ "natives acquainted with the business," namely, one supervisor (10 pagodas), one press man (4 pagodas), and one ball man (3 pagodas). English and Tamil type were in hand, but fonts for the other languages had yet to be found.

Two fonts of Telugu type had been cast, the first of which had been cut and cast at Madras about twelve years previous by the senior member of the Board—another tantalizing bit of information about Ellis, which tells us that his interest in Telugu started very early. This had been employed in the Government Press but "had long since been exhausted" (ibid., para. 160). The second Telugu font, cast in England and currently in use at the Government Press, was not suitable for more than "common work required in printing the regulations and occasional advertisement of Government" (ibid.) and could not be of use to the College. Hiring someone to cut 240 puncheons for all the characters and conjuncts, at a rate of one a day, would call for tools, five hundred pounds of type metal, hire of the cutter of puncheons for eight months at 10 pagodas, hire of someone to cast the type for four months at 4 pagodas, pay of a bellows boy for eight months at 1 pagoda, and purchase of charcoal—altogether 235 pagodas, 36 fanam, and 20 cash. For a slightly larger cost, the report said, the work could be speeded to a conclusion by hiring several cutters of puncheons working simultaneously.

While awaiting the Government's sanction for the making of a font of Telugu type, the College Press would start work with the existing English and Tamil fonts, beginning with Beschi's *Grammar of the low Tamil,* this being the most immediately useful of his two grammars for a beginner. Furthermore, "as a work of a more easy and elementary Nature was required for the use of the Native students belonging to the College," the Press also planned to print the *Tamizh Surucca Vilacum, brief exposition of the Tamil,* a Tamil grammar composed by the head Tamil master, Chidambara Pandaram (Chidambara Vadiyar), following the system of the *Tolkāppiyam.*

A complete bibliography of the works published by the College Press would be very valuable. The College and its head masters came to play a large role in the "revival of letters" in South India and the transition from the culture of the manuscript to the editing of printed works, and from royal patronage to patronage by government institutions and the market for printed works, as we shall see in chapter 6. Indeed, the study of publication and readership in nineteenth-century South India is woefully lacking and badly needed; we have a few catalogues published in the nineteenth century, such as those of John Murdoch (1865) for Tamil printed books and William Taylor (1857–62) for Oriental manuscripts, but more and better works are wanted, along the lines of what Kathleen Diehl has done for colonial Calcutta (Diehl 1964, 1969, 1971). As to the College Press, the difficulty is that the works were published in very small numbers and are rare or impossible to find. A place to begin is the "List of books printed, printing, or preparing for press at the College of Fort St. George," issued 22 December 1815, a few years after the Press's creation, which shows an ambitious plan for the Press. I give the list in paraphrase which follows the original quite closely, but with some abbreviation and summary.

TAMIL WORKS

Printed: *A Latin grammar of the low Tamil: Grammatica Latino-Tamulica, sive de vulgari Tamulica linguae idiomate kotuntamil dicto,* by J. C. Beschi.

Preparing for the Press: *A Latin grammar of the high Tamil, Grammatica Latino-Tamulica, ubi de elegantiori linguae tamulicae dialecto centamil dicto, cui adduntur Tamulica Poseos rudimenta,* also by Beschi.

Printing: *A Tamil and Latin dictionary.* A dictionary of the low dialect, forming with the next a perfect dictionary of the whole language, by Beschi.

Printing: *Caturakarati.* A dictionary in Tamil, in four parts, *peyar* (meanings of words), *porul* (synonyms), *tokai* ("the subordinate species of the technical and general terms of science and literature") and *totai* (a rhyming dictionary), by Beschi.

Printed: *Ramayana Uttarakantam.* The translation from Sanskrit into Tamil of the Uttarakanda of the *Ramayana* by Chidambara Vadiyar, Head Tamil Master of the College. A class book for Junior Civil Servants attached to the College.

Printing: *Tamilcurukkavilakkam.* A treatise on Tamil grammar for the use of beginning Native students at the College, by Chidambara Vadiar. A prose exposition of the meaning of the sutras of grammar, i.e., of the *Tolkappiyam.*

Prepared for the Press: *Mitaksharavivakarakandam.* A translation from Sanskrit into Tamil of the Vyavaharakanda of the *Ritu Mitakshara* of Vijnanesvara, begun by the late Porur Vadiyar, completed and revised by his brother, Chidambara Vadiyar. Verses of the *smriti,* gloss, and easy prose commentary to facilitate the memorization of the text and the comprehension of its meaning.

TELUGU WORKS

Prepared for the Press: *A grammar of the Teloogoo language, commonly termed Gentoo,* by A. D. Campbell, Member of the Board of Superintendence. The author has collected the substance of native grammars, but arranged the matter similar to that generally observed by European grammars. "This work, of which the copy-right has been purchased by Government, may be expected to appear in print, at an early period, as the fount of Teloogoo Types now casting for it in the College is nearly finished."

Prepared for the Press: *Andhradipaka.* A very voluminous and excellent dictionary of Telugu by Mamadi Venkayya, a learned Komati of Masulipatam, containing 30,000–40,000 words in alphabetical order. It will be of use to the student after he has overcome the first difficulties of learning the language, and will in some degree supply the want of a Telugu-English dictionary, "the compilation of which, if ever undertaken, must be a work of a great labour and time" (though, in fact, one was later made by A. D. Campbell and published by the College Press). "The work of Mamadi Venkaya is rather deficient in pure Teloogoo words, the columns of the Dictionary being filled chiefly by those of Sanscrit origin, and the illustration of the meaning of each word is also rather too concise, but the work is, on the whole, highly valuable, and, to encourage the composition of similar books by learned Natives, the copy-right has been purchased by the Government at a liberal price."

Preparing for the Press: *A vocabulary, English and Teloogoo,* the words of the common being distinguished from those of the classical dialect, by J. M'Kerrell [John McKerrell], Esq., of the Civil Service, Telugu translator to Government and ex officio member of the Board of Superintendence.

KANNADA WORKS

Preparing for the Press: *A grammar of the Carnataka language,* commonly called the Canarese, founded upon an approved treatise in the classical dialect. By M'Kerrell.

Preparing for the Press: *A vocabulary of English and Carnataca* to which is added a list of Carnataca roots. By M'Kerrell.

These two works, planned for publication as soon as the Telugu font of type was ready, would be "perhaps the first in any European language that treat of the elements of this useful tongue and when completed will prove a great acquisition to the College, as constituting a set of elementary works on one of the three grand dialects of the Peninsula at present less known then either of the other two."

ENGLISH WORKS

Preparing for publication: *Dissertations on the several modes of computing time observed by the inhabitants of the Indian Peninsula,* and on the method of converting time, computed according to any of these modes, into European time and vice-versa, by Captain J. Warren of the Madras 56th Regiment of Foot. Copyright purchased by the government. The three modes of computing time are the Hijri era of the Muslims, based on the Prophet's flight from Mecca to Medina in 620 A.D.; the Hindu solar year employed by the Saka era beginning 78 A.D., which is used where Tamil is spoken; and the Hindu soli-lunar year employing the Saka era used in the northern provinces, where Telugu is spoken. The work includes the translation of a tract by Beschi on the Hindu solar year reckoning, according to the methods of the *Vakiyam* and *Siddhantam,* the leading Tamil treatises on astronomy, with rules, tables, and examples for converting such time into "European time, and European time into the solar time of the Hindus."

Not preparing for the College Press, but about to be published in communication with the College and under immediate patronage of the Government: *A lexicon of that peculiar dialect of the Hindostanee language which prevails in the Dekhan of South of India,* by H. Harris, M.D., Second Member of the Medical Board at this Presidency. A dictionary of the dialect of Hindustani current in the Madras Presidency.

In this list we see again the primacy of Tamil and Telugu. Kannada, however, is not neglected, thanks to John McKerrell, and the College Press edition of his grammar was the first English grammar of Kannada to have been published. As for Malayalam, Ellis made several inquiries, with Erskine's help, trying to locate the font of type that had been used to print Drummond's grammar, but without success (Ellis to Erskine 10 Mar 1813, NLS Mss. 36.1.5, ff. 62–71). We also see in this list the impulse to use the College Press as an instrument to "promote the revival of letters" among Indian scholars of the Madras Presidency, using the newly introduced notion of copyright and encouraging the Government to make generous copyright purchases as a way of promoting scholarship.

The ambitions for the College Press far outran its shoestring budget. The scale of operations was ludicrously small. The presses were operated from the verandah of the College. The projects were complex and needed skilled compositors in Tamil, Telugu, Kannada, and English. Telugu type had to be made from scratch. The type was insufficient to do a whole book at once, and the type for several pages had to be torn down when they were struck off so the next grouping of pages could be set in type. The type was subject to battering and, because lead had some resale value, it was subject to theft as well, so its use had to be under constant supervision, and periodically it had to be weighed as a check against pilfering. Good paper had to be shipped from England; it was expensive and scarce.

We get a measure of the degree to which the reach of the Press exceeded its grasp in a letter written to the Government shortly after Ellis's death, proposing a revision in the rules of the College. The letter also gives us a sense of how the remaining members of the Board drew the balance of the Ellis years, and the problems that needed to be addressed. The teaching arrangements had worked well, and a body of competent teachers had been formed under the tutelage of the head masters; the College in its central function was a success. The two areas in which the College did not live up to expectations were the course of study, which I will discuss in the next chapter, and the College Press, "which it must be confessed is in an imperfect and defective state" (MPC 4 Dec 1819, para. 31).

Since the College was established in 1812, according to the Board, only four books had been printed, namely, Beschi's Latin grammar of the low Tamil, the Tamil translation of the Uttarakāṇḍa of the *Rāmāyaṇa,* Campbell's Telugu grammar, and a book of Telugu tales. Books still in press were (OIOC Mss. Eur.D.29; following the original wording):

1. Beschi's Tamil dictionary, the *Caturakaradi.*
2. The *Treatise on Tamil grammar* by the head Tamil Master, commenced in 1815 and only half printed.
3. A translation of the *Kural* of Tiruvalluvar, "accompanied by a full commentary by the late Mr. Ellis," commenced 1818 and two-thirds printed.
4. Babington's translation of Beschi's grammar of the high Tamil, just commenced.
5. A second edition of Campbell's Telugu grammar, one-fourth printed.
6. Campbell's Telugu dictionary, just commenced.
7. A work on Arabic grammar by the head Arabic master, commenced 1817 and two-thirds printed.

Works "which, with a proper establishment, might have passed through the press within two months, have not been completed within one or two years" (MPC 4 Dec 1819, para. 34). However, with some changes, not only these books but all the translations of the Regulations of Government into the native languages could well be done by the College Press, whose fonts of type for Persian and Telugu were greatly superior to those at the Male Asylum Press. The Board proceeded to show how the College Press could be improved, at minimal additional expense, by purchasing two new presses, hiring a superintendent of the Press at a salary suitable to attract a qualified candidate, and no longer using compositors from the Male Asylum, whose numbers had dwindled from eight or ten to one, causing the work to languish. With additional support, the College Press did manage to produce a series of important works, and Ellis's grand hopes for it were at least partially fulfilled.

MAMADI VENKAYYA

In his letters to Erskine, Ellis sent information about the College, which interested Erskine as a possible model for Bombay. Ellis made it clear that, while the College was established to educate the junior servants, it was also intended to promote learning among Indians, though it was necessary to keep this second purpose in the background. In a letter of 25 April 1812, when the College was just getting started, Ellis spoke of how it would give "encouragement to literary pursuit among the natives, which we know to have been greatly promoted by the establishment of the College at Calcutta." In this matter he felt that Madras has the greater chance of success than Calcutta, "as I have no doubt we have better materials."

> In truth a literary spirit always has been and to the present day continues to be prevalent in Southern India; besides poetical compositions, which, those of the lighter sort especially, here abound, we have recently seen works of considerable merit produced; among these may be reckoned, to mention no more, a compilation from nearly all the Sanscrit Dictionaries, arranged alphabetically, and a translation of the Commentary of Vijnáneswara into Tamil. These are works of considerable labor and were undertaken without any expectation of advantage, and scarcely any of fame. To what then may we look forward if works of utility are systematically encouraged by rewards and if the College Press is the certain road to notority? (NLS Mss. 36.1.5, ff. 76–77)

A year later, when the College had taken shape, Ellis, in a letter to Erskine of 10 March 1813, expressed pleasure in having got the necessary sanction of the Government to acquire new works for publication from outside the College staff. He sent a copy of the printed rules for the College and observed that the Government had placed it "on a very liberal footing" with regard to not only the junior servants, whose education was the immediate object of the College, but also "the natives attached to the Institution" and the program of encouraging the composition of literature:

> On this subject we agree perfectly; though it is not a point I must insist upon to others, I cannot help anticipating even greater benefits from the College by the influence it will have on the native character, than from that which is ostensibly its principal motive, the instruction of the Junior

> Servants. The influence has already begun to operate, we shall shortly have in the Press works on various subjects by natives attached to the Institution, and as we have begun to act on that part of the rules which authorizes us to purchase the copy right of Authors (see Table first Section XX) the encouragement to literary pursuits it is to be expected will extend itself beyond the bounds of our immediate superintendence (ibid., ff. 62–63).

One senses from this passage that the ostensible purpose of the College served, for Ellis, as a pretext for its true purpose, the one he most prized and strove for, namely, the "revival of letters" in South India.

We can get some sense of what the revival of letters meant under the changed circumstances of colonial rule by following the case of Mamadi Venkayya and the purchase of copyright on his Telugu dictionary. First, however, it needs to be said that the College actively sought to form a scholarly library that would include not only printed books—such as the language-learning texts it purchased from Calcutta, the products of its own publishing program, and the collection of Colin Mackenzie, when he was reassigned to Calcutta to become director of the Survey of India—but also manuscripts in Sanskrit, Tamil, and Telugu. Manuscripts were collected systematically by sending out two of the College's Indian staff, one to the north and one the south, to acquire copies of important texts in Telugu and Tamil. This happened in a period when the royal patronage of manuscript libraries, and therefore the entire machinery of manuscript production, was in decline. The College collection, therefore, was an important bridge to the new age of print editions of ancient texts supported by the market and the new cultural institutions, which served the functions previously served by royal courts.

Mamadi Venkayya (1764–1834) was a remarkable man, a Komati merchant supplying "clay goods," or crockery and the like, to the Dutch, French, and English factories until the year 1787, when he "was obliged to remain quiet for want of suitable employment" (MPC 28 Sept 1813, Mamadi Venkayya to Collector of Masulipatam 2 May). He had acquired a knowledge of Telugu and Sanskrit literature as a youth, and in his retirement from trade he became a scholar, compiling dictionaries of Telugu and Sanskrit. It took him fourteen years to complete these, and his scholarly ambitions were carried out against the opposition of local brahmins who, according to William Thackeray, Telugu translator to the Madras Government (and uncle of the novelist), twice pulled down his house to discourage him (MPC 15 Mar 1811). These two dictionaries the College wished to publish. The Government would not authorize purchase of the

Sanskrit dictionary, as Colebrooke was preparing to publish one at Calcutta, but it did authorize a sum of 1,000 star pagodas to purchase the copyright of Mamadi Venkayya's Telugu dictionary. The College Board, in its letter to the collector, asked that as much publicity as possible should be given to the matter, "as by the purchase of the copy-right of this work by Government being more generally known it may be expected that the exertion of literary talents similar to those of Mamadie Vencaya will be encouraged" (MPC 28 Sept 1813, Board to Collector 6 April).

At the time, Mamadi Venkayya was bedridden with a serious illness from which it was not certain he would survive. This complicated the negotiations, which were carried out by the College through the Collector of Masulipatam. The exchange of letters has been preserved, and it shows how perplexing the idea of copyright, possibly being introduced in South India for the first time, then appeared to a learned South Indian. The contract was a simple one, a notable feature being that while the author sold the copyright for a printed edition, he and his family could continue to copy and distribute the work in manuscript (MPC 15 Mar 1811). This shows just how tied to the technology and market conditions of print this novel form of property was, and how foreign, therefore, it was to the world of the manuscript and the scriptorium.

Mamadi Venkayya, writing the collector from his sickbed, rejected the offer of 1,000 star pagodas for the copyright of his Telugu dictionary. He said that he had composed his two dictionaries, Telugu and Sanskrit, with great labor, "intending them as a present to the Honourable the Governor in Council, and hoping by that means to merit his favour to such a degree as to get some durable allowance settled for the support of my family" (MPC 28 Sept 1813, letter of 2 May). He became ill just a few days before the works were finished, a fact that prevented him from proceeding to Madras for that purpose, as he had intended.

> This being Honored Sir, the wish I entertained in undertaking the work, I trust that the Honourable the Governor in Council will be so generous and benevolent as to grant it by settling what allowance he may think proper (either in money or land) for the support of my family; but in the event of his deeming it inexpendient to do so, I humbly entreat that he will at least accept of my works as a present and have them printed for the use of the public as I will by no means print them on my own account. (Ibid.)

Before the introduction of print and copyright, the publishing of a work of scholarship had involved its presentation to a patron in open court, in the presence of discerning critics and with the hope of liberal reward.

It is clear that Mamadi Venkayya expected the Governor of Madras to play the role of a discerning and liberal patron, a raja of sorts. But what, exactly, did he want in the way of a reward? The College Board asked the collector to ascertain this. In his second letter to the collector Mamadi Venkayya reiterates that in his letter "I left the matter entirely to the will and pleasure of the Government, but as the Board wishes to ascertain the same from myself, I can only intimate, that I have a family whose expences amount to one Pagoda pr. Day, but that I shall be satisfied with such quantity of land in the neighbourhood of Masulipatam, as the Government may deem an adequate compensation for the transfer already mentioned. I expect it will be granted to continue to all my posterity" (ibid., Mamadi Venkayya to Collector, 1 July)

The collector thought this would be impossible in light of the permanent settlement of the territory in that region upon a zamindar. He professed himself "at a loss to understand what you mean by requesting the grant of land near Masulipatam which you must well know is the property of the Zemindars and not that of Government" and requested a more explicit answer for the Board (ibid., Collector to Mamadi Venkayya, 3 July). Mamadi Venkayya coolly replied, "At the time when the Government granted the permanent Cowles [charters] to the Zemindars they retained the Authority to resume the land, when any occasion happened—'which circumstance is known to you'—as you are my superior. I wrote this to you, in hopes, that you have the authority of obtaining for me some maintenance in land permanently, so that it may be continued to all my posterity" (ibid., 10 July). The collector, in reply, repeated that his request had no chance of succeeding. The Government would not order lands which had been granted to the zamindars in perpetuity to be given to anyone, and there was no use in repeating those expectations (ibid., 11 July). Mamadi Venkayya, not entirely convinced that the era of tax-free grants of land in perpetuity was over, reluctantly replied,

> I have the honor to acknowledge the receipt of your orders of the 10th Instant, wherein it is stated that the Government would never order the lands to any one, which were granted to the Zemindars in perpetuity. As the Government can do any thing they please, I wish that the remuneration, which they offered to grant for the maintenance of my family may be in the description of lands. But as you have informed me that it is an inconvenient thing I beg you will be pleased to recommend to the Government that the remuneration should be fixed either in lands or in cash. I shall be satisfied with either of these which the Government think proper to approve. (Ibid., 14 July)

The Government considered a grant of land and a perpetual pension to be equally out of the question but sanctioned a monthly allowance for the remainder of his life and the lifetime of his widow.

Mamadi Venkayya had struggled mightily to construct his relationship with the Government along the lines of a scholar receiving an unasked-for gift from a liberal royal patron as a reward for writing a work of excellence. Such a patron would show his discernment and munificence by giving a permanent tax-free grant of land, a shrotrium. Mamadi Venkayya did not wish to take up the new role the Madras Government wished him to assume, that of an author selling his rights of intellectual property for a sum of money. But the new regime of property and government was hostile to privileged land tenures and committed to private property, including the property rights of authors bringing their works to print. The "revival of letters" was not the restoration of a previous regime of intellectual production but its reinvention under new conditions of property and government.

In his sparring with the collector, Mamadi Venkayya acutely noted that the Government had the powers in reserve, even under the permanent zamindari settlement, to make him a perpetual grant if it wished. The problem was that it did not wish to use these powers in that way. On another occasion the Court of Directors gave not a grant of tax-free land but a gold snuff box to Subbarayam Mudaliar, author of the *Tamil expositor* (MPC 8 April 1817). There are other such instances, as when the Board of Superintendence sought the sanction of London to give a pair of gold bracelets (valued at 120 pagodas) and a raise in salary to the deputy head master for Telugu, for having translated the *Tales of Vikramāṅka* (MPC 28 Apr 1819). However, the Government's reluctance to make grants of land that were tax-free and perpetual was not absolute, as it was allowed for charitable purposes. For example, when Chidambara Vadiyar completed the translation of the *Mitākṣarā,* the Government granted 1,000 pagodas for the erection of a choultry, or rest house, for the use of travelers in South Arcot district, and a grant of land rent free, "sufficient for the support thereof" (MPC 18 Dec 1818; 19 June 1819). But when Sankaraiah built another such choultry, to increase his spiritual merit, on lands granted by a zamindar, he had to petition the Government to confirm the arrangement and make provision to pay for the revenue lost to the Government by the grant (Madras Government 1934, p. 725, 20 May 1816).

Although the correspondence of the College Board often speaks of publishing Mamadi Venkayya's Telugu dictionary, it appears that the Board never actually did so. The problem, of course, was that the dictionary was entirely in Telugu, and so was not of use to British students learning Telugu until they had become advanced. In the meantime, A. D. Campbell published a grammar of Telugu, and went on to publish a Telugu-English dictionary that presumably incorporated some of Mamadi Venkayya's work. Much the most important impact of Mamadi Venkayya's dictionary, however, lay in his introduction, in which he surveyed the history and grammar of Telugu through the older Telugu grammars written in Sanskrit. Both Campbell and Ellis quoted this directly (in English translation) and at length in Campbell's work. It was a key proof text of the Dravidian proof, to which we now turn.

CHAPTER 5

The Dravidian Proof

We come now to the Dravidian proof itself, its argument, and the related argument of A. D. Campbell in the introduction to his Telugu grammar. But before doing so we need to contextualize the Dravidian proof's appearance by considering the public course that was designed as the centerpiece of the junior civil servants' education at the College, and the dissertations on the South Indian languages that Ellis intended to write and print up for the students' use as part of the course. This is necessary because the Dravidian proof is in fact the dissertation on Telugu. We need also to look more closely at the Prakrit grammarians, whose work we considered in chapter 2, since they were the creators of the chief analytical terms that structure the Dravidian proof. Then, after having analyzed the writings of Campbell and Ellis on the Dravidian concept, and the role of Mamadi Venkayya's text in the Dravidian proof, we shall look at the lists of roots for Tamil and Telugu—especially that of Pattabhirama Shastri for Telugu—composed in the College and show how they enter into the Dravidian proof. Finally, we will survey the manuscript record, examining both private papers and some surprising finds in the colonial archive, to probe the history of the idea of the Dravidian language family prior to its first publication by Ellis. One of the most interesting of these earlier, unpublished discussions appears in a quarrel about the history and nature of Telugu in which Sankaraiah played an important role.

THE PUBLIC COURSE AND THE DISSERTATIONS

To examine the public course we need to return to the plan for the College set forth in the report of the Committee for Examination of the Junior Civil Servants dated 20 October 1811 (in MPC 10 Dec 1811). The aim of the educational innovations proposed by Ellis and his committee was to impart "that fundamental knowledge of the relative connection and character of the several Southern Dialects . . . which, as it is always uncertain in what province a Junior Servant may be stationed, would be far more beneficial to the public service than the most intimate acquaintance with one dialect only" (ibid., para. 66). Here, in a word, is the colonial utility of the idea of a Dravidian language family: grasp the general structure of the Dravidian languages, and no matter which district one is stationed in, one will have the means of learning the local Dravidian language and its script, or "character." This accords with Ellis's own experience, for he had studied the languages of South India as an interrelated group, and for years at a time earlier in his career had been "continually in motion" from one language area to another while serving as a judge.

Indeed, the Committee thought that the junior servants' instruction in the languages of South India should begin in the East India College in England. A general knowledge of Sanskrit, sufficient to give aid in the inflection of Sanskrit loanwords in the South Indian languages, was already available there. Some arrangement should also be made to offer "the same elementary knowledge of the languages peculiar to the Peninsula" as was provided for Persian and Hindustani. Elementary books (by Beschi) for learning Tamil were "immediately obtainable," and "among the Christians of Pondicherry, many of whom rank among the best educated, and best informed, natives in this part of India, persons might be found well qualified to teach this language, who would not decline a voyage to England" to serve as teachers of the South Indian languages at the East India College. Although the recommendation that Tamil be added to the curriculum of Hertford College did not bear fruit, the Committee's recommendation that junior civil servants bound for Madras study Sanskrit was favorably regarded by the Court of Directors and duly put into effect, as we saw in chapter 4.

The Committee proposed the formulation of the public course as an arrangement for teaching the junior civil servants once they arrived at Madras. And, like the plan for the College itself, the Committee's rationale for the public course was a clear expression of the conception of a

Dravidian language family. The College would not absolutely interdict students from studying any language they wished (such as Persian or Hindustani), but they would be required to follow a certain course of study, the principal object of which would be, the report again says, "the attainment of a knowledge of those general principles of grammar and of the idiom and terms, which are common to all the vernacular dialects of the South of India, so that, in whatsoever province the student might be stationed, he might be enabled to acquire with equal facility the local language, although it might not have previously been the object of his particular attention." The course of study would follow the nature of and relations among the five cognate dialects: high Tamil, low Tamil, Malayalam, Telugu, and Kannada. The general grammar, idiom, "verbal collocation" (perhaps meaning conjugations), and especially the terms, or vocabulary, in all these languages are the same. Their grammar, idiom, and so forth "derive wholly from the Tamil"; the vocabulary, "with certain dialectic variations," from Tamil and Sanskrit (ibid., para. 67). In a note this pattern of the five vernacular dialects of the South is extended to "other languages of this same derivation" such as Kodagu, spoken in Coorg, and Tulu (Tuluvei) and Tigali spoken in Kanara, "but these are too local, and obscure to require notice" (ibid.).

The report goes on to say, "Hence it is of little importance in which of these five languages grammar is in the first instance studied, the knowledge of it once obtained is applicable, in its main branches, to all, and dialectic variation is the only difficulty remaining to be overcome." However, the report urged that the preference should be given to Tamil, not only because it was the only one for which elementary books then existed, but more especially because it was "the parent of the rest." Moreover, it was the language of nearly two-thirds of the population of the Madras Presidency and was used in religious ceremonies "over the whole peninsula, and, we believe, to a certain extent, throughout India." This last statement is, of course, wrong on both counts. Clearly the Committee, and Ellis as its leader, tended to inflate the importance of Tamil vis-à-vis the other languages of the South (ibid., para. 68).

The aims of the public course would be for the students to achieve the following: to perform exercises in Tamil grammar; to attain some knowledge of Sanskrit grammar, especially of nouns; to gain "a perfect acquaintance with all terms common to the Southern dialects, whencesoever derived, and with their more usual dialectic variations"; and to acquire a knowledge of the characters (i.e., scripts) in which these dialects are written. Concerning the last, the Committee believed that the various scripts were closely related, the Malayalam script being derived from the Tamil script, and the Kannada from the Telugu (ibid., para. 69).

These preliminary ideas of the plan for the College, discussed in the 20 October 1811 report, were elaborated upon in the proposed rules for the College of Fort St. George, set forth in the voluminous first report of the Board of Superintendence, discussed previously, dated 1 January 1813 (in MPC 2 Feb 1813). In these draft rules, four courses of public study were proposed, additional to the private study of particular languages.

The first course was to be the study of the scripts used in South India, grouped in families: the Tamil alphabet and the variations between it and the Grantha (for writing Sanskrit) and the Ariyam (for Malayalam) scripts; the Telugu alphabet and the variations between it and the Karnataka (for Kannada); the Nagari alphabet and its several variations, such as the Balabund, Maharashtra, (i.e., Marathi), Oriya, and so forth; and the Arabic, or Persian, alphabet and the several modes in which it is written (MPC 2 Feb 1813, para. 149, p. 895).

The second course was to consist of three parts: the study of Tamil grammar and as much Sanskrit grammar as would be useful for learning the languages of the South; the study of the variation of the grammars of Telugu, Kannada, and Malayalam from Tamil, and "the influence of the Sanscrit on each"; and the study of terms, "whether of Tamil or Sanscrit origin," common to all the South Indian languages, the general rules of derivation from Tamil and Sanskrit languages, and the distinguishing peculiarities of each dialect of South India (ibid., p. 896).

The third course would comprise the study of "Oriental literature" in general. Students had the choice of studying the grammar, prosody, and rhetoric of Sanskrit, high Tamil, Arabic, or Persian, and the literary works of these languages and of Telugu, Hindustani, and so forth. The wording here is cryptic, but the idea seems to be that Tamil is grouped with Sanskrit, Arabic, and Persian, and one studies the grammar, prosody, and rhetoric of these four as a key to the literatures of other languages such as Telugu and Hindustani. These four, we might say (although the report does not use the word), were treated as *classical* literatures that set the pattern for later literatures (ibid., p. 897).

The fourth course was to be the study of Hindu and Muhammadan law, to be studied both through English translations and in the original languages (ibid.).

According to the proposed rules of the College, the first two courses were obligatory, the last two optional. Students were to be examined twice a year in the public courses they had taken at the time. In addition to the four courses, the rules required, almost as an afterthought, that students must "make themselves acquainted with" the Regulations of Government concerning management of the revenues and the administration of justice and, as a catchall to that afterthought, "generally with all subjects tending to qualify them for the discharge of public duties," for which they would be provided with books (ibid., pp. 898–99).

The idea of the Dravidian language family, then, preexisted the College and gave it its plan, in both senses of that word: the *structure* of the College—its intellectual ground plan so to say—and its *intended future direction.* The public course was to be the medium through which that intention was accomplished, but it could not be implemented at once. In the first place, the students lived in lodgings scattered here and there in Madras, and it was not feasible to ask them to attend the College daily, with the result that they could not be massed for the purpose of taking the public course. In the second place, it was not at all evident by whom the public course was to be taught; the head masters were fully occupied instructing and supervising the teachers and teacher candidates, and the members of the Board of Superintendence had full-time jobs that made it out of the question that they could become teachers. In any event, the public course was never launched, and after Ellis's death it was removed from the rules. But even though it never came into being as a proper college course of study, it did get implemented, in a concentrated form, in the "dissertation on Telugu," that is to say, in the Dravidian proof.

It was for the public course, Ellis says, that he proposed to print a set of "dissertations on the languages of Southern India," as we have seen (Ellis to Erskine 24 March 1817). The plan of these dissertations marched with the plan of the public course; they were intended for the use of the students of the College as brief versions of what the public course would have contained. Ellis tells Erskine that the dissertations would "illustrate the origin and connection of the dialects"; that the dissertation on the Telugu had been printed, the one on Malayalam was being printed; and that the set when completed would number five dissertations: (1) on the alphabets of India in general and South India in particular, including the scripts of the Sinhalese, and of Burma and Java, all of which he believed were derived from the Tamil script; (2) on high and low Tamil; (3) on Telugu; (4) on Malayalam; and (5) on Kannada and the minor dialects of Kodagu, Tuluva, and so forth. It is in the context of elaborating his life plan that (in a passage cited previously) he speaks of the Dravidian proof: "I made many years ago a resolution not to publish anything until I was forty years old and I have kept it pretty well considering, for I shall not have completed that age until the conclusion of the current year, and the only thing like a literary production I have yet printed is the dissertation [on the Telugu] I shall send you." This was the Dravidian proof.

As we have seen, only the dissertations on Telugu and Malayalam were printed in Ellis's lifetime, and both survive in reprint, the Telugu one in A. D. Campbell's grammar of Telugu, published by the College in 1816, and the one on Malayalam, printed for the College but published much after Ellis's death, in the *Indian antiquary.* The latter was edited and annotated by A. C. Burnell, the great epigrapher of South India, who assesses the high importance of Ellis's achievements in the two dissertations in the following note:

> The above dissertation is of remarkable historical interest, for (taken with the essay on Telugu) it proves that before 1816 Mr. Ellis had already foreseen the possibility of comparative philology, not only as regards the so-called Aryan tongues, but also in respect of the Dravidian. Now it was not till 1816 (so Brunet says, and I must take his assertion for I cannot refer to the original) that Bopp published his *Conjugations System,* which was the beginning of comparative philology in Europe. Ellis could (considering the means of intercourse available in those days) hardly have seen or heard of this work at all, for he died early in 1819. He must then, in future, be considered one of the originators of one of the most remarkable advances in science in this century. His unfortunate end—he was poisoned by accident—prevented his doing much, for he was only forty when he died, but he cannot be robbed of his due fame by the success of others more lucky that he was. (Ellis 1878)

The essay on Malayalam is a closely reasoned argument for considering Malayalam to be derived from Tamil, specifically "high Tamil" (also called "pure Tamil" in this piece). It compares the lexicons of high Tamil, low Tamil, and Malayalam and the treatment of Sanskrit terms in the three languages, as well as the declension of nouns, the conjugation of verbs, and the comparison of idioms. The last section of the essay is illustrated by a passage from the *Keralotpatti,* Kerala's creation narrative, with an interlinear translation into Tamil, probably by Ellis himself, to highlight the similarities and differences between the two languages. Other passages quoted here are taken from the *Vyavahārasamudra,* a treatise on law, and the *Rāmāyaṇa,* showing a "hybrid language" in which Sanskrit terms retain their primitive form and rarely take Malayalam terminations. Some of the details of the argument now seem antiquated, especially when Ellis argues (ibid., 280–81) that "the general progress of human speech" is from complex to simple: "as far as history can ascend, language will ever be found more artificial, more fertile in terminations, more abounding in inflections, and more copious in terms, in proportion to its antiquity; and during the last fifteen hundred years every progressive change in language, either from desuetude or intermixture, in Asia as well as in Europe, has invariably tended to reduce this exuberance." This view is given in proof that the direction of change had been from high Tamil to Malayalam, much like the change from Latin to the Romance languages, and not the reverse.

Yet it was not the dissertation on Malayalam that was the site of the Dravidian proof. Malayalam and Tamil had differentiated themselves from one another so gradually and so recently in history that it was, one might say, too easy to demonstrate their relationship, and the demonstration did not have to work against strong resistance from existing beliefs. Telugu, not Malayalam, was to be the site at which the Dravidian proof was made in all fullness, for reasons which will shortly become apparent.

THE PRAKRIT GRAMMARIANS

Campbell's introduction to his grammar on Telugu and Ellis's dissertation that follows it conform to the same line of argument and the same rhetorical strategy, Campbell confining himself to Telugu, Ellis explaining Telugu within a comprehensive view of all the South Indian languages. The overall stance is polemic. Both pieces are directed against the arguments of the Orientalists at Calcutta, specifically against William Carey, whose Telugu grammar had been published by the Serampore Press two years previously (Carey 1814), and Henry Thomas Colebrooke, whose essay on Prakrit asserted the Sanskrit origin of the "polished" or literary languages of modern India, both north and south (Colebrooke 1801). Campbell and Ellis alike cite many Indian texts in support of their arguments, using them as authorities against Carey and Colebrooke. The nub of the matter is the status of the *deśya* vocabulary in Telugu. In a nutshell, the Dravidian proof consists of showing that the *deśya* words of Telugu are traceable to roots found not in Sanskrit but in the South Indian languages generally.

As we have seen in chapter 2, the word category called *deśya* emerged through the process of extending *vyākaraṇa* analysis, first devised for Sanskrit, to the Prakrit languages. This process assumes that Sanskrit and the Prakrits are related in some way, but there is a considerable difference of opinion about what that relationship is.

One of the early texts to comment on this question is the *Nāṭyaśāstra,* the foundational text for all the fine arts, since the Prakrit languages were regularly used in the Sanskrit dramas by characters of all but the highest status. Prakrit is characterized there as a language that is devoid of refinement, implying that Sanskrit is the refined language (*saṃskāraguṇavarjita,* 17.2 quoted in Acharya 1968:39) and playing upon the meanings of "natural" or "unrefined" for the word *prākṛta* and "polished," "perfected," "refined" for *saṃskṛta.* In this view, Sanskrit is a more refined register of natural, unrefined speech, and its refinement has to do with its being, as Pāṇini says, the language of the learned *(śiṣṭa bhāṣā),* being cultivated by the poets and having a proper grammar. But as the Prakrits became literary languages themselves—considered to have a refinement of their own as they were cultivated by poets and patronized by kings and recited in their courts—they came to have grammars of their own; or rather, the *vyākaraṇa* analysis of Sanskrit was extended to the Prakrits. Therefore, in the Prakrit grammars we get a different definition of Prakrit from that in the *Nāṭyaśāstra.* The Prakrit grammars as a class say or imply that the name "Prakrit" derives from *prakṛti,* "basis," because Sanskrit is the basis of Prakrit *(prakṛteh saṃskṛtād āgatam prākṛtam;* Siṃhadevagaṇin on *Vāgbhaṭālaṅkāra* 2.2, cited in Acharya 1968:39, and many other passages to the same effect).

The universal view of the Prakrit grammars—all of them written in Sanskrit—is that Prakrit derives from Sanskrit, and their analysis of the language follows suit. For example, in the earliest surviving Prakrit grammar, the *Prākṛtaprakāśa* of Vararuci, the treatment of Maharashtri, considered the Prakrit *par excellence* and the sole object, perhaps, of this text in its original form, concludes its *sūtras* for Maharashtri by saying that the remaining rules are as in Sanskrit (*śeṣaḥ saṃskṛtāt, Vāgbhaṭālaṅkāra* 9.18, cited in Acharya 1968:47). Subsequent chapters devoted to other Prakrits—which seem to have been added to the text at a later time—open by stating that Shauraseni is the *prakṛti,* or basis, of Paishachi and of Magadhi, while Sanskrit is the *prakṛti* of Shauraseni (*Vāgbhaṭālaṅkāra* 10.2, 11.2, 12.2, cited in Acharya 1968:47). Thus the overall stance is that Prakrit grammar is not complete in itself but takes Sanskrit grammar as its starting point and develops further *sūtras* to account for the transformation of Sanskrit into the Prakrit languages.

It is well to remember that the assumptions of the Prakrit grammarians—meaning those grammarians who derive the Prakrits from Sanskrit—did not go unchallenged, especially by the Jains and Buddhists, whose sacred languages were themselves Prakrits. Although the great Jain scholar

Hemacandra wrote his Prakrit grammar within the tradition I have just described, other Jain scholars took a very different view. In Acharya's valuable discussion (1968:54–55) we come across the interesting counterargument of Namisādhu, an eleventh-century Jain scholar (in a comment upon Rudraṭa's *Kāvyālaṅkāra* 1.12), in which he also derives the term "Prakrit" (Prākṛta) from *prakṛti,* but takes it in the sense of the natural speech used by all beings in the world, which is not refined by grammar. Prakrit, in this argument, means "first produced" *(prāk+kṛta),* the speech easily intelligible to children and women and the source of all other kinds of speech. It is also the speech of the gods and sages (i.e., the Jain scriptures). Prakrit is the same everywhere, like the rain, which is everywhere alike, the same in every country *(deśa)* in which it falls; it becomes specialized by refinement into Sanskrit and other languages by Pāṇini and others in their rules of grammar. Thus, inverting the relation as it is understood by the Prakrit grammarians, Namisādhu argues that Prakrit is the basis of Sanskrit.

The Jain belief that the Addhamāgahā Vāṇī, or Ardhamagadhi language, in which the oldest Jain texts are written, was the original Prakrit language from which all the others were derived is based on a statement in the Jain canon that Mahāvīra preached his doctrines in that language. It is also mentioned there that this language undergoes modifications when it is spoken by Aryans, non-Aryans, and other living beings such as the bipeds, the quadrupeds, the wild and the tamed animals, the birds, and the insects—opening up an enchanted world in which the languages of all creatures, even the crickets, have a common origin and, at bottom, a common structure (Acharya 1968:65). Similarly, in Buddhist writings and grammars of Pali, it is often Pali (or Magadhi as it is also called) that is named the mother of all languages. In short, there is among some Jain and Buddhist authorities a distinct opposition to the doctrine of the Prakrit grammarians that the Prakrits derive from Sanskrit.

Given the belief that the Prakrits are derived from Sanskrit, the project of the majority of Prakrit grammarians was to account for the literary Prakrits by means of supplementary *sūtras* that presuppose and add to the rules making up the body of Sanskrit grammar. In this connection the Prakrit grammars make a threefold distinction that is crucial for understanding how the Dravidian proof was reached. The first two classes of Prakrit words are "same as Sanskrit" (*saṃskṛta-sama,* shortened to *tatsama,* "same as that") and "originating from Sanskrit" *(saṃskṛta-bhava,* shortened to *tad-bhava,* "originating from that"). *Tatsamas* are Sanskrit words that are used in Prakrit unchanged except for the addition of

Prakrit endings; *tadbhavas* are Prakrit words that are thought of as altered forms of their Sanskrit cognates.

The third category consists of the *deśya,* or *deśi,* words, which in contrast to the *tatsamas* and the *tadbhavas* are not obviously and transparently derivable from Sanskrit. As Hemacandra says in his compendium of *deśya* words, the *Deśināmamāla,* they are not derived by grammatical rules *(lakṣaṇa),* not found in Sanskrit dictionaries, and not derived by metaphorical use of Sanskrit words. Moreover, unlike Sanskrit words, which in principle do not change across time and place, *deśya* words have had different usages in different countries from time immemorial (1.3–4, cited in Acharya 1968:41–42). Similarly, Rudraṭa says that *deśya* words lack the derivation from root and affix found in Sanskrit *(prakṛtiprayaya-mūlā vyutpattir nāsti yasya deśyasya; Kāvyālaṅkāra* 6.27, cited in Acharya 1968:44).

The admission of the *deśya* category introduces an element of tension into the analysis, as Acharya notes, a tension that is never fully resolved. For if Prakrit is defined as based on Sanskrit, it is somewhat contradictory to admit some words into the analysis that cannot be derived from Sanskrit roots (listed in the *Dhātupāṭha*) and affixes by means of the transformational rules of Pāṇini. Are we to understand from the fact that *deśya* words cannot be derived from Sanskrit roots that they are not somehow derived from Sanskrit? Perhaps not, but the Prakrit grammarians leave the matter ambiguous. It is symptomatic of that tension, for example, that Hemacandra treats of Prakrit and Apabhramsha grammar within his large treatise on Sanskrit grammar, but devotes a separate treatise, written in Prakrit, to the *deśya* words. This exemplifies well enough the fault line that Acharya has identified and that the Prakrit grammarians did not overcome.

This internal tension does not get out of hand, however, because the *deśya* words are only a limited part of the literary Prakrit lexicon. The purpose of the Prakrit grammarians was to analyze not ordinary speech but the literary languages used by the great poets, so only the *deśya* words the poets have sanctioned by use need be noticed by the grammarians. For that reason, the name *deśya* connotes something like "country" words, in the sense of nonstandard, less-refined words which are nevertheless adopted by the poets and in that way given a certain refinement. There is another reason as well. In the grammarians' works we find lists of names of the Prakrit languages in various groupings. The late Prakrit grammarian Mārkaṇḍeya, for example, recognized four categories: Bhāṣa, Vibhāṣa, Apabhraṃśa, and Paiśācika. Among these, especially the last, are many names that suggest a South Indian ambience, such as Kāñci-deśīya (of the region of the city Kanchipuram in the Tamil country), Dākṣiṇāṭya (of the Deccan), and Drāviḍa (of South India or Tamil Nadu). But in every case the Prakrits actually analyzed by the Prakrit grammarians are Indo-Aryan languages and not Dravidian ones; presumably those with South Indian names were also literary dialects of Indo-Aryan, used in South Indian courts. However that may be, the *deśya* class of words was kept within fairly narrow limits by the fact that the Prakrit grammars limited themselves to Indo-Aryan languages, derivable, for the most part, from the roots and affixes of Sanskrit by means of specifiable rules. Finally, with sufficient ingenuity a Sanskrit root can be found for any *deśya* word, and one often sees a tendency at work among these grammarians to find a Sanskrit origin for words clearly not Sanskritic. Taken altogether, the non-Sanskritic component of the literary Prakrits was minimized and the problems of accounting for them were not suffered to grow acute.

It is when the analytic machinery of the Prakrit grammarians is directed toward Telugu that the *deśya* element becomes large, and indeed dominates the lexicon. It was in connection with this aspect of the language that the Dravidian proof emerged.

CAMPBELL ON THE NON-SANSKRIT ORIGIN OF TELUGU

Alexander Duncan Campbell, whom I introduced in chapter 3, was young in the service, and something of a protégé of Ellis, with whom he worked closely. He passed the examination for the prize in Telugu only in 1813, after becoming secretary to the Board of Superintendence of the College. The College published his grammar and dictionary of Telugu for the use of its students, and the colonial record contains long, interesting reviews of these projects in their early stages, reviews in which Ellis participated and which he probably drafted.

Campbell's project was to give the students of the College of Fort St. George a grammar of "the superior dialect" of the Telugu language, following the existing native grammars, as distinguished from the "inferior or colloquial dialect in common use among all classes of the people" (1816:xvi). The distinction of *superior* and *inferior*—elsewhere, *grammatical* and *vulgar,* which agrees with Beschi's treatment of Tamil, whose work was an explicit model for Campbell—is common, Campbell says, to Telugu, Tamil, and Kannada. His plan for the grammar of Telugu was to give all the rules for the superior dialect, but to give only those aspects of the inferior dialect which depart from the superior dialect. Since the inferior dialect was used in conversation and official business, using the higher register of the language as the basis of the grammar may seem a poor choice for the education of English civil servants training to be judges and collectors; but to this objection (one which, as we shall see, was raised by the Governor of Madras against the language teaching policy of the College) Campbell replies that his aim is to teach *both* dialects, so the student can understand the rules governing the classical texts and also learn to speak and write common Telugu. To this end he has followed the native grammarians, tracing the language to its source in the superior dialect and at the same time giving instruction in "its more useful branches in the inferior dialect, which, as being Vulgar, Native authors have considered beneath the notice of the learned" (ibid., xvii). This approach was in complete accord with that Ellis took for teaching Tamil, which also followed Beschi, as previously described.

Accordingly, Campbell draws upon the tradition of Telugu grammar, said to have originated with Kāṇva, though the earliest work available to him was the *Āndhraśabdacintāmaṇi,* attributed to Nannaya Bhaṭṭa, an eleventh-century poet who translated the *Mahābhārata* into Telugu, plus Nannaya's commentators and successors. All of these grammatical works were written in Sanskrit by brahmins and directed toward the language of courtly poetry. Campbell acknowledges the help of one Mr. Stokes of the civil service for examining the manuscript before it was submitted to the Government; of the Board of Superintendence of the College, especially Ellis and Archdeacon Mousley, for helpful criticisms (the Board issued a long report on the manuscript to the Government, presumably mainly written by these two); and of Udayagiri Venkatanarayana and Pattabhirama Shastri. The first of these was Campbell's Telugu teacher, who guided Campbell through the Telugu grammars and gave aid and advice throughout his labors on the text; subsequently this young brahmin, a man "of superior intelligence and remarkable acquirements . . . by his own merits alone, subsequently rose to the situation of Head English master at the College of Fort St. George, and lately to the more honorable office of Interpreter to the Supreme Court of judicature at the Presidency" (ibid., xxv). The latter was head Sanskrit and Telugu master at the College. In brief, Campbell's grammar was very much a product of the Madras school of Orientalism formed around the College and was fully in harmony with the overall vision of Ellis.

In his introduction, Campbell attacks Carey of the Serampore Mission near Calcutta, "one of the learned Professors in the College of Fort William," who in the preface to his own Telugu grammar, published two years prior to Campbell's, argued that the languages of South India, namely, Telugu, Kannada, Tamil, Malayayam, and Sinhalese, derive from Sanskrit as do the languages of the North, but differ greatly in other respects, "especially in having a large proportion of words the origin of which is unascertained," that is, *deśya* words (Carey 1814). Campbell asserts, rather, that although Telugu contains many Sanskrit words, perhaps more than any other South Indian language, there is nevertheless reason to believe that the origins of Sanskrit and Telugu are "altogether distinct."

Campbell's proposition that Sanskrit and Telugu have different origins rests mainly on his reading of the Telugu grammarians. Some of them, he says (he cites the *Ātharvanavyākaraṇam* of the *Āndhrakaumudī*, Campbell 1816:xx), maintain that before King Āndhrarāyalu moved his palace from Srikakulam on the banks of the Krishna River to the environs of Rajahmundry on the banks of the Godavari, the only Telugu words were those of pure *(acca)* Telugu, called "the language of the land" *(deśya)*, considered primeval, created by the creator god Brahmā. This king's followers adopted Sanskrit terms with Telugu terminations (that is, *tatsamas*), "and by degrees corruptions from the Sanscrit crept into the language" (that is, *tadbhavas*) due to the ignorance of the people concerning their correct pronunciation. Campbell comments: "This would imply that the nation still retain some faint remembrance of those times, in which their language existed independent of the Sanskrit" (ibid., xvii). The proof is that every Telugu grammarian, from Nannaya Bhaṭṭa to the present, "considers the two languages as derived from sources entirely distinct," for they classify the words of the language under four headings: *deśya, tatsama, tadbhava,* and *grāmya,* or "provincial," terms. To these, Campbell notes, later authors added *anyadeśya,* for "foreign words or those from other lands."

Campbell's quarrel with Carey hinges on the interpretation of the *deśya* category. Carey said the *deśya* words were of unascertained origin, and we can see that this definition flows directly from the tradition of the Prakrit grammars, which say that *deśya* words are those not derivable by combinations of Sanskrit roots and affixes as governed by the rules of *vyākaraṇa.* Campbell thought Carey wholly wrong. Instead, he relied on the etymological connection of the term with *deśa,* country or region, interpreting *deśya* to mean "that which belongs to the country or land." This class is not merely a "large proportion" of the words of Telugu, as Carey said, but constitutes the most numerous class of words in the language, and it forms the model upon which words of the other classes are modified from their original languages. It will be obvious to a Sanskrit scholar reading this book, Campbell says, that many aspects of Telugu morphology and the whole of its syntax are entirely different from the Sanskrit, while the scholar of Tamil and Kannada "will at once recognize their radical connexion with each of these languages." Just as Jones had presented the idea of an Indo-European language family as occurring spontaneously to someone examining the sibling languages of the family, so Campbell presents the kinship of the leading Dravidian languages as a spontaneous product of direct inspection.

Campbell goes on to invoke explicitly the theory of the comparative vocabulary: "The reader will find all words denoting the different parts of the human frame, the various sorts of food or utensils in common use among the Natives, the several parts of their dress, the compartments of their dwellings, the degrees of affinity and consanguinity peculiar to them—in short all terms expressive of primitive ideas or of things necessarily named in the earlier states of society, to belong to the pure Telugu or *language of the land*" (ibid., xx; emphasis in original).

It is true, Campbell says, that Telugu has become so mixed with Sanskrit that derivatives or corruptions of the latter may occasionally be used to denote some of these primitive ideas or things. This, however, is not common. The majority of Sanskrit words admitted into the language are abstract terms and words connected with science, religion, or law, much like Greek and Latin words incorporated into English (as indeed the theory of comparative vocabulary leads one to expect). Moreover, Sanskrit words thus introduced into Telugu are not allowed to retain their original forms, but are made to undergo changes and assume terminations and inflections unknown to Sanskrit, that is, Sanskrit words are never admitted into Telugu unless they appear in the dress peculiar to *the language of the land,* meaning pure Telugu (*acca*-Telugu).

The rhetorical strategy of the piece is to show that the non-Sanskritic origin of Telugu is evident from the plain meaning of ancient texts by the Indian grammarians of a distant past, and from the unmediated inspection of the South Indian languages. Thus Campbell attacks Carey by showing that the ancient Telugu grammarians are on his side and not Carey's. But the real source of his argument is the theory underlying the method of the word list and the radical distinction it makes between primitive words and borrowed ones. Although the Telugu grammars function here as found objects that, as it were, confirm Campbell's argument even before it is made, in truth Campbell is reinterpreting the meaning of the *deśya* category through the theory of the comparative vocabulary. If this were not so, the non-Sanskritic origin of Telugu would have needed no demonstration. Although Campbell portrays his opponent, Carey, as simply misinformed, in fact Carey is expressing the view of the Prakrit grammarians. Campbell, in short, may think he is giving the plain meaning of ancient authors, but he is really expounding a new idea which came about when the European and the Indian traditions of analysis came together in British-Indian Madras.[1]

ELLIS AND THE DRAVIDIAN PROOF

Like Campbell, Ellis opens his essay (the text of which is reproduced in appendix B) with a statement directed against the Orientalists of Calcutta: "The real affiliations of the Telugu language appears not to have been known to any writer, by whom the subject has been noticed." Carey, Charles Wilkins, and H. T. Colebrooke are cited. Carey had provided a number of passages that made good targets. In the preface of his Sanskrit grammar (Carey 1804) he says that Hindustani and Tamil, and the languages of Gujarat and Malayala (Kerala, i.e., Malayalam), "are evidently derived from the Sanscrit," though "the two former are greatly mixed with foreign words," and that Bengali, Oriya, Marathi, Kannada, and Telugu "are almost wholly composed of Sanskrit words." In his grammar of Telugu (1814) Carey writes, "The languages of India are principally derived from the Sanskrit": the structures of the languages in the middle and north of India are generally the same, while those of the South, namely Telugu, Kannada, Tamil, Malayalam, and Sinhalese, though of the same (Sanskrit) origin as the northern languages, differ greatly from them in other respects, "especially in having a large proportion of words, the origin of which is unascertained"—virtually the definition of *deśya* words given by the Prakrit grammarians. Wilkins states in his grammar of Sanskrit that Tamil, Telugu, Kannada, and Malayalam, together with the idiom of the Maratha states and Gujarat, "so abound with Sanscrit, that scarcely a sentence can be expressed in either of them without its assistance" (Wilkins 1808). Colebrooke's important 1801 paper on the Prakrit languages more or less implies that all the main languages of the North and the South are derived from Sanskrit.[2]

Ellis plainly rejects this chorus of opinion emanating from Calcutta:

1. I have benefited from Lisa Mitchell's thoughtful reading of this text of Campbell, and of the one of Ellis which follows (Mitchell forthcoming). The object of her analysis is the development of a sense of linguistic nationalism, and accordingly her focus in this reading is on the *anyadeśa* category.

2. An earlier article on this topic (Trautmann 1999b) gives somewhat fuller details.

"It is the intent of the following observations to shew that the statements contained in the preceding quotations are not correct; that neither the Tamil, the Telugu, nor any of their cognate dialects are derivations from the Sanskrit; that the latter, however it may contribute to their polish, is not necessary for their existence; and that they form a distinct family of languages, with which the Sanskrit has, in latter times especially, intermixed, but with which it has no radical connexion" (Ellis 1816:2). The rejection of the Calcutta consensus could not be more plainly stated.

Ellis then lists the languages of the proposed family, which we now call Dravidian: high and low Tamil; Telugu, grammatical and vulgar; Kannada, ancient and modern; Malayalam which, according to Paulinus a Sancto Bartholomeo, is also divided into a higher and lower register, the higher one containing many Sanskrit terms and forms; and Tuluva of the Kanara country on the west coast of the peninsula. Besides these there are a few local dialects such as Kodagu (a variation of Tuluva and spoken in Coorg district), Sinhalese, Marathi, and Oriya, which, "though not of the same [Dravidian] stock, borrow many of their words and idioms from these tongues," thus quite correctly stating what has remained the consensus view of these (Indo-Aryan) languages. Ellis thought it an extraordinary fact that the language of the "mountaineers" of Rajmahal, an "uncivilized race" of the North, "if not of the same radical derivation," nevertheless "abounds in terms common to the Tamil and Telugu." Ellis's identification of this language, called Malto, as a member of the Dravidian family was very acute indeed. The material upon which he worked, although he does not name his source, must have been a word list of the language of Rajmahal sent to the Asiatic Society by one Major Roberts (1808) and published in the *Asiatic researches* as a supplement to an article on the inhabitants of the place published the previous year (Shaw 1807). From this short list—a distant relative of the list of Leibniz, testifying to the wide scope of the languages-and-nations project—Ellis drew the quite correct conclusion about the Dravidian nature of this northern language, spoken in the Ganges basin, far from the main body of Dravidian languages. Thus, the inclusions and exclusions Ellis states here are fully in accord with current expert opinion, nearly two centuries after his piece was published. The identification of Malto at this early date was a brilliant hit.

Telugu is formed, says Ellis, from roots of its own, which in general have no connection with Sanskrit or any other language except "the cognate dialects of Southern India," with which, allowing for "the occasional variation of consimilar sounds," they generally agree. The differences among Telugu, Tamil, and Kannada are found only in the affixes by which words are made from roots; "the roots themselves are not similar merely, but the same."

The doctrine Ellis here advances, of a radical difference between Sanskrit and the South Indian languages and the existence of a *single* stock of roots underlying *all* the Dravidian languages, is then developed. The first step is to make a comparison between the roots of Sanskrit and Telugu, making use of the Sanskrit *dhātumāla,* or list of roots (I presume this is the *Dhātupāṭha* connected with Pāṇini's grammar), and a *dhātumāla* for Telugu which had been compiled by Pattabhirama Shastri, an original work of great value.[3] In parallel columns Ellis gives a sampling of ten roots each beginning with the letters *a, k, p,* and *v,* and to make the comparison easier to follow he gives both the Sanskrit and the Telugu in the romanization scheme proposed by Sir William Jones, slightly modified. That the stock of roots in Sanskrit is completely different from that in Telugu is evident.

The second step is to show "that an intimate radical connection exists between the Telugu and other dialects of Southern India," again through a comparative table, this one showing likenesses rather than differences. Ellis takes the first fifteen roots in alphabetical order beginning with *a* and similarly the first fifteen beginning with *k,* from Pattabhirama's *dhātumāla* of Telugu, and corresponding roots of Tamil and Kannada, the Tamil ones from a list compiled by the head Tamil master of the College (Chidambara Vadiyar) and compared with Beschi's dictionary, the *Caturakarādi,* and the Kannada roots "from an old list explained in Sanskrit." The table—three columns of romanized Telugu, Kannada, and Tamil roots—is much more complex than the previous table, showing often close agreement in cognate roots among the three languages, and sometimes cognate roots shared between only two of the languages, in every combination of pairs of languages. Here again the table itself is the proof. The immense labor and skill that went into its construction is not so much as hinted at, though it is perfectly evident to readers.

The third step of the argument is a comparison of words made from Telugu, Kannada, and Tamil roots; for though a (literally) radical connection among the South Indian languages may be proved by showing the unity of the stock of their roots, their connection "may not be intimate" in respect of the words made from those roots. For this Ellis makes

3. N. Venkata Rao (1957) gives valuable historical information on this work, a copy of which exists in the Government Oriental Manuscripts Library.

much use of the Telugu dictionary *Āndhradīpaka* compiled by Mamadi Venkayya, the copyright of which had been purchased by the Government of Madras at the urging of the Board of Superintendence, which is to say, virtually at the urging of Ellis, as we have seen. This dictionary has a long introduction giving an analysis of Telugu grammar, based on the earlier Telugu grammarians, whom it cites. Ellis translates a large chunk of this introduction that concerns the categorization of words as *tatsama, tadbhava, deśya,* and *grāmya.* Once again, the rhetorical strategy is to show that the Indian grammarians agree with Ellis against the Calcutta Orientalists, and to show that the latter have misinterpreted them. I paraphrase Ellis's translation of Mamadi Venkayya, giving the gist of his reading of it.

Ellis writes that *tatsamas,* or "pure Sanskrit terms received into Telugu," are illustrated through a table of Sanskrit words and their corresponding *tatsamas* in Telugu, romanized, with glosses in English, for instance: Skt. *vanam,* Tel. *vanamu,* "a forest"; Skt. *gauḥ,* Tel. *govu,* "a cow." *Tadbhavas* are derived from Sanskrit either directly or through one of the six Prakrits, with alteration of letters as explained in the *Vaikṛtacandrika.* Lists are then given of *tadbhavas* derived from Sanskrit immediately, or from Sanskrit through Maharashtri, Shauraseni, Magadhi, Paishachi, Chulika or Chulika-Paishachi, and Apabhramsha. In a long note on the Prakrits, Ellis estimates that the proportions of the *tadbhava*s in Telugu are: Sanskrit *tadbhava*s one-half, Maharashtri one-quarter, Shauraseni one-tenth, Magadhi one-twentieth, and one-tenth for Paishachi, Chulika, and Apabhramsha taken together. Against Colebrooke's view that Apabhramsha is "a jargon destitute of regular grammar," Ellis quotes a Sanskrit passage from the Prakrit grammar of Lakṣmīdhara, the *Ṣaḍbhāṣācandrikā.* This text, though concerned only with the *tatsamas* and *tadbhavas* of the six Prakrit languages, expressly says that each possesses its own *deśya,* or native, terms. Of Paishachi, for example, Lakṣmīdhara says "These are the Paishachi countries *(deśa),* and the *deśya* terms of each have their own particular quality" *(ete paiśācadeśās syus, tad deśyas tad guṇo bhavati).*

Ellis notes that the third category, *deśya*—in other words, Telugu, or Andhra—refers to words of two kinds: the language which originated in the country of Telingana, and *anyadeśa,* or "the language of foreign countries intermixed with it." The text then cites the *Ātharvanavyākaraṇam* as to the boundaries of the Triliṅga-deśa (or Telingana). The *acca*-Telugu, or pure Telugu, spoken there is described in another text, the *Ap-*

pakāvīyam, as "pure native speech of Andhra" *(śuddha-āndhra-deśyam).* A list of *acca*-Telugu words, romanized and with English glosses, is then given: *pālu,* milk; *perugu,* curdled milk; *ney,* clarified butter (ghee); *rōlu,* a mortar; *rōṅkali,* a pestle; and so forth. Ellis explains the *anyadeśyas,* "terms introduced into Telugu from foreign countries," by quoting a verse from the *Appakāvīyam* to the effect that "the natives of Andhra, having resided in foreign countries, by using Telugu terms conjointly with those of other countries, these have become Andhra terms of foreign origin." The examples given in the *Āndhradīpaka,* Ellis says, are of *anyadeśya* terms (1) in which aspirates occur (since aspirates do not belong to the "thirty letters proper to the Telugu" but are for the expression of Sanskrit words), e.g., *bhalā,* a eulogistic exclamation; (2) which end with a final long vowel, such as *anā,* the sixteenth part of a rupee; and (3) "difficult words" such as *kalanu,* battle; *toyyeli,* a woman; *mēnu,* the body; *ullamu,* the mind. Ellis comments that the first (words with aspirates) are of uncertain derivation, the second (ending in a long vowel) are either Hindustani or terms whose last syllable has been lengthened "casually." Most of the third (difficult words), he says, "are common in the southern dialects," and he goes on to give Dravidian cognates for Mamadi Venkayya's list: Telugu *kalanu* answers to Tamil *kal,* from the root *kala,* to join, common to Telugu, Tamil, and Kannada; Telugu *toyyeli,* to Tamil *taiyel,* from *tai,* to beautify; Telugu *mēnu,* to Tamil *mēni,* from *mēl,* upward/outward; and Telugu *ullumu,* to Tamil *ul,* inward/mind.

The fourth category, the *grāmya* words, are "terms which cannot be subjected to the rules of grammar, and in which an irregular increment or decrement of letters occurs." This ends the translation of the long extract from Mamadi Venkayya's *Āndhradīpaka.* Ellis comments:

> In the preceding extracts, the author, supported by due authority, teaches, that, rejecting direct and indirect derivatives from the Sanscrit, and words borrowed from foreign languages, what remains is the *pure native language of the land:* this constitutes the great body of the tongue and is capable of expressing every mental and bodily operation, every possible relation and existent thing; for with the exception of some religious and technical terms, no word of Sanscrit derivation is *necessary* to the Telugu. This pure native language of the land, allowing for dialectic differences and variations of termination, is, with the Telugu, common to the Tamil, Cannadi, and the other dialects of southern India. (Ellis 1816:18; emphasis in original)

We see here again, in the distinction between the words that are necessary and native, and those that are technical and borrowed, the theory of the word list at work. Ellis quotes Mamadi Venkayya's text at such length because it gives untainted evidence of the correctness of this interpretation of Telugu's *deśya* words. This interpretation, which expands upon Mamadi Venkayya's analysis of Telugu by putting it in a larger, South Indian field of vision together with Tamil and Kannada, is then clinched by taking the list of *deśya* words that Mamadi Venkayya had quoted from the *Appakāvīyam,* against which Ellis juxtaposes columns of Kannada and Tamil words "expressive of the same ideas." This second three-column table is the basis for the third step of the argument, showing that not only are the *roots* of these three languages the same, but the *words* formed from the roots in these languages also correspond. Although, Ellis says, it would have been easy to draw up from the three languages a far longer list of words that exactly agree with each other, he chose to use Appakavi's list because it is an unimpeachable source, a work of recognized authority to which no suspicion of bias can attach, as the author, though a good Sanskrit scholar, was ignorant of all the languages of South India except his native Telugu. Appakavi's list of *deśya* words is the basis, then, of a list in three columns of cognate words in Telugu, Kannada and Tamil, words such as Telugu *pālu,* Kannada *hālu,* Tamil *pāl,* "milk" and so forth. Here again, the demonstration is brilliantly constructed and beautifully clear.

From this analysis Ellis concludes that the Telugu language may be divided into four branches, using the terms of the native grammarians but putting them in what he considers their natural order: *deśya,* or *acca*-Telugu, "pure native terms, constituting the basis of this language and, generally, also, of the other dialects of southern India"; *anyadeśya,* "terms borrowed from other countries, chiefly of the same derivation as the preceding" (i.e., from other Dravidian languages); *tatsama,* pure Sanskrit terms with Telugu affixes; and *tadbhava,* Sanskrit derivatives received directly from Sanskrit or through one of the six Prakrits, "in all instances more or less corrupted." *Grāmya,* the rustic dialect, is not a constituent part of the language but is formed from the *acca*-Telugu "by contraction, or some permutation of the letters not authorized by the rules of Grammar." The proportion of *acca*-Telugu terms is one-half, of *anyadeśya* terms one-tenth, of *tatsamas* three-twentieths, and of *tadbhavas* one-quarter. Thus, by putting the categories of the Prakrit grammarians, as embraced by the Telugu grammars, in a larger comparative framework that uses Tamil and Kannada as examples of the South Indian languages as a group, Ellis gives them a new reading, both historical and structural at once, that shows their underlying logic.

The Dravidian proof is an act of reinterpretation that validates the existing classification while revealing its hitherto hidden rationale. In this it is rather like the chapter on classification in Charles Darwin's *Origin of species,* which shows that the theory of natural selection validates and supplies the hitherto unknown logic of the Linnean classification of species. The likeness is by no means a distant one. Darwin employs the image of a branching tree to explain the relations among species through time, and he explicitly draws the tree image from the languages-and-nations project:

> It may be worth while to illustrate this view of classification, by taking the case of languages. If we possessed a perfect pedigree of mankind, a genealogical arrangement of the races of man would afford the best classification of the various languages now spoken throughout the world; and if all extinct languages, and all intermediate and slowly changing dialects, had to be included, such an arrangement would, I think, be the only possible one. . . . The various degrees of difference in the languages from the same stock, would have to be expressed by groups subordinate to groups; but the proper or even only possible arrangement would still be genealogical. (Darwin 1859:422–23)[4]

In a similar way, Ellis uses the idea of a genealogical tree to reinterpret the categories of the *vyākaraṇa* analysis of Telugu, showing their validity and their hitherto unknown logic.

In the final section of the Dravidian proof, Ellis, having dealt with roots and with words, turns to the third of his triad on language, the "idiom," a term largely meaning syntax but also including prosody, a subject in which Ellis had a deep interest. The preliminary, incorrect view from which this section sets out (the *pūrvapakṣa,* as the pandits would say) is that, though the roots and words may be the same in the cognate dialects of South India, "a difference in idiom may exist so great, that, in the acquisition of one, no assistance, in this respect, can be derived from a knowledge of the other" (Ellis 1816:22). The burden, of course, is to show the reverse, which he does in the conclusion (the *uttarapakṣa* or *siddhānta*). It is something of a bravura performance, for Ellis gives short passages from Sanskrit, which he translates into Telugu, Kannada, and Tamil, and

4. See also Trautmann 1987:215 and 1997:57 for the importance of this passage. It is often said that Darwin got the underlying treelike image of the relations among species from paleontology, but his text shows the influence of the languages-and-nations project upon his own. Note especially the interchangeability of race and language. The ultimate source of Darwin's diagram, tracing it all the way to its source, is the Tree of Nations in the book of Genesis.

the sentence structure of each is analyzed minutely. It ends with versified translations into these four languages of an English sentence: "When thou art an anvil, endure like an anvil; when a hammer, strike like a hammer," the Tamil in *kuṟaḷ veṇba* meter, the Telugu and Kannada in *dvipada,* the Sanskrit in *anuṣṭubh.* It is a brilliant coda to an argument of great power and beauty.

THE *DHĀTUMĀLA*

Although Ellis articulated the Dravidian proof, it will be evident by now that it did not emerge in a vacuum but was fashioned with the help of the community of scholars brought together at the College of Fort St. George. In particular, the central part of the proof is the two-column comparison of roots in Telugu and Sanskrit, showing their utter difference, and the three-column comparison of roots in Telugu, Kannada, and Tamil, drawn from the lists of roots, or *dhātumālas,* constructed for these languages, showing their close similarity. The list for Kannada was taken from an "old" list, presumably in manuscript. The other two were made by head masters of the College, the one for Telugu by Pattabhirama Shastri, the head Sanskrit and Telugu master, and the one for Tamil by Chidambara Vadiyar, the head Tamil master. The Telugu one was of special importance to the proof, and to the construction of Campbell's grammar. This emerges clearly when we examine the report on Campbell's manuscript that was submitted to the Madras Government and forwarded to the Court of Directors in London for approval.

This report, by the Board of Superintendence of the College, is a remarkable document. Since Campbell was secretary to the Board of Superintendence, it was hardly an independent review, and, as one would expect, its overall tone is one of praise for the manuscript and recommendation that it be published by the College Press. But it is not a perfunctory endorsement. What one does not expect from the close relation between the authors of the review and the author of the grammar being reviewed is the abundance of closely argued criticisms and suggestions for revision. There are abundant signs (including the careful use of the Jonesean romanization scheme for Indian words) that the body of the report was written by Ellis, and it displays a considerable knowledge of Telugu. The report is a long one, it is studded with Telugu words in Telugu script, and it argues with a formidable depth of detail. It is unlikely, therefore, that the Governor and Council of Madras, to whom it was addressed, would have understood it, and it is virtually certain that it was not understood by any member of the Court of Directors, to whom it was forwarded for approval of the report's recommendation to publish. However, the length and complexity of the report would have conveyed a sense of the seriousness with which the Board examined Campbell's manuscript, and this was sufficient to gain the sanction of the Court. The report was certainly closely read and acted upon by Campbell, and so in a sense its content has been incorporated into the printed grammar. In all likelihood, the report has not been read by anyone since that time until I came across it in the Madras Public Consultations.

The most penetrating criticisms, which concern Campbell's manuscript chapter on verbs, are "founded on, or are supported by a work composed, since Mr. Campbell's Grammar was finished" by head Sanskrit and Telugu master Pattabhirama Shastri. "In this, the form of the verb, according to its several variations, and as used in the grammatical and common dialect, are minutely explained, and a list compiled of all the roots of the language, shewing the treatment of each, on the plan of the Sanskrit Dhatu Malas" (MPC 22 Dec 1815). Pattabhirama's list of Telugu roots, then, which had been only recently composed, was much more than a bare list. It was also an analysis of the "form of the verb," and out of Pattabhirama Shastri's analysis was fashioned the Board's—which is to say, Ellis's—critique of Campbell's treatment of the verb.

The gist of the Board's critique is that all verb forms require three things: root, intermediate particle, and personal termination. The personal terminations are readily identified, but they are subject to modifications depending upon the particles placed between root and termination. The criticism of Campbell's manuscript treatment of this subject is that, "for the ease of the student," his table of terminations does not discriminate between the particle and the termination in some cases. And failure to do so

> destroys the simple and, if such a term may be so employed, the elegant system on which the Telugu verb is constructed, and, what is of material consequence to the persons for whose use the work is principally intended (the students in the College of Fort St. George) it destroys, also, the analogy which subsists in this respect between the Telugu and the Tamil, the Carnatuca, and other dialects of Southern India, the verbs of which are all constructed on the same model, and differ from each other, only by the variation of the intermediate particle, the root being the same, the termination the same, or similar. (Ibid., p. 3394)

Here again Telugu is illuminated by setting it within a larger, Dravidian comparative framework.

How valuable Pattabhirama's analysis of the Telugu verb was to the formation of the Dravidian proof may be inferred from the examples given in a long marginal note to this passage, using the regular root *pāḍu,* "to sing," and the irregular root *paḍu,* "to suffer." The note shows how the same root is variously inflected in the making of verbal forms in Tamil, Kannada, and Telugu. In Tamil, the past tense is formed by inserting the particle *in* or the particle *du,* or modifications of the latter, before the personal termination; thus *pāḍu,* "to sing," always takes *in,* never *du,* and forms the past tense *pāḍu+in+en* = *pāḍinen,* "I sang." Kannada rejects the particle *in* altogether and affixes *idu* (nearly the same as Tamil *du*), or some modification of it, to make the past tense from the root: thus, adding the Kannada first person singular termination, we get *pāḍu+idu+anu* = *pāḍinanu,* "I sang." Telugu retains both *in* and *itu* (nearly the same as Tamil *du* and Kannada *idu*) and makes two forms from *pāḍu,* namely, *pāḍu+in+anu* = *pāḍinanu* and *pāḍu+itu+ini* = *pāḍitini,* "I sang." "Here it is clear that it is not the variation of the root, which is the same, nor the termination which differs immediately, but the varied use of the inserted particles that occasions the difference of the form of the past tense in the three dialects." The three languages treat irregular verbs in the same way, as well. Thus the verb *paḍu,* "to suffer," inserts *du* to form the past but, dropping the final *u* of the root, the final consonant of the root and the first consonant of the particle coalesce, forming the double letter *ṭṭ* in Tamil and Kannada, and *ḍḍ* in Telugu, to which the personal terminations are added. Thus Tamil *paḍu+du+en* becomes *paṭṭu+en* or *paṭṭen,* "I suffered"; Kannada *paḍu+du+anu* becomes *paṭṭu+anu* or *paṭṭanu,* and Telugu *paḍu+du+anu* becomes *paḍḍu+anu* or *paḍḍanu.* This root also has the regular forms *paḍinnanu* and *paḍutine* in Tamil and Kannada (ibid., p. 3395).

The note concludes by drawing from this early adumbration of the Dravidian proof an Orientalist conclusion about the value for colonial rule of a deeply philological education: "These examples will sufficiently demonstrate that which they are intended to prove; namely the great advantage that will accrue to the student who is obliged to acquire more than one of these languages from the observation of correct theory in the grammar of each. If correct, the knowledge he has acquired by the study of one will be easily extended to the other; if incorrect, no assistance will be afforded him, and his labor, therefore, will be, to be renewed, not continued" (ibid.).

Thus the College head masters played a crucial role in formulating the published proof of the idea of the Dravidian language family. But, as we have seen, the Dravidian idea itself preexisted the College, providing the logic of its design in the plan of Ellis. We can, to an extent, trace the prehistory of the Dravidian *proof* by tracing earlier expressions of the Dravidian *idea*. One of the most remarkable among the government documents that help us do so concerns another Telugu grammar, that of William Brown.

HULLABALOO ABOUT TELUGU

Though Ellis was the first to publish what I have called the Dravidian proof, this does not mean he was the discoverer of it, or that the idea of the Dravidian family of languages originated with him. Examining the period leading up to the Dravidian proof, we find a number of glimmerings of what was to come.

The first glimmering originated with Ellis himself, in his early and, as the Government thought, premature proposal to write a grammar and dictionary of Tamil in response to a Government advertisement soliciting proposals early in 1800, to which I have previously referred (MPC 2 May and 27 June 1800). In this correspondence Ellis says that he has already commenced writing a grammar of Tamil, and he expresses his preference to understand the Indian languages in general rather than to confine himself to one in particular, since they are so intimately connected with one another "that to obtain a perfect Grammatical knowledge of one is to obtain a knowledge of all." As an example he comments that in translating Tamil into Telugu or vice versa, "the position of a single word in a thousand *need* not be changed" (MPC 27 June 1800). Although the Government did not accept his proposal, and the grammar of Tamil Ellis was writing has not survived, the ultimate fruit of his thinking was the Dravidian proof of many years later.

John Leyden, as we have seen, came to know Ellis shortly after his arrival in Madras in 1803, and it was from Ellis, we may suppose, that Leyden came to a rough approximation of the Dravidian idea. Leyden soon was assigned to the survey of Mysore, newly conquered from Tipu Sultan under Colin Mackenzie. Although his efforts were hampered by serious illness and he eventually went to Penang to convalesce, his work did get written up, though it was never published, as the first part of the four-part plan for investigating the languages of India and Indo-China that he presented to the supreme government at Calcutta, as I have discussed in chapter 3.

In part one of this ambitious project, the "Plan for investigating the languages, literature, antiquities and history of the Dekkan," Leyden even used the word "Dravida," following Colebrooke's 1801 essay on Prakrit, which had applied to languages the distinction made in the lawbooks *(dharmaśāstras)* between brahmins of the North (the five Gauḍas) and of the South (the five Drāviḍas). Leyden's list of the southern "Hindu tribes," as he calls them, consists of the Tamils, Telingas, Karnatas, Marathis, and Gujaratis, to which he adds the Oriyas, also following Colebrooke, as a "nation" of the Deccan. Right at the outset Leyden departs from Colebrooke, however, when he says that Sanskrit, being mainly a language of religion and science, "is not the native or indigenous language of the Dekkan but only superinduced by the propagation of religion and foreign conquest" (BL Add. Mss. 26,600, ff. 3–4). His overall conception is that the languages of the Deccan "graduate into each other by almost imperceptible shades as they extend from South to North till they finally blend with those of Hindustan proper." By fixing Tamil of the South and Sanskrit of the North as the two extremes, one can class and arrange the intermediate languages. Tamil "seems to be the most original in the southern peninsula and in its purest state exhibits little analogy to Sanscrit" (ibid., f. 5), and Malayalam is closely related to it, though the ancient form of Kannada also has considerable claims to being an original language (called Hullé Canara; ibid., f. 20). Telugu (called Telinga here) is of a more mixed character than Tamil, Malayalam, or Kannada and "seems to have borrowed freely from all quarters to add to the original stock of its vocables" (ibid., f. 27). The idea of an imperceptible shading of languages intermediate between Tamil and Sanskrit does not, however, allow for a clear delineation of the Dravidian family of languages such as we find in the Dravidian proof. Marathi, Gujarati, and Oriya are not clearly assignable to either side of the divide separating Tamil and Sanskrit, and indeed, there can be no definite dividing line under a conception of imperceptible shades of gradation between these extremes. Moreover, Leyden's model leads him into error when he says that Sinhala is closely connected in origin with ancient Tamil and that the morphology of its nouns and verbs are deducible from Tamil "with an occasional intermixture of Sanskrit" (ibid., ff. 30–31). Though Leyden gives a great deal of information about existing grammars and dictionaries in the course of a long disquisition on the Deccan languages, running to forty-one folios, when speaking of the historical relations he finds among these languages, he simply asserts them rather than demonstrating them with evidence and argument.

Leyden's reference to Hullé Canara gives reason to think that the inquiries into language made by Colin Mackenzie's assistants may have shaped

Leyden's views, though Leyden was also in communication with Ellis from the start and might have gotten his ideas from both sources. A circular letter of 1807, written by Mackenzie, which Rama Mantena has found in the Godavari District Records, giving a list of "Desiderata and enquiries connected with the Presidency of Madras," includes the following passages on the sought-for parent of the South Indian languages and their nonderivation from Sanskrit:

> It is certain that the Hindu languages of the south of India are not derived from the Sanscrit, and it is a tradition which this circumstance confirms that the Brahmans, with their religion and language, came from the north. The question regarding the time when the Vadamozhi or northern tongue (the Sanscrit) was introduced, is one of great interest.
>
> A comparison of the different languages of the south and an examination of what they have borrowed from the Sanscrit, with an accurate account of the geographical limits of these languages.
>
> Which is the most ancient character in use in the south of India?
>
> Is there any trace of a language which may be considered the parent of those now existing in Southern India? If so, what is its name? Where was it vernacular? And how far has it entered into the formation of the other peninsular languages?
>
> Does the Purvada Hali Canada answer in any degree this description? Some account of this language with a well written alphabet of its characters as appearing in inscriptions, it is believed, may be obtained from learned Jain Brahmans. One of this Sect, employed by Colonel Mackenzie, thoroughly understood it, and if still living, might probably furnish the information here desired. (Mantena 2002:58–59)

Thus it is clear that a version of the Dravidian idea informed the project of Colin Mackenzie, though it did not lead to a published proof, for which Mackenzie himself, being unfamiliar with the languages of the South, was not suited.

But the most interesting expression of the Dravidian idea in the period before the Dravidian proof was published comes from Sankaraiah, Ellis's chief of staff at the Madras Collectorate and a formidable scholar in his own right, judging from the praise accorded to him in the *Sarvadevavilāsa*. His views lay buried and forgotten in the colonial record as part of a response to a proposal by one William Brown to write a Telugu grammar for the Company, till I came across them while doing research for this book.

William Brown—not to be confused with the great Telugu scholar

C. P. Brown, who belongs to a later generation—wrote a grammar of Telugu which was published in 1817, the third to appear in a few years, following those of Carey (1814) and Campbell (1816). This mini-explosion of grammars testifies to the fact that by this time the British had come to recognize the importance of Telugu.

The Madras Government had made it known that it would subsidize the publication of grammars and dictionaries of the South Indian languages, and Brown submitted the draft of his grammar to the Government in about 1810 for that purpose. The Government formed a committee of two civil servants with knowledge of Telugu, William Thackeray and William Sanders, to evaluate the draft. Thackeray, who was later Telugu translator to the Madras Government, became a member of the Board of Superintendence when the College was formed. The committee tried to get evaluations of Brown's grammar from pandits of Masulipatam whom Brown had named in his manuscript as his advisors in the writing of it, and who were also known to Thackeray, namely, Chandragula, Gopal Rao, Purushottam Pantalu, and Mamadi Venkayya. The committee said they had already suggested bringing Mamadi Venkayya to Madras to supervise the teaching of Telugu in the Madrassah: "He is a very extraordinary man, a banian who in spite of the opposition of the Brahmins who, enraged at the presumption of a man of his cast [*sic*] in venturing to apply himself to literature, have more than once had his house pulled down, has persevered in his literary pursuits and has compiled two most curious Dictionaries from one of which Mr. Brown has taken the English and Gentoo Vocabulary which he has annexed to his Grammar" (MPC 15 Mar 1811, para. 20). However, they were unsuccessful in getting evaluations from these pandits.

The committee, in turn, sent the manuscript to a learned brahmin of the city, who was none other than Sankaraiah, soon to become sheristadar to Ellis, for evaluation. Sankaraiah was very critical of it. The committee's report, enclosing the report of Sankaraiah, both reports being long and detailed, was sent to the Government, which in turn sent a copy of the whole to William Brown, with a letter of rejection. Brown was extremely angry and sent a long rebuttal to the Madras Government, enclosing also a long rebuttal in response to Sankaraiah's critique by *his* pandit, Purushottam of Masulipatam, who was the vakil, or Hindu law expert, to the provincial court there (MPC 15 Dec 1818). But by then Campbell's grammar had been published, and Brown was obliged to publish his grammar himself, without government help. Buried in the Madras Public Consultations, the two hundred or so folio pages of the committee's report plus Brown's response, handwritten with a steel nib pen and probably not read since the time of their writing, comprise a splendid five-sided hullabaloo about Telugu grammar involving three British scholars and two Indian ones. In it we can see very clearly the cross-cutting ways in which Indian and European ideas about language were being combined and contested in colonial Madras.

By far the most interesting parts of the hullabaloo are the contrasting readings of Telugu given by Sankaraiah of Madras and Purushottam of Masulipatam.

Sankaraiah offers a number of criticisms of Brown's manuscript grammar of Telugu. One of them is that Brown uses the five cases of English grammar (or we should rather say, the five cases of Latin grammar that were conventional for grammars of English) for Telugu nouns rather than the seven cases plus vocative of the Indian grammatical tradition. Interestingly, Campbell also stuck to the five-case plan that would have been more familiar to the British beginner, and in the critique of Campbell's grammar Ellis made the same point as Sankaraiah makes here, arguing that the Indian analysis is more natural and in any case would facilitate communication between the Indian teacher and the British student. Sankaraiah also criticizes Brown for including as Telugu the naturalized Persian and English words used as technical terms in colonial courts and government. Sankaraiah prefers to coin new words from Sanskrit roots, a view Thackeray and Sanders do not endorse. Criticisms of this kind are fairly direct reflexes of the Indian tradition of language analysis.

However, Sankaraiah gives a very novel and imaginative reading of that tradition when he refers the words of Telugu to the roots of two different languages, Sanskrit and Tamil, concluding that Telugu is a *mixture* of the two. He states that part of the Telugu language is referable to Sanskrit roots, and supplies a list of such words, including *tadbhavas* such as *dīvi, kaṃcu,* and *pavaḍamu,* derived from Sanskrit *dvīpa* (island), *kāṃsya* (bell metal), and *pravāla* (coral bead). Of the *deśya* words, which of course make up the greater part of the Telugu lexicon, he gives a list with Tamil cognates: for instance, Telugu *mōru, mala, kaḍali,* and *ceppu* correspond to Tamil *mōr* (buttermilk), *malai* (mountain), *kaṭal* (ocean), and *cerappu* (sandal).[5] Sankaraiah further says that the four conjugations

5. V. Narayana Rao tells me that the Telugu word *mōru,* "buttermilk," is spoken only in the Telugu of Madras and is a local Tamil loanword. I am grateful to him for much help in the decipherment and interpretation of the records making up the "hullabaloo about Telugu."

of Telugu verbs consist of three conjugations of *accadeśyamu* origin, referable to pure Tamil and governed by rules of the Tamil *Nūl,* that is, the grammar called *Naṉṉūl,* while the fourth conjugation concerns verbs of Sanskrit derivation that are governed in part by the rules of Sanskrit grammar. He supplies detailed examples of the four conjugations.

Sankaraiah's view that Telugu is a mixture, derivable from roots in Sanskrit and Tamil, was, I venture to think, quite unprecedented, though it was entirely constructed with the tools of Indian grammatical analysis. What is unprecedented is that it combines the ancient traditions of grammatical analysis of Sanskrit and of Tamil (which are distantly but definitely related in some way) and applies them to a third language, Telugu.

Just how novel this was may be measured by the answering comments of Purushottam on Sankaraiah's report, which were hostile. Purushottam takes a position completely in keeping with that of both the Prakrit and the Telugu grammarians, in that he treats Telugu as the last term in a continuum beginning with Sanskrit, with Prakrit as the middle term. He illustrates this analysis with columns of *tadbhavas* showing the continuity from Sanskrit to Prakrit to Telugu. Examples from his list are: *siṃha* (Skt.), *siṃghā* (Pkt.), *siṃgamu* (Tel.) "lion"; and *lākṣā* (Skt.), *lakkā* (Pkt.), *lakka* (Tel.), "sealing wax." The intent here is to interpret as many Telugu words as possible as *bhavas* of Sanskrit. Puroshottam leaves the *deśya* residue unremarked, and it was generally the position of the Telugu grammarians to regard *deśya* words as having an ancient and mysterious origin (see Paravastu Venkata Ramanujaswami's very interesting and useful introduction to Hemacandra's *Deśināmamāla,* 1938 ed.).

Brown's grammar, even as it was written, was being superseded by the advances of language study under the new Orientalism at Calcutta and in Madras, and its out-of-dateness shows. It was a workmanlike primer of Telugu meant to give a British civil servant the ability to converse with a minimum of fuss and a maximum of colonial utility—a kind of Berlitz School approach based upon Samuel Johnson's grammar of English. One of the signs of Brown's resistance to new trends is his defensive clinging to the once-customary expressions "Gentoo" and "Malabar" as adjectives ("Gentoos" and "Malabars" as substantives), whereas by this time "Telugu" and "Tamil" were the normal names in English.

Brown's argument is, at bottom, not very coherent. He claims that his grammar is sound because it was written with the assistance of learned Telugu pandits of Masulipatam, and he also engaged one of them to counteract the authority of Sankaraiah; yet he is at the same time scornful of

Sanskrit, Sanskrit grammar, and its utility in learning Telugu, as well as the Sanskritic element in the Telugu language. Thus his view that Telugu "at one time flourished without those adulterations from the Shanskrit with which it is at present overwhelmed" (MPC 15 Mar 1811, para. 11) places him quite at odds with the Sanskritocentric position of his champion, Purushottam, and creates a contradiction within his own position.

The argument of Brown's critics, Thackeray and Sanders, has its own weakness. They extol the virtue of knowing Sanskrit as an aid to learning Telugu and its grammar and answer the charge that Sanskrit has adulterated Telugu by airily saying that these adulterations are in fact improvements, rather like the adulteries of Arabian stallions with English mares. But they admit that they do not themselves know much Sanskrit, remarking, also airily, that the volunteer (Brown) must be held to a higher standard than those (Thackeray and Sanders) who have been ordered to the service—ordered, in their case, to evaluate his manuscript by the Madras Government. This tells us that their grasp of the latest Orientalist scholarship relating to Indo-European and Dravidian languages (they cite, for example, Colebrooke 1801 and Hamilton 1809), and especially what they had learned from Ellis, ran ahead of their own acquaintance with Sanskrit. It is abundantly clear from their references to other scholars that their critique of Brown's manuscript was informed by this larger horizon of scholarship, especially by conversations with Ellis, and that Brown had not kept up with these developments or was out of sympathy with them.

Brown's view that Telugu once existed without Sanskrit borrowings, interestingly enough, is consistent with the Dravidian idea, and his quarrel with Thackeray and Sanders has only to do with whether, given that position, Sanskrit improved Telugu or disimproved it. In the course of their long discussion of the relationship between Sanskrit and Telugu, Thackeray and Sanders reimagine the way in which brahmin scholars of the past must have come to believe in the linguistic unity of India. The brahmins, they say, assert that all languages ultimately derive from Sanskrit, and, consistent with this view, "the similarity of words expressing objects which engage the attention of mankind in the Infancy of Society"—the method of the word list—has led European scholars to derive Greek, Latin, Gothic, and Persian from Sanskrit, "or from some language the Common Mother of all," in short, the conception of the Indo-European language family as propounded by Jones and developed by Hamilton. The method of comparative vocabulary does not sustain the view that Telugu is derived from Sanskrit, and perhaps other Indian dialects as well, and yet "almost every language in India . . . is so filled with Shanskrit words that any person well grounded in one Indian language will easily understand at least one half the terms used in any other" (MPC 15 Mar 1811, para. 13). Thus Thackeray and Sanders, like Brown, maintain that Telugu is radically different from Sanskrit, but on quite different grounds, namely, the differences between the conjugations of Telugu and Sanskrit verbs, and between the Telugu and Sanskrit words expressing "objects of early sensation, and common life"—words which must be classed as *deśya*.

Thackeray and Sanders go on to say that complex ideas connected with science, art, religion, and law are expressed in Sanskrit words throughout India (except in Tamil, as Ellis informs them), so it is hardly surprising that brahmins insist that Sanskrit was formerly universal. If a brahmin renouncer (a *vairāgi*) were to travel from the Indus to Pegu (in Burma), or from Cape Comorin to Tibet, he would find Sanskrit words denoting almost everything he thinks holy or important: every term in the sciences and the arts; every attribute of the deity; every quality and operation of the human mind; every part of the human body; the sun, moon, and stars; the years, days, weeks, and months; ceremonies and books. These terms, moreover, are in common use "among those who have the least pretensions to education." He would find, to be sure, that the words used by the vulgar for father, mother, cow, dog, horse, river, fire, water, and other such entities (i.e., the simple words of the comparative vocabulary) seem to have no connection with Sanskrit, "and if he were quite unprejudiced and addicted to philology, he would endeavor to decide whether these words were Corruptions, which had crept into a language derived immediately from Shanskrit, or whether they were the remains of an original dialect which prevailed before the Shanskrit was known [i.e., *deśya* words]" (ibid., para. 16).

Mr. Brown, they continue, thinks the Sanskrit is an innovation and the original Telugu was a rich and copious language, yet he has overlooked the principal argument for this, namely, that Telugu terms expressing "those things and ideas which in the infancy of society are first named" are not from Sanskrit. It is exactly such words that have been fastened upon by scholars who have been struck by the similarity among Sanskrit, Persian, Latin, Greek, and Gothic, arguing therefrom the probability of a common origin of these languages and nations, while the terms of science and art, which developed later in these languages, are heterogeneous. The authors quote Hamilton's review of Wilkins on the theory of the word list: "There are things which must have been named in the very infancy of Society and before the first dawn of Civilization where these names correspond. Therefore in different Countries we may confidently infer that the one has been peopled by the same stock as the others" (Hamilton 1809:372). By this rule, they argue, Telugu and several other Indian dialects might be set down as of an origin radically different from that of Sanskrit, since the Indo-European situation is here inverted, words of science and art in South India being pure Sanskrit but terms expressing primitive ideas seeming to be quite unconnected with Sanskrit. This is the idea, in a nutshell, of the Dravidian family of languages, though the analysis is directed to only one of them.

Thackeray and Sanders imagine, they say, that the existence of non-Sanskritic words of this kind (i.e., *deśya* words) has led Sir William Jones and other scholars who have discussed the subject in India to think that such words are traces of an original language antecedent to or independent of Sanskrit; and they think that either an original Telugu dialect may be traced in such words or "the opinion of some learned natives who assert that these independent words are Tamil, is to be adopted"—the opinion, in short, of Sankaraiah and apparently some others (MPC 15 Mar 1811, para. 17). But they consider it pretty certain that the arts, knowledge, and civilization followed the Sanskrit language, which has left its imprint throughout India, from the Indus to Pegu.

This is the burden of the report on Brown's manuscript, to which, as we have seen, Brown vigorously objected. But Brown's complaint was not only directed to the substance of the report. He also claimed that a malign influence had been working upon Thackeray, coming from unnamed outsiders who overvalued Sanskrit. He offered in proof a letter which Thackeray wrote him when Brown first submitted the grammar, along with a vocabulary of Telugu, to the Government in 1809. In this letter Thackeray had expressed the opinion, unofficially and on a cursory examination to be sure, that he "highly approved" of both, and thought they would be of the "greatest practical utility to a student." Why had Thackeray turned against Brown's grammar in the report? The committee's objections seemed "to have arisen from the opinion of others, whose fanciful and ostentatious predilection for Shanscrit, prevented them from judging dispassionately of a work, which professed no blind devotion to that sacred & mysterious tongue." Had Thackeray's opinion been "unshackled by a superfluous display of Shanscrit rules with which that report has been crowded to an excess," Brown complained, the merits of his "humble production" would have been better appreciated (MPC 15 Dec 1818, para. 9). This seems essentially right. I believe Thackeray had consulted Ellis after his initial, favorable reading of Brown's manuscript, and Ellis persuaded him otherwise. Ellis is cited favorably as an authority three times in the report, and there are a number of other clues that link the report and its "take" on Telugu to Ellis and his circle. The most important of these, of course, is Sankaraiah himself, who had been sheristadar to Ellis at Kumbakonam and would shortly be sheristadar to Ellis as Collector of Madras and, briefly, English head master at the College. Ellis and Sankaraiah would certainly have discussed the relationship among Tamil, Telugu, and Sanskrit, and these discussions must have informed Sankaraiah's report on Brown's grammar.

Did Ellis share Sankaraiah's view that Telugu is a mixture of Sanskrit and Tamil? Ellis doesn't quite put it like that. In his analysis he presents a list of roots *(dhātumālas)* for *each* of the three languages, Telugu, Tamil, and Kannada, while Sankaraiah argues that the roots of the *deśya* words in Telugu are to be found in the Tamil *Naṉṉūl.* Yet Ellis goes on to say that the roots of the three languages are not simply similar, they are the same; that is, they are not three stocks of roots, but one. And elsewhere he makes it clear that he believes Tamil preserves the South Indian language with the greatest purity and that other languages are, on the whole, deviations from Tamil. Putting these statements together, we come to a view that is virtually indistinguishable from that of Sankaraiah.

Brown suspected that his grammar had fallen victim to a conspiracy when the College published Campbell's Telugu grammar and the Government declined to subsidize the publication of his own. To give him his due, Brown had, I believe, identified more or less accurately the author of his difficulties. Ellis and his circle at the College and in Madras generally, including Campbell, Sankaraiah, Pattabhirama Shastri, Chidambaram Vadiyar, and Udayagiri Venkatanarayana, were engaged in discussions leading to innovative ideas about the South Indian languages and Sanskrit, in the course of which the grammatical traditions of Pāṇini and Tolkāppiyar were mixing with the language-nation obsession of Europe, and strange, unanticipated hybrids were being born. One of these was Sankaraiah's view of Telugu.

Brown and Purushottam could make much of the fact that Sankaraiah was a native of Madras, not of the Telugu country proper, yet he was being taken as the expert on the Telugu spoken to the north, while Purushottam, as "an able expounder of the merits of his own language, . . . must of course be supposed superior to a stranger and a southern man" (ibid., para. 3). But of course Sankaraiah's strength was exactly that he was a Telugu brahmin of Madras, on the borderland between the Telugu and Tamil regions, conversant in Telugu, Tamil, Sanskrit, and English. That Purushottam lived in Masulipatam in the Telugu-speaking region, with little exposure to Tamil, is consistent with the argument he makes, which is within the *vyākaraṇa* tradition. The novelty of Sankaraiah's analysis has to do with the fact that it is the view from Madras, a colonial metropolis where Telugu, Tamil, and English mingled, and where *vyākaraṇa,* the Tamil *Nūl,* and the linguistic analysis that had grown out of the Mosaic ethnology conversed, clashed, and converged. In this mixed British-Indian space something quite new came into being.

Thackeray and Sanders' report is structurally similar to A. D. Campbell's argument in the introduction to his grammar of Telugu, published by the College in preference to that of Brown, in that it directs itself to the analysis of Telugu alone among the Dravidian languages and Telugu's relation to Sanskrit; while Sankaraiah's report within the report, with its three-cornered analysis of the relation of Telugu to Sanskrit and Tamil, is structurally similar to Ellis's Dravidian proof, though of course less extensive in its scope—the Dravidian proof in a nutshell. Two Dravidian languages plus Sanskrit provide the minimum material for a proof that languages of South India are related to one another and not derived from Sanskrit. Tamil and Telugu need not have been those two languages, but they were in many ways an ideal pair for the purpose.

A pleasing aspect of this story, as with many stories of origin, is that we cannot, in the end, get to the bottom of it. We cannot say for certain whether Sankaraiah got the idea of a Dravidian family of languages from Ellis, or Ellis got it from Sankaraiah. To be sure, as early as 1800, much earlier than we can trace the relationship between Ellis and Sankaraiah, Ellis had expressed something like the Dravidian idea in his letter to the Government proposing that it subsidize him in the writing of a Tamil grammar and dictionary, but where that idea came from we do not know. In the end, all we can say is that the Dravidian idea emerged from the conjuncture of certain ideas and a certain network of scholars in colonial Madras.

CHAPTER 6

Legacies

Ellis was involved in generating a whole array of new understandings of South Indian history and culture concerning such matters as law, land, literature, religion, and caste. Some of these were highly consequential, especially his work on land tenure, which included writing, with Sankaraiah, the *Treatise of mirasi right,* and introducing the ryotwari system (over which Ellis clashed with Thomas Munro), which brought a new mode of government to bear on the South Indian countryside. This is not the occasion to go into these dimensions of Ellis's work. I have chosen to concentrate in this book on the Dravidian proof, which was certainly the heart of his project, but it is well to keep in mind that it was part of a larger vision about the past of South India.

The legacy of the Dravidian proof most evident today is the Dravidian political movement in Tamil Nadu, which began with the Justice Party of the 1920s and continued with the DMK (Dravida Munnetra Kazhagam) Party and its offshoots. The very word "Dravidian" is strongly associated with that political formation. Assuredly, there is a lineal connection between the Dravidian proof and the Dravidian political movement, but the nature of the connection is not self-evident, and it is not simple. The political movement came about nearly seventy years after Caldwell's comparative grammar of the Dravidian languages (1856) and a full century after the Dravidian proof (1816). To derive it from the Dravidian proof directly would be to evacuate the large time interval and the many historical developments that mediated between them. The Dravidian movement, moreover, was largely successful in only one part of the Dravidian language region, Tamil Nadu, and in its origins was associated with the attempt to overcome brahmin hegemony in government. These features do not flow directly from the Dravidian proof. Indeed, in the light of the Dravidian movement, it is something of a paradox that it was two Telugu brahmins, Sankaraiah and Pattabhirama Shastri, who were the most closely involved with Ellis in the proof's formulation.

In this chapter we will examine not the well-studied Dravidian movement of the twentieth century but the Dravidian proof's more immediate legacies: for Indians of the College of Fort St. George, and for the College's philological activity in the years following Ellis's death, for these legacies are little-known yet momentous in their own way. We will first take up the death of Ellis and the fortunes of the College before and after. Then we will turn to the Indian students of the College and their program of instruction, especially in law, as an indicator of the effects of the College upon this class of its Indian constituents. Finally, we will sketch the publications of the College's head masters and their contributions to Tamil and Telugu letters. As we shall see, these scholars had a significant role in the recovery of the classics, the publication of first printed editions of the literature of the past, and the transformation of the written language itself. These were the very real legacies of the "revival of letters" that the making of the College had put in train.

THE DEATH OF ELLIS

At the College's creation and for its first few years, both the institution and Ellis enjoyed the full confidence of the Government of Madras. It was during the governorship of Sir George Hilaro Barlow (1807–13) that Ellis and his fellow members of the Committee for the Examination of the Junior Civil Servants had been invited to devise and present proposals for the improvement of language instruction, and the plan for the College of Fort St. George which the Committee put forth was sanctioned with alacrity. The Government of Madras smiled on the early accomplishments of the College, and so did the Court of Directors in London.

This situation did not last. On 16 September 1814, Hugh Elliot arrived to assume the governorship of Madras, accompanied by Mrs. Elliot, Miss Emma Elliot, Miss Harriet Elliot, Miss Caroline Elliot, Mr. Martin Frederick Elliot, H. Elliot Esq., aide de camp, and H. M. Elliot Esq., writer, as well as Colonel Thomas Munro and Mrs. Munro. The new governor came ashore under a nineteen-gun salute from the battery near the northeast angle of the Fort, and was met on the beach by various dignitaries (*Bombay courier* 1 Oct. 1814).

Under the governorship of Elliot the atmosphere changed abruptly for the worse, and the College could no longer count on the Government's ready assent to its actions. The change was partly due to a growing concern on the part of the Government that the College was too philological and insufficiently directed to the practical ends of colonial rule in its language instruction, and partly owing to an unfortunate happenstance that got entangled with this question. The report of the Board of Superintendence on the first examination of students in 1815, submitted 15 June, listed all the students in order of their proficiency in the various languages, and commented on the progress and attainments of most of them in considerable detail. But the report gave only a laconic reference to those at the bottom of the list for Tamil. "In the hope that the four Gentlemen whose names are entered last on the list of Tamil students will enable us at the next examination to report favorably on their progress, we refrain from any particular mention of them at present," said the report (MPC 3 Nov 1815, para. 28). Included in this list of the bottom four in Tamil was Mr. H. M. Elliot, the governor's son.

The problem would not have arisen if the governor's son had been an apt student of Tamil, but he was not. The next report to which this report looked forward so hopefully would have been in December, but trying to ease a delicate situation, the Board gave a special examination for young Mr. Elliot and another writer in September. It sent a short letter to the Governor in Council, the burden of which was to report on the satisfactory progress of two of the four students, "this day examined at their own request":

> Mr. Crowley and Mr. Elliot have very materially improved their knowledge of Tamil Grammar, and they are now tolerably well versed in the elements of this language; but their command of words is yet very limited, and consequently their translations of even the most easy papers very incorrect and defective, and their means of colloquial intercourse with the natives restricted to the most common and simple questions. The laudable attention, however, which these two Gentlemen have lately evinced to study, and the success with has attended their assiduity and application, induce us to recommend that the Right Honourable the Governor in Council may be pleased to confer upon each of them the increased allowance of Pagodas 75 pr. Mensem, which we trust will not fail to encourage them to further exertion. (Ibid., para. 2)

In short, the Board of Superintendence proposed to promote the governor's son to the second stipendiary level not because he had reached the expected level of proficiency but because he had made some progress and was now applying himself. It was hardly a strong record of attainment. The report was not signed by Ellis, who was in Bengal on a three-month leave at the time (MDR 22 Aug 1815). The leave completely explains the absence of his signature, but we may wonder whether the giving of an ad hoc examination in Tamil, his special passion, and the writing of this less than honest letter might not have been rushed through by the Board members while Ellis was away. Had Ellis been present, he might have been an obstacle to the shabby solution the Board was offering for the problem, though this must remain pure speculation in the absence of any direct evidence. The letter closed with a gentle reminder that its report of 15 June had not yet been acted upon by the Governor in Council.

Two months passed before the governor replied, in a minute of 3 November. In his apology for having taken so long to reply he cited "a very long and severe illness," on the one hand, and, on the other, the newness to him and the importance of the subject, that is, the instruction of the junior civil servants. Expanding ominously on this theme, he said that before departing from England he had heard complaints about the expense of the College, and been asked to investigate how far the expense of the College could be reduced without injury to its principal object, namely, procuring the means for junior servants of the Company "to acquire a sufficient knowledge of the vernacular languages of this country, to be usefully and practicably employed in the different departments of Government" (MPC 3 Nov 1815, para. 3). There was, he continued, a considerable difference of opinion among those expert in the details of the Madras Government as to the course of studies that the students should follow.

> On the one hand Gentlemen deeply versed in Indian literature, conceive that the student ought to be grounded in the knowledge of some of those original languages, from which they contend that the idiom at present in use in various parts of the Peninsula, have been originally derived, altho' these roots must be traced back with great labour, to a deep antiquity. On the other hand it is asserted, that to become useful servants of the Company, it is merely requisite in the first instance, to understand the different languages, as they are now written and spoken, by the natives over whom the Government presides, and whose relations with them are principally included in the Judicial and Revenue branches of the service. (Ibid., para. 4)

The first of these opposing visions was of course the plan of Ellis. It cannot have been much of a relief to the College Board that the governor said he was deferring consideration of the main question to a future time. In the meantime, he spoke to the issues at hand, of which the one that concerns us is the treatment of his son. In its letter of 7 September, said Governor Elliot, the Board stated that Mr. Crowley and Mr. Elliot "have very materially improved in their knowledge of Tamil Grammar, and that they are tolerably well versed in the elements of the language; but attached to this statement in their favour the same sentence contains a list of various deficiencies, which did not accompany the approbation which was given to the Gentlemen recommended in the former report for the increased allowances" (ibid., para. 13). This being so, he declined recommending increased allowances of 75 pagodas per month for Mr. Elliot and Mr. Crowley till they received from the Board a recommendation equal to that given to others named in the report of 15 June, "to whose deficiency in the command of words, in translation of papers, and in the means of Colloquial intercourse with the Natives, it was not thought necessary to advert" (ibid., para. 14). The Board's attempt to smooth over a difficult situation was so transparently dishonest that the governor felt obliged to reject it. Far from defusing the problem, it caused it to blow up in their faces. It stirred the governor's anger and provoked him to look more closely at the College with a less friendly eye. In the end, young Mr. Elliot gave up the attempt to master Tamil and left the service.

Ellis had anticipated such developments two years earlier and expressed this to his friend Erskine at Bombay, and he planned to return to England in order to lobby for the College with the Court of Directors:

> I foresee that my presence in Europe at no distant period will be of great advantage to the College of Fort St. George and as my prospects in the service are bounded at present by the situation I now hold, the temporary relinquishment of which could affect my primary concerns only and then not permanently, I am resolved to proceed thither about the commencement of next year. Sir George [Barlow, the then Governor of Madras] indeed has done everything in his power for the Establishment, and as busy as he remains will no doubt continue to do so, but how the Court of Directors may feel, or what may be the opinions of the new Governor which the revolution of two or three years must, in the customary routine send us, it is not so easy to anticipate. It is certain, however, than an advocate on the spot must be greatly advantageous, and I have no doubt that when in England I shall be able to make arrangements which will be much more beneficial to the Institution, and to my own interests, which of course it behooves me not to leave out of the calculation, than could result from my remaining in India. (Ellis to Erskine 10 March 1813)

He asked Erskine to get him information about the overland journey from Bombay, especially the best season of the year for crossing the Syrian desert from Basra, at the head of the Persian Gulf in Iraq, and whether there might be a party making the journey which he could join to lower the expense.

From this first mention, the overland journey to England became a leitmotiv in Ellis's letters to Erskine, much discussed but never acted upon. In August of the same year, Ellis wrote that he would not be able to join Captain Digby, who, Erskine had informed him, was to make the journey. After much thought he had decided to wait till the next year, as "certain irons which I have now in the fire require to be beaten out, and I am allowing myself another year." The College needed his attention—"the printing of books, for instance of which we have many in hand and which I find so much slower than I expected." He also felt a certain ambivalence about returning to England after having lived so long—by now the greater part of his life—in India:

> A man is at no period of his life sure of the continuance of his prevailing habits and dispositions, however fixed he may consider them; on this point I feel very diffident with respect to myself, and I think it, therefore, better to accomplish as much as I can in India before I quit it. Whether Europe with respect to myself will operate any material change I know not but it is probable that many objects I now hold in estimation may by a residence there lose their value. I have every thing indeed to learn with respect to Europe and as I become acquainted with it, therefore, as I europeanize, I think there is a great chance that I shall deindianize in proportion." (Ellis to Erskine 24 August 1813).

In a letter to Erskine of 1815, Ellis speaks again of the plan to make an overland journey, "which after nine cancellations, I am positively determined to undertake in the course of the coming year, 1816." The easiest way, he understands, is to take passage on one of the Arab ships that leave the ports of Malabar and Kanara in February and March, proceeding directly to Morcha; but he prefers to go via Basra over the great desert, making a tour of Syria through Damascus to Jerusalem, which he is resolved to see, though it is off the beaten track (NLS Mss. 36.1.5, ff. 88–98). The following year he writes thanking Erskine for information he had sent concerning the overland route, which, "unless disease, death, or some other accident intervenes to prevent it," he will surely make use of, a facetious statement that is more somber for us, knowing that death indeed intervened to prevent the journey. His visit to Bengal in the autumn of 1815 he had intended as a preparation for leaving India, but he again found, "for at least the fifth time," that he had to postpone the journey for some months, if not more. One of the greatest difficulties was the settlement of official accounts; his accounts for his first year as Collector of Madras were not yet finally adjusted—"adjusted or not, however, I intend certainly to be off in the Autumn of 1817, and this time I think I shall not fail." Speaking of the College, he thinks its reputation is everywhere increasing except at Madras, by which he means the governor, Hugh Elliot. "The old Gentleman at the head of affairs here regards us with no complacent eye. We reported too honestly on the progress or rather the non-progress of his son, and he thought proper to remove him from the service, a result which he attributes to us—he has thought proper also, as you must have observed, to prevent the publication of our reports on examinations, though his son being now removed he has not the same reason for continuing as for originating the prohibition"(ibid., ff. 112–18). The College would flourish, but it needed the sanction of higher authority, that is, of London.

If only Ellis had made that journey to England! Instead, a medical mishap brought him to an early grave in Ramnad. Writing to Leyden in 1808, he had spoken of ill health that might drive him to England or to death. At that time he was serving as judge in the zillah of Masulipatam, in the Telugu country, to which he had been sent two years previous after his brief, disastrous appointment in Tanjore. Over the past several years, he tells Leyden in the letter, he has been travelling constantly and camping out. "During this period I have at times met with a check or two in my progress, but two only have been of sufficient consequence to give me a shock of any violence; one of these was my removal from Tanjore and consequent banishment from the southern provinces, and the other is a damnable fit of Dyspepsia, which has tormented me for the last five months, and I fear will ultimately drive me either to England or out of the world" (Ellis to Leyden 7 Aug–28 Sept 1808, OIOC Mss. Eur.D.30, pp. 127–28). One gets a sense from this what a hardship it had been for Ellis, a scholar of Tamil, to have been banished from the Tamil region to the Telugu country (though he was not prevented from traveling through Tamil Nadu on his way from Jagannath in Orissa to Kumari at the southern tip of India). The shock of his removal from Tanjore stuck with him, and so did the dyspepsia.

Ten years later, when he was applying for three months' leave from his labors as Collector of Madras, the grounds of the request were the "restoration of my health." He enclosed the certificate of a surgeon, which refers to attacks of dyspepsia "accompanied by considerable derangement of the liver" and recommending "a change of air towards the cooler climate of the interior" (MDR 18 Nov 1818). But Ellis went to Madurai, where he stayed with the collector, Rous Petrie, rather than to the hills, as one might have expected, and from Madurai he went to Ramnad in the deep south. So, although the chronic stomach problems were genuine, the itinerary may have had more to do with his research interests than with seeking cooler air. In Ramnad he unexpectedly died.

We know little of his final trip except what we learn from the three documents he wrote as he lay dying in Ramnad. We know of course that the dyspepsia from which he had suffered so greatly in 1808 was a continuing problem, and he tells us while dying that he took "poison instead of medicine," which caused his death. His dying took several hours, during which he dictated his will, in three parts (OIOC L/AG/34/29/219, pp. 44–45). The first, dated Ramnad, 9 March 1819, says.

> I give all my property to my mother Elizabeth Hubbard except.—
>
> Item 5000 £ to my Brother George Item 2000 £ to the elder daughter of John Howeth, 1000 £ to the Son of John Howeth & 500 £ to each male and female child of the said John Howeth, 100 £ to John Howeth Sen to buy mourning and 500 £ to my Aunt Dianna Howeth.

The second is as follows:

> I request that what remains after paying my funeral charges to give fifty (50) Pags. To Sangera Sixty Pagodas to Veerasawmy Thirty Pagodas to Vencatraswamy & Daniel if there is not enough they will apply to my dubash Mambharangayanag who has property of mine in his possession.

The third is a letter to this dubash:

> My Dear Rungiah Nack
>
> Pay the whole of my Bond to the Register of the Court. I take poison instead of Medicine at Ramnad and I am at point of death.

These three brief writings were evidently dictated and written out by someone else, as the handwriting and the vernacular spellings of Indian names show. Each was signed by Ellis. The witnesses were A. Campbell—presumably not his protégé A. D. Campbell—and D. Schreyvoyd.

Since Ellis died without having named an executor and had not left any next of kin in India, his estate was administered by the Registrar of the Supreme Court. It was a goodly estate—worth over two lakhs (200,000) of Madras rupees—including an excellent library, the inventory of which, as we would expect, is strong on philology; it lists over 550 books and manuscripts in both Sanskrit and Tamil, and includes a number of guidebooks for the overland journey to England he never took (OIOC L/AG/34/29/22/ pp. 123–37). The whole of his effects were sold at public auction in Madras and Madurai. It is a great pity that his library was broken up and scattered, but at least (one supposes) the books found readers and contributed in that way to the improvement of knowledge at Madras. The papers were another matter. I have already recited the story circulating years later in Madras, which Walter Elliot reports, that the Ellis papers went up in smoke, one at a time, in the kitchen of Rous Petrie, "to kindle fires and singe chickens." A year after Ellis's death, the Court of Directors gave George Hubbard and John Howorth [*sic*] Jr. permission to proceed to Madras to settle the estate (MPC 1 Nov 1820, paras. 5–6).

According to a historian of the Madras Literary Society, the Society foundered following the death of Ellis, who had been its most active and able member, and was resuscitated only some years later (Ramaswami 1985). When it revived and published the first volume of its transactions, the manuscript of Ellis's lectures on Hindu law provided material for the first article, published as a tribute to the Society's most illustrious scholar. The Society continues to this day, but the episode reminds us of the fragility of life in colonial India, and the fragility of institutions of this kind, sustained by the energy and interest of a few.

The College, on the other hand, was by this time, seven years after its founding, a viable government institution, well able to survive its founder's demise. Ellis's report on the manuscript of Campbell's Telugu-English dictionary was one of his last contributions to the work of the College, and when the dictionary came out, Campbell dedicated it to him in these words: "To the memory of the late Francis Whyte Ellis, Esq. of the Madras Civil Service, who planned the establishment of the College of Fort St. George, and, while he lived, was it's [*sic*] chief ornament and support, this work, the offspring of that institution, is inscribed; as a tribute of friendship due from the author."

Ellis did not make the mark on scholarship he certainly would have, had he lived. Nevertheless, his accomplishments were considerable. In Madras his reputation lingered, and several people sought to keep his memory green and record his accomplishments. Walter Elliot, a prize-winning student of the College of Fort St. George in Tamil and Hindustani who went on to be a distinguished civil servant and Orientalist, as we have seen, rescued and published Ellis's dissertation on Malayalam. G. U. Pope, the missionary and professor of Tamil at Oxford to whom Elliot bequeathed the Ellis papers, published Ellis's work on the *Kuṟaḷ* and *Nālaḍiyār,* and deposited the papers in the Bodleian Library. Even the Rev. William Taylor, who regarded Ellis as an atheist, acknowledged his greatness as a scholar, and C. P. Brown, himself a great scholar of Telugu, who rarely had a good word to say about other Orientalists, mixed his blame with praise when it came to Ellis. As we have seen, A. C. Burnell, the great paleographer and historian of grammar, considered Ellis's Dravidian proof the equivalent of Bopp's famous pamphlet of the same date (1816) on Indo-European.

At the College some changes were immediate. The course of study that had been written into the rules of the College had never been actuated; shortly after Ellis's death the rules were revised and the course of study was dropped. The work of the College Press, which was proceeding very slowly, was reorganized and put under a full-time supervisor. A new member of the Board of Superintendence was needed, especially one who knew Sanskrit, in which the remaining members were deficient.

The College long outlived its founder, but it too was not immortal. It continued till 1854, when it was closed along with Haileybury and the College of Fort William, and the business of preparing the junior civil servants was thrown on the universities of England. Moreover, it continued according to the original plan only till 1836, when it was reduced to an examining body, its staff let go, and its library dispersed as a result of an anti-Orientalist revolution stemming from the much-described victory of the Anglicists, led by Charles Trevelyan and Thomas Babington Macaulay, over the Orientalists at Calcutta. In its relatively short lifespan its effects on Indian society were nevertheless substantial, as I will now try to show, not with any hope of making a definitive assessment but, in a preliminary way, opening the matter for further study.

NATIVE STUDENTS

In a letter to Erskine early in 1812, Ellis laid out his plan for the College in a manner that revealed his deeper, hidden reasons for its design: in a word, not only to contribute to the education of the junior civil servants but also to encourage the pursuit of letters among South Indians. I paraphrase here what he said.

Ellis announced to Erskine that, in imitation of Bengal, they were establishing a college at Madras for the instruction of the junior civil servants in the various dialects of South India. It would differ from the college at Calcutta both in being very much less expensive and in the staffing, as the instruction would be given not by European professors but by Indians; and in order to do this there would be provision for the instruction of a certain number of native students in English, Sanskrit, Tamil, and the like. The college was to be superintended by a board consisting of senior civil servants with pertinent knowledge. Another object of the college would be the publication of textbooks for the languages of southern India, as well as works in all subjects useful to civil servants in Madras, such as Indian literature, religion, history, and customs. They had at their disposal an excellent font of type for English, purchased for them by the Government, also fonts for Tamil and Telugu, and would in time add those for other scripts. Erskine would no longer have to prod Ellis to publish, for, Ellis said, he would now be doing so at the College Press. Though the Catholic missionaries had left many valuable books on the languages of southern India, there were still many lacunae that Ellis would have to fill. However, Erskine need not expect voluminous publication like that of Gilchrist (who had undertaken the composition and publication of Hindustani textbooks at Calcutta as a moneymaking venture), though it would be more excusable at Madras, inasmuch as displaying the hidden beauties and literary wealth of languages that had been "at one period highly cultivated, is more beneficial and praiseworthy than licking into form a barren jargon" (NLS Mss. 36.1.5, Ellis to Erskine 25 April 1812, f. 74). Apparently Ellis considered Hindustani nothing better than a pidgin, and not a cultivated language.

After discussing the project to improve the Abbé Dubois's text on the manners and customs of the South Indians—essentially a work on caste—and mentioning the *History of Mysore* of Wilks, recently noticed in the *Edinburgh review,* Ellis goes on to speak of the effect he hoped from the college, namely, "the encouragement to literary pursuit among the natives." This had been greatly promoted at Calcutta by the college there; and he believed that at Madras they had a greater chance of success than at Calcutta, "as I have no doubt we have better materials," meaning, of course, the South Indians themselves.

The prospects, then, for a revival of literary endeavor in South India appeared boundless, the College and the Government supplying the stimulus.

The "encouragement to literary pursuit among the natives," or "the revival of letters," in South India was Ellis's great overall objective for the College, cleverly engineered into the structure of a plan to provide for the instruction of British civil servants. As we have seen, to an unsympathetic observer such as Governor Elliot, dead to the delights of philology and uninterested in the revival of letters in Madras, the expense, small as it was, would appear greater than needed to achieve the College's practical colonial purposes. But for the moment Ellis and his plans for a simpler, cheaper version of the college at Calcutta that nevertheless took on a large body of "Native students" and placed them under the instruction of the head masters enjoyed the warm encouragement of the Government.

The phrase "revival of letters" presumes a former greatness and a decline in recent times. Campbell expressed his sense of former greatness in Telugu literature in the introduction to his Telugu grammar. Telugu, he says, was a cultivated language at a very early period, though few Telugu works have survived the violent political and religious changes through which the Deccan has passed. A great number of books composed under Kṛṣṇadevarāya, the great king of Vijayanagara, are still to be found in the libraries of the poligars, their former vassals; but "the intolerant zeal of the Mahommedans" who extinguished the Vijayanagara empire has left of the ancient Telugu works "little else remaining than the name" (Campbell 1816:xiii). "Under the fostering auspices of the British Government," he goes on to say, " it is confidently hoped that the Teloogoo may recover that place which it once held among the languages of the East, and that the liberal policy of the Legislature may be successful in renewing, among the Natives of Telingana, that spirit of literature and science, which formerly so happily prevailed among them, and still so much endears to their remembrance the days of the most enlightened of their Hindoo rulers" (ibid.). In a note he quotes from the Parliamentary legislation giving the Governor-General in Council power to spend a sum not less than one lakh of rupees annually on "the revival and improvement of literature, and the encouragement of the learned Natives of India, and for the introduction and promotion of a knowledge of the science among the Inhabitants of the British Territories in India" (ibid., xi, xiii).

The Parliamentary act in question was the 1813 renewal of the charter of the East India Company for a further twenty years. The "revival and improvement of literature," the "encouragement of the learned Natives of India" in knowledge of science, and the miniscule sum of a lakh of rupees for education for the whole of British India were to become the battleground for the education wars provoked by the Anglicists Trevelyan and Macauley against the Orientalists in the 1830s, long after the death of Ellis. That battle, which deeply affected the College and its personnel, lies beyond the scope of this book, though I must touch on the positions of the two sides.

"Revival of literature," or "revival of letters," was the phrase the British used to describe the Renaissance brought about in Europe by the recovery of ancient Greek learning—"literature" or "letters" meaning not only art literature but formal, written learning in all its branches. In the minds of Ellis and Campbell, South India's past literary greatness had occurred before the "Muslim intrusions," and the establishment of a British government in India was in the nature of a disestablishment of Muslim rule and a restoration for Hindus. The renaissance it promised was the revival of ancient literary greatness through the recovery of the classics and the composition of new works in the languages of South India. The Anglicists contested this Orientalist viewpoint with their own version of renaissance imagery: As Latin education had civilized the Anglo-Saxons now English was the most highly cultivated language in the world, and its study would raise the overall level of civilization in India. It would be an Anglicist renaissance for India (cf. Trautmann 1997:109–13). It was the Orientalist position, however, that underlay Ellis's goals for the native staff and students of the College.

On 7 April 1813 the College held the first examination of the native students and subsequently reported the results to the Government. The report stressed these students' low level of education at the starting of the College. It had been difficult, the report said, to find even a few persons tolerably well qualified to be teachers, most being entirely ignorant of English grammar, having very limited knowledge of Tamil grammar, and no acquaintance whatsoever with Telugu grammar since all the original treatises on that grammar were composed in Sanskrit and the teachers were not sufficiently acquainted with that language. Head masters had been engaged to direct the studies in these subjects, one for English (Udayagiri Venkatanarayana, acting), one for Tamil (Chidambaram Vadiyar), and one for Telugu and Sanskrit (Pattabhirama Shastri). They had been lecturing to the students daily on these languages. In addition, the acting English master had translated one of the most esteemed Sanskrit treatises on Telugu grammar; the Tamil master has composed an easy Tamil grammar for the use of the native students, now at the College Press; and the Telugu and Sanskrit master has nearly completed a similar work on Telugu grammar in verse. Thus the College, from the start, was actively producing new literary works in the languages of the South.

Examinations of Indian teachers and students were held on three successive days, with questions on English, Tamil, Telugu, Persian, and Hindustani grammar, and translations of very difficult compositions from native languages into English. Though the more learned Indian students had only begun the study of English, the report said, the results in the

Tamil and Telugu papers showed a complete knowledge of the principles of these languages. The Board considered the result highly satisfactory and found great improvement in the knowledge of Indian teachers and students alike. "It presents to us as nearly accomplished, one of the principal objects for which the College was originally instituted, and shews in prospect other benefits thence resulting in the revival and encouragement of a taste for literature, and the extension of a correct knowledge of the English, and of their own languages among the Natives generally, and in the formation of a body of well educated men whose abilities may hereafter be found as useful in other branches of the Public Service, as in that in which they are at present employed" (MPC 22 June 1813, para. 6).

The report went on to praise the exertions of Udayagiri Venkatanarayana, whom it described as an able young brahmin holding the acting English headmastership at half pay, and it recommended his promotion to full pay. He understands Sanskrit and Telugu fully, the report said, and is well acquainted with colloquial Tamil, has completely mastered English grammar, and has competent knowledge of several other languages.

Besides arranging for competent teachers, the other objective of the College was the provision of elementary books. The Board asked for 150 pagodas for the purchase of "native books" (manuscripts, that is) for that purpose, with the idea of deputing "an intelligent native" into the country to find and purchase them. It asked for an additional 240 pagodas for cupboards or presses to store books in. Thus began the College library and its manuscript collection.

The Government replied, in a curious locution which raised, as if anticipating the later complaint of Hugh Elliot, a concern about an excess of grammar at the College, only to answer it in the Board's favor:

> The Governor in Council is satisfied that both in educating those Teachers and in employing their Services, you will keep in view the substantial object of the Institution, which is to qualify the Junior Civil Servants of this Establishment for the discharge of the duties hereafter to be imposed upon them, and that the study of such grammatical niceties as may be more curious than useful will not be allowed to supersede or obstruct the acquisition of that practical knowledge of the languages, which is all that the purposes of the public service can in ordinary cases require. The Governor in Council has principally been led to make the foregoing observation in consequence of the great improvement in the study of the native languages which has taken place since the College was established, and of his earnest solicitude that this improvement should not have any tendency to defeat the important public end which it is naturally calculated to promote, and he is happy to observe that the course of instruction described in your letter now replied

> to does not in any respect disagree with the view of the subject which he has taken. (MPC 22 June 1813, para. 1)

The teaching of law to native students was begun later. The rationale for teaching law to Indians was that the colonial courts required pandits and maulvis as sources of expert knowledge on Hindu and Muslim law, principally on such family matters as marriage, adoption, and inheritance, of which the court of Sadr Adawlet was perpetually in need. Raising the quality of training for pleaders, or courtroom lawyers, was a secondary objective that fit well with the primary one. The College proceeded to institute the teaching of Hindu and Muslim law, and although existing histories of education in South India that I have examined do not mention this, it became thereby the first colonial school of law in South India. At the same time its annual examination became a mechanism for certification, which was made a requirement for government service. And since pandits and maulvis had long been gaining their skills in many different ways that preexisted British rule, the annual examination of native students in Muslim and Hindu law was thrown open to anyone who, "having prosecuted their studies in the interior," considered themselves qualified. Thus the College also quickly became the gateway, through the certification process, to positions as court pandits and maulvis and to the profession of pleader.

The Board proposed new rules to regularize the practices it had instituted in its report on the examinations in law for 1816. The proposed rules, which were duly sanctioned by the Government, provided for three classes of law students, each consisting of six brahmins and six Sunni Muslims, and a separate class of an unlimited number open to all Muslims and Hindus "of pure caste" as a fourth class for aspiring pleaders. The head masters' duties were now to include the instruction of the law classes. Students in the first three classes received salaries of 4 to 10 pagodas per month, while those in the pleader class received no salary. The annual exam was to be held by the Board, assisted by the head masters and the Hindu and Muslim law officers of the court of Sadr Adawlet, and reported to the Governor in Council. Students of the superior class and those brahmins and Sunni Muslims who had not studied at the College but appeared for the annual examination would, upon passing the examination, be issued a certificate qualifying them to serve as law officers and to have their names entered on the list of candidates. While waiting for openings in the court, their salaries would continue, and they would be employed teaching other students. Students in the unsalaried pleader class and others not trained in the College would sit for the examination for a certificate, and if they passed, their names would be put on a list of candidates for the office of pleader (MPC 23 April 1816).

In the same report the Board reported a "highly satisfactory" result in the 1816 examinations of native students on law, "evincing in the examined zealous application to study, honourable emulation to be distinguished by the success of their labours, and confidence that talent and assiduity would receive their merited reward" (ibid., para. 3). This was particularly true of the Hindu students. In all their answers and disputations they used Sanskrit, and they and the head masters earned the praise of the law officers of the court. Certificates issued to both Muslim and Hindu law students were reported. The Board was so pleased with its own success in the native law branch of the College that it was led to contemplate reviving the traditional titles used in the South to honor literary achievement, titles "still in use, but greatly abused by being derived from hereditary succession, and not from individual merit" and of conferring them, with a certificate "under the seal of the College," on persons who have established "their claim to these honours" before the Board of Superintendence and the head masters, Muslim and Hindu. (ibid., para. 13). In other words, the College was contemplating taking on the traditional function of the royal assembly at which scholarly eminence was publicly rewarded.

> The emulation which had already been manifested by the [law] candidates of different and distant provinces has appeared to us to establish a fair claim to distinctions which have formed a part of the institutions of every civilized Society, and which, although greatly changed in India from the original intention, under a succession of revolutions, we have no doubt may be revived with success in peaceable and prosperous times. Consulting several learned natives on this subject, we were pleased to find them entirely concurring with us in opinion, that titles of honour so conferred would be received with gratitude, and acknowledged with respect. (Ibid., para. 14)

The Board proposed to gather more information and submit a proposal for the revival of traditional scholarly honorific titles at a later time, and the Government encouraged it to do so. The College's achievements in teaching law and becoming an examining body and certifying authority for students coming from all parts of the province, then, had encouraged the Board to think of extending that mechanism to all branches of literary learning in its ancient but now decayed forms—a projected Orientalist renaissance.

How greatly this ambitious program depended upon Ellis's extraordinary skills, especially in Sanskrit, and how difficult, indeed impossible, it was to carry it out without him, became apparent after his death. A letter of the Board to the Government (MPC 29 Nov 1819) spoke at length of the "unrelaxing attention" Ellis had paid to the interests of the College and the value of his intimate knowledge of the languages, literature, and habits of the people of South India. His death, above all, left the study of Sanskrit without benefit of supervision by a member of the Board. Young gentlemen destined for service in Madras were studying Sanskrit at the East India College at Haileybury—and this was so because of the express recommendation of the Board, endorsed by the Government of Madras and accepted by the Court of Directors. The Board noted the rapid progress made in the languages of South India by those gentlemen whose proficiency in Sanskrit was the most distinguished (ibid., para. 4). Sanskrit, the Board went on to say, was also the only medium through which to study logic and law according to the Hindu shastras. The Board, in its reports on the law examinations of Indian students, had noted the increased number of those qualifying as candidates for positions as pandits and pleaders, and the extraordinary rapid advances they had made in the knowledge and use of Sanskrit, "in which disputations are now held with unimpeded fluency of expressions for any length of time that the discussion may require or admit of" (ibid., para. 5). The use of Sanskrit in speaking on philosophical subjects, the Board held, was further evidence of the acquisition of clear and definite ideas, since Sanskrit best supplies precise terms.

Whether that high standard of Sanskrit at the College continued after Ellis's time we do not know. But while he lived, and for many years thereafter, the College educated a substantial number of young South Indians in grammar, literature, and law, and promoted the composition of works in these fields among its head masters. The College's role in the education of Indians has been largely if not completely forgotten and deserves further study. But it is through consideration of the head masters who did the educating that we can see most clearly the importance of the College. We turn now to them.

THE TAMIL RENAISSANCE

Long after his death, and indeed to this day, Ellis is remembered as Ellis Durai ("Lord Ellis," approximately) in Tamil publications, and the Madras College as the Chennai Kalvi Sangam, a new *saṅgam,* or college of learned persons, not entirely unlike the *saṅgams* of old, in which poets recited their works before persons of learning and discrimination whose judgments formed the canon of Tamil literature. It was the head masters who presided over this new *saṅgam*.

We have already seen, from the encomia of Pattabhirama Shastri and Sankaraiah in the *Sarvadevavilāsa,* that they were admired by their contemporaries both for their learning and for the influence they had through the important positions they held in the Government service. We can get a fix on the historical significance of this class through consideration of Kamil Zvelebil's pioneering work on this question.

The sixth chapter of Zvelebil's *Companion studies to the history of Tamil literature* (1992) is called "Rediscovery of ancient Tamil literature: The Tamil Renaissance." He argues that the period spanning the late nineteenth and early twentieth centuries was a time in which the ancient, classical "Sangam literature" was recovered. Between roughly 1850 and 1925, most of the Tamil classics, hitherto forgotten and neglected or considered lost, were recovered and put into print for study and research, and scholars became aware that India had a second ancient classical language in addition to Sanskrit; indeed, the Tamil Sangam literature is claimed to be very much older than any other non-Sanskrit literature. The beginning of the period identified by Zvelebil coincides with the closing of the College of Fort St. George. Its culmination was the work of U. V. Swaminatha Iyer (1855–1942), for whom the first generation of makers of print editions, scholars such as Arumuga Navalar, Malavai Mahalinga Aiyar, and Simon Casie Chitty, were a generation of "forerunners" in Zvelebil's account. But Zvelebil goes on to say that the story really began fifty years before this formative period: "To trace the initial stages of editing and printing the classics in Tamil, however, we have to go back half a century before Simon Casie Chitty, to a man almost forgotten in our days, called Muttusami Pillai" (1992:158). This takes us directly to the College of Fort St. George.

It was at the College, indeed, that the process of recovering and preparing the first printed editions of Tamil classics of ancient and medieval times was initiated. According to Zvelebil, the key figure was Appu Muttusami Pillai (d. 1840), to give his full name, librarian of the College and later head Tamil master (1992:158–59). Muttusami Pillai was one of the Pondicherry Tamil Christians educated at the Jesuit college there whose training Ellis so admired. Besides his native Tamil, Muttusami Pillai had some knowledge of Sanskrit, Telugu, English, and Latin. It was he whom the Board sent, in 1816, on a tour of the southern provinces to collect

Tamil manuscripts, and in this way he created the manuscript collection of the College—or at any rate the Tamil part of it, since Telugu manuscripts were collected at the same time by another agent of the College. From this we see that the College's collection of manuscripts must have been an important source for the Tamil renaissance of the nineteenth century. It is a great pity that we have only a sketchy and imperfect knowledge of this collection. The reconstruction of its contents is a great desideratum for advancing our knowledge of the Tamil renaissance. Some of the items of this collection appear among the manuscripts in William Taylor's bafflingly written *Catalogue raisonné of Oriental manuscripts in the Government Library* (3 vols., 1857–62), which would be the starting point for such a reconstruction. After the winding-up of the College in 1854, the collection was eventually included in the Government Oriental Manuscripts Library, now at Madras University. The published catalogues of the latter do not identify the provenance of its manuscripts, making it difficult to identify manuscripts that came from the College library.

It is worth looking closely at Zvelebil's account, because it gives a well-documented and persuasive overview of the process of the recovery and formation of print editions of the classics of Tamil, though there are slight inaccuracies here and there. Zvelebil writes of the munshis, or language teachers, appointed for Tamil, but we need to understand that the persons he is talking about were not teachers of Tamil to the British junior civil servants but were the head masters for Tamil supervising the education of the Tamil teachers—the teachers of the teachers, so to say. These men occupied important positions in the College, and their influence extended widely. The succession of head Tamil masters, according to Zvelebil, was as follows:

> Chidambara Pandaram
> Tandavaraya Mudaliar
> Muttusami Pillai
> P. Naranappa Mudaliyar
> Sivakolundu Desikar
> M. Kandasami Pillai
> and a few others. (1992:159 n. 36)

These scholars published a considerable amount, some of it through the College Press, some of it at the other publishing venues for Tamil printed books that were sprouting up during that period. The Tamil renaissance, then, was a matter of recovering ancient Tamil literature from oblivion and of making it newly and widely available in print, giving it the new formats and the breadth of circulation that print made possible. The College was triply involved in this renaissance through the collection of Tamil manuscripts, the scholarly work of its head masters, and the publication of Tamil books by the College Press. To get some sense of the process we can follow the publications of some of these Tamil head masters as discussed by Zvelebil.

Chidambara Pandaram (Chidambara Vadiyar, of the Pandaram caste), according to Zvelebil, "translated into Tamil two parts of the Sanskrit lawbook *Mānavadharmaśāstra,* and is said to have been awarded the prize of one thousand gold pieces *(varāha)* for the job; as far as we know, his translation was not published" (1992:160). This is slightly inaccurate; it was not the lawbook of Manu that he translated but Vijñāneśvara's great commentary on Yājñyavalkya, the *Mitākṣarā.* As we have already seen, the translation was begun by Chidambara's brother, Puriar Vadiyar, who died before completing it. The Board urged the Government to purchase the copyright of the work, which the author and his brother's widow were willing to part with for 1,000 pagodas (the English term for the Tamil *varāha*) for the erection of a choultry for travelers on the inland road from Madras to Trichinopoly, "where accommodations of that kind are particularly wanting," plus a grant of rent-free land sufficient for its maintenance. This was approved by the Court of Directors, and land was so granted in the village of Anunyare, Vellarpuram taluk, of South Arcot district (MPC 19 Jan 1819).

Ellis says that the greater part of the translation was made by Puriyar Vadiyar, and that "what he left unfinished and a general revisal of the whole" was done under his brother's supervision. It included original texts of Yājñavalkya and of other fundamental law texts, or *mūlasmṛtis,* in verse translation, followed by a paraphrase of the text and commentary in prose. Every effort was made to make the text intelligible to persons of moderate education, and it was put "in the plainest style, which a proper attention to elegance of expression and grammatical propriety would admit." Ellis adds:

> The importance of this work in those countries of which the Tamil is the current language, now that a System of regulated law has superseded the arbitrary proceedings, which, since the abolition of the Hindu Governments, had obtained, is too evident to require illustration; not the least of the benefits which will result from it is it's [*sic*] tendency to diminish the influence of the Brahmans by enabling the Sudras to attend to a knowl-

> edge of law independently of them, and without that gloss which their peculiar pretensions and prejudices ever incline them to give to the text. Of this influence the people of Southern India have always been jealous, and though it is assuredly not the policy of our Government entirely to abrogate it, of the propriety of abating it, of being able, should it be expedient, to act without the interference of this class, there can be no doubt. (Ellis, "Memorandum respecting the proposed translation of the Rju Mitacshara," Erskine Collection, OIOC Mss. Eur.D.30, pp. 294–55)

This work was to have been printed with the Tamil and the English translation in the same book, "rendering thereby the provisions of the Hindu law at once intelligible to the Judge and the Suitor." Ellis elsewhere says that he had translated much of the *Mitākṣarā*, and possibly it was he who was preparing the English text for this projected publication. Printed sheets had been made up as a sample, but I have not been able to locate a copy and cannot verify that the book was ever published. We may suppose, at the least, that the manuscript was used in the classes of native law students.

Tandavaraya Mudaliar (d. 1850) was a student at the College before becoming head Tamil master, a position he held till 1839, when he was appointed a judge of the court in Chingleput, according to Zvelebil (1992:161–62; 1995:652). He was an outstanding scholar of the College, well educated in Tamil, English, Telugu, Kannada, Marathi, Hindustani, and Sanskrit. In 1824 he edited Beschi's Tamil dictionary, the *Caturakarāti*. His treatise on Tamil grammar, *Ilakkaṇaviṉāviṭai*, was completed in 1825 and published in 1828. He translated the well-known collection of fables, the *Pañcatantra*, from Marathi into Tamil (published 1826). His collection of these fables, called *Kathāmañjari* (Katāmañcari), Zvelebil says, is "one of the earliest books of Tamil narrative prose" and was reprinted many times in various forms. Both books would have been textbooks for the British students studying Tamil. He edited the first ten parts of a tenth-century Jain lexicon of Tamil, the *Cūṭāmaṇi nikaṇṭu* (1856), and, with K. Ramasami Pillai, edited eight parts of the earliest (ninth-century) Tamil lexicon, the *Divākaram (Cēntaṉ tivākaram)*, published in 1835 and many times reprinted. He collaborated with Muttusami Pillai on the collection of grammatical texts called *Ilakkaṇa pañcakam* (1835), which included the *Naṉṉūl*, *Akapporuḷ viḷakkam*, and *Puṟapporuḷ veṇpāmālai*. Zvelebil adds that Tandavaraya Mudaliar also wrote many original plays and poems.

Of Appu Muttusami Pillai's invaluable work of collecting manuscripts for the College I have already spoken. Besides the work on grammar in which he collaborated with Tandavaraya Mudaliar, he was author of a book of Catholic prayers, rituals, and doctrines, the *Āttumavuttiyāṉam,* 1817; a defense of Christianity against the attacks of Ponnampalam *(Tikkāram)*; a defense of Ellis *(Taravu koccakakkalippā),* about which one would like to know more; a lexicon of Tamil on the model of the old *nighaṇṭus,* or lexicons, of Sanskrit and Tamil *(Nāṉārtta tīpikai,* published by Madras University in 1936); and a biography of Beschi (*Brief sketch of the life and writings of Father C. J. Beschi or Vira-Mamuni,* 1840; Tamil version 1822) (Zvelebil 1995:453). P. Naranappa Mudaliyar (1779–1845), according to Zvelebil, "was a true pioneer of Tamil critical editing" (1992:160), taking note of textual variants and making emendations in his printed editions of texts he collected and collated. Among his editions were the *Tañcaivāṇaṉkōvai* of Poyyāmoḻippulavar (1834), *Nēminātam* (1836), *Nālaṭiyār* (1844), *Tivākara nikaṇṭu,* parts 9 and 10, and parts of the *Cūṭāmaṇi nikaṇṭu.* He was preparing an edition of the Tamil version of the *Mahābhārata,* Villiputturar's *Pāratam,* when he died suddenly at age 46.

T. Sivakolundu Desikar of Kottaiyur was court poet to Raja Sarfoji of Tanjore. He transferred to the College during the headmastership of Tandavaraya Mudaliyar with the Raja's consent. His most memorable labor, according to Zvelebil, was the first printed critical edition of Māṇikkavācakar's massive work of Shaiva devotionalism, *Tiruvācakam* (1857). He also published several older *purāṇas* and *prabandhas* (Zvelebil 1992:163–64).

One might add to Zvelebil's recitation of forerunners the name of Sankaraiah. He was of course only briefly at the College, as head English master, and most of his career was spent in administration, as sheristadar to Ellis at the Collectorate of Madras. And of course he is not known for preparing editions of Tamil works of literature, as are the others of this list. But he was certainly a very visible public figure, known for his Sanskrit learning. Susan Neild, for example, in her history of Madras, records that he published a refutation of Rammohan Roy's account of Vedanta in the *Madras courier* of 31 December 1816 (Neild 1976:235). He was also involved in an early attempt to create a literary society (Mantena 2002:94), and was memorialized in the *Sarvadevavilāsa.* So far as I know, however, apart from the article in the *Courier,* his only published piece was his set of answers to questions on land tenure in Madras in the *Treatise of mirasi right.*

In Zvelebil's analysis we see that the College was the single most important locus for the "revival of letters" in the Tamil country, a project its founders had aimed for from the institution's creation until the mid-nineteenth century, when it was closed, after which the sites and projects in this recovery of the literary works of the past become many and various. The Tamil renaissance had the two aspects of recovering old works and of casting them into the new medium of print. The College occupied a strategic moment, when the old forms of patronage of letters associated with the royal courts had, for a while, devolved upon the great dubashes and merchants but were soon to take on new institutional forms of which the College itself was a leading example. As patronage declined, and with it the copying of manuscripts so essential to the transmission of the literary works of the past to future generations, the College undertook to copy and preserve works in manuscript, providing a new institutional frame for manuscript collection and preservation and in this way contributing to the essential foundation for the casting of Tamil literature into print. The collection of manuscripts for the College library and the publication of printed editions of ancient works both at the College Press and elsewhere, by its illustrious head masters, made the College a significant site at which the Tamil Renaissance was begun, in the first half of the nineteenth century.

THE MODERNIZATION OF TELUGU

The head Telugu masters of the College were no less figures of importance than their Tamil colleagues, especially in the struggles over Telugu grammar in the era of print and prose. From the research of Lisa Mitchell (2003), on whose valuable work I draw in the following paragraphs, we learn that three leading Telugu head masters of the College each published a grammar of Telugu, presumably for the instruction of the Indian students preparing for positions as teachers of Telugu in the College. They were Vedam Pattabhirama Shastri (1760–1820), Ravipati Gurumurti Shastri (1770–1836), and Paravastu Chinnayasuri (1802–60).

Pattabhirama Shastri was, as we have seen, the first Sanskrit and Telugu head master of the College, and he remained in this joint position till his death, teaching Hindu law *(dharmaśāstra)* as well as grammar. His eminence during his lifetime was considerable; he appears on a list of "respectable native inhabitants" among the notable residents of Madras from whom testimony was taken by the committee investigating the causes of the right/left caste riots of 1809, and, as noted previously, is the first of a series of able and influential scholars eulogized in the *Sarvadevavilāsa*. Ellis refers to him several times in his Dravidian proof, and clearly had a great regard for Pattabhirama Shastri's scholarship. The list of Telugu roots that Pattabhirama composed was highly regarded by C. P. Brown and others, and was an essential resource for the Dravidian proof. His grammar of Telugu, *Āndhra vyākaraṇamu,* was published in 1825 and reprinted in 1951.

Ravipati Gurumurti Shastri's *Telugu vyākaraṇamu* appeared in 1836 (reprinted 1951), and Chinnayasuri's *Bāla vyākaraṇamu* was published in 1858 (reprinted 1967), according to Mitchell (ibid.). It is evident, then, that the College, through its learned head masters and their publications, had considerable influence on Telugu grammar. The nature of that influence is for others, more knowledgeable in these matters than I, to determine. One has the impression that there was considerable tension between the high formalism of the *vyākaraṇa* tradition and the desire for a printed prose Telugu closer to speech and the prose of workaday documents—the prose of the *karaṇam,* or scribe, of which Velcheru Narayana Rao, David Shulman, and Sanjay Subrahmanyam have written (2003:93–139; 239–48).

These tensions, and other ones as well, can be seen in the writings of the great Telugu scholar C. P. Brown, whose role in the recovery, editing, and printing of classic Telugu works was immense, as one learns from Peter Schmithenner's excellent biography (2001; see also 1991). Brown was a product of the College and learned Telugu from A. D. Campbell's grammar in 1817, while Ellis was still at the helm of the Board of Superintendence. But his relations with the College and with Campbell's work were extremely fraught. Anyone reading Brown's works soon becomes aware that he was a contrarian with strong views, and that he was quick to criticize and slow to praise anyone whom he considered a rival. This was most emphatically the case with regard to Campbell and his grammar, as we may see from Brown's furious, obsessive annotations in a copy now in the British Library (OIOC Mss. Eur.D.867). The feelings about Campbell that are revealed therein are of a kind a clinician would probably label as oedipal. His marginal comments include: "lost labour," "silly nonsense," "wrong," "rubbish," "useless." He did grant Campbell certain merit as a pioneer and for surpassing the grammar of Carey ("a deplorable affair . . . wrong in every page, nearly in every sentence"), but for the most part he heaped scorn upon the grammar of Telugu from which he had his first lessons, from a man who, though proud, "was a kind man and always treated me with respect" (ibid., 23). His greatest satisfaction was that his own grammar (1840, 1857) replaced Campbell's; he became, by a kind of cannibalism, the new Campbell.

Brown became Postmaster General of Madras at a high salary, high enough to keep a coach and four, give lavish parties, and maintain a sizable company of pandits, whom he referred to as his college, to assist him in the preparation of his several grammars, dictionaries, and editions of Telugu works (Schmithenner 1991:253–65, 325–26). The conditions of his scholarship, unfettered by any institutional structure, fostered an eccentricity of manner and judgment on which many commented and allowed for the free play of his unique scholarly genius, resulting in a veritable flood of books, many of them still in print.

In these works one sees a back-and-forth over which register of Telugu to recognize. Brown's critique of Campbell was, among other things, that his grammar was too tied to the high register of the *vyākaraṇa* tradition and too distant from everyday spoken Telugu. On the other hand, Brown himself created a dictionary for what he regarded as pure Telugu, colloquial and poetic (Brown 1852), and consigned "mixed Telugu," including foreign borrowings used in speech and legal documents, to an appendix, subsequently issued as a separate dictionary (Brown 1854). This shows an impulse to separate pure, native Telugu from foreign accretions, a purism somewhat at odds with his criticism of Campbell for following the native authorities too slavishly.

C. P. Brown is a fascinating figure over whom one would like to linger. He was a brilliant linguist and admirer of Telugu, but his Christian beliefs made him strongly disapproving of Hinduism, as was Leyden, in a way we do not see in Campbell or Ellis, and this kept him from gaining a sympathetic understanding of certain areas of his chosen field of endeavor. He had characteristic Protestant Christian beliefs critical of brahmins, but he employed several and was on the best of terms with them as individuals. He was very much a product of the College and became an Orientalist in the tradition of Ellis and Campbell, yet he entertained strong feelings of rivalry toward them. Eventually he retired from the service and became professor of Telugu at University College, London. He is greatly admired among scholars of Telugu literature for his many scholarly editions of Telugu works, which began the process of producing print editions of the literary heritage of Telugu and created pioneering models of scholarly editions to be followed by others.

In addition to commenting on the students and head masters of the College, I should say a word about the personnel for Colin Mackenzie's project, the other institutional pole of the Madras School of Orientalism. Rama Mantena's interesting study of the Telugu speakers among Mackenzie's assistants, especially the three Kavali brothers, opens up an investigation of their contribution to the development of history writing in Telugu prose, especially the history of Telugu literature (Mantena 2001). And Phillip Wagoner's recent study examines the role of Telugu Niyogi brahmins, that is, secular brahmins whose traditional occupation is to work with documents in the chancelleries of kings, on Mackenzie's staff (Wagoner 2003). Wagoner argues that these scholars had formidable linguistic skills, which, however, differed from those of grammarians of the *vyākaraṇa* tradition, being oriented toward the assessment of diplomatic and legal documents in many languages, including the detection of forgery. Wagoner argues that these abilities were the crucial ones around which the Mackenzie project devised practices for surveying, collecting, and registering masses of inscriptions, a culture of practice that was carried over into the Archaeological Survey of India when it was formed at mid-century by Alexander Cunningham.

These, then, are a few of the lines of influence connecting the head masters and students of the College with wider cultural developments in the Tamil and Telugu regions of South India. I must leave it to others to work out these connections more fully. The College's contributions to Kannada and Malayali cultural developments were assuredly less; the College Press published the first grammar of Kannada in English, that of John McKerrell (1820), and Ellis, as we have seen, printed a treatise on Malayalam for the use of students in the College (Ellis 1878). There were no head masters for these languages in Ellis's lifetime. The College's great and lasting effects were in Tamil and in Telugu. It was in respect of these two languages that the College made a distinct contribution to the "revival of letters" in South India.

CHAPTER 7

Conclusions

Having completed our analysis of the Dravidian proof, the conditions of its emergence, and its effects in India, we return to the larger phenomenon of the languages-and-nations project in relation to India and the Indian tradition of language analysis. I begin by reprising the analysis of the languages-and-nations project as it now appears, in the light of the Dravidian proof as an illuminating instance of British-Indian Orientalism, showing the specific authority claim upon which the new Orientalism of British India based itself and the rhetoric of proof that followed from it. Then I take up two concluding topics: One is the emergence of the "race science" idea and the racial theory of history as the assumption of a tight connection between languages and nations came increasingly into question in the nineteenth century. The other is the matter of theory, specifically, the place of Indian theories of language in modern thought.

PHILOLOGY, ORIENTALISM, AND THE DRAVIDIAN PROOF

The languages-and-nations project, as we have seen, was not a matter of pure science freeing itself from the shackles of religion, as it has often been represented. To the contrary, its deep roots are in the Bible, in the genealogy of the nations that descended from Noah and his three sons. Because of these biblical roots, the project is found in Christian Europe and not in pagan Greece and Rome. The genealogical paradigm of the Bible for locating the nations in relation to one another, the Mosaic ethnology as I have called it, was shared by the Peoples of the Book: Jews, Christians, and Muslims; but only in Europe did it also become a model for the locations of *languages* in relation to one another and, conversely, a key to the lost bits of the genealogy of nations. The study of languages could make good the imperfections of the historical record, based on collective memory, and extend the reach of history back four thousand years to the Tower of Babel and the Confusion of Tongues.

From the fact that the languages-and-nations project has arisen only in a part of the world that adheres to the biblical religions we draw the inference that it does not arise spontaneously from the Bible but rather is a specific way of *interpreting* the Bible narrative, arrived at through many mediations that might have led to a different result. It is the product of historical contingencies that occurred in a specific part of the world and under specific circumstances. These circumstances can be identified once it is recognized that the prevailing representations of this history have obscured aspects of the story by drawing too sharp a line between religion and science and making that line a threshold for passage from one to the other.

In this book we have explored but a portion of this development, and assuredly there is much more to be learned. Comparing the way the Indo-European idea appears in the work of Sir William Jones and the work of Father Coeurdoux, we see that Jones's *genealogical* (or as linguists now say, genetic) conception of the relations among Sanskrit, Greek, Latin, and the others, and Coeurdoux's narrative of the linguistic *mixing* between neighbor nations, were alternative interpretations of their time. I have no doubt that Jones and Coeurdoux were not the first to use the ideas of genealogical relations among languages and language mixture as interpretative means, and it is certain that the Indo-European idea had yet earlier anticipations. It is not my purpose to trace these anticipations, which doubtlessly lead as far back as J. C. Scaliger, if not further, and may have no absolute starting point.[1] My purpose has been merely to

1. Max Müller, in his *Science of language* (1899), traces early European knowledge of Sanskrit prior to Wilkins and Jones, mostly through Catholic missionaries. Success has a thousand fathers, as they say, and virtually every nation of Europe has some claim to the formulation of the Indo-European idea. George van Driem, in a recent publication (2001: 1039–51), makes an argument for Marcus Zuerius van Boxhorn (1612–1653) of Leiden as the first to recognize the existence of the family of languages now called Indo-European, comprising Persian, Greek, Germanic, and others, which he derived from a protolanguage he called Scythian. Von Driem further argues that Boxhorn's friend Claudius Salmasius added Sanskrit to Boxhorn's Indo-Scythian family on the basis of Indian words recorded in the fragments of Ctesias's lost work, the *Indica,* because of their resemblance to mod-

identify genealogy and mixture as competing theories. In the long run, comparative philology developed in such a way that mixing came to be seen as a secondary and late phenomenon, and genetic relations were taken to indicate what is early and at the core of a language. Indeed, the idea of a "mixed language" came to be ruled out as a possibility in nineteenth-century comparative philology, even though all languages are, in truth, mixed. A language was identified with its unmixed, original core, as known through its grammar.

The striking similarities among the Indo-European languages that Jones pointed out in his famous pronouncement are found in "the roots of verbs and in the forms of grammar," elements that constitute the inner cores of those languages—which suggests genealogical relations between them rather than a process of language mixture. Jones asserts that the mere examination of these affinities would lead philologers spontaneously to infer their co-descent from a parent language, "now perhaps lost." In so saying he naturalizes a process that is, shall we say, highly processed, through the prior formulation and writing of grammars. By implication, to determine the genealogical relations among all languages, this writing of grammars needs to be universalized to all languages, and this industry—this "explosion in the grammar factory"—which was well under way in the eighteenth century, continues apace today.

The comparative vocabulary or word list that was the starting point for so much language comparison in the eighteenth and nineteenth centuries, and was the substance of Marsden's work on Malayo-Polynesian and the Romani language, is another example of a naturalizing rhetoric of mere inspection, a pure empiricism, that needs to be deconstructed so we may see the complex work of abstraction from which it is made. As I have shown, the seemingly simple word list for comparisons of vocabulary among languages is not an arbitrary list made up of words chosen at random, but one whose inclusions and exclusions implement a series of

---

ern Persian words. He further argues that Jones picked up on these findings through the work of William Wotton. It is clear from the evidence given that ideas of genetic connection of languages were already in play, and that ancient Indian languages were being connected with those of Persia and Europe by these Dutch scholars. Plainly, the Indo-European idea was the product of a long evolution involving many, rather than the discovery of a lone genius. Von Driem sees the Biblical story of the descent of Noah and the dispersal of nations as having contributed to "obscuring the overall picture" of the genetic connections among languages for European scholars leading up to the Renaissance. But it is my view that the development of the Indo-European idea presupposed the genealogy of nations in the Bible and applied it to languages; in other words, the idea of a family of languages and of genetic connections among them was not naturally given and had to be fashioned from the idea of a genealogical tree of nations.

contrasting binaries of core/periphery, native/foreign, original/borrowed, simple/complex, unlearned/learned. An implication of these binaries is that a language is identified by its core, and its periphery is secondary. The genealogical relations among languages are relations among cores of languages, which are found only after identifying and clearing away borrowed words, setting aside their misleading testimony about the affinities of languages. We have traced the structure of the word list and the conception of its method back to Leibniz, though doubtless it, too, has earlier beginnings. My purpose in this analysis is to dispel the rhetoric of simple empiricism that surrounds these proofs of genealogical relations among languages and to show how very highly processed the languages that enter into such comparisons are. They are, in fact, abstractions from real, living languages.

It is because this exercise requires a high degree of prior processing of the material of comparison, specifically the composition of written vocabularies or dictionaries and grammars, that British India was especially favorable for carrying out the languages-and-nations project, given India's long, rich tradition of phonological and grammatical analysis. Carried to India by the imperial expansion of European power, the languages-and-nations project found rich soil there in which to grow. And because Jones's essay on the Hindus in which he outlined the concept of the Indo-European language family was in the form of a lecture, and is therefore very brief, while Ellis's Dravidian proof is a "dissertation," a formal written demonstration of a proposition worked out at some length, it is in the latter that we see more clearly the relation between the languages-and-nations project and the properly Orientalist scholarship of the British in India.

Orientalism, in the expansive definition of Edward Said, is "the corporate institution for dealing with the Orient—dealing with it by making statements about it, authorizing views of it, describing it, by teaching it, settling it, ruling over it: in short, Orientalism as a Western style for dominating, restructuring, and having an authority over it" (1978:3). Virtually everything said by Westerners about the Orient can be called Orientalism in this sense. But in British India, while Orientalism meant something fitting this description, it also had a much more narrow scope; it meant scholarship that derived its claim to authority from knowledge of Indian languages.[2]

2. I discuss the Saidian revolution at greater length in Trautmann 1997, chapter 1.

In British India, Orientalism was a self-conscious intellectual formation with a definite ideology. It staked its claim to authority upon mastery of the languages of Asia as giving access to the minds and intentions of Asians, in contrast to the authority of what the Greeks called autopsy *(autopsia)*, or self-sight, which had authorized ethnographies and histories going back to the times of Herodotus and Thucydides. John Zephaniah Holwell, in his *Interesting historical events, relative to the provinces of Bengal* (1765–71), states the Orientalist position well in his attack upon "all the modern writers" who represent Hindus "as a race of stupid and gross *Idolaters*":

> A mere description of the exterior manners and religion of a people, will no more give us a true idea of them; than a geographical description of a country can convey a just conception of their laws and government. The traveller must sink deeper in his researches, would he feast the mind of an understanding reader. His telling us such and such a people, in the East or West-Indies, worship this stock, or that stone, or monstrous idol; only serves to reduce in our esteem, our fellow creatures, to the most abject and despicable point of light. Whereas, was he skilled in the languages of the people he describes, sufficiently to trace the etymology of their words and phrases, and capable of diving into the mysteries of their theology; he would probably be able to evince in us, that such seemingly preposterous worship, had the most sublime rational source and foundation. (Holwell 1765–71, 2:9)

As this statement shows, the claims of British-Indian Orientalism were, in the first place, language-based, although language served not as an end in itself—that is, their interest was not linguistics—but as a means of accessing the thoughts and purposes of, in this case, the Hindus. In this respect Orientalism was a pure product of the languages-and-nations project, resting as it does upon the presumption that languages and nations are so closely identified with one another that the one is the gateway to the inner meaning and constitution of the other. Second, this Orientalism presented itself as a new formation, replacing the writings about India of the "philosophical traveler" and the Catholic missionary, dismissing them, (quite unfairly, actually, especially the language-based knowledge of the Jesuits) as based solely upon the ancient authority of autopsy, the mere "I-was-there-and-saw-with-my-own-eyes" kind of authority. The critique, then, was founded upon a differentiation of inner and outer. Finally there was a distinct note of empathy, both as source and as consequence of this style of inquiry, in contrast to the lack of engagement and the contempt that derive easily from the mere observation of externals.

This spread an appealing glow of humanism over British-Indian interactions, which, in truth, were inescapably hierarchical.

It is worth saying that while in theory the style of Orientalism that came into being in British India canceled out the Orientalism of the traveler and the missionary that preceded it, in practice it drew upon this prior fund of knowledge. Nevertheless, the Orientalism of Calcutta constructed itself as a New Orientalism (my term, but the sense of newness is explicit in the writings of the Calcutta Orientalists), quite different from the older Orientalism of Europe, which had been an extension of Bible study into the wider philological terrain of Hebrew, Aramaic, Arabic, and Persian. While the first Orientalists of British-Indian Calcutta initially approached India through Persian and Hindustani, they hoped to reach an entirely new understanding of India through access to the Sanskrit language and the recovery of the Veda, thought to have been composed very shortly after the dispersal of humanity over the face of the earth and therefore a precious testimony of the primitive state of humankind independent of the Bible and offering, therefore, an unimpeachable test of its truth. There was, then, something distinctly new about the Orientalism of Calcutta, even though it overstated its newness in relation to the knowledge production of missionaries such as Nobili and Beschi, for example. Raymond Schwab's classic study of this formation shows how the Sanskrit-and-Veda-based New Orientalism emanating from Calcutta was expected to be the foundation for a second renaissance in Europe—an Oriental renaissance, in the coinage of Edgar Quinet (Schwab 1984:11)—which, like the first Renaissance, based on the recovery of ancient Greek literature, would lead to some higher level of civilizational development. This hope sustained a considerable wave of Indomania in Europe, of which British-Indian Calcutta was the point of origin and over which it held monopolistic powers for several decades (Trautmann 1997:62–98).

From the authority claim of Orientalism, deriving as it did from Indians and Indian texts, it follows that the rhetoric of Orientalist scholarship was a rhetoric not of *discovery* or *imposition* but of *derivation.* We see this especially clearly in the *Treatise of mirasi right,* which presents itself as deriving knowledge of land tenures in the Tamil country by eliciting responses to the Board of Revenue's questions from an authoritative source, Ellis's sheristadar, the learned Sankaraiah, quoting them in Tamil (although he was perfectly capable of rendering them in English) along with Ellis's English translation. This proof text is ranged alongside other, older proof texts in the form of inscriptions collected from the various parts of South India by the Mackenzie project and others.

The same rhetorical structure is evident in the Dravidian proof. A large portion of the text is given over to Ellis's translation of the words of Mamadi Venkayya. Far from presenting his work as a heroic act of discovery or personal genius, Ellis is at pains to show that the Dravidian idea is already implicit in the Indian tradition of grammatical analysis, and needs only to be displayed and made comparative by a few transparently simple operations, making use of the technical means already present in the Indian tradition or, in the case of Pattabhirama Shastri's inventory of Telugu roots, indigenous methods for the teaching of Telugu grammar to the native teachers of the College of Fort St. George.

Here again a certain naïve empiricism is at play. The Indian tradition of grammatical analysis, which is presented in the Dravidian proof as if it speaks for itself and is self-explanatory, is in fact being interpreted in a very specific way, toward a *history* and *comparison* of languages—the tendency, that is, of the European languages-and-nations project.

Putting it very broadly, we may say that the European tradition of language analysis was strongly oriented toward language history, and that of India toward language structure. This formula is no sooner stated than it needs to be qualified. On the European side of this contrast, I hasten to say that there was also a strong tradition of "universal grammar" that sought to identify the categories of grammar found in all languages. While the languages-and-nations project searched out the historical connections among *languages,* universal grammar studied the structure of *Language* as a universal singular and without reference to time-bound phenomena. This "Cartesian linguistics," revived in our own time by Noam Chomsky (1966), takes no great interest in the differences among languages and their genealogical affinities, and may be pursued through the study of a single language, which in principle might be any language of the world but in practice has generally been a language of Western Europe.[3] Paradoxically, universal grammar has tended to stay at home.

But in many respects the languages-and-nations project was the stronger tendency of the two in eighteenth-century in Europe. Not only was the genealogy of languages newly seen as the key to the genealogy of nations; no language was to be taken as a wholly self-contained entity. It could be explained not entirely on its own, from within itself, so to say, but only in reference to its historical relation to other near-kindred languages. This required a vigorous development of etymology. We see both these trends—

3. For an overview of universal grammar at the time of Sir William Jones, see Beattie 1788: 125 ff.

to explain a language in the context of its related languages and to explain it through etymology—for example in the grammar of English that prefaces Samuel Johnson's great dictionary (Johnson 1755), written well before the discovery of Grimm's law and the other regular sound-shift principles that characterize the historical progression of Indo-European languages. Jacob Grimm's *Deutsche Grammatik* (1819) explained the grammar of German by seeing it through the wide-angle lens of Indo-European, and the lawlike rigor of the sound changes which he propounded, identifying different historical stages of the Indo-European languages leading to modern German, energized the new scholarship and created its self-confident sense of being a new science. His work marked the beginning of the German takeover of comparative philology. But even before Grimm had deepened the analysis of German by putting it in an Indo-European frame of reference and formulating the sound shifts we call Grimm's law, Johnson's dictionary showed the same aspiration to explain a language in the context of its related languages and through etymology.

Historicization and the energetic pursuit of etymology in the European tradition of language analysis thus long preceded the development of exact means of attaining these ends. The eighteenth century was indeed a period of "wild" etymologizing, in which everyone had a scheme of etymology and no one scheme prevailed over all others. Sir William Jones, for instance, lampooned the etymologies of Jacob Bryant, but his own were indeed little better and included some real howlers (Trautmann 1997:43–47). As Hans Aarsleff's fine book *The study of language in England, 1780–1860* (1967) has shown, the British had a vigorous indigenous scholarship of Anglo-Saxon, nourished by the etymological system of Horne Tooke, whose system eventually proved to be a blind alley and was swept aside and forgotten. Meanwhile, a younger generation of British scholars was learning anew how to read their ancient texts in German universities and in the illumination cast by Grimm's law. In a very real sense, the accomplishment of nineteenth-century comparative philology was to domesticate the wild etymology of the eighteenth century by creating a single standard, based on the lawlike sound shifts it had identified, that was seen to be scientific and that put an end to the exuberant and endless proliferation of systems of etymology in eighteenth-century Europe.

In the Indian tradition of language analysis there was considerable variation as well; we have seen, for example, that there was complete disagreement about whether Prakrit was the *source* of Sanskrit (Jain and Buddhist grammarians) or its *descendant* (the Prakrit grammarians writing in Sanskrit)—a question that continues to be debated. There are historical elements in the grammatical analysis at several points, and many analytic procedures can be read both historically and structurally. Nevertheless, there is nothing in the Indian grammatical tradition like the European rage for creating a family tree of all languages.

At the same time, the former did have what the latter was badly in need of. The Prakrit grammarians had identified a large body of words that could be derived from the grammar of Sanskrit by the addition of further *sūtras* to those of Pāṇini, thus treating those words as further transformations of Sanskrit morphological changes applied to Sanskrit roots. The British Orientalists regularly read these essentially structural changes as historical ones, and indeed, while the *sūtras* of Pāṇini seem entirely structural in nature, the supplementary *sūtras* of the Prakrit grammarians are, or can be read as, historical sound shifts of a kind not unlike Grimm's law. Thus the analysis of *tatsamas* and *tadbhavas* in Prakrit lend themselves to a historicizing interpretation. The *deśya* category is outside this kind of analysis and cannot be derived from the Sanskrit list of roots. When the Telugu grammarians conceptualized *deśya* words as entirely confined to a particular region *(deśa)*, this could again be, and was, interpreted historically. The Indian tradition of language analysis was very useful to the Orientalists because it contained within itself what the languages-and-nations project of Europe most needed: ideas of regular sound shifts and a systematic etymological procedure. *That* was the nub of the conjuncture that produced such strikingly new and enduring knowledge in British India.

LANGUAGE, NATION, RACE

Orientalism, then, was one of the products of the close relation of languages and nations in eighteenth-century European thought. The key idea, that language mastery is the conduit to the inner lives of other nations, continues in many forms, including social or cultural anthropology and area studies. It is still very much a living idea. But by the middle of the nineteenth century, the belief that was the source of that idea, the close connection of languages and nations, came under scrutiny and began to loosen, creating new possibilities. The decay of the languages-and-nations idea had a certain timing and shape, and the products of that decay, some of them toxic, others valuable, are also still with us. Although these outcomes go beyond the purposes of this book, a sketch, at least, is necessary to complete the fixing of the Madras School of Orientalism in its largest context.

The loosening of the languages-and-nations relation became evident in two interconnected developments. The first of these was the swelling chorus of voices saying what is common sense today: that languages and nations or races are not *necessarily* connected, that the relation between them is contingent. Thus people of the same nation or race may speak different languages, and the same language may be spoken by people of different nations or races. We now take this idea for granted, but by about 1860 various writers were putting it forth as a new concept that was by no means obvious; indeed, it was stated as a novel and surprising truth. This tells us that the taken-for-granted quality of the languages-and-nations relation was coming under skeptical examination for the first time, and a new common sense was being formed on the ruins of an exploded common sense. Of course, to say that languages and nations or races have no *necessary* connection is not to say there is *no* relation between them, but it leaves the relation problematic and dependent upon historical circumstances. This quality of throwing the question open is what I mean by the "loosening" of the relation.

The second development was that the concepts of nation and race, hitherto virtually interchangeable, began to differentiate themselves and acquire distinct valences. In eighteenth-century British writing, "nation" and "race" are little different from one another, and, if anything, the word "nation" is the more usual term. For this reason I have preferred the word "nation" in treating what I have called the languages-and-nations project, but it should be understood that "nation" here is not used in its modern sense or as distinct from race. After the American and French revolutions, the sense that the nation was the subject of a progressive march of history grew ever stronger, becoming normative in the nineteenth century, when "nation" acquired a strong political charge as the idea of a people whose proper destiny was to form a state based on popular representation, a nation-state, as we say. At the same time, "race" became ever more connected with the body and its visible signs; it was biologized. The rapid expansion of the race concept, unhampered by a connection with languages, was now a possibility and in fact is what occurred.

The view I am proposing departs from the general understanding, which was articulated by Max Müller and has been repeated ever since. Max Müller said, in 1854, that the same blood flowed in the veins of the soldiers of Clive that flowed in the veins of the "dark Bengalese," and that this truth, contrary to the testimony of skin color, was guaranteed by the linguistic connection between English and Bengali as members of the same Indo-European language family (1854:29). Thus language, not complexion, is a sign of the inner and invisible entity called race and symbolized by blood. Later in life, however, alarmed by the growth of racial doctrines, Max Müller repented of having identified race and language, and he proposed an amicable divorce between philology and ethnology. There are, he now acknowledged, "no dolicocephalic languages." Great mischief, he believed, had come about through mixing race and language, and the two needed to be kept separate. This is the common view of the matter today, that the nineteenth-century roots of, above all, the Aryan doctrine as the centerpiece of the politics of racial hatred had to do with the fatal conflation of language and race. This is the view, for example, in Léon Poliakov's very interesting book *The Aryan myth* (1974). Much as I like the book, I believe this view of the matter is mistaken and virtually the reverse is true; that the real mischief began not with the close identification of race (or nation) and language in the first half of the nineteenth century (though that caused mischief enough), but with their disconnection at mid-century. Since this interpretation is so very opposed to the prevailing view, and since it can easily be misunderstood, let me explain it as clearly as I can.

The best illustration of the relation of language and race *before* the great divorce of philology and ethnology is provided by James Cowles Prichard, whose two great works on the races of man (*Researches into the physical history of man,* 1813; *The natural history of man,* 1843; 4th ed. 1855), several times expanded and reissued, dominated the scientific study of race in Britain through nearly the whole of the first half of the nineteenth century. Prichard was a physician and attentive to the physiological attributes of race, but he was deeply read in contemporary work on the classification of languages, including the Indo-European and Dravidian families, and he himself contributed to the comparative philology of Celtic in a book called *The eastern origin of the Celtic nations proved by a comparison of their dialects with the Sanskrit, Greek, Latin and Teutonic languages* (1831), written as a supplement to his *Researches.* More than that, he had subordinated the physiological study of human bodily variations to the broad classifications of languages into families, which supplied the highest level of classification for races in his work. That is, language dominated physiology as a sign of race, not because of some perceived tension between them but, to the contrary, because Prichard assumed language was intimately connected with race and that language provided signs of race every bit as decisive as bodily signs, if not more so. His book is a grand synthesis, harmonizing the growing knowledge of language history and the accumulations of new information on the physiological variations of humankind. Prichardian ethnology was very much a child of the languages-and-nations project.[4]

The breaking apart of the assumed connection between language and race is evident in the work of the next generation of British ethnologists, especially Robert Gordon Latham and John Crawfurd. Latham was a scholar of the English language who wrote extensively on languages and races (Latham 1850, 1859a, 1859b, 1862); Crawfurd had been a medical officer in North India, subsequently spent most of his career in Southeast Asia at Penang, and wrote memoirs of his diplomatic services and a grammar and dictionary of Malay (Crawfurd 1830, 1834, 1852). Both were philologists, both were admirers and successors of Prichard, and both departed from the languages-and-nations assumptions of the Prichardian formula for drawing up a natural history of man. Both, moreover, were leading figures of the Ethnological Society of London—Crawfurd was its president—in which (as also in the rival Anthropological Society of London) the fledgling "race science" formula was trying its wings, and the close relation of language and race was being contested, especially as concerns the Indo-European family. Latham located the homeland of Indo-European in Lithuania, arguing that when philologers determined the age of the Vedas at three thousand years and derived Latin and its (Indo-European) relatives from Asia, they were wrong by at least a thousand years and as many miles (Latham 1862:619). He especially attacked Max Müller, opposing English common sense to the idea that language could prove what complexion denied: a relationship between the English and the Bengalis. Crawfurd came to the heart of the matter in an article on what he called the Aryan or Indo-Germanic [i.e., Indo-European] theory, which he characterized as the view that the nations and tribes from Bengal to Europe are of a single race, excepting the Arabs, Jews, and others who speak cognate (Semitic) languages. He argued that the theory fails because it is founded on a supposed conformity of language and nationality "without regard to physical form or intellectual capacity" (Crawfurd 1861:268). Here we see the explicit rejection of the foundational assumption of the languages-and-nations project and the freeing of the idea of race from its constraints. For Crawfurd as well as Latham, Max Müller's pronouncement was the provocation, and he attacked it explicitly:

> From the facts I have adduced in the course of this paper I must come to the conclusion that the theory which makes all the languages of Europe and Asia, from Bengal to the British Islands, however different in appearance, to have sprung from the same stock, and hence, all the people speak-

4. On the work of James Cowles Prichard, see Stocking's introduction to his edition of Prichard 1813 (Stocking 1973) and Stocking 1987, ch. 2.

> ing them, black, swarthy, and fair, to be of one and the same race of man, is utterly groundless, and the mere dream of learned men, and perhaps even more imaginative than learned. I can by no means, then, agree with the very learned professor of Oxford [Max Müller], that the same blood ran in the veins of the soldiers of Clive as in those of the Hindus whom, at the interval of two-and-twenty ages, they both scattered with the same facility. (Ibid., 285)

Later writers, notably Isaac Taylor in his book reviewing the new race science work being done in France and Germany, *The origin of the Aryans* (c. 1889), wrote of "the tyranny of the Sanskritists"—one cannot doubt that Max Müller is the type case—that interfered with a true and scientific understanding of race. For such writers, the languages-and-nations project was based on a false premise and race science was emerging from its ruins. It is in this sense that race only truly emerged after the great divorce of languages and nations (see Trautmann 1997:165–85).

Race came fully into its own as a fundamental cause in history in Arthur de Gobineau's *Essay on the inequality of the human races* (*Essai sur l'inégalité des races humains,* 4 vols., 1853–55). This is the mother lode of all modern racist theories. Racially based antipathies, of course, existed long before Gobineau, and he was not the first intellectual to theorize about race, but he was the inventor of the racial theory of history. By this I mean that he invented a theory of history in which race acted not as one factor of history among others but as the prime mover, the cause of causes, in the process of history.

According to Gobineau, there have been ten civilizations in the history of the world, and all are the work of the white race. Racial whiteness, in this theory, has some mysterious virtue which brings about the rise of civilizations, and the mixture of the races which the great empires inevitably bring about is the cause of their fall. All of the great empires, including the Roman Empire, on whose ruins Europe was built, have come to grief because of the mixture of races that follows their success, since peoples of different races are encompassed as empires expand their frontiers. Race and race mixture have been obscured as keys to history by the attention devoted to language, but language and race have no necessary connection. Thus Gobineau's theory is based on the explicit rejection of comparative philology as a key to ethnology and of the languages-and-nations connection that comparative philology had assumed. The rejection of language as a sign of race enabled Gobineau to argue that among speakers of Indo-European languages, all are of mixed race except the Germanic race, the last pure remnant of the civilization-building white race. In this way, the Aryan concept became a purely racial one, and Gobineau's theory became the precursor to Nazi race doctrine.

The new European view of race as a fundamental force of history had a deep effect on the interpretation of Indian history, and what I have called the racial theory of Indian civilization (Trautmann 1997, ch. 7) is the result. By this theory, Indian civilization is the product of a clash and partial mixture of two races: the fair-skinned, Sanskrit-speaking, civilized Aryan invaders and the dark-skinned, Dravidian-speaking, savage indigenous inhabitants. The outcome of this originary clash is the caste system, the central institution of the new civilization that emerged. This view, which for a very long time has been the master narrative of the history of Indian civilization, is only now coming under skeptical scrutiny. I have shown elsewhere (ibid.) how much text torturing is necessary to sustain the idea of the encounter of Indo-European and Dravidian languages in India as racial in character, and how false is its racially essentializing identification of civilization with whiteness and savagery with dark complexion. What I had not then seen is Gobineau's central role in the transformation of the languages-and-nations project into a racial theory of history, with profound effects on the history of Indian civilization. But that is a long story whose full elucidation must be left for another time.

INDIA IN THEORY

It remains to say a word about the fate of the Indian tradition of language analysis in the modern world. This raises the question of theory, which in various ways has been hovering over this study and needs now to be confronted directly, even though I cannot hope to do more than scratch the surface of the matter.

I begin with a passage from Dipesh Chakrabarty, who puts the problem of theory in the study of India (in the social sciences, at any rate) in a particularly arresting way:

> Today the so-called European intellectual tradition is the only one alive in the social science departments of most, if not all, modern universities. I use the word "alive" in a particular sense. It is only within some very particular traditions of thinking that we treat fundamental thinkers who are long dead and gone not only as people belonging to their own times but also as though they were our own contemporaries. In the social sciences, these are invariably thinkers one encounters within the tradition that has come to call itself "European" or "Western." I am aware that an entity called "the European intellectual tradition" stretching back to the ancient Greeks is a fabrication of relatively recent European history. Martin Bernal, Samir Amin, and others

> have justly criticized the claim of European thinkers that such an unbroken tradition ever existed or that it could even properly be called "European." The point, however, is that, fabrication or not, this is the genealogy of thought in which social scientists find themselves inserted. Faced with the task of analyzing developments or social practices in modern India, few if any Indian social scientists or social scientists of India would argue seriously with, say, the thirteenth-century logician Gangesa or with the grammarian and linguistic philosopher Bhartrihari (fifth to sixth centuries), or with the tenth- or eleventh-century aesthetician Abhinavagupta. Sad though it is, one result of European colonial rule in South Asia is that the intellectual traditions once unbroken and alive in Sanskrit or Persian or Arabic are now only matters of historical research for most—perhaps all—modern social scientists in the region. They treat these traditions as truly dead, as history. (Chakrabarty 2000:5–6)

This passage asserts that India had theory but it is dead, and offers a criterion of that deadness: that great thinkers of India's past are not treated today as our contemporaries, are not argued with seriously. Thus they become wholly past, no more than data for historical study or objects of veneration.

Is this deadness of Indian theory—of ancient theorists of logic, language, and aesthetics, topics on which ancient Indian theorists had very profound things to say—a fact? And if so, how did it come about? How did Indian theory become, at best, data for analysis by theories emanating from Europe?

It seems to me that in the early phase of Orientalism, Indian theory was by no means wholly dead, either for Indians or for Europeans. In the first anniversary discourse, Sir William Jones laid out a program of study for the Asiatic Society that included examination of Asiatic improvements and methods in arithmetic, geometry, trigonometry, mensuration, mechanics, optics, astronomy and general physics, systems of morality, grammar, rhetoric and dialectic, surgery and medicine, and anatomy and chemistry, among other things (Jones 1788b). However, the early Orientalists were not in doubt about the far greater advancement of Europe. In the second discourse Jones spoke of "the superiority of European talents" and "our superior advancement in all kinds of useful knowledge" in relation to those of Asia, while in the sciences, on the other hand, the Asiatics, "if compared with our Western nations, are mere children." He added that, on the whole, "reason and taste are the grand prerogatives of European minds, while the Asiatics have soared to loftier heights in the sphere of imagination," which is to say, in the arts (Jones 1788c). Accordingly, expectations of what an examination of Asiatic science might yield was limited. Jones's greatest enthusiasm was for the Hindu system of music, "formed on truer principles than our own," a knowledge of which might assist in the recovery of much of the ancient Greek musical theory, much as Ellis, as Erskine tells us, thought that Indian prosody (of Sanskrit and Tamil, presumably) could improve the European understanding of the topic (see chapter 3). On the other hand, Jones's examination of an ancient Sanskrit book of mathematics was disappointing, as he found it to contain only elementary material; and he believed the Europe of Newton could anticipate no new methods or the analysis of new curves from examining the works of the geometricians of Iran, Turkistan, or India. The history of modern mathematics might be improved, Jones thought, through knowledge of the works of Asia, but not its substance. Nevertheless, the search for the sciences of India should be continued and rewards held out for those Indians writing the best essays or dissertations. Indian literature held out the brightest promise of new value, both for the elucidation of the past and for the stimulus it might offer to the European present. Indeed, through Jones, Indian literature had a role in the Romantic movement in Europe, though Indian aesthetic theory remains surprisingly neglected by critics, even in India.

Thus Indian, indeed Asiatic, theory was consigned largely to the past by the leading Orientalist of his day, its various writings serving primarily as data for historical reconstructions and only in limited ways offering theories for Europeans to argue seriously with. It was for Indian scholars such as Rammohan Roy (1772–1833) to keep alive the theorists of the past and bring them into relation with Enlightenment categories of knowledge coming into India through the British.

As I have suggested at the beginning of chapter 2, however, the true architects of the death of Indian theory were neither the Orientalists nor Indian modernizers but the anti-Orientalists James Mill and G. W. F. Hegel. Both undertook systematic reviews of Indian civilization, drawing upon the writings of the Orientalists with an impressive thoroughness and degree of engagement; both rejected the Orientalists' enthusiastic and positive appraisals of Asian civilization; both thought that Indian civilization would be elevated by British rule. Mill's evaluation of the place of Hindu India on the scale of civilization in his influential *History of British India* (1817; see Majeed 1992 and Trautmann 1997:117–24) found it to be very low indeed; in his view, and contrary to the Orientalists, it had been raised by Muslim rule, as it was being further raised by the British.

Hegel, who was a leading figure in what Chakrabarty calls the fabrication of an unbroken European tradition beginning with the Greeks, stressed that *theoria* and *philosophia* are Greek words. In his palindromic works, the *Philosophy of History* (1878) and the *History of Philosophy* (1892–96), Hegel determined that India had no historical consciousness, and what passed for Indian philosophy—what he knew of it through the existing Orientalist scholarship, which he examined with care—did not rise to the level of the ancient Greeks (Hegel 1878; 1892–96, vol. 1). The limited accomplishments that Indian history and philosophy had achieved belonged to a pre-Greek or early-Greek horizon of development, and, along with the contents of all past philosophies, were objects of historical contemplation from the raised height of Europe, which had been built up by the accumulation of learning. For Hegel there could be no question of a living Indian theoretical tradition, of Indian contemporaries worth arguing with. Schopenhauer was the major dissenter from Hegel's view, and his followers formed something of an opposition to it, but theirs was a minority position, marginalized by the success of Hegel and the Hegelians (see Halbfass 1988, ch, 6; Droit 1989).

Karl Marx, writing for the New York *Daily Tribune,* endorsed Hegel's judgment against India in his own way. He did not share, he said, the opinion of the Orientalists, who believed in a golden age in India's past; he held that the pattern of Indian history was one of constant political change—"civil wars, invasions, revolutions, conquests, famines, strangely complex, rapid and destructive"—that did not, however, bring about social change and improvement. This unprogressive history was the result of the peculiar relation between a despotic, centralizing government needed for vast irrigation works and an unchanging village community, largely self-sufficient and indifferent to its rulers. These idyllic and apparently inoffensive village communities were the solid basis for an Oriental despotism. They "restrained the human mind within the smallest possible compass, making it the unresisting tool of superstition, enslaving it beneath traditional rules, depriving it of all grandeur and historical energies." "We must not forget," he continues, "the barbarian egotism which, concentrating on some miserable patch of land, had quietly witnessed the ruin of empires, the perpetration of unspeakable cruelties, the massacre of the population of large towns, with no other consideration bestowed upon them than on natural events, itself the helpless prey of an aggressor who deigned to notice it at all." Thus the "undignified, stagnatory, and vegetative life" of the village was dialectically related to the "wild, aimless, unbounded forces of destruction" that governed political life (Marx 1853). Between Hegel and Marx, then—from the right to the left across the political spectrum of European thought—it came to be a settled fact that theory was, at best, a thing of India's past, and that a progressive dynamic was missing from its history. The marginalization of Orientalist scholarship within the European tradition by Mill and Hegel coincided with the denigration of Orientalism's object, Asiatic learning, carrying Jones's limited appreciation to an extreme negative conclusion. The trial had taken its course and the verdict was out: no theory outside Europe.

Is this the last word? Hegel and Mill have influenced Western thinking for a very long time, but there remains room for another way of looking at the matter. Confining ourselves to the question of language analysis, there are, it seems to me, two things that need to be said.

The first is the hope that it may not always remain so. I have already cited Fritz Staal's optimistic statement that Pāṇini is becoming the Aristotle of linguistics, a living presence of past theory and a thinker with whom it is worthwhile to engage again and again. Whether this will truly come to pass is a question; many linguists know of Pāṇini as a revered intellectual ancestor, but few engage with him intellectually. Partly because of the difficulty of the text but mainly because of the great marginalization of the knowledge of India specifically (Mill) and the non-West generally (Hegel), scholarship on Pāṇini tends to be confined to specialist books and journals and is not found in the mainstream publications of disciplinary linguistics. This could possibly change, but for the present it remains a hope.

The second is that Indian theoretical ideas are nevertheless present, often unknown and unremarked, in the living body of modern thought, and ancient Indian analysts of language are, in some measure, contemporaries with whom we interact, even if they remain nameless and unrecognized. Much as the Indian system of place notation of numbers, the concept of the zero, and Indian accomplishments in algebra and trigonometry have become part of what every child and high school student learns and are essential parts of modern life, so too, Indian language analysis has been folded into modern ideas and remains alive today. I have already remarked on how the Indian analysis of the sounds of Sanskrit has been concretized in the alphabetical order of the Brahmi script and its descendant scripts in India and beyond, carried wherever Indian religions and cultural influence spread in Central Asia, East Asia, and Southeast Asia. We have seen how, on the basis of the phonological analysis concretized in Indian scripts, in the very first article published by Jones in the

Asiatic researches, the Indian analysis of the sounds of Sanskrit provided the crucial means for the formation of a scheme for transliteration of Asian languages into the roman script. This in turn has contributed to modern schemes of phonology such as the International Phonetic Alphabet. We have seen as well that because of its language analysis and especially because of the work of the Prakrit grammarians, India was an exceptionally privileged site for the languages-and-nations project and its search for more precise ideas of phonology, morphology, and etymology.

Without the European encounter with India, and above all with Sanskrit, comparative philology, which crystallized around the concept of the Indo-European language family, could scarcely have come about in the form we know it. Comparative philology and historical linguistics contain within them the sedimented structures of Indian language analysis to which Europeans were exposed at a crucial moment in history. Even if we do not acknowledge and engage with the Indian analysts of language of ages long past, Pāṇini, Tolkāppiyar, and the others are our contemporaries nevertheless. Colonial rule did not kill them off; it incorporated them, often silently, into the public domain of modern thought. Their work continues to live, whether we know it or not, by being put to use, again and again, in the present.

APPENDIX A

The Legend of the Cow-Pox

By F. W. Ellis, Esq.

Ellis first wrote this curious text, "The Legend of the Cow-Pox," in Tamil and then translated it into English. It was meant to aid in the promotion of the new vaccination for smallpox, a project on which the colonial government had embarked in a big way shortly after the vaccine's discovery. Indeed, as David Arnold (1993) points out, the vaccination campaign was the first way in which the British-Indian government impinged directly on the lives of ordinary Indians in the mass. Edward Jenner had developed the vaccination after discovering that milkmaids exposed to cattle infected with cowpox had immunity to smallpox. This connection with cattle gave Ellis an opening. He devised a *purāṇa*-like text consisting of a colloquy between Dhanvantari, the physician of the gods, and Śakti, the spouse of Śiva, in which the Goddess declares that she has created a new, sixth *gavya,* or purifying product of the cow, to relieve the suffering of humanity from the smallpox. (The five traditional *gavyas* are milk, curd, butter or ghee, urine, and dung.) The text gives a very specific description of how the vaccine is harvested from the cowpox pustule and administered to a person's arm.

Dominik Wujastyk published a piece (1988) based on newspaper reports about Ellis's text, though he had not seen the English text published here and thought the original was in Sanskrit. I found a copy of the text in the William Erskine Collection of the OIOC, and another copy in the Leyden Papers of the British Library.

In 1812, Erskine read two papers before the Asiatic Society of Bombay, in whose Minutes they are described as "a Translation of a Tract written in the Tamil Language by F. W. Ellis on the subject of vaccine inoculation" and "a plan by Mr. F. W. Ellis for compiling and translating a Body of Hindu Law suited to the South of India, with preliminary remarks" (Minute Book 13 Jan 1812).

The following year, in a letter to Erskine of 10 March 1813, Ellis described the tract on vaccine inoculation thus:

> I have neither heard nor seen anything of the researches of your Society though from what you say in your last you appear, so far back as the date of it, the 5th July, to have been in possession of materials for a volume or two. With respect to my treatise on the Cow-pox you are at liberty to do with it what you please; it is, you will remember, a translation, the original having been composed in Tamil. It is in my opinion much more easy to write in the Indian dialects than to translate into them from the European tongues; even translation from one European language to another, though the mode of thinking, the immediate derivation of terms, and, often, the idiomatic expression be the same, is, unless a person has acquired a knack of it, much more irksome than original composition. With respect, however, to the Indian dialects, though frequently the derivation and idiom be the same with those of Europe, the mode of thinking is so different, that it is not the distaste only that attends all translation which makes it disagreeable, but the mind finds it almost impossible to recur from one mode to another with sufficient celerity—hence it is that we have had so few good translations from the Indian Dialects, scarcely any, excepting Sir W: Jones version of Menu, in which the spirit of the original is in any degree maintained, and thus it is, also, that all our translations into the Indian Dialects of Proclamations, Regulations &c. are hardly even intelligible to those for whose information they are made—indeed I have often wished that these, the Regulations especially, were composed originally in the Indian Dialects; this might be done, presuming of course competent skill on the part of the Composer, if the themes only of the intended provisions were given to him and he was left to amplify and explain them according to his own judgement. (NLS Mss. 36.1.5, ff. 66–67)

Erskine did not publish the article in the transactions of the Literary Society of Bombay but took it with him when he left India.

The transcription of Ellis's tale that follows is based on the copy in the William Erskine Collection (William Erskine Collection 290, OIOC Mss. Eur.C.9, pp. 51–65), collated with the version found in the Leyden Papers ("The Aramavara Vilaccam by F. E.," John Leyden Papers, BL Add. Mss. 26,568, ff. 41–44). Both were apparently written out by copyists, since they are not in Ellis's handwriting. I have edited the text slightly, mostly for punctuation and capitalization, which varies considerably between the two copies. Marking of vowels for length and other diacritics are imperfectly rendered by the copyists, and differ between them as well. I have thought it better to omit them than to insert marks that in many cases are missing from the copies.

VERSE

Salutation and reverence to the Child who delighted in sporting among cows!
Salutation and reverence to the Guardian protector of the herds!
Salutation and reverence to her whose colour is of the purest gold, whose eyes are lotoses; whose horns are like the lunar crescent; who affordeth Ambrosia; whose sweet breath, ascending into the air, throws around the perfume of Sandal to the Holy Cow Cama Dhenu!
Salutation and reverence to the great Mother, who giveth prosperity to the three worlds; to her who has no equal, the most high Sacti!
Salutation and reverence to him by whose assistance were produced those repositories of physical science, which teach the means of resisting every disease that afflicts mankind, to the divine Dhanvantarih!

PROSE

In ancient times when the Gods, unable to overcome their invincible enemies the Demons, fled to the ornamented Caves of the Mountain Mandharam and concealed themselves from the sight of their foes; Brahaspatih, the sacred preceptor of Indrah, came to the retreat of his defeated disciples and said: "O ye Gods! why do ye remain thus, as if deprived of reason, without attempting to relieve yourselves? Our refuge is that all-worshipped deity, the Lord of the Lotos-throned Lacshmi. He alone can afford us protection," he said, and obeying the command of their sage instructor, the Gods repaired to the presence of the divine archer; and, beseeching protection, reverentially addressed him: "O Foe of the Demons!" said they, "O thou to whom the universe is as a garment! We have suffered much from the force of the Demons: protect us, O Supreme Spirit!" The Lotos-eyed God, whose mercy is boundless as the Ocean, replied: "Take ye the Mountain Mandharam as a churn and the serpent Vasuki as a rope, and churn the Ocean of Milk: then shall ye obtain the means of repressing the pride of the Demons." The Gods, hearing these words, prostrated themselves before the divinity, and when they departed to do as he had said, the being who reclines on the immortal serpent, on account of the great weight of the mountain took upon him the form of a tortoise, and supported it on his hard back. Then, while the Gods and Demons churned the sea, black clouds arose, from which burst forth terrible thunder and lightnings, and, filling the heaven with profound darkness, covered the whole world; then arose the black poison which terrified the universe, which Sivah swallowed at the request of the Gods.—When the Gods and the Demons again returned to churn the ocean, the holy gifts arose, which together with the black poison are in number fourteen[:] they are Sudhacarah, the moon with nectarine beams; Camala Devi, the goddess of prosperity; Cabila Devi (the holy cow) the goddess of plenty; Sura Devi, the goddess of wine; Jeshtha Devi, The goddess of adversity; the choir of Apasaras, or divine nymphs; Caustabham, the breast jewel of Vishnuh; Parijatam, the tree that fulfills every desire; Uccesravah, the horse of Indrah; Airavatah, the white elephant of Indrah; Abramuh, the consort of Uccesravah; Dhanvantarih, the Celestial Physician, Amrtam, the beverage that confers immortality: among these the Amrtam; the physician Dhanvantarih, who brought the Amrtam from the Milky Sea; and the giver of Amrtam, the holy cow Camadhenu were the three most excellent gifts. The Gods alone possess the Amrtam; Camadhenu and Dhanvantarih are common to Gods and Men. To give immortality to the Gods was the Amrtam produced; Dhanvantarih to protect the Gods from the arrows of their foes, the Demons; and Men from the excruciating tears of the Goddess Death.—From Cabila, who benignantly fulfills all desires, came five other great gifts; Gomutram, Gomayam, milk, curds, and butter; these are the five Gavyams, or sacred productions of the Cow.—By Gomutram and Gomayam, purity is maintained, by milk, curds, and butter, life: these give equal delight to Gods and to Men.—Thus, in former times it was established by the most merciful will of the supreme spirit, but in the present times, he who preserves the World, and protects all beings; by the pronunciation of whose holy names, Acchutah, the immutable; Anantah, the eternal; and Govindah, the preserver of the world, and protector of cows, all diseases are cured: this holy being has created a sixth Gavyam, and united it to the former five. From the udders of the cow, which produce milk, curds, and butter, there flows also, a crystal fluid, similar in its effects to Amrtam; which, being inoculated into the body of a man, prevents forever the ravages of that disease, which causes terror and anguish to all on whom it seizes, the cruel small pox.—If thou desirest to know how that most wonderful dispensation came into the World, attend—and I will instruct thee in every circumstance relating to its origin, its nature, power and effects, and the benefits resulting from it.—Should any one disbelieve what I shall relate let him make trial of the virtue of this most admirable remedy, he will then be convinced of its power to resist the small pox, and, having experienced its benefits, let him determine then if it can be of less than divine origin.—

Reverence and salutation to him who knows every thing that is contained in all the worlds, to the great Muni Naradah! Without confusion of Mind attend, while I relate every circumstance respecting the origin of the vaccine disease. While the king Acampah, overwhelmed with grief for the death of his son Aricarsanah, who had been slain in battle, wept like an ancient woman who had lost all her relations by the cruel ravages of the small pox, and tears flowed from his eyes like the large drops of rain which fell when the general deluge inundated the whole earth, the divine Naradah came to afford him consolation, and said, "O King! why art thou weighed down with grief? Had thy son been as renowned as Vishnuh or Sivah, had he been as powerful as the six-faced deity, who leads the celestial armies, could he have escaped from the all-conquering Goddess of Death? To die in the field of battle is the principal duty of a king. Had your son lived to old age he would have drunk the bitter tears of the Goddess of Death, and expired undistinguished by fame, like a common man," he said, and the King, attentively listening to his words, replied, "O God! to dissipate the black clouds of grief which lour over my spirits, graciously deign to inform me of every circumstance relating to the Goddess of Death and the tears which she shed." Naradah complied, and thus displayed what was concealed in his sacred mind. "In the Krita Yugam, men and animals, not being subject to death, the Goddess of the Earth was not able to support the great weight that oppressed her. Brahma, therefore, at the request of Sivah, created the Goddess of Death, with a red countenance, and a black body, from the fire of divine anger, and commanded her to destroy all beings without partiality, the wise as well as the foolish, the rich and the poor, the young and the old. The Goddess, trembling with terror, her joined hands lifted up in supplication, and without daring to look Brahma in the face, thus addressed him: "O God! O most merciful! O Creator! I am created by you a female, and this office, therefore, does not befit my nature. O Spirit supremely virtuous! most graciously be pleased to remove from me this most heavy guilt." While she thus earnestly supplicated, she shed tears like the large drops of rain that fall from the banyan tree after a long continued shower; but Brahma refused to hear her prayers as a deaf snake refuseth to hear the pipe of the serpent-taker. The Goddess of Death, therefore departed, and with continual tears, performed the severest penance to Brahma in Dhenucasramam, in the river Ganga, and in all other places where the Gods of old had offered sacrifices. At length the lord of the universe again appeared, and thus declared the ordinances of Destiny. "O Death, why dost thou vainly perform penance in opposition to the purpose of thy creation?

Murder shall not be guilt to thee: but what is wrong to all other created beings, to thee shall be right. The reward of the penance thou hast now performed is this: thy hands shall not be stained with blood, but all the tears thou hast shed during this penance shall receive the force of different diseases, and all living be destroyed thereby. From that day the lingering pain of disease and sharp anguish of women came into the world. From that day mothers have bewailed their children, who have died by the enemy, by the cruel small pox; by tigers, serpents and other pernicious animals, or by the several diseases which originated from the tears of the Goddess of Death, and which are in number upwards of four thousand." All this was declared by Naradah.—

After the creation of the Goddess of Death by Brahma as here related, by the power of her destroying tears she tyrannized, as if she were the empress of the universe, alike over Gods and Demons, men and animals. Sucracharyah, therefore, having learnt the form of incantation which alone resists the power of Death and preserves the utterer from dissolution, imparted it to his disciples the Demons and thereby brought great affliction on the Gods. Wherefore the Deities as before related, having obtained from him who reclines on the waters a promise of the beverage which confers immortality, thus again reverentially addressed him: "O supporter of the Universe! although the Amrtam will resist the ultimate power of the Goddess of Death, how shall thy creatures be preserved from the anguish of her tears?" He replied, "To wipe away the tears of the Goddess of Death, and to instruct the world in the science of physic by my divine mercy the celestial physician Dhanvantarih shall arise with the Amrtam from the Ocean.—According to his holy will Dhanvanarih arose, and by the means I am about to relate, obtained the knowledge of the science of physic.—The seats of disease in animal bodies are five, the blood; the flesh; the serum; the bones; and the skin: over the two last, presides Sivah; over the three former Sacti. When, therefore, Dhanvantarih desires to acquire the knowledge of a remedy for any particular disease, if that disease originate from the blood, the flesh, or the serum, he performs his adorations to Sacti; if from the bones, or skin, to the lord of the senses.—His penance is in this wise. As Pulastyah had told it to Bishmah, Naradah has declared to Dherma Raja, the virtue resulting from a Pilgrimage to the Holy Springs: "Whatever rewards," said he, "are obtained by those who invariably adhere to truth; by those who fast daily; by the humble and lowly of heart; by those who are of an equanimous, and contented disposition; by those who offer sacrifices; and those who observe all the duties of life, equal regards will result to those who perform a pilgrimage to all the holy springs. There are a hundred million of holy springs; if a person bathe in each, he shall obtain as great a reward as if he had performed all the different species of sacrifices, and of alms, and had daily read the whole Vedam. Because Brahma every day descends into the holy spring of Pushcaram, and in former times all the Gods have performed penance there, distinguished persons perform penance principally in this spring. This spring, therefore, is the most sacred of springs; three times a day, at morning, noon and night, the virtue of all holy springs is centered in this, and, if a person bathe in it, during the month of Cartica, at these periods, he will obtain the reward of innumerable sacrifices. Thus the Bharadam.

Wherefore, Dhanvantarih, desiring to know the remedies for all those disorders, which proceed from the blood, the flesh, & serum went on pilgrimage to all the holy springs, and performed the most severe penances in each, to the supreme Sacti—at length he arrived at the spring Pushcaram, and when he had therein performed penance for a long time, thrice every day, the mother of nature, Mahasacti, appeared in that form which terrifies mortals, and causes the deities themselves to tremble; and demanded what he desired to obtain. He replied: "O all powerful mother! thou presideth over diseases which proceed from the blood, the flesh, or the serum, graciously instruct me in the proper remedies for these diseases. According to his request, the merciful Goddess informed him of many admirable specifics, and afterwards thus declared to him her sacred mind. Most sage physician! now I will instruct thee in a method by which the cruel small pox may be entirely removed from the world; attend!—

Sacti.—By my divine favour, I will infuse a virtue into the body of cows: a virtue by which shall arise on the place whence flows milk, curds, and butter, an eruption of pustules resembling small pearls set in a breast-case of gold, containing a limpid fluid, like liquid crystal, the admirable power of which shall prevent the fatal effects of small pox, by protecting from its ravages; and it shall be considered as a sixth Gavyam.—

Dhanvantarih.—O all-powerful Mother! by what means shall this divine fluid prevent the cruel ravages of the small pox? Mercifully inform me.—

Sacti.—By my divine favour I have already taught thee that the small pox, being inoculated into the bodies of men, the disease takes a mild form, and as the Indrachi mantram protects the possessor of it from the pain and danger of wounds, protects from the pain of the small pox; thus also, if the clear fluid in the pustules arising by my power in the teats and udder of the cow be inoculated into the body of man, he shall never be liable to suffer from the small pox.—

Dhanvantarih.—O all powerful Mother! if this fluid be inoculated into the body of a man, will it not cause pain? What will be the degree of that pain, and what means are to be used to alleviate it? Mercifully inform me.—

Sacti.—By my divine favour this disease shall be very mild, generally there will only be one pustule on the place of inoculation; there will sometimes be a slight degree of fever, sometimes a pain in the armpits, and sometimes three or four pustules in different parts of the body.—

Dhanvantarih.—O all powerful Mother! in what manner is the inoculation to be performed? Mercifully inform me.—

Sacti.—By my divine favour, let the fluid be taken from the pustule on the udder of the cow, or from the body of a man, who has been inoculated, in the time between the fifth and eighth day of the disease on the point of a sharp instrument: let this instrument be held perpendicularly in the hand, that the fluid may flow down to the point: let an incision be then made obliquely in the thin outward skin, until a very small quantity of blood flows out, and the instrument for a short time kept in gentle motion, so that the fluid may properly insinuate itself; before taking it out, press the instrument with the finger, while under the skin, for the purpose of wiping the fluid off it, but let the drops of blood remain and dry in the place.—This is when the fluid is fresh. If the fluid be dried on the instrument, moisten it before inoculation with water, and then proceed as above directed. But if the fluid remain dry longer than five or six days, as divine power cannot by its nature continue long inert, the subtile virtue of this fluid will escape, and as the human soul is absorbed in the Essence of the Godhead, be absorbed into my virtue.—

Dhanvantarih.—O all powerful Mother! What part of the body is most proper for inoculating this divine fluid? Mercifully inform me.—

Sacti.—By my divine favour, the proper place for inoculating is in the fleshy part of the arm between the shoulder and the elbow, to secure the inoculation taking effect; when dry matter is used, the inoculation should be made in both arms.—

Dhanvantarih.—O all powerful Mother! What is the properest season for inoculation; and in what case should it not be performed? Mercifully inform me.—

Sacti.—By my divine favour the cow pox may be inoculated at any season with equal benefit; but in case of itch or any similar disorder originating from the skin, inoculation should not be performed, unless there be immediate fear of small pox.—

Dhanvantarih.—O all powerful Mother! after inoculation what shall be the symptoms and progress of this disease, the beneficent gift of the deity? Mercifully inform me.—

Sacti.—By my divine favour, there are among men three different complexions, the red, the black, and the brown; the symptoms and progress of the vaccine disease in those of the red complexion, is as follows. On the third day a small inflamed spot shall appear on the place where the puncture has been made, resembling the young bud of a red lotos: this shall progressively continue to increase in size, as the red lotos increases by degrees until the sixth day, when a tumor will be formed, filled with a clear discoloured [var. colourless] fluid; in this state it resembles the lotos half-blown, and partly discovering the shining calix in the middle from the sixth day to the tenth, in like manner it shall increase and shall then appear like a red lotos fully blown, the middle or calix, being pure white, and the surrounding circle, or spreading leaves, of a bright vermillion: thus it shall continue, like a red lotos, flourishing in perfect beauty, for two days; from this time it shall gradually fade away for four days, like a red lotos decaying, from the water in which it grows being dried up by the heat of the weather; until nothing remain in the place of inoculation but a hard seal of a glossy brown, resembling the small stone within the tamarind. The vaccine disease shall thus appear in red complexions: in brown complexions the red inflammation and other symptoms shall scarcely appear: in black although the pustules shall regularly pass through the several stages as above described, it shall in no respects be different from a small pox pustule. These are the symptoms, and thus the vaccine disease should be finished in sixteen days, but sometimes on account of the difference of constitution there may be a variation of a day or two in the progress of the disease, and it may continue seventeen or eighteen days.

Dhanvantarih.—O all powerful Mother! by inoculating the disease from the cow, though the small pox be prevented thereby, may it not introduce a new disease among men, and may not others suffer by catching it from those that have been inoculated? Mercifully inform me.

Sacti.—By my divine favour, the cow pox shall not be contagious; it shall never be communicable by the air, the breath or effluvia. The only means by which it shall be possible to communicate it to the body of man shall be by actual contact with the pustule on the teats of a cow, or by the inoculation of the fluid in those pustules:—thus a man, having the vaccine disease, shall lie on the same bed as his wife, and not communicate it to her; a child shall lie on its mother's breast, and the mother not receive the disease.—

Dhanvantarih.—O all powerful Mother! O most merciful Mother! Thou hast beneficently revealed to me a method by which one of the most cruel of diseases may be removed from the earth, one of the most acrid tears of the Goddess of Death dried up; but of what avail is it that I should make it known to the world, the inhabitants of which are obstinate in their opinions, and entangled in their minds! Many will not believe it, and many being prejudiced, although the truth of it be demonstrated before their eyes, will not submit to the operation.—

Sacti.—By my divine anger! the same sin shall fall on those who do not believe the truth of this sacred remedy, as on him who should tell his spiritual preceptor, he lied; on him that, knowing the truth, shall oppose it, through prejudice; as on him that should refuse to fulfill a penance he had vowed to perform.—Whatever virtue arises to a Brahmanah from instructing others; whatever virtue to a Raja from affording protection; whatever virtue to a Vaisyah from accumulating Wealth or rendering an unproductive soil productive; whatever virtue to a Sudrah from performing servile duties with fidelity; whatever virtue to a man of any cast from protecting the life of a cow, or from charitably affording food and raiment to those who are hungry and naked; such virtue shall be to him, who, with clear mind and humble heart, receiving what I have revealed to him shall submit himself to the vaccine inoculation, and endeavour, by every means in his power, to extend the practice among others. Let those who can afford it, when any in the family are inoculated for the vaccine disease, make the same gifts and perform the same ceremonies as they would, had the inexorable Ammei, under the shape of the small pox, taken up her dwelling in their houses; and let them especially propitiate me under my attribute of Cali:—Thus shall they be safe from the practices of any cruel demon who may endeavour to counteract the inestimable benefits of the cow pox.—To those who do this I will recapitulate in a few verses what the fruit of the cow pox shall be:—Whoever commits these to memory, the same reward shall be to him, as if he repeated a thousand times the holy names of Sivah or Vishnuh.—

VERSE

By my sacred mercy! to destroy the small pox,—the vaccine disease,
as an antidote, shall be spread through the world; though millions

shall undergo this inoculation not one shall suffer death or pain from it: this I have predestined.—This is truth.—

By the sacred mercy beaming from my eyes! at all seasons, men, women or infants shall obtain health and safety by this inoculation, and such virtue will I bestow on it, that if weak children be inoculated, it shall frequently restore their strength.—This is truth.—

By my sacred mercy! not only milder than the small pox, shall be the vaccine disease; but with those infected, though there be others living in the same house or lying in the same bed, it shall never be caught by them: this benefit I have conferred.—This is truth.—

By my sacred mercy! many consequences of the small pox shall not ensue: such as blindness; swellings in the arms or the joints; in the legs, lameness, and other complaints shall be prevented; and thus from the vaccine disease numerous benefits shall be derived; this I have revealed.—This is the truth.—

By my sacred mercy! hear again another excellence of the vaccine disease! both before and after inoculation into the body, neither magicians, nor physicians, to administer medicines shall by any means be required in this disease.—This is the truth.—

The merciful divinity thus said, and while Dhanvantarih bent in humble devotion, disappeared, like a flash of brilliant lightning and ascended to Cailasam.

APPENDIX B

The Dravidian Proof

I reproduce here the text of the Dravidian proof, that is, the "Note to the introduction" by F. W. Ellis printed in A. D. Campbell's *A grammar of the Teloogoo language* (1816). This text is also referred to as the "Dissertation on Telugu," one of a set of projected dissertations on the South Indian languages which Ellis intended to have printed at the College Press for the use of students. The only other completed dissertation is the one on Malayalam (Ellis 1878), published posthumously from a copy found at the College in later years.

Ellis shows here that Telugu and Sanskrit roots are different, and that Telugu shares a set of roots with Tamil and Kannada. These two propositions are illustrated with columns of roots and words, and they form the two parts of the proof that concern vocabulary or lexicon. The last part of the proof extends the inquiry from lexicon to "idiom," or syntax. It makes numerous four-way comparisons among Sanskrit, Telugu, Tamil, and Kannada verses or sentences.

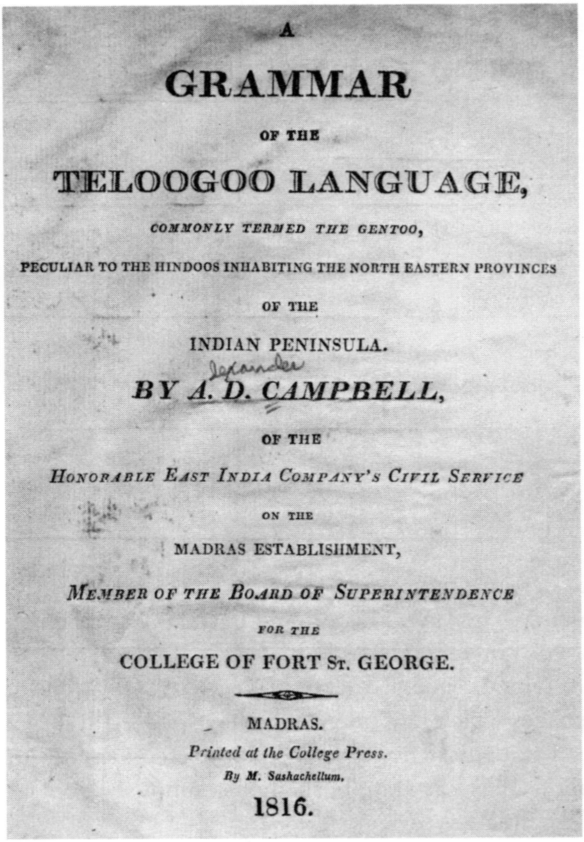

A

GRAMMAR

OF THE

TELOOGOO LANGUAGE,

COMMONLY TERMED THE GENTOO,

PECULIAR TO THE HINDOOS INHABITING THE NORTH EASTERN PROVINCES

OF THE

INDIAN PENINSULA.

BY A. D. CAMPBELL,

OF THE

HONORABLE EAST INDIA COMPANY'S CIVIL SERVICE

ON THE

MADRAS ESTABLISHMENT,

MEMBER OF THE BOARD OF SUPERINTENDENCE

FOR THE

COLLEGE OF FORT ST. GEORGE.

MADRAS.

Printed at the College Press.

By M. Sashachellum,

1816.

NOTE TO THE INTRODUCTION.

In support of what I have ventured to advance, in the preceding introduction, on the subject of the structure and derivation of the Teloogoo *language, it is peculiarly gratifying to me to be allowed to quote the high authority of my friend Mr. Francis W. Ellis, at the head of the Board of Superintendence for the College of Fort St. George, as contained in the following observations with which he has favoured me. The knowledge which this Gentleman possesses of the various spoken dialects of the Peninsula, added to his acquirements as a Sanscrit scholar, peculiarly qualify him to pronounce a judgment on this subject.*

The real affiliation of the Telugu language appears not to have been known to any writer, by whom the subject has been noticed. Dr. Carey in the preface to his Sanscrit Grammar says—"The Hindoostanee and *the Tamil,* with the languages of Gujarat and *Malayala, are evidently derived from the Sanscrit, but the two former are greatly mixed with foreign words.* The Bengalee, Orissa, Maratta, *Kurnata, and* Telinga languages *are almost wholly composed of Sanscrit words.*" In the preface to a Grammar of the Telugu lately published by him he, also, says—"The languages of India are principally derived from the Sanscrit": &c. "The structure of most of the languages in the middle and north of India, is generally the same, the chief difference in them lies in the termination of the nouns and verbs, and in those deviations from Sanscrit orthography which custom has gradually established in the countries where they are spoken. The languages of the south of India, i. e. *The Telinga, Karnatic, Tamil, Malayala,* and Cingalese, *while they have the same origin with those of the north,* differ greatly from them in other respects: and especially in having a large proportion of words, the origin of which is unascertained."—To this testimony Dr. Wilkins adds the weight of his authority, when he says in the preface to his Grammar of the Sanscrit—"*the Tamil, the Telugu, the Carnatic, the Malabar,* together with that" (the idiom) "of the Marratta states and of Gujarat so abound with Sanscrit, that *scarcely a sentence can be expressed in either of them without it's assistance.*"—Mr. Colebrooke, also, in his dissertation on the Sanscrit and Pracrit languages in the 7th Volume of the Asiatick Researches, though he has not given so decided an opinion, yet, by including these under the general term Pracrit, appropriate only to dialects of Sanscrit derivation and construction, and by the tendency of his remarks, appears to favor the received notion of their origin; he states indeed in express terms that the *Tamil* (which word he writes Támla, deducing it from Támraparnà the Sanscrit name of the river of Tirunelvéli) is written in a character which is greatly corrupted from the present Dévanágari, and that both the "*Carnata*" and "*Telingana*" characters are from the same source. In arrangement the two latter, which are nearly the same, certainly follow the Nágari, but in the form of the letters, mode of combination, and other particulars, there is no resemblance; and the *Tamil is totally different,* rejecting all aspirates, and having many sounds which cannot be expressed by any alphabet in which the Sanscrit is written.

It is the intent of the following observations to shew that the statements contained in the preceding quotations are not correct; that neither the Tamil, the Telugu, nor any of their cognate dialects are derivations from the Sanscrit; that the latter, however it may contribute to their polish, is not necessary for their existence; and that they form a distinct family of languages, with which the Sanscrit has, in latter times especially, intermixed, but with which it has no radical connexion.

The members, constituting the family of languages, which may be appropriately called the dialects of Southern India, are the high and low Tamil; the Telugu, grammatical, and vulgar; Carnátaca or Cannaḍi, ancient and modern; Malayálma or Malayálam, which, after Paulinus a St. Bartholomæo may be divided into Sanscrit (Grandonico-Malabarica) and common Malayálam, though the former differs from the latter only in introducing Sanscrit terms and forms in unrestrained profusion; and the Tuluva, the native speech of that part of the country to which in our maps the name of Canara is confined.

Besides these, there are a few other local dialects of the same derivation, such as the Coḍugu, a variation of the Tuluva spoken in the district of that name called by us Coorg; the Cingalese, Mahàrástra and the Oḍḍiya, also, though not of the same stock, borrow many of their words and idioms from these tongues. A certain intercommunication of language may indeed, always be expected from neighbouring nations, however dissimilar in origin, but it is extraordinary that the uncivilized races of the north of India should in this respect bear any resemblance to the Hindus of the south; it is, nevertheless, the fact, that, if not of the same radical derivation, the language of the mountaineers of Rájmahàl abounds in terms common to the Tamil and Telugu.

The Telugu, to which attention is here more specially directed, is formed from it's own roots, which, in general, have no connexion with the Sanscrit, nor with those of any other language, the cognate dialects of Southern India, the Tamil, Cannaḍi &c. excepted, with which, allowing for the occasional variation of consimilar sounds, they generally agree; the actual difference in the three dialects here mentioned is in fact to be found only in the affixes used in the formation of words from the roots; the roots themselves are not similar merely, but the same.

The roots of the Telugu Language, like those of the Sanscrit, are mostly the themes of verbs, but they may often be used in the crude form, or with a single affix, as nouns or adjectives, and many of them are used only in the latter acceptation; thus గుద్దు, as a noun, signifies *a blow with the fist* and is the root of the verb గుద్దడము *to strike with the fist*; thus also, నడు *nadu*, with the affix క *ca*, నడక *Nadaca*, signifies, as a noun, *a step, progress, conduct, manner*, and is the root of the verb నడవడము *nadávadamu to walk*. In this use of the roots, all the dialects differ; the root that is used as a noun only in Tamil and Telugu may serve as the theme of a verb in Cannadi, and *vice versâ*: thus in Tamil the term அக்கறை, *accarei* is used as a noun in such impersonals sentences as எனக்கக்கறையில்லை *yenac' accareiyillei, it is not a* want *to me—I do not require it*; in Cannadi అక్కఱియ *accariy* is the root of the verb అక్కఱియుడు *accariyudu to be desired—to be endeared to*. It frequently happens, also, that a term occurs which cannot be referred to any root of the tongue to which it belongs, though it is readily traced to a radical in one of the cognate dialects; thus in the compound అగుపడడము *agupadadamu*, (which signifies in Telugu *to take* in the sense in which it is used in such sentences as అదిధూమముగానాకుఅగపడింది *adi d,húmamugà nácu agupadindi, I* take *it to be smoke* - దానికినర్థమునాకగపడలేదు *dánikin art,hamu nác' agapada lédu, I do not* take, *or comprehend, the sense of it*, but in Tamil *to take* in general, *seize, obtain*, as குருவியெனக்ககப்பட்டது *curivi yenac' agapattadu, I have* caught *the bird*) the first member అగ *aga* or అగు *agu* has no separate meaning in Telugu, in Tamil அகம் *agam* signifies the *interior* and, in both languages, the root படு *padu to suffer*.

To shew that no radical connexion exists between the Sanscrit and Telugu, ten roots in alphabetic order, under the letters *A, C, P*, and *V*, have been taken from the common d,hátu-málà or list of roots, and with them have been compared ten Telugu roots, under the same letters taken from a Telugu d,hátu-málà compiled by Patáb,hi-ráma Śástri, the Head Sanscrit and Telugu Master at the College; these will be found in the following lists, the mere inspection of which will shew, that, among the forty Telugu roots, not one agrees with any Sanscrit root. To facilitate a comparison of the several languages treated on, each of which has a distinct alphabet, the Roman character is used throughout:

the orthography is generally that of Sir Wm. Jones, as explained in the 1st Volume of the Asiatic Researches, but the grave accent is used instead of the acute, to mark a naturally long syllable when final or formed by *Sand,hi*, and *K*, is occasionally substituted for *C*, before *i* and *e* in words belonging to the southern dialects only: other variations of trifling importance will be observed.

ROOTS UNDER THE LETTER

SANSCRIT.	TELUGU.
A.	
Ac *to mark-move-move tortuously.*	Accaĺu *to contract the abdominal muscles.*
Ag *to move-move tortuously.*	Agalu *to separate - break.*
Anca or Anga } *to mark.*	Aggu *to worship.*
Ag,h *to move - despise - begin - move quickly.*	Aggalu *to be insufferable - be excessive.*
Ag,ha *to sin.*	Ats *to give by compulsion - incur debt.*
Ach *to honour - serve.*	Ańtu *to touch or stick - adhere - anoint the head.*
Anch *to move - speak unintelligibly - speak intelligibly.*	Ad́angu *to be destroyed - submit - be subdued, or suppressed.*
Aj *to throw - move - shine.*	Ad́aru *to shine - shoot at.*
At́ or At́,h *to move.*	Ad́alu *to weep bitterly.*
Ad́ *to occupy - undertake.*	Ad́u *to slap.*

ROOTS UNDER THE LETTER.

SANSCRIT.	TELUGU.
C.	
Cac *to hint desire - go.*	Caccu *to vomit.*
Cacc *to laugh.*	Cats *to play dice, chess &c.*
Cac,h *to laugh.*	Crats *to want.*
Cacc,h *to laugh.*	Cat́t́u *to tie - build - become pregnant.*
Cag *to move.*	Cad́ugu, *to wash.*

SANSCRIT.	TELUGU.
Cach *to tie - shine.*	Cad́angu or Cạnangu *to swell, boil.*
Caj *to hiccup.*	Cat́acu or Cad́agu *to lick as a dog.*
Cat́ *to move - skreen - rain.*	Cad́aru *to call aloud - exclaim.*
Cạt́,h *to fear - recollect anxiously.*	Cad́alu *to move or shake.*
Cad́ *to eat - rejoice - divide - preserve.*	Cad́i *to approach - obtain.*

ROOTS UNDER THE LETTER

P.

SANSCRIT.	TELUGU.
Pach *to cook-explain-stretch.*	Pagalu, or Pangalu *to break - make forked.*
Pad́ *to shine - move.*	Panchu *to devide into shares - send away - appoint - divide by figures.*
Pat,h *to speak.*	Pat́t́u *to seize - touch - begin - knead the limbs - understand - contain - unite intimately, as colour with that which is coloured, &c.*
Pań *to traffic - praise.*	Padu *to suffer - fall.*
Pat *to rule - move.*	Pand́u *to reprove - produce - lie down.*
Pat,h *to move.*	Pad́ayu *to obtain.*
Pad *to move - be fixed.*	Pantangu *to vow.*
Pan *to praise.*	Pad́āru *to act precipitately - speak nonsense - threaten.*
Pamb *to move.*	Pannu *to join steers to a plough - prepare.*
Parbb *to move.*	Panatsu *to send - employ.*

ROOTS UNDER THE LETTER

SANSCRIT.	TELUGU.
	V.
Vak *to be crooked - move.*	Vaga or Vagu *to grieve - pretend grief - consult.*
Vag *to be lame.*	Vagir *to speak deceitfully - bark as a dog.*
Vach *to speak - order.*	Vangu *to stoop.*
Vaj *to move - renew or repair.*	Vats *to come.*
Vaṫ *to surround - share - speak.*	Vantsu *to bind - pour water from a vessel.*
Vaṫa *to surround - share.*	Vrats *to divide.*
Vaṅta *to share.*	Vaṫu *to become lean.*
Vaṫ,h *to go alone - be able.*	Vaṫṫu *to dry up.*
Vaḋ *to shine - surround.*	Vaṫṫru *to shine.*
Vaṅ *to sound.*	Vaḋḋu *to serve food.*

To shew that an intimate radical connection exists between the Telugu and other dialects of Southern India, fifteen roots have been taken in alphabetical order from the Dhàtu-màla above mentioned, under the first vowel and first consonant, with which the correspondent roots of the Tamil and Cannaḋi are compared: the Tamil roots are from a list compiled by the Head Tamil Master at the College, compared with the Sadur Agaràdi and other dictionaries and the Cannaḋi roots are from an old list explained in Sanscrit.

TELUGU.	CANNAḊI.	TAMIL.
	Accarey *to feel affection for, love.* This root, in Telugu *accara* and in Tamil *accarei*, is used as a noun, only in these languages.	
Accaḷu *to contract the abdominal muscles.* This root is never used without the formative syllable intsu in Telugu, isu in Can. which gives an active sense to primitive roots, and a causal sense to the derivative themes of verbs.	Accaḷu *as in Telugu.*	
Aggalu *to separate.*	Agalu *as in Telugu*-also, *to become extended- to extend - lament.*	Agal *as in Telugu* - also, *to keep at a distance - pass beyond.* Agavu *to call, play.*

TELUGU.	CANNADÍ.	TAMIL.
	Agaĺu *to dig.*	Agaźh *as in Cannadí* in which language the Tamil *źh* is usually converted into *ĺ.*
	Agey *to be afraid - be pleased.*	Agei *to beat - cut - break in two.*
Aggalu *to become insufferable - be excessive.*		
Aggu *to worship.*		Ahgu *to decrease.* Angar *to gape.*
Ats *to give by compulsion-incur debt.*	Atchu *as in Telugu.* The consonant in this root, which agrees with the first of the second series of consonants in the Sanscrit alphabet, is pronounced *tsa* and *cha* in Telugu; *cha* in Can. and *sa*, *sha*, *cha*, and *ja* in Tam. according, as it is final or medial, single or double.	
	Anju *to be alarmed - fear - frighten.*	Anju *as in Can.*
Ańtu *to touch - stick or adhere - anoint the head.*	Ańtu *to join - stick together.*	Ańtu *to join - adjoin - approach - befit.* This root, spelt with the same letters in the three dialects, is in Tamil pronounced *Ańdu.*
Ad́angu, Ańangu, Aańugu *to be destroyed - submit - be subdued or suppressed.*	Ad́agu or Ad́angu *to be contained - enclosed - subdued or suppressed - submit-recede.*	Ad́angu *as in Can.*
Ad́aru *to shine - shoot at.* In the second sense it takes the formative *intsu.*	Ad́aru *to ascend - climb ride.*	Ad́aru *to throng - press together - be connected.*
Ad́alu *to weep bitterly.* Ad́u *to slap.*	Ad́u *to cook.* This root with a final *e ade,* means the same as in Telugu, and, also it *to obtain-move.*	Ad́u *to join - be near - be connected - to kill - fight - cook.* With a final *ei* this root means, as in Can. *to obtain* and, also, to *tie-unite.*

NOTE. This root is the primitive of all those in the three languages commencing with the letters *ad*, in which the leading idea of *nearnes -junction*, variously modified, is very apparent : the several modes of forming the secondary root by inserting a nasal before the final syllable, as in Andú, or Ántu, or by adding the syllables *ei* or *e, ar, al, gu, angu, &c.* as here exemplified, is common to them all. This formation of a number of secondary roots from a primitive by the adjuncts mentioned, is constantly observable under every letter of the alphabet: the primitive is found sometimes in Tam. sometimes in Can. and sometimes in Tel. sometimes it exists in all three, sometimes in none of them.

TELUGU.	CANNADÍ.	TAMIL.
Ádugú *to ask - beg alms.*		
Áddagu *to interrupt - prevent.*	Áddagu *as in Tel.*	
Caccu *to vomit.*	Caccu *as in Tel.*	Caccu *as in Tel.*
	Cangedu *to become lean.*	
	Cargu *to become black, by fire &c.*	Carugu *as in Can.*
Cats *to play dice, chess &c.*		Casa *to be modest, or diffident.*
		Casangu *to be bruised by the hand - squeezed.*
	Cachini *to join together two things of the same kind - pair.*	Casi *to be moist or damp - to weep - entreat.*
	Carchu *to bite-wash rice.*	Cada *to pass beyond.*
		Cadavu *to pay - fulfil - give attention - reflect - nail up.*
Cattu *to tie - build - become pregnant,* said of cattle only.	Cattu *to tie - build.*	Cattu *as in Can.*
Cadugu *to wash off,* as dust from the hands *- wash out,* as stains from a cloth.		This root in Tamil is pronounced Cazhavu; *da* in Tel. and *la* in Can. are constantly substituted for the Tamil *Zh* ழ and roots of which the final is *gu* in the former end in the latter in *vu*; thus the root meaning to *stroke gently - caress* is in Tam. Tazhavu in Tel. Tadugu &c.
Cadangu or Canangu } *to swell - boil or bubble.*	Cadangu *as in Tel.* In both languages this verb is primarily used of water, and secondarily of the affections of the mind, in expressions similar to *the sea swells, his anger boils, his wealth overflows.*	This root is not in Tam. but it is evidently the same in meaning and derivation with the two following, the last of which, Cadu, is the primitive of all those commencing with Cad in the three languages.

TELUGU.	CANNAD́I.	TAMIL.
	Cad́i *to cut - bite.*	Cad́i *to cut - bite - guard- swell or be angry.*
		Cad́u *to cut - plough - snatch or seize suddenly - steal - be angry.*
	Cad́ekey *to hurry - hasten.*	Cad́agu *as in can.*
	Cadé *to churn.*	Cad́ei *to stir up with a stick &c. - to turn by a lath.*
	Cańmalei *to think - conceive in the mind.* This is evidently a compound of the simple root *cań*, but the second member, *malei*, has no separate meaning.	Cań or Cańi *as in Can. also to consider - mark - determine.*
	Cattu *to kill.*	Cattu *to call aloud - roar or bellow - croak.*
	Cadad́u *to dissolve in liquids.*	
Cadaru - *to call aloud from any affection of the mind - to exclaim.*	Cadaru *to call or weep aloud - bellow as a beast.*	Cadaru *as in Can.*
	Cadalu *as in Tel.*	Cadalu *as in Tel.*
Cadalu or Cadulu *to move or shake.*	Cadi *to steal.*	Cadi *to sound - make a noise - be haughty.*
Cadiy *to approach - obtain.*		
Cadu *to draw gold or silver.*		
Cadumu *to push away.*		
		Caduvu *to be confused or perplexed.*
	Cadrucu or Cadruncu *to peck as a bird.*	

TLUGU.	CANNADÍ.	TAMIL.
Candu *to fade or decay* as flowers and fruit by heat.	Candu *as in Tel.*	Candu *as in Tel. & Can.* It has this meaning in Tam. when the last syllable is writen *ru* but pronounced *du*; when written with the same final consonant as in Tel. and Can. it signifies *to be spoiled - to perish* generally.
	Canam *to become rancid - to acquire a bad taste or smell by smoke or keeping.* This root is used as a noun in Telugu in the same sense.	
Canalu *to become angry - fade.*	Canalu *to kindle as fire - to become angry.*	Canal and Candal } *to become angry.* Used as a noun, Canal means fire.
Canu *to see - to bring forth a child.*	In the first sense, *to see*, this root in the present and future of the Can. and Tam. is written with a long *á* and with the nasal of the third series of consonants *Càń* and *Cáńu*; in the past it is short *Candén-Candenu*, as in Tel: the second sense is peculiar to the latter language; but *Candu a calf* in Tamil is evidently derived from it.	
Cappu *to cover.*	Cappu *to dig a pit - excavate - hollow out.*	This root is not used in Tam. either in it's Tel. or Can. sense, but it is evident that from it in the latter acceptation is derived the Tamil terms, *Capparu a hollow bason* carried by beggars, and *Cappel a ship.*

But though radical connection may be proved to exist between languages, their actual connection, as regards terms used for the expression of ideas, may not be intimate and it becomes necessary, therefore, to establish this point, to enter further into detail and compare the words of the three cognate dialects, as well as the roots whence they are derived. Mámidi Vencaya, the author of the Ándhra Dìpaca, an excellent Dictionary of the Telugu, has, in the preface to this work, introduced a concise analysis of the language, the substance of which, as affording the means of making this comparison, is translated in the following paragraph.

" The modes of derivation in the Ándhra language are four; they are Tatsaman, Tadbhavan, Désyam and Grámyam.

12 NOTE TO THE INTRODUCTION.

" OF PURE SANSCRIT TERMS RECEIVED IN TELUGU."

" Tatsamam consists of Sanscrit terms, pure as spoken in heaven, the Telugu terminations being substituted for those of the original language, of which the following are examples.

SANSCRIT.	TATSAMAM.	
Rámah	Rámandu	*a proper name.*
Vanam	Vanamu	*a forest.*
Gangá	Ganga	*the river.*
Harih	Hari	*a proper name.*
B, hagavatì	B, hagavati	*a goddess.*
'Srìh	'Srì	*prosperity.*
Sambuh	Sambuvu or Sambundu	*a proper name.*
Vad, huh	Vad, hu	*woman.*
Gauh	Govu	*a cow.*
Glau	Glau	*the moon.*
Vác	Váccu	*a word.*
Bishag	Bishacu	*a physician.*

SANSCRIT.	TATSAMAM.	
B, hub, hrüt	B, húb, hrüttu	*a king.*
Hanuman	Hanumá, hanumantudu and hanumánudu	*a proper name.*
Sampad	Sampadu and Sampattu	*wealth.*
Cshut...... and Cshud......	Cshuttu	*appetite.*
Ápah	Appu	*waters.*
Dyau	Divamu	*the heavens.*
Payah	Payassu	*milk.*
Anadwán	Anadwáhamu	*an ox.*

" OF TERMS DERIVED FROM THE SANSCRIT.

" Tadb,havam consists of terms formed, either from the Sanscrit direct, or through one of the six Pracrits, varied by the interposition of syllables, and by the substitution, increment, and decrement of letters, as explained in the Vaicrüta-chundrica : the several modes of derivation, here indicated, are exemplified in the following lists.

" TADB,HAVAM TERMS DERIVED IMMEDIATELY FROM SANSCRT.

SANSCRIT.	TADBHAVAM.	
Samudrah	Sandaramu	*the sea.*
Chandrah	Tsandurundu	*the moon.*
Cánanam	Cána	*a forest.*
Cudyam	Góda	*a wall.*

SANSCRIT.	TADBHAVAM.	
Yátrà	Dzatara	*pilgrimage.*
Áturam	Átramu	*hurry.*
Pangtih	Banti	*a line or row.*
C, huralí	Garidí	*a fencing school.*

NOTE TO THE INTRODUCTION. 13

" TADB,HAVAM TERMS DERIVED FROM SANSCRIT THROUGH THE PRACRUTAM SPOKEN IN THE COUNTRY OF MAHARASTRA.

SANSCRIT.	PRACRIT.	TELUGU.	
Chacravácah	Chaccaváyò	Dzaccavu	*a species of water fowl.*
Upád,hyáyah	Ojjháo	Oddza	*a preceptor.*
Brahmà	Bamhà	Bomma	*Brahma.*
Dwípah	Dívo	Dívi	*an island.*
Cámsyam	Camso	Cantsu	*bell metal.*
Yaśah	Jaso	Asamu	*fame.*

" TADB,HAVAM TERMS DERIVED THROUGH SAURASENI, THE LANGUAGE OF THE COUNTRY OF SURASENA.

SANSCRIT.	SAURASENI.	TELUGU.	
Yejnópavítam	Dzannóvídam	Dzannidamu	*the Brahminical thread.*
Prátijnyátam	Padinńádam	Pannidamu	*a vow.*
Hintálah	Hindálò	'Indu	*a date.*
Haritálah	Haridálò	Aridalamu	*orpiment.*
D,hátu	Dádu	Dzádu	*colour.*

" TADB,HAVAM TERMS DERIVED THROUGH THE MAGAD,HI, SPOKEN IN THE COUNTRY OF MAGAD,HA.

SANSCRIT.	MAGAD,HI.	TELUGU.	
Nédisht,ham	'Nédistam	Nés	*friendship.*
Géhast,hah	Géhastè	Gésta	*a householder.*
Cashtam	Castam	Casti	*difficulty.*
Rámà	Láma	Léma	*a woman.*

" TADB,HAVAM TERMS DERIVED THROUGH THE PAISACHI, SPOKEN IN THE COUNTRIES OF PANDYA AND CECAYA.

SANSCRIT.	PAISACHI.	TELUGU.	
Alactah	Alatto	Latuca	*lac-dye, prepared for painting the feet.*
'Sashculì	Sack,huli	Tsackilamu	*a contorted cake.*
Urnà	Unná	Unni	*wool.*
Trilingah	Tilingo	Telungu Telugu Tenugu	*the Telugu Language.*
Śwernam	Sannam	Sonna	*gold.*
Niśréní	Nísena	Nittsena	*a ladder.*

" *TADB,HAVAM TERMS DERIVED THROUGH THE CHULICA OR CHULICA-PAISACHI, SPOKEN IN THE COUNTRIES OF GANDARA, NEPALA AND CUNTALA.*

SANSCRIT.	CHULICA.	TELUGU.	
Bründah	Pundo	Pindu	*an assemblage.*
Bud,hah *intelligent*	Puddo	Pedda	*great*; peddavandu *a wise man &c.*
Swernam	Panaò	Ponnu	*gold.*
Mrügah	Mícò	Mécamu	*a beast.*
Brad,hnah	Paddo	Produ & Poddu	*sun rise.*

" *TADB,HAVAM TERMS DERIVED THROUGH THE APAB,HRAMSA SPOKEN IN THE COUNTRY OF AB,HIRA AND THE COAST OF THE WESTERN OCEAN.*

SANSCRIT.	APABHRAMSA.	TELUGU.	
Bráhmanàh	Bamb,hadu	Bápadu	*a Brahman.*
Abad,ham	Abadd,hu	Baddu	*an untruth.*
Stanam	Tanu	Tsannu	*the bosom.*
'Srutam *heard*	Sudu	Tsaduvu	*reading or learning.*"

Note. Apabramśa means, literally, *corrupted language*; but the author says the word is not to be taken in this sense, but as the proper name of the dialect, and to this purpose quotes a verse from Appacavi, one of the commentators on the Nannayab,hattiyam, who states the same, and adds it was the speech of the goddess Saraswati in her youth, and that it's terms, therefore, are without exception, pure. Words which have passed through this dialect to the Telugu are, however, more frequently used by the 'Súdra tribes than by the Bráhmans.

The proportion of corrupt, or, more appropriately, permuted terms in Telugu of the several derivations above noticed, may be stated as follows; Sanscrit Tadb,havam *one half*; Prácrit, *one quarter*; Sauraséni *one tenth*; Mágad,hi *one twentieth*; the Paisáchi, Chúlicà, Apabramśa together *one tenth.* Mr. Colebrooke, in his dissertation on the Sanscrit and Pracrit languages, admits but of three distinctions; these two and the Magad,hi, or Apabramśa, which he considers the same. The six Prácrits here enumerated, however, are six distinct dialects, each formed, as to terms, according to it's own rules of permutation, but all following the idiom, collocation and, with special exceptions, the general grammar of the Sanscrit: in the Shadbáshà-chandricà by Lacshmid,hara, a joint grammar of the six Prácrits, after general rules applying to all, the Prácrit κατ' ἐξοχὴν (*Pracrütam mahàrástr' ódb,havam*) is deduced immediately from the Sanscrit, the Sauraséni from the Prácrit and Sanscrit and so on; the Mágadhi, Paisáchi, Chúclica - Paisáchi, and Apabraḿsa, each declining a degree in purity and the last varying more than any of the rest from the parent stock; this, however, the author does not allow to be, as Mr. Colebrooke considers it, "a jargon destitute of regular Grammar," for he says-*Apab,hraḿsas tu b,háshà syàd ab,hiràdi giránchayah - cavi prayóg'ànerhetwàn n'àpasabdas sa tu cwachit, Apabraḿsa is the language spoken in Ab,hira and other countries, and, as it is used by the poets, it is not in any respect corrupted*—and he proceeds, accordingly, to detail it's grammatical rules.

The work here noticed is confined to these dialects, as they now exist in the Nátacas, and treats, therefore, only of Tatsamam and Tadb,havam terms of Sanscrit origin; it is expressly stated, however, that each possessed its proper Désyam, or native, terms, and it is probable, as many of these dialects prevailed in countries far distant from each other, that each was connected with Désyam words of various derivations, in conjunction with which they produced spoken languages differing considerably from each other; this in fact is declared to be the case with respect to Paisáchi in the following passage - *Pisácha désa niyatam Paisáchi dwitayam viduh - Pisácha desàstu vrüdd,hair uctáh-Pándýa Cécaya Cháhlica Sahya Népála Cuntalàh Sud,hésha B,hóta Gánd,hára Haiva Canójanàs tat,hà-, Etè paisácha désàs syus tad désyas tad guno b,havati.* The two Paisáchi dialects are said to prevail in all the countries here mentioned, commencing with Páńdyam at the southern extremity of India, and extending to Canoj (*Canójána*) in the north, and Siam (*Sayha*) to the east, and it is added. *These are the Paisáchi countries, and the Désyam terms of each have their own particular quality.*

"Desyam, in other words 'And,hra, or Telugu, is of two kinds; the language which originated in the country of Telingana and Anya-désyam, or the language of foreign countries intermixed with it.

"*OF TERMS WHICH ORIGINATED IN TRILINGAM.*

"Previously to shewing what part of the language originated in Trilingam, the following stanzas from the Ad,haravana Vyácaranam are here inserted, to describe the country to which this name applies."

A quotation from the Adharavana Vyácaranam is omitted: the author explains that part which relates to the boundaries of Trilingam as follows:

"As it is here said, in the country between Srisailum, the station of Bhímeswara at Dracharámam, the greater Cálèswaram and, as the fourth, the mountain of Mahéndra, in these holy places were three Lingams, and the language which originated in the country known by the name of the Trilinga Désam, is that now under consideration; this is the *Atsu* or pure Telugu, and is thus described in the Appacavíyam.

VERSE.

"*All those words which are in use among the several races who are aborigines of the Country of A,nd,hra, which are perfectly clear and free from all obscurity, these shine forth to the world as the pure native speech of A,nd,hra (Sudd,ha A,nd,hra Dés,yam.)*

"*OF THESE THE FOLLOWING ARE EXAMPLES.*

Pálu	*milk.*	Nela	*the moon, a month.*
Perugu	*curdled milk.*	Vésavi........ and Vésangi........	*sultry weather.*
Ney	*clarified butter.*	Gudi	*a temple.*
Rólu	*a mortar.*	Madi	*a field.*
Róncali	*a pestle.*	Puli	*a tyger.*
Utti	*a long net for holding pots &c.*	Tsali	*cold.*
Pudami	*the earth.*	Madugu	*a natural pool or lake.*
Padatuca	*a woman.*	U'ru	*a village.*
Pasidi-paindi	*gold.*	Magavandu	*a man.*
Bangáru	*gold.*	'Andadi	*a woman.*
Coducu	*a son.*	Aluca	*vexation-displeasure.*
Códalu	*a daughter in-law.*		
Tala	*the head.*		

"*OF TERMS INTRODUCED INTO TELUGU FROM FOREIGN COUNTRIES.*

"The following verse is from the Appacavíyam.

"*O Césava, the natives of A'nd,hra having resided in various countries, by using Telugu terms conjointly with those of other countries, these have become Ánd,hra terms of foreign origin.*

"The people of 'And,hra, otherwise called Trilingam, have, as Appacavi states above, frequented other countries and mixed their language with that of these several contries; of such Anya-dés yam terms the following are examples.

The examples are of Anya-dés yam terms in which aspirates, not belonging to the thirty letters proper to the Telugu, occur: such as, *b,halà* an eulogistic exclamation; *avad,háru* an exclamation of entreaty; *t,havu a place-station*; *d.háca a haughty, high spirited man*: of those which have a final long vowel; such as, *anà the sixteenth of a Rupee*; *navalà an excellent woman*; *códì a flag*; *jirà armour*: and, lastly, of difficult words, inappropriately ranked among Any-adés yam terms; such as, *calanu battle*; *toyyeli a woman*; *ménu the body*; *ullamu the mind.* Of the list given by the author as examples of the several kinds of Anya-désyam terms, the whole of the words in the first are of uncertain derivation: those in the second are either Hindustáni or they are terms the last syllable of which has been casually lengthened; thus *códì*, is the same as *códi* and *navalá* is either of Sanscrit derivation from *nava new*, or a native term from the Tamil *navam affection*. Most of those in the last list are common to the southern dialects; thus *calanu*, in Tamil *cal*, is derived from the root *cala to join*, common to the three dilalects; *toyyeli*, in Tamil *taiyel*, from *tai to beautify*, *ménu*, in Tamil *méni*, from *mêl upward-outward*, and *ullumu* from *ul inward-mind.*

" *OF TERMS AND FORMS OF RUSTIC OR VULGAR SPEECH.*

"Terms which cannot be subjected to the rules of Grammar, and in which an irregular increment or decrement of letters occur are called Grámyam; they are corruptions, and are described in the following verse from the Appacaviyam.

VERSE.

" *Such Tenugu words as are commonly used by rustic folk are known as Grámyam terms; these lose some of their regular letters and are not found in poetry, unless, as in abusive language, the use of them cannot be avoided, for example,*

Vastádà Hari Somulu

Destádà golladanti dittaca carunan

Tsústádà caungili níd'

Istádà tsepamannan ivi grámyoctul."

In this verse *vastádà* for *vatstsunnándà*; *testádà* for *tetstsutsunnándà*; *tsústádà* for *tsútsutsunnádà*; *istádà* for *itstsutsunnándà* and *tseppamu* for *tseppumu*, are Gràmyam terms

In the preceding extracts, the anther, supported by due authority, teaches, that, rejecting direct and indirect derivatives from the Sanscrit, and words borrowed from foreign languages, what remains is the *pure native language of the land*: this constitutes the great body of the tongue and is capable of expressing every mental and bodily operation, every possible relation and existent thing; for, with the exception of some religious and technical terms, no word of Sanscrit derivation is *necessary* to the Telugu. This pure native language of the land, allowing for dialectic differences and variations of termination, is, with the Telugu, common to the Tamil, Cannadi, and the other dialects of southern India: this may be demonstrated by comparing the Désyam terms contained in the list taken by Vencaya from the Appacavíyam, with the terms expressive of the same ideas in Tamil and Cannadi. It has been already shewn that the radicals of these languages, *mutatis mutandis*, are the same, and this comparison will shew that the native terms in general use in each, also, correspond.

It would have been easy to have selected from the three dialects a far greater number of terms, than these, exactly agreeing with each other; but it is considered preferable to follow a work of known authority, and to which no suspicion of bias to any system can attach: the author, though a good Sanscrit scholar, was ignorant of all the dialects of southern India, his native tongue excepted.

TELEGU.	CANNIDI	TAMIL
Pálu *milk*	Hálu When *P* begins a word in Tamil or Telugu, it is in Cannadí changed to *H*, as Tamil *Palli* Tel; *Palle*. Can. *Halli a small village*: but in the old Can. all such words may, also, be written with a *P*.	Pál.
Perugu *curdled milk*		Perugu.
Ney *clarified butter*	The Telugu term is not used by itself in Can. but is found in compounds as *Bennè, white ghee-butter*.	Ney. Of these terms the fist and last are common to the high and low Tamil, the second is confined to the high dialect.
Rólu *a mortar*	Orulu	Urul. High Tamil.
Róncali *a pestle*	Onake	Uroncali. H. Tam. The Telugu terms are contractions of these: many similar instances might be adduced, thus *irà* night in Tamil becomes *rè* in Telugu, *irandu two rendu*; *aven that man, iven this man become vándu and víndu*.
Ut́t́i *a long net for holding, pots or other household utensils.*	This term may be used in Can. but nelu is more correct.	Uri In Tamil when the letter r̄ (ற) is doubled it, it is pronounced t̄ t̄ and in similar Tel. terms, is written t́t́ (ట్ట)
Puḋami *the earth*	Poḋavi	Puḋavi. H. Tam.
Paḋatuca *a woman* This term is probably a compound, but it is not easy to reduce it to its elements.		
Pasiḋi or Painḋi *gold*	Pasaru or Hasaru with which the Telugu term is derivatively connected, is used in Can. in the acceptation of *green colour* only.	Pasuppu *golden colour.* *Pasamei green colour*, whence this term is derived, means, also, *beauty-purity*; *pasum*, the adjective derived from it is frequently contracted to *paim as pasumpon-paimpon pure gold* and from this contraction the secon of the Tel. terms is derived.
Bangáru *gold*	Bangáru	Bangáru L. *Tam*.

TELUGU.	CANNDI.	TAMIL.
Codúcu *a son*........ } Códalu *a doghter in law*........ }	....	Cuźhandi } Cuźhavi... } *H. Tam.* and Coźhandei *L. Tam.* signify *a child of either sex.* These are the same as the Tel. terms the anomalous letter z'h (ழ) being, as usual, changed to d́ and the dialectic terminations added.
Tala *the head*	Tale.	Talei. A short *a* enus all words in Tel. which in Tamil end in *ei.*
Nela *the moon, a month*		Nilavu *the moon.*
Vésavi } *sultry weather-* and } *the hot sea-* Vésaugi } *son*	Besagi As usual in Cannadi the Telugu V is here changed to B.	This compound is not used as a noun in Tamil, though it may be as in epithet. as *vésavi calam* it is derived from *Vé* heat and *savi* light.
Gud́i *a temple*	Gud́i	Cudi or Gud́i. This used in Tamil signifies any *habitation* ; *tiru-gudi*, or *dever-cudi is a temple* ; the first member of the latter compound may be added or omitted in Tel.
Mad́i *a field*	Mad́i In Can. this word properly means *beds in which vegetables are sown* ; *the subdivision of salt pans.*	Mad́i This word may be used in the same sense as in Tel. but it means, derivatively *a section*, from the root *madu* to *devide into sections.*
Puli *a tiger*	Huli	Puli.
Tsali *cold*	Chali	....
Mad́ugu *a natural pool or lake*	Mud́ugu	Mad́u.
U'ru *a village*	U'ru	U'r.
Magavánd́u *a man* *Vańd́u* is here merely the personal termination equivalent to *en* in Tamil ; without this termination the word means a male of any species, and *magad́u* in the Mas. therefore, is a *husband*	Magenu This word in Can. has exclusively the second of the Tamil meanings.	Magen. This word in Tamil [illegible]s, first, *a man, a male of the human species*, secondly, *a male child, a son.*

TELUGU.	CANNADI.	TAMIL.
'Andádi *a woman.*	....	'Adável. The termination only differs; the nasal in the first syllable of the Telugu Word being scarcely heard in pronunciation.
Aluca *vexation - displeasure.*	....	Alappu. The only difference is the termination.

From the preceding extracts and remarks on the composition of the Telugu language, as respects terms, it results that the language may be divided into four branches, of which the following is the natural order. Dés'yam or Atsu-Telugu *pure native terms*, constituting the basis of this language and, generally, also, of the other dialects of southern India: Anya-dés'yam *terms borrowed from other Countries*, chiefly of the same derivation as the preceding: Tatsamam, *pure Sanscrit terms*, the Telugu affixes being substituted for those of the original language: Tadb,havam, *Sanscrit derivatives*, received into the Telugu, direct, or through one of the six Prácrits, and in all instances more or less corrupted. The Grámyam (literally the *rustic* dialect from *Grámam* Sans. *a village*) is not a constituent portion of the language, but is formed from the Atsu-Telugu by contraction, or by some permutation of the letters not authorized by the rules of Grammar. The proportion of Atsu-Telugu terms to those derived from every other source is *one half*; of Anya-dés'yam terms *one tenth*; of Tatsamam terms in general use *three twentieths*; and of Tadb,havam terms *one quarter.*

With little variation, the composition of the Tamil and Cannadi are the same as the Telugu and the same distinctions, consequently, are made by their grammatical writers. The Telugu and Cannadi both admit of a freer adoption of Tatsamam terms than the Tamil: in the two former, in fact, the discretion of the writer is the only limit of their use; in the high dialect of the latter those only can be used, which have been admitted into the dictionaries by which the language has long been fixed, or for which classical authority can be adduced; in the low dialect the use of them is more general—by the Bráhmans they are profusely employed, more sparingly by the Súdra tribes. The Cannadí has a greater and the Tamil a less proportion of Tadb,havam terms than the other dialects; but in the latter all Sanscrit words are liable to greater variation than is produced by the mere difference of termination, for, as the alphabet of this language rejects all aspirates, expresses the first and third consonant of each regular series by the same character, and admits of no other combination of consonants than the duplication of mutes or the junction of a nasal and a mute, it is obviously incapable of expressing correctly any but the simplest terms of the Sanscrit; all such, however, in this tongue are accounted Tatsamam when the alteration is regular and produced only by the deficiencies of the alphabet.

But, though the derivation and general terms may be the same in cognate dialects, a difference in idiom may exist so great, that, in the acquisition of one, no assistance, in this respect, can be derived from a knowledge of the other. As regards the dialects of southern India this is by no means the case, in collocation of words, in syntaxical government, in phrase, and, indeed, in all that is comprehended under the term idiom, they are, not similar only but the same. To demonstrate this and to shew how far they agree with, or differ from, the Sanscrit, the following comparative translations of examples taken from the section on syntax in Dr. Wilkins Sanscrit Grammar have been made into Tamil, Telugu, and Cannadí; from these, also, will appear the relation these languages bear to each other in the minuter parts of speech and in casual and temporal terminations.

SANSCRIT.

1 2, 3 4 5 6
Cumáràs seratè swairam rórúyantè cha náracàh
7 8 9 10 11
Jégíyantí cha gitajnyà mémriyanti rujájitàh.

TRANSLATION.

1 2 3 5 6 6 4 4 4
The children sleep freely and the infernal beings are continually crying;
9 7 7 7 8 11 11 11 11 10 10
The songsters are always singing, and those overcome by disease are always
10
dying.

TELUGU.

1 3 2 6 6 , 5 4
Cumárulu swéch,hagà nidrintsutsunnáru naracamulón undedivarunnu mickili
4 9 7 7 , 11 11 , 8
arutsutsunnáru gayaculu mickili pádutsunnáru rogamuchéta cottabaddavárunnu
10 10
bahu tsattsutsunnáru.

CANNADI.

1 3 2 6 6 4
Cumáreru yad,héchch,héyági nidrisut'táré naracadalli iruvarunnu héral'a
4 9 7 7 , 11 11
cúguttárè gayacaru ad,hicavági háduttárè rogadinda hodeyel-pattaverunnu
10 10
bahala sayiltárè.

TAMIL.

1 3 3 3 2 6
Cuz'hendëigal' tam manadin padiccu nitterei-pannuchirárgal naragattil
6 5 4 4 , 9 , 7 7
ullavergálum nillámel cúppidugirárgal' páduvàr migavum páduchirárgal'
11 11 , , ,8 10_ 10
rogottinàl oducca-pattavergalum cureiyámel shágirárgal'.

The construction of the Sanscrit sentence is as follows. The figures throughout refer to the collocation of the Sanscrit.

1. A noun in the 1st case plural governing 2 a verb in the 3rd. per. plu. pres. of *sétè he sleeps.* 3 a noun in the 2d case neu. used adjectively, composed of *swa own* and *iram motion.* 4 the 3d per. plu. pres. of the reiterative form, medial voice, of *rauti he roars.* 5 a conjunction. 6 a derivative from *naracah* by the *tadd,hita* affix *an* with the meaning of the 7th or locative case, *being in a place.* 7 the same as 4 from *gáyati to sing.* 8 the same as 5. 9 a compound formed of *gítah* a song and *gnyah* part. past act. (*capratéya*) from *jánáti* to know. 10 the same as 4 from *mrityati to die.* 11 a compound from *rujà* disease fem. and *jitah* past part. pas. (*ctapratéya*) from *jayati to conquer.*

The construction of the Telugu sentence is ;

1. Sans. a noun in the first case plural. 3 an adverbial phrase, formed from *swéchch,ha,* of Sanscrit derivation, being from *swa own* and *ichch,hà desire,* and *gà,* changed from *cà* by *sandhi,* the inseparable part. from *cávadumu to be-become.* 2 the 3rd pers. plu. of the compound present, formed by *nidrintsutsu,* the gerund of the present tense, derived from *nidrà* Sans. *sleep,* and *unnáru,* the third per. plu. pres. of *undadamu to be-exist.* 6 Sans. a noun in the seventh

or locative case. 6. a compound formed by the aorist part. of *undádamu* and the plu. pro. *vádu he- that man.* 5 a conjunction ; it is inseparably attached to the word it conjoins. 4 an adverb qualifying the following verb. 4 the same as 2 from the Telugu verb *aravadámu to roar.* 9 the same as 1. 7 an adverb. 7 the same as 2 from the Telugu verb *pádadámu to sing.* 11 Sans. a noun in the 3d, or instrumentive case. 11 a Telugu compound from *cótta* the inf. of *cóttadámu to beat, báddá,*by *sand,hi* for *páddá,* the past part. of *pádádamu to suffer,* used to form the passive voice, and the plu. of *vádu.* 8 the same as 5. 10 Sans. an adverb. 10 the same as 2 from the Tel. verb *tsávadámu to die.*

The construction of the Cannadi is exactly the same as the Telugu, one or two of the compounds only differing

3 is composed of Sans. adverb *yathá as* and *ich,ha.* The verbs marked 2,4,7 and 10 are not compounds. 6 the 7th case is formed by the adjunct *alli place,* united to *naracadá* the genitive form of *naracam.* 7 is a compound used adverbially from *ad,hica excessive,* a Sans. crude noun, and *ági* the gerund of the past tense *agavadu to become.* The compound marked 11 is from the verbal noun *hodeyel the beating,* instead of the inf. as in Tel.

The construction of the Tamil is ;

1 as in Tel. 3. the gen. plu. of the pronoun *tàn himself.* 3 the gen. of *manadu,* from the Sans. *mannas mind, will.* 3. the dat. of *pádi a measure,* used as a preposition and signifying *according to.* 2 a hybrid compound formed from *nitterei,* the same as *nidrà* Sans. and *pánnudel to do-make,* the Tamil seldom allowing a simple verb to be formed from a Sanscrit word with a long final vowel. 6 as in Tel. 6 a compound formed by *ul'la,* indefinite part. of the defective verb *ul' to be- have,* and *avergal'* the plu. of the pro. *aven he- that man.* 5 as in Tel. 4 the neg. part. of *nilludel to stand-stay.* 4 this with 7 and 10 are simple verbs, as in Cannadi, not compounds, as in Tel. 9 an attributive noun from *pádudel to sing.* 7 the inf. of *migudel to increase,* with the conjunction *um* used adverbially. 7 as in Cannadi. 11 as in Telugu. 11 a compound from *oducca* the

inf. of *oduccudel to oppress* and *pat'ta* the same as in Tel. and Can. 8 as in Tel. 10 the neg. part. of *cureidel to lessen.* 10 as in Can.

In the preceding sentence the Sanscrit differs in every point from the southern dialects; in the following, the variation, except in the formation of cases, is not so great.

SANSCRIT.

1 2 3 4 5 6
Samyamáya s'rutam d,hattè narò dhermáya samyamam,
7 8 9 10 11 12
D,hermam mócsháya mèd,hávì d,hanam dànáya b,huctayé.

TRANSLATION.

9 4 3 2 2 1 6 5
A wise man keepeth the divine law for constraint, constraint for religion (and)
7 8 10 11 12
religion for salvation; wealth for donation (and) for enjoyment.

TELUGU.

9 4 1 2 5 6
Méd,haviyaina narudu samyamamucoracu srutamunu dhermambucoracu samyama-
8 7 11 12 10
munu mócshambucoracu d,herrmamunu dánamucoracunu bhucticoracunu dhana-
3
munun dharintsutstunnádu.

CANNADI.

9 4 1 2 5 6
Méd,háviyáda manushyenu samy amaccóscara srutavannu d,hermaccóscara samya-
8 7 11 12
mavannu mócshaccóscara d,hermavanna dánaccóscaravágiyu b,huctigóscaravágiyu
10 3
d,hanavannu d,harisuttánè.

TAMIL.

9 4 1 2 5 8
Arivall'a manaden adaccattaccága vedatteiyun deramattuccága adacatteiyum mattic-
7 11 12 10 3
cága derumatteiyum dánattuccágavum bógattaccàgavum danatteiyung càchirán.

CONSTRUCTION OF THE SANSCRIT.

1 a noun sub. neu. in the 4th or dative case. 2 the same in the 2d, or ac. governed by the following verb. 3 the third person sing. pres. medial voice, governing the several accusatives in the sentence. 4 noun sub. masc. in the 1st or nom. 5, 6, 7 and 8 the same as 1 and 2 respectively. 9 a noun of quality agreeing with *narah*; this word *méd,hávì*, has the force of an adjective, though it is actually a substantive. 10 the same as 2. 11 and 12 the same as 1 &c.

CONSTRUCTION OF THE TELUGU.

9 a compound having the force of an adjective, formed by affixing, to the Sanscrit word, *aina* the past part. of *cávadamu to become.* 4 as in the Sans. formed by affixing the Tel. termination *udu.* 1 as in Sans. except that, in place of being declined, the case is formed from the sixth in *cu* by the adjunct *orucu for the sake of;* when *orucu* or *ósaram,* which has the same meaning, are added to this case the *drüttam* or nunnation, if interposed between the theme and affix is dropped; thus these compounds, though derived from *danamunucu,* become *danamuc' orucu* and *dánamuc' ósaram.* 2 as in the Sans. 5,6,8,7, 11 and 12, as in the Sanscrit, with the Tel. terminations and affixes; the two last are connected by the conjunction *nu and,* repeated after each. 10 as in the Sans. it takes the *drüttam* before the following *d,ha.* 3 the third person sing. pres. *of d,harintsadamu to dress - assume,* from the Sanscrit.

NOTE. The compound dative, answering to the Tádarthya chaturt, hi of the Sanscrit and to the noun governed by the proposition *for* in English, is formed in the three dialects from the fourth case in *cu* by the addition of the same or similar adjuncts; in Tel. by *ai, orucu* and *ósaram*; in Can. by *ági* and *óscaram,* and in Tamil by *ága* and *ósaram : ai* and *ági,* are the gerunds and *ága* is the inf. derived from the root *á be - become ; ósaram* in Tel. signifies *a side, inclination, bias,* but this and *orucu,* from *oray to join - obtain,* intimately correspond with the English term *sake,* as, like the latter, they are used only in the formation of this dative, the meaning of which may always be appropriately expressed by the phrase *for the sake of.*

The Canadi construction is exactly the same as the Tel. the datives are formed by adding *óscara for the sake of* to the fourth case in *cu.* 11 and 12 *ági,* the gerund of the past tense of *ágavadu to become,*is added to these datives, and the conjunction copulative *nu* is changed to *yu,* to mark their special connection with the following word.

CONSTRUCTION OF THE TAMIL.

9 a compound having the form of an adjective from *arivu knowledge* and *ul'lu* the part of the defective *ul' to have.* 4 as in Sans. 1 the dative case formed by adding *ága,* the inf. of *ádel to become,* to the dative of declension in *cu.* The sentence does not differ, otherwise than as here noticed, from the Telugu.

In the following short sentence and all similar constructions the Sanscrit agrees exactly with the southern dialects.

SANSCRIT.

1 2 3 4
Tasya bahu d,hanam esti.

TRANSLATION.

" *He possesses, or hath much wealth:* " or, nearer in Latin, *Illi multa res est.* (1 2 3 4)

TELUGU.

2 3 4
Vániki bahu d,hanam unnadi.

CANNADÍ.

1 2 3 4
Avenge héral'a d,hana vide.

TAMIL.

1 2 3 4
Avenuccu micca porul' undu.

Again, in constructions like the following, when the *sati saptami*, or ablative case absolute, is used, as in Latin, or when the relative pronoun occurs, the Sanscrit idiom is totally different from that of the southern dialects; in these there is no relative pronoun, but the interrogative may, as these examples will shew, be used for it.

SANSCRIT.

1 3 4 5 6 7
Yas sa, servéshu b,hútéshu nasyetsu, na vinás'yeti.

TRANSLATION.

1 3 5 7 6 7 2 2
" *He who upon all things perishing does not perish:* " or in Latin *Ille qui,*
3 3 5 7
omnibus entibus periuntibus, non perit.

TELUGU.

1 4 5 1 67 2
Samastamaina b,hùtamulu nasintsutsnudagà yevadu nas'intsadó ? vándu.

CANNADÍ.

1 4 5 1 2
Samasta b,hútangal' unasisuttirel ági yávenu nasisenò ? avenu.

TAMIL.

1 3 5 5 5 7 1 2
Bútangal' ellámum násam adeiyum pozhudil násamadeiyán eveno ? avené.

In the Sanscrit sentence 3-4 and 5 have the form of the 7th or locative case and are in the grammatical connection denominated the ablative case absolute;

in Tel. this meaning is expressed by the gerund of the present tense of the verb *nasintsadámu*, united with the inf. of *undádámu to be*, and followed by the inseparable gerund of *Cávadamu to become*; literally *the destroying becoming to be*. The Can. is the same execpt that instead of the inf. the verbal noun *the being*, is used. The Tamil differs ; in this the future part. of the verb compounded of *násam* Sans. *destruction* and *ádeidel to obtain-arrive* is followed by the 7th case of *poz,hadu time*, and the literal meaning, therefore, is *in the time in which* (*when*) *destruction shall have reached*. Again 1 and 2, the relative and it's antecedent, is in each of the southern dialects expressed by the interrogative pronoun *yevadu* with ò, the sign of dubitative interrogation, added, either to it, or to the verb it governs, followed by the words respecting which the doubt is expressed, or the question asked, so that the sense is *who may it be that is not destroyed? he*. The relative, however, may be as well, if not better, expressed, by any of the participles followed by the word which in the Sanscrit connection, would be the antecedent ; thus this example is properly in Telugu translated by
3 4 5 1-2-6 7
samastamaina bh,útamaulu nasintsutsundagá nasintsanivándu the last term being composed of *nasintsani* the negative of *nasintsadámu* united with the indicative pronoun *vándu*.

The preceding translations have been made into what may, not inappropriately, be called the Sanscrit dialect of the southern tongues; the terms employed being chiefly from that language, and, when they could be used without affectation, the same as in the original passages : in the translations of the following sentence, the pure native terms of the three dialects only are used.

SANSCRIT.

1 2 3 4 5 6
Dadátu sadbhyah sa suc,ham Haris smarát
7 8 9 10 11
Gopi ganó suyati cupyati irshàti,
12 13 14 15
Sma-róchatè druhyati tisht,'hatè hnutè
16 17 18 19 20
'Slaghista yasmai spriihayaty as' apta cha.

TRANSLATION.

1 5 1 4 2 2 2 11 7 7
"*Let Hari grant happiness to the just, for whom the females of the cowherds*,

6 6 9 9 10 10 12 11 17
from desire, were calumnious, shewed anger, were pleasant, shewed malice,
15 13 16 18 20 19
waited, were sly and insidious, flattered, hoped & cursed."

NOTE. It will be observed that the English translation does not exactly express the meaning of the original, and, as this is carefully preserved in the other versions, it of course, disagrees with them.

TELUGU.

17 17 7 6 8 6 6 9
Yeveni gurinchi golla-ádavari gumpu tamacamu vella leni-tappul-encheno-
10 11 12 13 14 15 16
alegenò ortsaccapoyenò impayenò chedocórenò cálsiyundenò bonkenò pogadenò
18 19 3 5 2 1 2
córenò tit'tenò á Hari ped'dalacu hayn'itsugáca.

CANNADÍ.

17 17 7 8 6 9 10
Yávanan curittu gollatica gumpu soccuninda al'càjum-pattidò muniytó
11 12 13 14 15 16 18 19 3
sanasitò baitó keda-gorittó cădaconditt6 bonkitò hogal'itò gorittò baytò, antà
5 6 1 1
Harí val'l'evange sompannu codali.

TAMIL.

17 7 8 6 9 10
Evenuccága videiyàl' cùt'tam naseiyenàl az'haccàru-pattadidò munindadò
11 12 13 14 15
poràd'irundadó vinb'ànadò kèdaccorinadó càttucond'irundadó poccan-chon-
16 18 19 3 5 2
nadópugez'hndadò coradò túvinadò averri nellavugal' uccuchelvam coduccavum

The observations made on the preceding example, respecting the construction of the relative and antecedent in Sanscrit, and the modes of supplying it in the southern dialects, may be made on this. The original, in the work whence it is taken, exemplifies the government of the fourth or dative case by the several verbs which therein occur; in Telugu and Cannadí these verbs do not govern this case, but the *upapada dwitiya* of the Sanscrit with the *upaserga prati*; this, in these languages, is expressed by the accusative governed by *gurinchi or curitu-mark, determine,* used as a preposition: in Tamil these verbs may have the same government, or as in the translation into this language, they may govern the dative, as in the Sanscrit, with the preposition *for* as explained in the note on the foregoing example.

In translating this last sentence into the southern dialects, the difficulty has rather been in the selection of appropriate terms whereby to express the shades of meaning which the verbs, in tho original, convey; in general, however, it ill be found difficult to express any sentiment clearly and precisely in Telugu or Cannadi, without using Sanscrit words in a greater or less proportion, while in Tamil, in the higher dialect (*Shen Tamiz'h*) especially, this may always be done with facility. Thus in the present examples, *smarah,* a name of the Indian Cupid, but signifying, the cause being put for the effect, *love,* is appropriately translated in Tamil *nasel*. *sexual love* : in the other two dialects, however, there is no such native word, the Sanscrit *cámam* being used for it; *tamacamu,* the word substituted in Telugu, means *lust* merely, and *soccu* in Cannadi *desire* in general. Again, *asapta* the third person of the past tense *lang* of *sapati he curses,* cannot be rendered strictly into any of the three dialects, except by a term from the same root; *tittádamu* in Telugu, and *bayvadu* in Cannadi, mean to *vilify-abuse,* either of these, *v* being substituted for the *b* of the last, may be used in Tamil, but *túridel* is preferred, as it is more frequently applied when abuse by women is meant. Again *hnuti* in Sanscrit means to *dissemble* this is exactly rendered by *bonkadamu* in Tel. and Can. but *poccam* in Tam. though derived from the same root, scarcely extends to this meaning, nor is it in common use.

To enable a comparison to be made of the superior dialects of the southern languages with each other, and with the Sanscrit, the following versions of an English sentence have been made; they are necessarily in verse as this is the appropriate style of the three dialects and, and with the preceding observations, will sffiuciently establish the positions maintained at the commencement of this note, relative to the affiliation of the Telugu.

1 2 3 4 5 6
When thou art an anvil, endure like an anvil ;
7 8
when a hammer, strike like a hammer.

TAMIL.

CURAL-VENBA.

6 5 4 41 2 3
Adeiyel'át't at'tel ád ngi ad'eiyelày
12 11 10 10
Suttiyel at't àt'tel ad i.

TELUGU.

DWIPADA.

6 5 4 1·2·3 10
Dáy velan an'igi diyyai venca
12 11
Tíyaça suttiya tiruna cot'tu.

CANNADÍ.

DWIPADA.

Ádigallu sari baggi yági yà gallu.
Man'di tirasada chamalige saribadi.

SANSCRIT.

ANUSH'TUP-VRUTTAM.

Cútò b,hútwà cúta iva vinamya twam ayóg,hanah
B,hùtwà'yog,hanavad gad,ham d,hairyavàn prahara dwishah.

Bibliography

ABBREVIATIONS

BC	Board's Collections
BL	British Library
NLS	National Library of Scotland
OIOC	Oriental and India Office Collections, British Library
MBR	Madras Board of Revenue
MDR	Madras District Records
MJC	Madras Judicial Consultations
MPC	Madras Public Consultations

MANUSCRIPT COLLECTIONS

Tamil Nadu State Archives, Chennai
Madras Board of Revenue Proceedings
Madras Board of Revenue Miscellaneous
Madras District Records
Madras Public Consultations
Asiatic Society of Mumbai, Mumbai
Minute Book
Oriental and India Office Collections (formerly India Office Library and Records), British Library, London
Walter Elliot Collection
William Erskine Collection
John Leyden Collection

Colin Mackenzie Collection
Board's Collections
Board of Revenue Proceedings
Madras Despatches
Madras Judicial Consultations
Madras Public Proceedings
National Archives of India, New Delhi
National Library of Scotland, Edinburgh
William Erskine Collection
Letters of Ellis to Erskine Mss. 36.1.5, ff. 27–124
John Leyden Collection
Oriental Manuscripts Library, Bodleian Library, Oxford University
F. W. Ellis Papers
School of Oriental and African Studies, London University
William Marsden Collection
Harry Ransom Library, University of Texas, Austin
William Jones Collection
Angus Campbell
Alexander Duncan Campbell diary

PUBLICATIONS OF FRANCIS WHYTE ELLIS

1810 Note, by Mr. Ellis, on the 239th and 243d verses of the eighth chapter of Menu. In *Historical sketches of the south of India,* by Mark Wilks, 2nd ed., 2 vols. (Mysore: Government Board Press, 1930), appendix 1, 817–21.

1816 Note to the introduction. In *A grammar of the Teloogoo language,* by A. D. Campbell, 1–20. Madras: College Press of Fort St. George.

1818 *Replies to seventeen questions proposed by the Government of Fort St. George relative to mirasi right with two appendices elucidatory of the subject.* Madras: Government Gazette Office. Reprinted in C. P. Brown, ed. 1852, and in Bayley and Hudleston, eds. 1862. Generally called *The treatise of mirasi right.*

c.1819 Translation of Tirukurral of Tiruvalluvar. 304 quarto plates without title or date. Madras: College of Fort St. George. Copies are in the Indian Institute Library, Oxford, and OIOC.

1822 Account of a discovery of a modern imitation of the Védas, with remarks on the genuine works. *Asiatic researches* 14:1–59.

1827 On the law books of the Hindus. A selection from the papers of the late F. W. Ellis, Esq. of the H. C. Civil Service, Collector of Madras. *Transactions of the Literary Society of Madras,* pt. 1 (1827):1–25. Part 1 of the *Transactions* published a selection of papers previously given to the Madras Literary Society but not hitherto published due to the death or removal from India of several of its most able contributors shortly after its formation.

1844 Analysis of the copper grant in possession of the Jews of Cochin. By the late F. W. Ellis of the Madras Civil Service. *Madras journal of literature and science* 13.2, no. 31:1–11. Note initialed by WE (Walter Elliot): "Since the publication of No. 30 we have met with the following translation of the Jewish Sasanam by the late Mr. Ellis among some old papers in the College. . . ."

1878 Dissertation on the Malayalam language. *The Indian antiquary* 7:275–87. Preceded by a note by Walter Elliot: "The late F. W. Ellis's essays on South-Indian languages," which explains that this piece is printed from proof-sheets found by Elliot in the College of Fort St. George.

1955 *Tirukkural: Ellis' commentary.* Ed. R. P. Sethu Pillai. Madras: University of Madras.

1958 *Naladiyar; with translations in English by G. U. Pope, and F. W. Ellis.* Foreword by M. Varadarajanar. Tirunelveli, Madras: South India Saiva Siddhanta Works Publishing Society, xxiv, 214 p. port. (publication no. 927).

OTHER PUBLICATIONS

Aarsleff, Hans

1967 *The study of language in England, 1780–1860.* Princeton: Princeton University Press

1982 *From Locke to Saussure: Essays on the study of language and intellectual history.* Minneapolis: University of Minnesota Press.

Abu'l Fazl

1783–86 *Ayeen Akbery, or, the institutes of the Emperor Akber.* 3 vols. Trans. Francis Gladwin. Calcutta: n.p.

1908 *The Akbar Nāma of Abu-l-Fazl.* 2 vols. Trans. H. Beveridge. Reprint, Delhi: Ess Ess Publications, 1977.

Acharya, Krishna Chandra

1968 Introduction to Mārkaṇḍeya's *Prākṛtasarvasva,* ed. Acharya. Ahmedabad: Prakrit Text Society.

Allen, W. S.

1953 *Phonetics in ancient India.* London: Oxford University Press.

Anderson, Perry

1979 *Lineages of the absolutist state.* London: Verso.

Anquetil-Duperron, Abraham Hyacinthe

1808 Le Premier fleuve de l'Inde, le Gange, selon les anciens, expliqué par le Gange, selon les moderns. *Mémoires de littérature, tirés des registers de l'Académie Royale des Inscriptions et Belles-Lettres,* 1784–93, vol. 49, 519–646; Supplément au mémoire qui précède, 647–712. The Supplément publishes correspondence of G-L. Coeurdoux with the Académie des Inscriptions of about 1768.

Arnold, David

1993 *Colonizing the body: State medicine and epidemic disease in nineteenth-century India.* Berkeley: University of California Press.

Asiatic Society

1995 *Proceedings of the Asiatic Society 1801–1816.* Vol. 2. Ed. P. Thankappan Nair. Calcutta: The Asiatic Society.

1996 *Proceedings of the Asiatic Society 1817–1832.* Vol. 3, bk. 1. Ed. P. Thankappan Nair. Calcutta: The Asiatic Society.

Barton, Benjamin Smith

1797 *New views on the origin of the tribes and nations of America.* Philadelphia: the author.

Bayer, Gottlieb Siegfried

1738 *Historia regni Graecorum Bactriani in qua simul Graecarum in India coloniarum vetus memoria explicatur.* St. Petersburg: Academy of Sciences.

Bayley, W. H., and W. Hudleston, eds.

1862 *Papers on mirasi right selected from the records of government and published by permission.* Compiled by W. H. Bayley of the Madras Board of Revenue. Madras: Pharoah and Co. Athenaeum Press.

Baxter, William H.

1992 *A handbook of old Chinese phonology.* Trends in linguistics: Studies and monographs 64. Berlin: Mouton de Gruyter.

Beattie, James

1788 *The theory of language.* Facsimile reprint, Menston, England: The Scolar Press, 1968.

Belvalkar, Shripad Krishna

1915 *An account of the different existing systems of Sanskrit grammar.* Poona: the author.

Beschi, Constantius Josephus

1822 *The adventures of the Gooroo Paramartan: A tale in the Tamul language: accompanied by a translation and vocabulary, together with an analysis of the first story.* By Benjamin Babington of the Madras Civil Service. London: J. M. Richardson.

1920 *The adventures of the Gooroo Paramartan.* Trans. Benjamin Babington. Ed. Charles Clinch Bubb. Cleveland: The Rowfant Club.

1971 [1728]. *A grammar of the common dialect of the Tamil language called koutamil,* tr. George William Mahon. Thanjavur: The Tanjore Maharaja Servoji's Sarasvati Mahal Library.

1974 [1730]. *A grammar of the high dialect of the Tamil language called centamil,* tr. Benjamin Guy Babington. Thanjavur: The Tanjore Maharaja Servoji's Sarasvati Mahal Library.

Bombay Branch of the Royal Asiatic Society

1954 *Sardha-Satabdi celebrations (150th anniversary) (1804–1954)*. Bombay: Bombay Branch of the Royal Asiatic Society.

Bopp, Franz

1816 *Über das Conjugationssystem der Sanskrit Sprache in Vergleichung mit jenem der griechischen, persischen und germanishen Sprache*. Frankurt: Andraeäischen Buchhandlung.

1833 *Vergleichende Grammatik des Sanskrit, Zend, Grieschischen, Lateinischen, Littausischen, Gothischen und Deutschen*. Berlin: F. Dummler.

1845–53 *A comparative grammar of the Sanskrit, Zend, Greek, Latin, Lithuanian, Gothic, German and Slavonic languages*. 3 vols. Trans. Lieut. Eastwick. Ed. H. H. Wilson. London: Madden and Malcolm.

Boswell, James

1791 *Life of Johnson*. Reprint, Oxford: Oxford University Press, 1970.

Brimnes, Niels

1999 *Constructing the colonial encounter: Right and left hand castes in early colonial South India*. Richmond, Surrey: Curzon.

Brown, Charles Philip

1840 *A grammar of the Telugu language*. Madras: Vepery Mission Press.

1852 *A dictionary, Telugu and English, explaining the colloquial style used in business and the poetical dialect, with explanations in English and Telugu*. Madras: CKS Press.

1854 *A dictionary of the mixed dialects and foreign words used in Telugu, or dictionary of mixed Telugu, with an explanation of the Telugu alphabet*. Madras: CKS Press.

1857 *A grammar of the Telugu language*. 2nd ed. Madras: CKS Press. Reprint, New Delhi, Asian Educational Services, 1981.

Brown, Charles Philip, ed.

1852 *Three treatises on mirasi right: By the late Francis W. Ellis, collector of Madras, A.D. 1817*. Lieutenant Colonel Blackburne, Resident at Tanjore, 1804. Sir Thomas Munro, Governor of Madras, 1824. With the remarks made by the Hon'ble the Court of Directors, 1822 and 1824. Madras: Christian Knowledge Society's Press, Vepery.

Brown, I. M.

c.1965 John Leyden (1775–1811): His life and works. Ph.D. dissertation, University of Edinburgh.

Brown, Lloyd A

1949 *The story of maps*. New York: Little, Brown and Co. Reprint, New York: Dover Publications, 1977.

Brown, William

1817 *A grammar of the Gentoo language; as it is understood and spoken by the Gentoo people; residing north and north-westward of Madras*. Madras: The Commercial Press.

Bryant, Jacob

1744–76 *A new system; or, an analysis of antient mythology*. 3 vols. London: T. Payne.

Bühler, Georg

1907 *Indian palaeography*. Reprint, Calcutta: Indian Studies Past and Present, 1959.

Burnell, A. C.

1875 *On the Aindra school of Sanskrit grammars*. Reprint, Varanasi: Bharat-Bharati, 1976.

Burrow, T., and M. B. Emeneau

1984. *A Dravidian etymological dictionary*, 2nd ed. Oxford: Clarendon Press; New York: Oxford University Press.

Caldwell, Robert

1856 *A comparative grammar of the Dravidian or South-Indian family of languages*. London: Harrison.

1913 *Comparative grammar of the Dravidian or South-Indian family of languages*. 3rd ed. Rev. and ed. J. L. Wyatt and T. Ramakrishna Pillai. Reprint, New Delhi: Oriental Books Reprint Corporation, 1974.

Campbell, Alexander Duncan

1816 *A Grammar of the Teloogoo language, commonly termed the Gentoo, peculiar to the Hindoos inhabiting the North Eastern provinces of the Indian Peninsula*. Madras: College Press.

1820 *A Grammar of the Teloogoo language, commonly termed the Gentoo, peculiar to the Hindoos inhabiting the North Eastern provinces of the Indian Peninsula*. 2nd ed. Madras: College Press. 3rd ed., 1849.

Cardona, George

1976. *Panini: A survey of research*. The Hague: Mouton

Carey, William

1804 *A grammar of the Sungscrit language, composed from the works of the most esteemed Hindoo Grammarians*. Serampore: Mission Press.

1814 *A grammar of the Telingana language*. Serampore: Mission Press.

Chakrabarty, Dipesh

2000 *Provincializing Europe: Postcolonial thought and historical difference*. Princeton: Princeton University Press.

Charlevoix, Pierre-François-Xavier de

1994 [1744] *Journal d'un voyage fait par order du roi dan l'Amérique septenrtionnale*. 2 vols. Critical ed. Peirre Berthiame. Montreal: Presses de l'Université de Montréal.

Chomsky, Naom

1966 Cartesian linguistics: A chapter in the history of rationalist thought. New York: Harper & Row.

Cockburn, Lord Henry

1974 *Memorials of his time*. Ed. Karl F. C. Miller. Chicago: University of Chicago Press.

Coeurdoux, Gaston-Laurent

c.1768 Réponse au memoire de M. L'Abbé Barthélemy. In Anquetil-Duperron 1808: 647–67.

Cohn, Bernard S.

1966 Recruitment and training of British civil servants in India, 1600–1860. In *Asian bureaucratic systems from the British imperial tradition*, ed. Ralph Braibantim, pp. 87–109, Durham, N.C.: Duke University Press. Reprinted in Cohn 1990.

1985 The command of language and the language of command. In *Subaltern studies IV*, ed. Ranajit Guha, 276–329. Delhi: Oxford University Press.

1990 *An anthropologist among the historians and other essays*. Delhi: Oxford University Press.

1996 *Colonialism and its forms of knowledge: The British in India*. Princeton: Princeton University Press.

Colebrooke, Henry Thomas

1801 On the Sanscrit and Pracrit languages. *Asiatic researches* 7: 199–231.

Crawfurd, John

1830 *Journal of an embassy from the governor-general of India to the courts of Siam and Cochin China*. London: H. Colburn.

1834 *Journal of an embassy from the governor-general of India to the court of Ava*. London: H. Colburn.

1852 *A grammar and dictionary of the Malay language*. 2 vols. London: Smith, Elder & Co.

1861 On the Aryan or Indo-Germanic theory. *Transactions of the Ethnological Society of London* n.s., 1: 268–86.

Daniels, Peter T., and William Bright, eds.

1996 *The world's writing systems*. New York: Oxford University Press.

Danvers, F. C., et al.

1894 *Memorials of old Haileybury College*. London: Constable.

Das, Sisir Kumar

1978 *Sahibs and munshis: An account of the College of Fort William*. New Delhi: Orion Publications.

Darwin, Charles

1859 *On the origin of species*. Facsimile reprint, Cambridge: Harvard University Press.

Davis, John

1987 *Libyan politics: Tribe and revolution, an account of the Zuwaya and their government*. London: I. B. Tauris.

Deshpande, Madhav M.

1993 *Sanskrit and Prakrit: Sociolinguistic issues*. Delhi: Motilal Banarsidass.

1997 Introduction to *Śaunakīyā caturādhyāyikā, a prātiśākhya of the Śaunakīya Atharvaveda*, ed. Deshpande. Harvard Oriental Series vol. 52. Department of Sanskrit and Indian Studies, Harvard University.

Diehl, Katherine Smith

1964 *Early Indian imprints*. New York: Scarecrow Press. Based on the William Carey Library, Serampore College.

1969 *Serampore pamphlets (secular series)*. Serampore: Serampore College.

1971 The role of government and introduction of type printing to South Asia. In *Primary printed and manuscript sources for sixteenth to nineteenth century studies available in Bengal, Orissa and Bihar libraries*, ed. Diehl. pp. 221–32. Calcutta: American Institute of Indian Studies, Calcutta Center.

Dirks, Nicholas B.

1993. Colonial histories and native informants: Biography of an archive. In *Orientalism and the postcolonial predicament: Perspectives on South Asia*, ed. Carol A. Breckenridge and Peter van der Veer, pp. 279–313. Philadelphia: University of Pennsylvania Press.

2001 *Castes of mind: Colonialism and the making of modern India*. Princeton: Princeton University Press.

Dodson, Michael S.

2002 Re-presented for the pandits: James Ballantyne, "useful knowledge," and Sanskrit scholarship in Benares College during the mid-nineteenth century. *Modern Asian studies* 36: 257–98.

Dodwell, Edward, and James Samuel Miles

1839 Alphabetical list of the Honorable East India Company's Madras civil servants from the year 1780 to 1839. London: Longman, Orme, Brown and Co.

Douglas, James

1900 Glimpses of old Bombay, and western India: with other papers. London: Samson Low & Co.

Dresch, Paul

1988 Segmentation: Its roots in Arabia and its flowering elsewhere. *Cultural anthropology* 3: 50–67.

1989 *Tribes, government, and history in Yemen.* Oxford: Clarendon Press; New York: Oxford University Press.

Drewitt, Frederic George Dawtry

1907 *Bombay in the days of George IV: Memories of Sir Edward West.* London: Longmans, Green and Co.

Driem, George van

2001 *Languages of the Himalayas.* 2 vols. Leiden: Brill.

Droit, Roger-Pol

1989 *L'Oublie de l'Inde: Une amnésie philosophique.* Paris: Presses Universitaires de France.

Dubois, Abbé J. A.

1906 *Hindu manners, customs and ceremonies.* 3rd ed. Trans. Henry K. Beauchamp, with a prefatory note by F. Max Müller. Oxford: Clarendon Press.

Du Ponceau, Peter Stephan

1838 *Mémoire sur le système grammatical des langues de quelques nations indiennes de l'Amérique du Nord.* Paris: A. Pihan de La Forest.

East India Company

1804 *Report of the committee appointed to enquire into the plan for forming an establishment at home for the education of young men intended for the Company's Civil Service in India, 26 October 1804.* Published in Farrington 1976: 14–21.

Elliot, Walter

1875 Mr. F. W. Ellis. *The Athenæum,* 10 April, 489. Reprint, *The Indian antiquary,* 219–21.

1878 The late F. W. Ellis's essays on South-Indian languages. *The Indian antiquary,* 274–75.

Emmerick, Ronald E., and Edwin G. Pulleyblank

1993 *A Chinese text in Central Asian Brahmi script: New evidence for the pronunciation of Late Middle Chinese and Khotanese.* Roma: Istitito italiano per il Medio ed Estremo Oriente.

Erskine, William, and John Leyden

1826 *Memoirs of Zehuir-ed-Din Muhammed Baber, emperor of Hindustan.* London: Longman, Rees, Orme, Brown, and Green.

Evans-Pritchard, E. E.

1940 *The Nuer: A description of the modes of livelihood and political institutions of a Nilotic people.* Oxford: Clarendon Press.

Farrington, Anthony

1976 *The records of the East India College, Haileybury, and other institutions.* India Office Records: Guides to Archive Groups. London: Her Majesty's Stationery Office.

Firishtah, Muhammad Qasim Hindu Shah Astarabadi

1768 *The history of Hindostan; from the earliest account of time, to the death of Akbar.* 2 vols. Trans. Alexander Dow. London: T. Becket and P. A. De Hondt.

Firth, J. R.

1957 The English school of phonetics. In *Papers in linguistics, 1934–1951,* pp. 92–120. London: Oxford University Press. (Orig. pub. 1946.)

Frykenberg, Robert Eric

1969 Village strength in South India. In Frykenberg, ed., pp. 227–47.

1977 The silent settlement in South India, 1793–1853: An analysis of the role of inams in the rise of the Indian imperial system. In Frykenberg, ed., *Land tenure and peasant in South Asia, pp.* 37–53. New Delhi: Orient Longman.

Gobineau, Joseph Arthur, comte de

1853–55 *Essai sur l'inégalité des races humaines.* 4 vols. Paris: Firmin Didot Freres.

1856 *The moral and intellectual diversity of races.* Trans. H. Holtz. Appendix by J. C. Nott. Philadelphia: J. B. Lippincott & Co. Facsimile reprint, New York: Garland Publishing, 1984.

Greenberg, Joseph

1955 *Studies in African linguistic classification.* Bradford, Conn.: Compass.

1987 *Language in the Americas.* Stanford: Stanford University Press.

2000 *Indo-European and its closest relations: The Eurasiatic language family.* 2 vols. Stanford: Stanford University Press.

Grierson, George Abraham Sr.

1903–27 *Linguistic survey of India.* 11 vols. Calcutta: Office of the Superintendent of Government Printing.

Grimm, Jacob

1819 *Deutsche Grammatik.* Excerpted in *A reader in nineteenth-century historical Indo-European linguistics,* by Winfred P. Lehmann. Bloomington: Indiana University Press, 1967.

Gulya, Janos

1974 Some eighteenth century antecedents of nineteenth century linguistics: The discovery of Finno-Ugrian. In Hymes 1974, pp. 258–276.

Halbfass, Wilhelm

1988 *India and Europe: An essay in understanding.* Albany: State University of New York Press.

Halhed, Nathaniel Brassey

1778 *A grammar of the Bengal language.* Facsimile reprint, Menston, England: The Scolar Press, 1969.

Hamilton, Alexander

1809 Review of Wilkins's *Sanscrit grammar. Edinburgh review* 13 (Oct): 366–381.

1820 Sanscrit and Greek—Sanscrit Poetry. *Edinburgh review* 33 (May):431–42.

Hegel, Georg Wilhelm Friedrich

1878 *Lectures on the philosophy of history* [*Die Philosophie der Geschichte,* 1830–31]. Trans. J. Sibree. London: G. Bell and Son.

1892–96 *Lectures in the history of philosophy* [*Vorlesungen über die Geschichte der Philosophie,* 1840].) 3 vols. Trans. E. S. Haldane and Frances H. Simson. London: K. Paul, Trench, Trübner. Reprint, Lincoln: University of Nebraska Press.

Hemacandra

1938 *The Deśīnāmamāla of Hemachandra.* Ed. R. Pischel. 2nd ed., ed. Paravastu Venkata Ramanujaswami. Bombay Sanskrit series no. 17. Bombay: Department of Public Instruction.

1994 *Apabhraṃśa vyākaraṇa.* Ed. Harivallabha Bhāyāṇī. Ahmedabad: Smrti Samskara Siksananidhi.

1997 *Prākṛta vyākaraṇa.* Ed. Udayachandra Jain and Suresh Sisodiya. Agama Samsthana granthamala 15. Udaipur: Prakrta Samsthana.

Hodgson, Brian Houghton

1833 Origin and classification of the military tribes of Nepal. *Journal of the Asiatic Society of Bengal* 2: 217–24.

1847 On the aborigines of the sub-Himalayas. *Journal of the Asiatic Society of Bengal* 16: 1235–44.

1848 The aborigines of Central India. *Journal of the Asiatic Society of Bengal* 17: 550–58.

1849 Aborigines of Southern India. *Journal of the Asiatic Society of Bengal* 18: 350–59.

Holwell, John Zephaniah

1765–71 *Interesting historical events, relative to the provinces of Bengal, and the Empire of Indostan.* 3 vols. London: T. Becket and P. H. De Hondt.

Hymes, Dell, ed.

1974 *Studies in the history of linguistics: Traditions and paradigms.* Bloomington: Indiana University Press.

Irschick, Eugene F.

1994 *Dialogue and history: Constructing South India, 1795–1895.* Berkeley: University of California Press.

Jacobsen, Thorkild

1974 Very ancient linguistics: Babylonian grammatical texts. In Hymes 1974, pp. 41–74.

Jefferson, Thomas.

c. 1782 *Notes on the state of Virginia.* N.p.: n.p.

Jones, Sir William

1788a A dissertation on the orthography of Asiatick words in Roman letters. *Asiatic researches* 1: 1–56.

1788b A discourse on the institution of a society, for inquiring into the history, civil and natural, the antiquities, arts, sciences, and literature, of Asia, by the President. (The first anniversary discourse). *Asiatic researches* 1:ix–xvi.

1788c The second anniversary discourse, delivered 24 February 1785, by the President. *Asiatic researches* 1: 405–14.

1788d The third anniversary discourse, delivered 2 February, 1786, by the President. (On the Hindus). *Asiatic researches* 1: 415–31.

1792 The eighth anniversary discourse. *Asiatic researches* 3: 1–16.

1807 *The works of Sir William Jones.* 13 vols. Ed. Anna Maria Jones. London: G. G. and J. Robinson, and R. H. Evans.

1993 *The collected works of Sir William Jones.* 13 vols. Ed. Garland Cannon. New York: New York University Press.

Johnson, Samuel

1755 *A dictionary of the English language.* Reprint, London: Times Books, 1983.

Karlgren, Bernhard

1926 *Philology and ancient China.* Oslo: H. Aschehoug & Co.

1963 [1954] *Compendium of phonetics in ancient and archaic Chinese.* Göteborg: Elanders Boktryckeri Aktiebolag.

Kejariwal, O. P.

1988 *The Asiatic Society of Bengal and the discovery of India's past, 1784–1838.* Delhi: Oxford University Press.

Kemp, J. Alan

1981 Introduction of Lepsius's 'Standard alphabet'. In *Standard alphabet for reducing unwritten languages and foreign graphic systems to a uniform orthography in European letters,* by Richard Lepsius, ed. Kemp, pp. 1–87. Amsterdam studies in theory and history of linguistic science 5. Amsterdam: John Benjamins.

King, Ross

1996 Korean writing. In Daniels and Bright 1996, pp. 218–27.

Kopf, David

1969 British Orientalism and the Bengal Renaissance: The dynamics of Indian modernization 1773–1835. Berkeley: University of California Press.

Kuipers, Joel C., and Ray McDermott

1966 Insular Southeast Asian scripts. In Daniels and Bright 1996, pp. 474–84.

Kynynmound, Gilbert Elliot-Murray, first earl of Minto

1874 *Life and letters of Sir Gilbert Elliot, first earl of Minto, from 1751 to 1806.* Ed. by the countess of Minto. 3 vols. London: Longmans, Green and Co.

1880 *Lord Minto in India: Life and letters of G. Elliot from 1807 to 1814.* Ed. by his great-niece the countess of Minto. London: Longmans, Green and Co.

Latham, Robert Gordon

1850 *The natural history of the varieties of man.* London: John van Voorst.

1859a *Descriptive ethnology.* 2 vols. London: John van Voorst.

1859b *Ethnology of India.* London: John van Voorst.

1862 *Elements of comparative philology.* London: Walton and Maberly.

Lariviere, Richard

1989 Justices and *panditas:* Some ironies in contemporary readings of the Hindu legal past. *Journal of Asian studies* 48: 757–69.

Leibniz, Gottfried Wilhelm von

1718 Desiderata circa linguas populorum, ad Dn. Podesta, interpretem Caesareum transmissa. In *Otium Hanoveranum,* ed. Joachimis Fridericus Fellerus. Leipzig: J. C. Marini. Reprinted in *G. W. Leibnitii opera omnia,* ed. L. Dutens, vol. 6, part 2, *Collectanea etymologica,* pp. 228–31, Geneva: Fratres de Tournes, 1768.

1981 [1765] *New essays on human understanding,* ed. and tr. Peter Remnant and Jonathan Bennett. Cambridge: Cambridge University Press.

Leyden, John

1810 *A comparative vocabulary of the Barma, Maláyu and T'hái languages.* Serampore: Mission Press.

1812 On the languages and literature of the Indo-Chinese nations. *Asiatic researches* 10: 158–289. Reprint, New Delhi: Cosmo Publications, 1979.

1819 *The poetical remains of the late Dr. John Leyden, with memoirs of his life, by the Rev. James Morton.* London: Longman, Hurst, Rees, Orme and Brown.

1821 *Malay annals: Translated from the Malay language, by the late Dr. John Leyden [Shajrat Malayu].* With an introduction by Sir Thomas Stamford Raffles. London: Longman, Hurst, Rees, Orme and Brown.

1858 *Poems and ballads by Dr. John Leyden: With a memoir of the author by Sir Walter Scott, Bart., and supplement by Robert White.* Kelso: J. and J. H. Rutherfurd.

Locke, John

1975 [1689] *An essay concerning human understanding,* ed. Peter H. Nidditch. Oxford: Clarendon Press.

Lopez, Donald

2004 The ambivalent exegete: Hodgson's contributions to the study of Buddhism. In Waterhouse 2004. Pp. 49–76.

Mackenzie, Colin, and Kaveli Boria

1811 Account of the Jains, collected from a priest of this sect, at Mudgeri: Translated by Cavelly Boria, Brahmen, for Major C. Mackenzie. *Asiatic researches* 9: 244–86.

Mackenzie, W. C.

1952 *Colin Mackenzie: The first surveyor-general of India.* Edinburgh: W. and R. Chambers.

Madras Government

1934 *Guide to the records of the Chingleput District from 1763 to 1835.* Madras: Government Press.

Mahalingam, T. V.

1972–76 *Mackenzie manuscripts: Summaries of the historical manuscripts in the Mackenzie Collection.* 2 vols. Madras historical series 25, 26. Madras: Madras University.

Majeed, Javed

1992 *Ungoverned imaginings: James Mill's* The history of British India *and Orientalism.* Oxford: Clarendon Press.

Malcolm, John

1811 [Memorial of John Leyden]. *Bombay courier,* 2 November 1811.

Manaster Ramer, Alexis

1993 On Illic-Svitic's Nostratic theory. *Studies in language* 17: 205–50.

Mantena, Rama Sundari

2002 Vernacular futures: Orientalism, history, and language in colonial South India. Ph.D. diss., University of Michigan.

Marsden, William

1782 Remarks on the Sumatran languages, by Mr. Marsden. In a letter to Sir Joseph Banks, Bart. President of the Royal Society. Read 22 February 1781. *Archaeologia: or, miscellaneous tracts relating to antiquity* 7: 154–58.

1783 *The history of Sumatra, containing an account of the government, laws, customs, and manners of the native inhabitants, with a description of the natural production, and a relation of the ancient political state of that island.* By William Marsden, F. R. S. late secretary to the President and Council of Fort Marlborough. London: the author.

1785 Observations on the language of the people commonly called Gypsies. In a letter to Sir Joseph Banks, Bart. F. R .S. From Mr. Marsden, F. R. S. *Archaeologia: or, miscellaneous tracts relating to antiquity* 7: 383–86.

1796 *A catalogue of the dictionaries, vocabularies, grammars and alphabets of all languages and dialects.* London: the author.

1801 *A dictionary of the Malay tongue.* 2 vols. London: Arabic and Persian Press.

1812a *A dictionary of the Malayan language,* to which is prefixed a grammar, with an introduction and praxis. London: Longman.

1812b *A grammar of the Malayan language, with an introduction and praxis.* London: Longman.

1823–25 *Numismata orientalia illustrata,* 2 vols. London: Longman.

1827 *Bibliotheca Marsdeniana philologica et orientalis, a catalogue of works and manuscripts collected with a view to the general comparison of languages and to the study of Oriental literature.* London: J. L. Cox.

1834 *Miscellaneous works of William Marsden, F.R.S.* Art. 1: On the Polynesian, or east-insular languages; art. 2: On a conventional Roman alphabet, applicable to Oriental languages; art. 3: Thoughts on the composition of a national English dictionary. London: the author.

1966 *The history of Sumatra.* Reprint of the 3rd ed. with introduction by John Bastin. Oxford in Asia historial reprints. Kuala Lumpur: Oxford University Press.

Marx, Karl

1853 The British rule in India. New York *Daily Tribune,* 25 June. Reprinted in Shlomo Avineri, ed., *Karl Marx on colonialism and modernization,* pp. 83–89. Garden City, New York: Doubleday & Co. 1968

Max Müller, Friedrich

1854 *Suggestions for the assistance of officers in learning the languages of the seat of war in the East.* London: Williams and Norgate.

1855 *The languages of the seat of war in the East, with a survey of the three families of language, Semitic, Arian, and Turanian.* 2nd ed. London: William and Norgate.

1892 *Address delivered at the opening of the Ninth International Congress of Orientalists held in London, September 5, 1892.* Oxford: Oxford University Press.

1899 *The science of language, founded on lectures delivered at the Royal institution in 1861 and 1863.* 2 vols. London: Longmans, Green.

McKerrell, John

1820 *A grammar of the Carnátaka language.* Madras: College Press.

Meillet, Antoine

1952 *Les langues du monde.* Paris: Centre national de la recherche scientifique.

Meiners, Christoph

1780 *Historia doctrinae de vero Deo.* Lemgo: n.p.

Meenakshisundaram, K.

1974 *The contribution of European scholars to Tamil.* Madras: University of Madras.

Michalowski, Piotr

1992 Sumerian. In *International encyclopedia of linguistics*, ed. William Bright, vol. 4, 94–97. New York and Oxford: Oxford University Press.

Mill, James

1817 *The history of British India*. 3 vols. London: Baldwin, Cradock, and Joy.

1858 *The history of British India*. 5th ed., 6 vols. With notes and continuation by Horace Hayman Wilson. Facsimile reprint, with introduction by John Kenneth Galbraith, New York: Chelsea House Publishers, 1968.

Misra, Vidya Niwas

1966 *The descriptive technique of Panini: An introduction*. The Hague, Paris: Mouton & Co.

Mitchell, Lisa

2003 From medium to marker: The making of a mother tongue in modern South India or, feeling Telugu: language, culture, and affect in southern India. Ph.D. diss., Columbia University.

Forthcoming Making the local foreign: Shared language and history in southern India. In *Adventures in heteroglossia: Navigating terrains of linguistic difference in local and colonial regimes of knowledge*, ed. Lisa Mitchell and Ben Zimmer. To appear in a special issue of the *Journal of linguistic anthropology*.

Murdoch, John

1865 *Classified catalogue of Tamil printed books, with introductory notices*. Madras: The Christian Vernacular Education Society.

Murr, Sylvia

1977 Nicolas Desvaulx (1745–1823) véritable auteur des Moers, institutions et cérémonies des peuples de l'Inde, de l'abbé Dubois? *Puruṣārtha* 3: 245–67.

1987 *L'Inde philosophique entre Bosuet et Voltaire*. Vol. 1: *Moeurs et coutumes des Indiens (1777)*; vol. 2: *L'Indologie du Père Coeurdoux: stratégies, apologétique et scientificité*. Publications de L'École francaise d'Extrême-Orient, vol. 146. Paris: École francaise d'Extrême-Orient.

Nālaḍiyār

1963 *Naladiyar, with translations in English by Rev. Dr. G. U. Pope and Mr. F. W. Ellis*. Foreword by Dr. M. Varadarajanar. Madras: South India Saiva Siddhanta Works Publishing Society.

Neild, Susan Margaret

1976 Madras: The growth of a colonial city in India, 1780–1840. Ph.D. diss., University of Chicago.

Neild-Basu, Susan

1984 The dubashes of Madras. *Modern Asian studies* 18: 1–31.

Pāṇini

1966 *La grammaire de Pāṇini* 2 vols. Ed. Louis Renou. Paris: École Française d'Extrême-Orient.

1987 The *Aṣṭādhyāyī of Pāṇini.* Ed. Sumitra M. Katre. Austin: University of Texas Press.

Pallas, P. S.

1786–89 *Linguarum totius orbis vocabularia comparativa.* 2 vols. St. Petersburg: Carl Schnoor.

Pingree, David

1963 Astronomy and astrology in India and Iran. *Isis* 54: 229–46.

1978 History of mathematical astronomy in India. *Dictionary of scientific biography,* ed. Charles Coulston Gillispie, vol. 15 supp. 1, 533–633.

Playfair, John

1790 Remarks on the astronomy of the brahmins. Read by the author, 2 March 1789. *Transactions of the Royal Society of Edinburgh* 2, art. 13: 135–92.

Poliakov, Léon

1974 *The Aryan myth: A history of racist and nationalist ideas in Europe.* Trans. Edward Howard. London: Chatto, Heinemann for Sussex University Press.

Prichard, James Cowles

1813 *Researches into the physical history of man.* Ed. with an introductory essay by George W. Stocking, Jr. Chicago: University of Chicago Press, 1973.

1831 *The eastern origin of the Celtic nations proved by a comparison of their dialects with the Sanskrit, Greek, Latin and Teutonic languages. Forming a supplement to Researches into the physical history of mankind.* Oxford: Oxford University Press.

1843 *The natural history of man; comprising inquiries into the modifying influence of physical and moral agencies on the different tribes of the human family.* London: H. Baillière.

Prinsep Charles C.

1885 *Record of services of the Honourable East India Company in the Madras Presidency from 1741 to 1858.* London: Trübner & Co.

Raffles, Thomas Stamford

1965 [1817] *The history of Java.* 2 vols. Kuala Lumpur: Oxford University Press.

Raghavan, V., ed.

1957–58 The Sarva-deva-vilasa. Pts. 1 and 2. *Adyar Library bulletin* 21: 314–414; 22: 45–118.

Ramaswami, N. S.

1985 *Madras Literary Society: A history: 1812–1984.* Madras: Madras Literary Society.

Rao, Velcheru Narayana, David Shulman, and Sanjay Subrahmanyam

2003 *Textures of time: Writing history in South India.* New York: Other Press.

Robb, Peter

1998 Completing "our stock of geography", or an object "still more sublime": Colin Mackenzie's survey of Mysore, 1799–1810. *Journal of the Royal Asiatic Society,* ser. 3, 8: 181–206.

Roberts, Major R. E.

1808 Specimen of the language of the people inhabiting the hills in the vicinity of Bhagulpoor. *Asiatic researches* 5: 127–30.

Rocher, Ludo

1986 *The Puranas.* Vol. 2, fasc. 3 of *A history of Sanskrit literature,* ed. Jan Gonda. Wiesbaden: Otto Harrassowitz.

Rocher, Ludo, and Rosane Rocher

1994–95 The *Purāṇārthaprakāśa:* Jones's primary source on Indian chronology. *Bulletin of the Deccan College Post-graduate & Research Institute,* Pune, 54–55: 47–71.

Rocher, Rosane

1961 *Alexander Hamilton (1762–1824): A chapter in the early history of Sanskrit philology.* American Oriental Series, vol. 51. New Haven: American Oriental Society.

1983 *Orientalism, poetry and the millennium: The checkered life of Nathanial Brassey Halhed, 1751–1830.* Delhi: Motilal Banarsidass.

Said, Edward

1978 *Orientalism.* New York: Pantheon Books.

Scharfe, Hartmut

1977 *Grammatical literature.* Vol. 5, fasc. 2 of *A history of Indian literature,* ed. Jan Gonda. Wiesbaden: Otto Harrassowitz.

Schedel, Hartmann

1493 *Liber chronicorum* (the Nuremberg chronicle). Nuremberg: Anton Koberger.

Schlegel, Friedrich

1808 *Über die Sprache und Weisheit der Indier: Ein Beitrag zur Begründung der Alterthumskunde.* Heidelberg: Mohr und Zimmer.

Schmitthenner, Peter Lee

1991 Charles Philip Brown, 1798–1884: The legacy of an East India Company servant and scholar of South India. Ph.D. diss., University of Wisconsin, Madison.

2001 *Telugu resurgence: C. P. Brown and cultural consolidation in nineteenth-century South India.* New Delhi: Manohar.

Schwab, Raymond

1984 *The Oriental renaissance: Europe's rediscovery of India and the East 1680–1880*. Trans. Gene Patterson-Black and Victor Reinking. Foreword by Edward Said. New York: Columbia University Press.

Selby, Martha

2000 *Grow long blessed night: Love poems from classical India*. Oxford: Oxford University Press.

Seshadri, P.

1912 *An Anglo-Indian poet, John Leyden*. Madras: Higginbotham & Co.

Shaw, Lieutenant Thomas

1807 On the inhabitants of the hills near Rajamahall. *Asiatic researches* 4: 31–96.

Shulman, David.

2001 First grammarian, first poet: A south Indian vision of cultural origins. *Indian economic and social history review* 38, 4: 353–71.

Smith, G.

1848 John Leyden. *Calcutta review,* September.

Smith, Janet S.

1996 Japanese writing. In Daniels and Bright 1996, pp. 209–17.

Staal, J. F.

1976 Sanskrit philosophy of language. In *History of linguistic thought and contemporary linguistics,* ed. Herman Parret. Berlin: Walter de Gruyter.

Staal, J. F, ed.

1972 *A reader on the Sanskrit grammarians*. Cambridge: MIT Press.

Stepan, Nancy

1982 *The idea of race in science: Great Britain 1800–1960*. London: Macmillan.

Stevenson, John

1841–44a An essay on the language of the aboriginal Hindus. *Journal of the Bombay Branch of the Royal Asiatic Society* 1: 103–26.

1841–44b An essay on the vernacular literature of the Marathas. *Journal of the Bombay Branch of the Royal Asiatic Society* 1: 1–10.

1843 Observations on the Maráthí language. *Journal of the Royal Asiatic Society,* pp. 84–91.

1849–51 Observations on the grammatical structure of the vernacular languages of India. *Journal of the Bombay Branch of the Royal Asiatic Society* 3, pt. 1: 71–76; pt. 2: 1–7, 196–202.

1853a A comparative vocabulary of the non-Sanscrit vocables of the vernacular languages of India. *Journal of the Bombay Branch of the Royal Asiatic Society* 4: 117–31.

1853b Comparative vocabulary of non-Sanscrit primitives in the vernacular languages of India, part II. *Journal of the Bombay Branch of the Royal Asiatic Society* 4: 319–39.

1853c Observations on the grammatical structure of the vernacular languages of India, no. 4—the pronoun. *Journal of the Bombay Branch of the Royal Asiatic Society* 4: 15–20.

Stewart, Dugald

1827 *Elements of the philosophy of the human mind.* Vol. 3. London: John Murray.

Stocking, George W.

1973 Introduction to Prichard 1813.

1987 *Victorian anthropology.* New York: The Free Press; London: Collier Macmillan Publishers.

Subramaniam, T. N.

1953–57 *South Indian temple inscriptions.* 3 vols. Madras: Government Oriental Manuscripts Library.

Subrahmanya Sastri, P. S.

1934 *History of grammatical theories in Tamil and their relation to the grammatical literature in Sanskrit.* Reprint, Chennai: Kuppuswami Sastri Research Institute, 1997.

Taylor, Isaac

1883 *The alphabet.* 2 vols., London:

c. 1889 *The origin of the Aryans; an account of the prehistoric ethnology and civilisation of Europe.* London: Walter Scott.

Taylor, Rev. William

1838 *Examination and analysis of the Mackenzie manuscripts deposited in the Madras College Library.* Reprinted from the *Journal of the Asiatic Society.* Calcutta n.p.

1857–62 *A catalogue raisonné of Oriental manuscripts in the Government Library.* 3 vols. Madras: H. Smith.

Tiruvalluvar

1980 *The 'sacred' Kurral of Tiruvalluvar-Nayanar, with introduction, grammar, translation, notes, lexicon and concordance (in which are reprinted Fr. Beschi's and F. W. Ellis versions).* Trans. G. U. Pope. New Delhi: Asian Educational Services.

Trautmann, Thomas R.

1981 *Dravidian kinship.* Cambridge Studies in Social Anthropology, 36. Cambridge: Cambridge University Press.

1987 *Lewis Henry Morgan and the invention of kinship.* Berkeley: University of California Press.

1992 The revolution in ethnological time. *Man* n.s. 27: 379–97.

1997 *Aryans and British India.* Berkeley: University of California Press.

1998 The lives of Sir William Jones. In *Sir William Jones 1746–94: A commemoration,* ed. Alexander Murray, pp. 91–121. Oxford: Oxford University Press.

1999 Hullabaloo about Telugu. *South Asia research 19.1,* pp. 53–70.

1999b Inventing the history of South India. In *Invoking the past: The uses of history in South Asia,* ed. Daud Ali, pp. 36–54. New Delhi: Oxford University Press

2001a Kinship, language, and the construction of South India. In *Structure and society in early South India: Essays in honour of Noboru Karashima,* ed. Kenneth R. Hall, pp. 181–97. New Delhi: Oxford University Press.

2001b Dr. Johnson and the pandits: Imagining the perfect dictionary in colonial Madras. *The Indian Economic and Social History Review* 38, 4: 375–97.

Forthcoming Explosion in the grammar factory.

Trevelyan, Charles, J. Prinsep, et al.

1834 The application of the Roman alphabet to all the Oriental languages. Serampore: Mission Press.

van der Kuijp, Leonard W. J.

1996 The Tibetan script and derivatives. In Daniels and Bright, 1996 section 40, pp. 431–41.

Venkata Rao, N.

1953 Dissertation on the Telugu language by Ellis—(1816). *Annals of Oriental research* (University of Madras) 11:1–6.

1957 History of Telugu linguistics. *Annals of Oriental research* (University of Madras) 13:16–25.

1957–58 Word classification in the Telugu language. *Annals of Oriental research* (University of Madras) 14:1–14.

Volney, C-F.

1804 *View of the climate and soil of the United States of America.* London: J. Johnson.

Wagoner, Phillip

2003 Precolonial intellectuals and the production of colonial knowledge. *Comparative studies in society and history* 45: 783–814.

Warren, (Lieutenant Colonel) John

1825 *Kala Sankalita: or, A collection of memoirs on the various modes according to which the nations of the southern parts of India divide time: to which is added, three general tables, wherein may be found by mere inspection the beginning, character, and roots of the Tamul, Telinga, and Mahommedan civil year, concurring, viz. the two former with the European years of the XVIIth, XVIIIth and XIXth centuries, and the latter and these from A.D. 622 (A.H. 1) to 1900*. Madras: College Press.

Waterhouse, David, ed.

2004 The origins of Himalayan studies: Brian Houghton Hodgson in Kathmandu and Darjeeling 1820–1858. London: Royal Asiatic Society.

Whitefield, Peter

1994 Image of the world: 20 centuries of world maps. London: British Library.

Wilkins, Charles

1808 *A grammar of the Sanskrita language*. London: n.p.

Wilks, Mark

1805 *A report on the interior administration, resources and expenditure of the government of Mysoor, under the system prescribed in the orders of the Governor-General in Council, dated 4th September 1799*. Calcutta: Fort William. Reprint, Bangalore: Mysore Government Press, 1864.

1810–17 *Historical sketches of South India, in an attempt to trace the History of Mysoor: from the origin of the Hindoo government of that state, to the extinction of the Mohammedan dynasty in 1799. Founded chiefly on Indian authorities collected by the Author while officiating for several years as political resident at the court of Mysoor.* 3 vols. London: Longman, Hurst, Rees and Orme. Reprint in 2 vols., with notes by Murray Hammick, Mysore: Government Branch Press, 1930.

Wilson, H. H.

1828 *Mackenzie Collection: A descriptive catalogue*. 2 vols. in one. Calcutta: Asiatic Press.

n.d. Francis Ellis. *The imperial dictionary of universal biography,* vol. 2, s.v. London, Glasgow and Edinburgh: William Mackenzie.

Wujastyk, Dominik

1988 A pious fraud: The Indian claims for preJennerian smallpox vaccination. In *Studies in Indian medical history,* ed. G. J. Muelenheld and D.Wujastyk, vol. 2. Groningen: Groningen Oriental Studies.

Wyatt, J. L., ed.

1894 *Reminiscences of Bishop Caldwell*. Madras: Addison and Co.

Zvelebil, Kamil

1992 *Companion studies to the history of Tamil literature*. Leiden: E. J. Brill.

1995 *Lexicon of Tamil literature*. Handbuch der Orientalistik, zweite Abteilung: Indien, Band 9. Leiden: E. J. Brill.

Index